C0-AVY-187

GANGS AND YOUTH SUBCULTURES

edited by

Kayleen Hazlehurst
Cameron Hazlehurst

GANGS AND YOUTH SUBCULTURES

International Explorations

Transaction Publishers
New Brunswick (U.S.A.) and London (U.K.)

This book is printed on acid-free paper that meets the American National Standard for Permanence of Paper for Printed Library Materials.

Library of Congress Catalog Number: 97-46823
ISBN: 1-56000-363-4
Printed in the United States of America

Library of Congress Cataloging-in-Publication Data

Gangs and youth subcultures : international explorations / edited by Kayleen M. Hazlehurst and Cameron Hazlehurst.
p. cm.
Includes bibliographical references and index.
ISBN 1-56000-363-4 (alk. paper)
1. Gangs—Cross-cultural studies. 2. Youth—Cross-cultural studies. 3. Subculture—Cross-cultural studies. I. Hazlehurst, Kayleen M., 1949– . II. Hazlehurst, Cameron, 1941– .
HV6437.G35 1998
302.3'4—dc21 97-46823
CIP

Contents

Illustrations

Acknowledgements

This international collection on gang phenomena was conceived in Brisbane in 1992. We would like to thank successive Deans of the Faculty of Arts at Queensland University of Technology, Professor Paul Wilson, Professor Peter Lavery, and Professor Roger Scott, who encouraged this and a series of related publications. A grant from the QUT Centre for Community and Cross-Cultural Studies funded the final editing of the manuscript.

During the gestation of this volume we have greatly benefited from opportunities for research, writing, and consultation with colleagues as Visiting Fellows at Trevelyan College, University of Durham, UK (jointly); the Australian National University, Canberra, Australia (CH); and as a Rockefeller Fellow in the Institute on Violence, Culture, and Survival, Virginia Center for the Humanities, Charlottesville, USA (KMH).

Our research has been aided by the sustained and resourceful assistance of Paula Callan of the QUT library in searching for obscure publications. Michael Belicic took time from his postgraduate studies to help locate elusive material.

We are especially grateful to Gail Turnbull and Glenda Wiltshire, who prepared the manuscript for publication with unfailing patience and expertise; Sally Whitehead for compiling the index; and Irene Hilleard, who was crucial as ever in doing everything that was needed to keep this project moving amid far too many other commitments.

Kayleen M. Hazlehurst and Cameron Hazlehurst
The Editors

1 Gangs in Cross-Cultural Perspective

Cameron Hazlehurst and Kayleen M. Hazlehurst

THE AMERICAN CONTEXT

Nearly four decades ago, the International Criminal Police Organisation (Interpol) and the United Nations General Assembly expressed concern over the worldwide prevalence of juvenile delinquency and gang behaviour. In 1965, after five years of deliberation and planning, Interpol conducted a survey of 32 countries. Defining a gang as a group of four or more young people who engage in anti-social or illegal activities, Interpol concluded that gangs were an urban phenomenon, most common in industrialised countries, especially since the end of the second world war.

Reflecting widespread fears, Interpol reported that many of their respondents related the growth of gangs to post-war urban devastation, homelessness, and 'lack of family unity'. Police in more affluent nations spoke of aimless young people with excess leisure and money. Gangs were observed to be largely male, often recent migrants into cities. They varied in size, with an average age of fifteen to seventeen. Offences against property predominated. Vandalism was common in prosperous industrialised countries. Offences against persons were frequently sexual. Many jurisdictions had preventive programs—youth clubs, police media campaigns, youth training schemes, and specialised police units. But no country had enacted special legislation providing sanctions against gangs. Delinquency laws were generally felt to be sufficient to cope with gangs (Interpol 1967). If there was a suggestion of complacency in many national responses, it would be difficult in the ensuing decades to remain indifferent either to the reality or to the community fear of gangs and criminally-oriented youth subcultures.

In the following 30 years, experts in many countries observed, reported, and analysed disturbing phenomena relating to law-violating behaviour by groups of young people. Regrettably, as with so many issues of common interest internationally, much of the official documentation and research in languages other than English has been inaccessible to the majority of scholars who are not poly-lingual. The invaluable bibliographical database of the U.S. Department of Justice's National Criminal Justice Reference Service has English language abstracts of many non-English publications. But helpful as they are—and our own work has been aided by them—they are for the most part signposts to foreign fields tilled only by indigenous researchers.

In this collection we draw attention to attempts in many countries to understand behaviours which have significant similarities as well as instructive differences. Nowhere until recently has 'the street gang' or 'the youth gang problem' been a more salient social and political concern than in the United States. Nowhere, to our knowledge, are the nature and activities of juvenile or street gangs studied more extensively and intensively. Nowhere does there seem to be greater or more justified pessimism about the efficacy of society's response to gangs.

As more American scholars have studied gangs, theories of gang behaviour and character have multiplied. A burgeoning textbook literature attempts to reconcile a range of explanatory constructs: strain and cultural deviance theories, social learning and social development approaches, subcultural and underclass analyses, and so on (Shelden et al. 1997; Miller and Cohen 1996). One conclusion is enunciated by many and denied by none. Whether as objects of social inquiry or targets of welfare programs or law enforcement, gangs remain enigmatic and unyielding. 'There is no generally accepted explanation of the origins and characteristics of youth gangs' (Miller 1983: 1676). 'Because research has been limited and because researchers have no real consensus on the definition of a gang or gang incident, the scope and seriousness of the youth gang problem are not reliably known' (Spergel et al. 1994: 1). In 1990 Walter B. Miller took as the starting point of his contribution to a major collective volume (Huff 1990) the assumption that the United States had failed to solve its youth gang problem. Miller, a veteran of gang research, asked why. He found answers in the absence of comprehensive, national, gang control strategies; shortcomings in program design, implementation, evaluation, and co-ordination; inadequate resources; and, most important, 'a deep-rooted, reluctance to face up to the implications of the social context of gang life' (Miller 1990: 283). Four years later Daniel J. Monti reminded us that deficiencies in knowledge and understanding remain vitally important.

> Researchers like myself are still trying to put together a broad outline of all that gangs do and mean to their members ... it seems that we can do little more than offer poor guesses as to how gangs can be made less threatening (Monti 1994: 131).

Although scholars complain perennially about insufficient funding, research on gangs in the United States is a multi-million dollar industry. The Office of Juvenile Justice and Delinquency Prevention (OJJDP) of the U.S. Department of Justice recently produced a 'Topical Bibliography' of abstracts of 'the most relevant literature on juvenile gangs'. This highly selective bibliography includes 198 items, only one of them more than five years old (OJJDP 1995). The American research effort is underpinned by substantial funding from justice agencies and foundations. Confronted by endemic social dysfunction, American federal, state, and local government authorities, police, educational and welfare officials, spare little expense in their efforts to understand gang phenomena. Studies of every conceivable kind are supported. Justice system data collections are analysed. Surveys of police, of prosecutors, of educators, of health and welfare professionals are commissioned. Gang members and delinquents in and out of jail are interviewed. So too are young people in schools, clubs, and neighbourhood recreational facilities. Ex-gang members, families, friends, and acquaintances are asked to tell what they know. Yet still the experts say they cannot confidently explain the 'astounding proliferation' (Klein 1995: 203; Curry, Ball and Decker 1996) of American street gangs or demonstrate agreement on effective strategies of prevention and suppression.

As gang research multiplies, the ingenious compete with the ingenuous in affirming the innovative design or 'startling new evidence' of their studies. There is an increasing abundance of intensive case studies of specific gangs or localities and of comprehensive reviews of previous research (Conly et al. 1993; Klein 1995b; Spergel 1995). What is undoubtedly neglected in American research, however, is a comparative perspective. The lack of interest in other national experiences is not accidental. The majority of American scholars, justice system officials, and policy makers appear to share the conviction that their gangs and gang problems are unique. As one of the leading authorities, Professor Malcolm W. Klein, put it emphatically in 1991 'The street gang is basically an American product'. Professor Klein distilled his thesis of American 'exceptionalism' in a foreword to the first comprehensive college textbook, *An Introduction to Gangs*, by George W. Knox:

> The United States is not alone in being an industrialised nation, nor in having major urban areas with denotable inner cities, nor in having sizeable minority populations, nor in having failed social policies for the urban poor, nor in relinquishing much responsibility for social control to the criminal justice system. Yet, with very few exceptions, the United States *is* alone in its development of the urban street gang. Our gangs are like no others in the world—ours are far more prevalent, more permanent in their communities, larger and more complex, and more criminally involved by far (Klein, in Knox 1995: iii).

American uniqueness could perhaps be defended with definitional agility. Curiously, in his latest major work, Klein himself has qualified his argument and tabled an odd assortment of observations and reports from other continents. He identifies 'analogues to the U.S. pattern' in Brussels, Mexico City, Port Moresby, and Berlin (Klein 1995b: 213-28) but makes no attempt to interpret 'the U.S. pattern' in the light of the analogous phenomena.

Meanwhile a thriving ancillary enterprise in debating the most useful way to define gangs shows no signs of abating. Recent debates about definitions have contributed to a greater conceptual awareness but no consensus among gang researchers (Conly et al. 1993). The state of knowledge—or, more accurately, the state of uncertainty—about gangs in America is distilled in the series of 28 questions which conclude James C. Howell's review of gang research (Howell 1994). Howell points to a large research agenda beginning with the elementary need to distinguish 'true gangs from other collective youth groups' and to differentiate between types of gangs. Is the quest for definitional precision worth pursuing? Ruth Horowitz has argued cogently that there are benefits from the fresh questions and thinking that arise from definitional flexibility:

> The search for parameters of what constitutes a gang ... may have important implications for policy-making ... but it is unlikely that social scientists will ever agree to one definition, let alone be able to persuade practitioners and officials of its merits (Horowitz 1990: 47).

Unhappy at leaving the matter there, Richard Ball and David Curry have provided a 20-page conspectus of logical flaws, inconsistencies, and tautologies in gang literature before concluding that they 'have only tried to clear the ground somewhat'! (Ball and Curry 1995: 241). In clearing the ground, Ball and Curry have warned against 'conflating correlates with intrinsic, analytic properties'. The most important correlate they contend, is 'illegal activity'. Others, they say, are adolescent male membership, lower socio-economic status, urban areas, territoriality, violence, and drug dealing (Ball and Curry 1995: 236). There is continuing controversy over the extent to which gangs are responsible for violent crime, homicide, and drug trafficking for example (Shelden et al. 1997: 137-54). But, if a definition emptied of all 'correlates' might satisfy a fastidious sociological theorist, its value to justice professionals would be limited.

Adolescent male membership is incontestably, almost tautologically, a defining element of the juvenile or youth gang. While female gang members, even female gangs, are not unknown (Knox 1995: 340-65; Shelden et al. 1997: 155-77), there is no disputing that many gangs still consist exclusively of males who are best thought of as pre-adults. Moreover, there is much more to be said about the age profiles of gangs in America and elsewhere. Diego Vigil's illuminating accounts of barrio gangs have shown how they may have 'age-graded cliques' as well as older members, 'sages of the street' who remain 'mired in the barrio' (Vigil, in Cummings and Monti 1993: 104-05). John Hagedorn (1988) delineated four main age groupings in Milwaukee gangs. The possibility of making a generalisable distinction between 'youth gangs' and 'young-adult gangs' was suggested by the analysis of Joe and Robinson (1980) in their study of immigrant Chinese youth gangs in Vancouver in the late 1970s. The status advantage enjoyed by those who had greater contact with young-adult gangs resonates with what is known about gang hierarchies elsewhere. The proximity of established older gangs provides role models and career paths. But, as another researcher has found, 'many Asian groups cannot be considered "groups of youngsters" since the age range is greater than adolescence (14-34), and many participants are in their twenties and thirties' (Toy 1992a: 17; Toy 1992b: 657).

Mixed-age membership is not unique to Chicano and Asian gangs. Indeed, George W. Knox goes so far as to argue that the notion of youth gang is out of place in the 'real world of criminal justice' (Knox 1995: 8). One of the most respected veterans of American gang research reported a quarter century after his first investigations that the modal age of gang members had apparently changed from sixteen to 20 (Klein paraphrased in Knox 1995: 58). Klein and his associates no longer restrict their conception of gangs to groups of adolescent youngsters. They argue that the term 'street gang' is now a better descriptor, as 'setting and style' are more defining characteristics than age (Klein 1995b: 21). Perhaps street gang would always have been more appropriate. For, as Ruth Horowitz cautions, there is no conclusive evidence about the changing age composition of American gangs: 'there may have been older youths who were affiliated with gangs, but no one may have noticed because gang members were defined as "juvenile"' (Horowitz 1990: 44). Definitional exclusion of older offenders who were not recognised as gang members could have unduly shaped Miller's conclusion in 1975 that longitudinal arrest data showed no 'age expansion' (Miller, quoted in Lasley 1992: 436).

More recently, some theorists have contended that the growth of an urban underclass is linked directly with the emergence of post-adolescent gang membership. Ronald Huff's proposition (1992: 33) that the American gang problem 'overwhelmingly involves members of the urban underclass' is undeniable (Jackson 1991). But underclass theorists provide no satisfactory explanation either of the absence of gangs where theory suggests they should be or of the majority of youth who apparently remain immune to the gang-generating conditions in which they live (Miller and Cohen 1996: 15). Attempts to bring greater precision to the phenomenon of aging youth gangs that is supposedly evident in numerous locations and ethnic groups have produced mostly inconclusive or negative results (Lasley 1992). Alicia Rand's exploration of 'Transitional Life Events and Desistance from Delinquency and Crime' suggests the potential of more sophisticated analytical procedures (Rand 1987). But the idea of the 'juvenile gang' or 'youth gang' remains unproblematic in much recent literature (Covey et al. 1992; Shelden et al. 1997).

ACROSS CULTURES

The contributors to this volume were unconstrained by rigid definition or disciplinary boundaries. Implicitly, however, all proceed from the premise that it is their orientation to illegal activity which animates our interest in gangs. Gangs are recognised as different from other adolescent (and post-adolescent) groups in the greater frequency of their illegal activities, the leadership and purposeful nature of their offending, and their turf claims (not necessarily related to neighbourhoods) (Huff 1992: 21). There may be advantages in the American context in excluding skinheads, bikers, prison gangs, 'copy-cat' gangs, 'wannabe' groups, and even 'so-called drug gangs' (Klein 1995b: 23) so as to leave a residual category of street gangs. The Chicago researchers Irving Spergel and David Curry make subtle distinctions between 'gang', 'street gang', 'traditional youth gang', and 'posse' or 'crew' (quoted in Shelden et al. 1997: 15). But what we knew of international experiences suggested that it would be inappropriate, certainly premature, to impose an American schema (Stelfox 1996: 4). Thus, neither the American scholars nor those whose research interests are focused on other continents, were explicitly requested to use the United States as a touch-stone. Yet the recent histories reported here from Germany, Russia, South Africa, the United Kingdom, Australia, New Zealand, Papua New Guinea, and Canada constitute an eloquent commentary on the thesis of American exceptionalism. Klein's initial emphasis on urban location, prevalence, permanence, size, complexity, and degree of criminality limited the bases for comparison. But, even if his criteria alone are applied, the case for American difference requires considerably more nuance and qualification than it usually receives. It rests more on ignorance of possible comparisons than on a comprehensive examination of comparable phenomena elsewhere.

Apart from isolated, and seemingly randomly acquired, references, the bibliographies of American texts generally provide little guidance to international literature. In a valuable review of 'Historical Perspectives of Gang Research' Dale Hardman pointed in 1967 to a number of scholars who had followed the pioneer Frederick Thrasher in believing that 'ganging is an adolescent phenomenon in all cultures' (Hardman 1967: 7). Block and Niederhoffer's comparison of four 'primitive cultures' with New York gangs was suggestive but far from definitive (Block and Niederhoffer 1957). And Hardman asked two questions which he concluded were unresolved in the then current scholarly literature: 'Are some cultures more conducive to ganging than others? If so, why?' (Hardman 1967: 26). Hardman's questions have been largely ignored.

It is of course difficult to answer Hardman's questions unless there is prior agreement on exactly which phenomena are to be examined. When Klein asks 'Is the American street gang unique?' we need to be aware that what he calls 'our pattern' (Klein 1995b: 214) does not comfortably encompass the 'new entrepreneurial gangs' in the United States described by Carl S. Taylor (1990) and Martin Sanchez-Jankowski (1991). Klein's tests seem contrived so as to exclude from consideration many groupings which other scholars, justice professionals, and group members themselves think of as gangs. They do not envisage an evolving gang morphology even though he himself recognises the recent 'taggers-to-tagbangers-to-gangs progression' (Klein 1995b: 211). Klein asks:

- Are they territorial, with gang rivalries?

- Do they acknowledge themselves as criminally oriented groups?
- Do they exhibit cafeteria-style crime patterns rather than crime-specific focuses?
- Are their structures moderately cohesive, neither very tight and structured nor quite amorphous?
- Are they the seeming products of current or growing inner-city areas of poverty, alienation, and discrimination; do they display the cultural signs that provide special identification—the attire, tattoos, argot, and overall posture of the street gang? (Klein 1995b: 214).

After a somewhat perfunctory survey of fragmentary information from about 20 countries, Klein concedes that 'other spots have developed their own variants on ganglike structures, and a few ... have given birth to genuine street gangs of the American sort' (ibid: 228). But he evinces no interest in the possibility that understanding of American gangs might be enhanced by international comparison.

There are only scattered examples over the past 30 years of explicit 'cross-cultural' comparative studies. In most cases the comparisons are between the United States and one other country. Thus Baur (1964) compared 'the trend of juvenile offences' in the United States and the Netherlands; in a tribute to the pioneer gang researchers Harry McKay and Clifford Shaw, Weinberg looked at delinquency in Accra and Clinard and Abbott examined two slum communities in Kampala (1976); Campbell and Muncer (1982, 1989), Whitfield (1982) and Campbell et al. (1992) examined American gangs and British sub-cultures; Westermann and Burfeind (1991) provide a fairly comprehensive overview of crime and justice in Japan and the United States; Sarnecki (1986) engaged robustly with American theoretical literature and concluded that 'Swedish gangs cannot be compared to the American either in number, violence or in any other respect'; Wikstrom (1991) broadened the canvas by placing the Swedish experience of 'Urban Crime, Criminals, and Victims' in an Anglo-American comparative perspective.

Irving Spergel's outstanding literature review refers to Japanese, Chinese, Italian, New Zealand, and East European studies and reports and concludes that youth gangs 'apparently are present in both socialist and free-market societies and in both developing and developed countries' (Spergel 1990: 171-3 cf Spergel 1995: 3-6). A notable general survey is Covey, Menard, and Franzese's *Juvenile Gangs* which devotes a 20-page chapter to 'comparative perspectives' and another fourteen pages to 'gangs in western history'. Covey et al., offer useful observations on the implications of an eclectic assembly of studies from every continent and every decade since the 1940s. They rightly emphasise the difficulties in comparing data compiled on incommensurate bases. Failures to distinguish between youth subcultures, gangs, and other law-violating groups—where such distinctions might have enhanced understanding—are a further admitted compounding factor. Undeterred by these limitations, or by the arbitrary chronological range and geographical locations of the studies they cite, Covey and his colleagues venture ten 'generalisations' derived from their cross-national and historical evidence.

The generalisations of Covey et al. (1992: 122-5) are as interesting for what they omit as for what they include. They note characteristics relating to social disorganisation, urbanisation, and industrialisation, gender, age, status and class, internal structure, activities, aetiology, and international impacts. They note an apparent consensus among researchers on the supposedly greater violence of American gangs. (The sole reference here is to a comparison with the Netherlands published in 1964.) What is conspicuously missing in this analysis is any attempt to compare official perceptions and responses to gangs. The sociological differences catalogued by scholars may be less significant for policy makers and law enforcement agencies than the behavioural similarities. Another dimension glimpsed in some studies but not pursued is the extent to which gangs can be seen in different times and places as having political motivation and objectives. Covey et al. (1992: 101) acknowledged that in America in the 1960s the 'Vice Lords', 'Black Panthers', 'Youth Lords', and 'Black Liberation Arm' 'provided politically conscious alternatives to traditional gang activity'. A more nuanced account had been given by James F. Short (1975); and Mike Davis (1992: 299) has detailed 'a radical permutation of Black gang culture' in the Los Angeles of the early 1970s. Spergel and his associates have commented on the 'symbiotic relationship' which has developed in more recent years between politicians and gangs in some low-income American communities. Youth gang members have been assigned tasks in local politics including obtaining signatures for petitions, putting up and tearing down posters, transporting and persuading voters. Gangs have been used in attempts to calm communities on the verge of tumult or riot. 'Gangs and gang members have received income, acceptance, status, and occasionally a limited degree of influence for their services' (Spergel et al. 1994: 4). In Chicago in 1994 some gang members actually ran for local office, perhaps foreshadowing a new trend towards political advocacy (Todd R. Clear, in Shelden et al. 1997: xii). All of these modern developments are in fact a replay of what Knox calls 'the enduring relationship between politics and gangs'—a relationship prominent in the works of pioneer scholars but subsequently often unnoticed (Knox 1995: 115 and 116-39). Spergel (1995: 124), comparing Japan and the United States, concludes that 'the dynamics of gang formation and the basic tendency of gangs to relate symbiotically to the political structure are remarkably similar'.

The international evidence of gang politicisation and the role of gangs in political violence and the disturbance of public order is abundant but must be interpreted with caution. The gangsterism associated with certain political organisations must not be confused with the political disguise sometimes adopted by essentially criminal groups. Yakuza syndicates may adopt right-wing political colouration but these are tactical adjustments and mergers not character transformations (Shikita and Tsuchiya 1992: 89; Friedland 1993). Moreover, the line is not always clear between those groups for which micro-territoriality or the accumulation of wealth are primary objectives and those like the Red Brigades, the Tamil Tigers, and the I.R.A. whose acts of murder, hijacking, kidnapping, and theft, have an avowed political goal which may sometimes cloak apolitical criminality (Lavey 1990). Italian researchers, for example, were puzzled in the mid-1970s by a decline in serious violent crime (murder, felonious assault, rape) among juveniles. This unexplained pattern and the relative absence of purposeless gang violence were in marked contrast to the emergent new form of political violence, kidnapping for ransom (Italian Society of Criminology 1977). On the other hand the symbiotic relationship of the Mafia and the Italian political system is now amply documented (Jamieson 1994; Schneider and Schneider 1994).

There are a number of elements in the reported experience of widely separate nations and disparate cultures which suggest that American scholars may have some way to go before they can be sure about what really makes American gangs unique. Consider, for example, the political dimensions in what have been described as 'social outlawry' in urban Jamaica and township violence in South Africa. Faye V. Harrison, writing of observations in the late 1970s, cast some violent crime in Jamaica as opposition to 'the oppression manifest in chronic unemployment, police repression, and partisan victimisation'. The complex relationships between 'corner' gangs and political parties—with particular groups switching 'from non-partisan outlawry to clientelist entanglement'—illustrated, Harrison suggested, a variety of principled forms of resistance to established authorities. A mass emigration of Jamaican criminals to the United States through the 1970s diminished but did not extinguish the political impetus behind their activities. Jamaican posses, recognised by the early 1990s as the most ruthless and deadly of organised criminal groups in the United States, focused on one major objective: control of street-level distribution of crack/cocaine. To this end they developed relationships with West Coast street gangs, as well as traditional organised crime groups and the Colombian cartels. In the absence of research or justice system data it was difficult to determine whether the profits of posse enterprise crime 'are being used to support political factions in Jamaica, used exclusively for narcotics trafficking, or for both' (Gay and Marquart 1993: 162).

If much modern Jamaican gang activity in the United States has roots in Caribbean political struggles, there is nothing new or unique about links between 'homeland' conflicts and violent clashes in immigrant communities. The Chinese in America are another case in point. Notwithstanding the obtrusive jargon of their Marxist analysis, Takagi and Platt persuasively argued nearly 20 years ago that it was important to distinguish between delinquency and organised political violence in San Francisco's Chinatown. While there was undoubtedly an upsurge in Chinese youth crime in the 1970s, the underlying tensions arising from Kuomintang influence were crucial to an understanding of the wave of murders that seized media attention. Indiscriminate use of the term gang by police and newspapers blurred the distinction between youth characterised by Takagi and Platt as aspiring for a better way of life, and those 'being paid to keep things as they are' (Takagi and Platt 1978).

At about the same time as Jamaican criminals were being interpreted by sociologists and anthropologists in the context of political resistance, similar perceptions were being advanced in New Zealand. As a new Maori political party sprang up in the early 1980s fears were voiced that it might become the political expression of the growing street gang violence in New Zealand's major cities. Matiu Rata, the leader of the Mana Motuhake party, had earlier acknowledged that the gangs were a symptom of 'a general urban crisis which Maori and Island people face'. And one of Rata's principal lieutenants, a senior Maori academic, linked gangs with protest groups as 'manifestations of the stifled desire of the Maori people for self-determination in the suffocating atmosphere of political domination and Pakeha [White] paternalism' (Hazlehurst 1993: 45, 58). But, apart from well-publicised and inconclusive talks with one large gang, Mana Motuhake and the gangs went separate ways. Both gangs and radical political groups made gains in membership and influence without finding much common ground.

The political challenge from New Zealand's indigenous minority has not been a major threat to stability and public order since the nineteenth century. Gangs have in some cases provided an ethnic identity for deculturated youth. Some have become organised criminal enterprises with international links (Justice and Law Reform Committee 1996). The rhetoric of social disadvantage can be heard on the lips of gang apologists and sympathetic liberals. But the gangs have not been radicalised. Nor have they used political agendas to veil criminality. In South Africa, with an indigenous population itself fundamentally in conflict, the story is more complex. Much gang violence in South African township and squatter camps in the 1980s might have had political inspiration or rationalisation. The majority of youth were militant participants in township eruptions (Straker 1992: 21). But, as one acute observer noted in 1989: 'No one's too sure any more how much politics has to do with the killings ... the basic reality, beyond and alongside politics and everything else is the gang' (Johnson 1989: 14-15). In a frightening report foreshadowing future community disintegration, R.W. Johnson wrote of the area between Durban and Pietermaritzburg where an estimated 1000 African children lived wild in the bush. Forced out by squatter-camp gang wars, these homeless young people were often described as pirates or flocks of wild birds. They had become 'violence-entrepreneurs, operating protection rackets and hiring themselves out as fighters in various community conflicts' (ibid: 15).

What would become of these feral youngsters? Johnson speculated that they would in time develop a leadership structure with 'the emergence of strong men or, at least, strong children' (ibid). More chillingly he recounted:

> A pharmacist friend told me how, driving through a township to deliver some medical supplies ... he was cheerfully greeted by a crocodile of uniformed school children marching unaccountably down the road in the middle of the school day. Later he found that an intruder into their school had attempted to rape one of the schoolgirls and, when she had resisted, had knifed her. Her classmates voted to suspend classes while they went off to burn the intruder's house down and kill him if they could. It was while they were on their way to do this errand that they had encountered my pharmacist friend and shown such good humour (Johnson 1989: 15).

Four years later, another British scholar described a typical Soweto weekend of fifteen murders, over 40 armed robberies, and up to 20 reported rapes. These predatory crimes were interspersed with sporadic 'political' assassinations for which payment was based on a quota for the killing of members of rival groups. Like justice reformers in many other parts of the world South Africa's National Institute for Crime Prevention and Rehabilitation of Offenders (NICPRO) was developing restorative programs aimed at reintegrating offenders into their communities rather than driving them into street gangs (Cooper 1993). Meanwhile, the transition to a democratic regime has been accompanied by a crime wave that has overwhelmed a demoralised and understaffed police force. Private security businesses flourish. Moslem vigilantes seek to reclaim their communities from gangs dealing in drugs, prostitution, robbery, and car-jacking. Senior law officers speak of anarchy in the streets of the nation's main cities (Beresford 1996).

South African history directs our attention to a question that is all too rarely asked: what is the impact of trans-generational influences on gang formation and maintenance? In this volume, Sinclair Dinnen argues that contemporary urban gangs in Papua New Guinea, exhibit 'a rich mixture of social traditions'. They are not explicable solely in terms of urbanisation and modernisation since the 1960s. In the South African context, although the precise linkages remain to be discovered, it is hard to believe, for example, that township violence in the 1980s could be adequately explained without reference to gang antecedents in the mining compounds and prisons of earlier decades.

Breckenridge's demonstration of the role of criminal organisation in buttressing ethnic solidarity among Mpondo mine workers suggests several lines of inquiry. In the first place he notes how the so-called Isitshozi gangs of the 1920s onwards resembled the Zulu-dominated Ninevite gang of an even earlier period. The Ninevites were mostly dead or dispersed. But it is conceivable that those serving long prison terms might have supplied inspiration and leadership to a new generation of offenders. The Isitshozi were themselves for the most part older men in their 30s. But as Breckenridge, following Moodie (1988) and Beinart (1987), shows: 'the gangs specifically recruited youths known to participate in homosexuality ... Establishing control over the supply of youths within the compounds was probably the gang's chief priority'. Youths not only performed domestic duties they were instructed to commit burglaries and robberies, and participate in 'a reign of terror on the paths leading to and from the mines' (Breckenridge 1990: 60-63). By the late 1930s the small Isitshozi gangs (usually about ten members) were undergoing a transformation as they drifted into the urban underworld and drew recruits from the large numbers of marginalised urban youth. More frequent violence and an increasingly hierarchical structure in the more youthful contemporary Indlavini groups in the 1950s may have reflected the 'exposure of young Mpondo migrants to Isitshozi organisation and activity' (ibid: 76). Speculative though it may be, Breckenridge's conclusion points to a potentially fruitful research agenda. 'It is perhaps here, amidst the violent control of the compounds, the exhausting mine work routine and the urban underworld, that we should seek an explanation for the so-called traditional hostility between the ethnic segments of the African working class' (ibid: 78).

What is manifest in environments as distant and dissimilar as South Africa and Russia is that the growth and expanding impact of gangs has a direct relationship with the reach, strength, and resolve of law enforcement agencies. In spite of strict censorship and a pervasive internal security and police presence, street violence and delinquency were visible problems in Russia by the mid-1970s. Moscow youth gangs made their own weapons, including long knives and guns. A *New York Times* correspondent concluded in 1978 that the 'picture emerging is that much Soviet violence, perhaps most of it, is the work of young people aged 14 to 18' (Shipler 1978: 42). By the late 1980s *glasnost* had led to the replacement of anecdotes and unsubstantiated journalistic estimates with remarkable data. The *USSR Crime Statistics and Summaries: 1989 and 1990* contained the astonishing admission that 'the Board of the MVD USSR, as a result of operative activities for 1989, noted that the internal affairs organs on the whole were incapable of maintaining proper order in the country, unable to deliver a decisive blow against extremist and criminal elements'. In some regions it was stated 'the worsening of the criminal situation was related to a great extent to the increased activities of anti-social teenage and youth street gangs'. This was particularly so in Uzbekistan, Kazakhstan, the Ukraine, in Moscow and many cities of the Volga region (Serio 1992).

Soviet authorities increasingly focused on organised crime in the late 1980s as gang shoot-outs in central Moscow drew attention to the rapid growth of what was officially described as 'group criminality'. Youth group criminality also became a preoccupation of authorities elsewhere who looked for underlying social and economic explanations of growing youth crime (Volobuev and Chebotarev, in Buckwalter 1990: 75-82, 95-9; Pilkington 1994: 141-60, 257-60). With the manifest breakdown of public order in Russia in the 1990s, Marxist explanatory formulas cast in terms of deepening 'contradictions existing in our society' (Borodin 1990: 5 cf Handelman 1994; Vesselinovitch 1996) seemed increasingly threadbare.

In examining the official and scholarly literature from countries with varying legal and juridical frameworks, it is necessary to be alert to the local particularities of definition, labelling, statistical compilation, and theory. Chinese scholars, for example, have predictably drawn attention to the surge of crime in the special economic zones where trade is more open and the influence of alien 'bourgeois morality' and 'underworld societies from outside the mainland' most marked (Curran and Cook 1993; Bojin 1992: 57). Unsurprisingly, official policy and public opinion have identified 'migrants' or 'blind roamers' converging from the interior on the rapidly growing coastal cities as responsible for threats to public safety. In Guangdong province police claimed that they had smashed 843 gangs in two days during a 'Strike Hard' campaign against 'groups of hoodlum powers' (McGregor 1996). An earlier study of 'Youngsters' Unlawful and Criminal Cliques' found that over 80 percent of the youngsters in a Xhanghai juvenile facility were in custody for committing crimes in groups (Zhou and Zia 1988, in Curran and Cook 1993: 306-07). The data is thin, the background information sparse, and the accompanying theory is simplistic. Historic continuities are conveniently overlooked (Epstein 1986). But there is clearly a prima facie case for exploring further the kinds of explanations which point to changing family and community values, in addition to growing temptations, as among the keys to understanding the increasing group criminality of Chinese youth. Nor should we be too quick to dismiss as 'a subjective factor' the 'yearning' for 'respect and love' which has been discerned among young Chinese offenders. 'Those who have lost respect and love need to be respected and loved the most, and the more respect and love for them are the antecedent and preconditions for their recovery' (Lui and Fu 1988, in Curran and Cook 1993: 305).

Absence of love is an undeveloped explanatory category in American studies, although it has an unspoken presence in much that is written about the underclass and 'fatherless' children. Elsewhere the connections are explicitly made. Twenty years ago, father deprivation—as a result of polygamy and large families—was seen as an important cause of delinquency in Iran and Iraq. Recommended modifications to the Iranian and Iraqi family systems, had they been seriously attempted, could scarcely have had as great an impact on youth behaviour as the socio-political revolutions that were to convulse both nations (Lynn 1978). In many so-called 'countries in transition' (United Nations 1995: 17), exemplified by the Russia and South Africa studies in this volume, juvenile delinquency and gang crime have grown dramatically over the past decade and a half (Finckenauer and Kelly 1992). In understanding the social pathologies of these turbulent environments conventional academic distinctions between delinquency and gang behaviour, gangs and subcultures, can be useful but other templates are also needed. As a recent United Nations Expert Group (1994: 39) noted, what distinguishes gangs in these situations is that they do not engage primarily in subsistence delinquency. While they may not be dedicated criminal enterprises, neither are they criminal for survival. Rather, they are more likely to be afflicted by what a German writer characterised as the 'murder of the soul', the abandonment of any ideals other than self-interested materialism (Stelling 1972). Such deracinated youth in Russia form 'an attractive labour pool' for criminal organisations operating in a world which 'offers a kind of spiritual satisfaction for the younger generation' (Handelman 1994: 17).

Where love and respect have gone, fearful admiration might fill the void. 'No one is going to steal my "rep"' proclaimed a Los Angeles gang member, recently arrested for the slaying of a rival. Individual manifestations of 'moral poverty' may not impress some criminologists although a host of American observers have pointed out the danger of allowing money and violence to buy dignity, making racketeers and gang veterans role models for youth (Zoglin 1996; Martens 1990: 113). It no longer seems a profound perception that the absence of kinship ties 'encourages the formation of adolescent peer groups which fill the social vacuum between the nuclear family and the community' (Joe and Robinson 1980). Yet policy-makers have so far failed to diminish one of the major assaults on the nuclear family which is of their own making: the incarceration of thousands of low-level non-violent drug sellers (Massing 1996; Tonry 1995). After two or three 'fatherless' generations, the concern is not simply that youth gangs can be surrogate families. In many cases, young people in gangs need to be understood as victims as well as offenders. As the line between gangs and organised crime is progressively blurred, a 'nefarious chain' is forged 'in which seasoned criminals enlist younger "associates", who in turn recruit still younger ones for proscribed and hazardous acts' (United Nations Expert Group 1994: 52). The example of the Neapolitan Nuovo Camorra Organizzata is salutary. Led by 'men of respect' it recruited many young people to whom it 'furnished real, proper work and has encouraged a sense of pride; if you're tough you can have dignity, you can escape your poor background, you can be a camorrista: you can be somebody' (Ruggiero 1993: 152).

No one should be under any illusions that attempts to extend our knowledge of these matters will be easy. The pitfalls and dangers of research into violent group criminal behaviour are obvious. The repertoire of research strategies includes a range of direct and indirect methods (Hamm 1996). But unique cultural patterns and societies in ferment call for inventiveness as well as courage. We had hoped, for example, that this collection might have included a study of the relationship between youth crime, delinquency, and adult criminal organisations in Japan. Joachim Kersten's valuable essay on 'Street Youths, Bosozoku, and Yakuza' (1993) had delineated the distinctions between youth gangs, Bosozoku (hot-rodders), and the major 'corporate' yakuza. The crucial question of the nature and extent of overlap between the three categories is yet to be adequately explored. And we were unable to identify a scholar with relevant recent expertise to undertake the task. At the end of the 1980s, Japanese authorities published official data indicating that the percentage of 'Boryokudan' (gang) members under 30 had declined from 56.1 to 30.4 between 1966 and 1987. The absolute number had fallen from 82,520 to 26,195. While there must be some scepticism about the astonishing precision of these figures (the derivation of which is not disclosed) they were consistent with the conclusion that 'gangsters are steadily ageing since young people try to stay away from gangs' (Shikita and Tsuchiya 1992: 91-3). They were also consistent with emerging evidence that some younger gangsters were developing free-lance drug operations giving them independence from established crime lords and making themselves less visible to police surveillance (Hills 1993). Criminological research is an underdeveloped field in Japan (Johnson 1996: 179). There has been little official encouragement for inquiries into the criminal justice system or studies which, by implication, might question its effectiveness and spotlight the inter-dependence of criminal, business, and political interests. Nevertheless what is clear from Kersten's synthesis of recent research is that cultural explanations of Japan's low official crime rates are at best problematic. The notion that 'reintegrative shaming' is a dominant social response in Japan which inhibits the development of criminal subcultures is plainly in need of careful qualification (Braithwaite 1989: 61-6, 136-7; Becker 1988; Tanioka and Glaser 1991).

Thinking about the nature and evolution of juvenile gangs is slowly coming to terms with the changing environment of organised crime and international criminal networks. The influence of major groups like the Hell's Angels, Triads, Yakuza, Posses and Yardies, the Colombian cartels, and the Mafia reaches down through a multitude of channels to street-corners and school grounds. Newer eastern European and Russian groups compete for influence. For Italy, Pino Arlacchi (1991) has described a 'pattern of territorial and sectorial [sic] franchises' which draw in gangs of neighbourhood youths as providers of 'information, logistical support, and specialized personnel' for the Mafia. In Denmark, where outlaw motorcycle gangs have fought for control of the east European drug market, Hell's Angels use associates and candidates for 'dirty work' (Devlin 1992: 86). Elsewhere they are known to use 'puppet clubs' (Campbell 1993: 5). In the United States, ethnic organised crime groups in particular have the capacity to use immigrant youth as disposable foot-soldiers and small-scale entrepreneurs in narcotics distribution, burglary, and extortion. Long established Chinese and Japanese criminal organisations operate on a multinational scale. They recruit young members and use members of youth gangs to carry out assignments as contract killers, extortionists, and drug peddlers. American law enforcement authorities had not until recently discerned comparable adult organisations among Vietnamese, Cambodian, and Korean immigrant communities (Jan 1993: 38-9). But police and intelligence agencies have very limited capabilities in penetrating ethnic criminal groups. Scholars fare little better (Sanders 1994: 155-63). So little is known about the organisation of Colombian, Vietnamese, Chinese or Cuban criminal enterprises, Martens (1990: 111) concluded, 'that comparisons and analyses are relatively meaningless'. As late as 1993, it was possible for an American scholar to write that 'ethnic specific research on gangs is sparse' (Joe 1993: 20). And a call four years earlier for research into variations in gang behaviour across ethnic lines (Jackson 1989) could be cited with barely a hint of embarrassment that such research was not already well advanced (Joe 1993: 20). In fact there has been a growing body of research over the last decade devoted to examining Vietnamese, Chinese, Chicano, African-American, Jamaican, Filipino and other ethnically specific law-breaking groups in the United States. But even the best scholarly syntheses conclude with as many questions as answers.

As more is learned about the ever-expanding links between Chinese, Japanese, Jamaican, Sicilian, Vietnamese, Colombian, Calabrian and other criminal organisations which flourish in several continents, research which is directed at trying to explain juvenile gangs by reference exclusively to endogenous socio-economic factors seems increasingly less adequate. The conclusion of Gay and Marquart (1993: 162) is persuasive: 'more research, in general, is needed on the impact of economic, social, cultural, and political factors in the native country upon the genesis of organised crime groups in the United States'. The standpoint we take embraces this view, but goes further. What is now imperative is an international research strategy that encompasses both a myriad local studies and, as William F.

McDonald (1995: 6) argues, 'global processes, global units of analysis, and global institutions'.

COMPARISONS AND CONTRASTS

Issues which have preoccupied American scholars must inform but not dominate international research agendas. What we can learn from examining trends in many different places should also caution us against complacency. It may be tempting to draw optimistic policy conclusions when official exaggerations or misconceptions are refuted but the temptation must be resisted. Malcolm Klein may have been right to say that the gangs he studied were neither well-organised nor persistent, and that most crime committed in gang territories is not perpetrated by gangs (Klein 1995b). One can almost hear the sigh of relief accompanying the conclusion that 'little evidence exists to show that traditional L.A. street gangs have deserted their turf focus to operate primarily as drug distribution networks' (Sullivan and Silverstein 1995: 28). Anxiety is further diminished by the argument that by their very nature, lacking in discipline and organisation and prone to high levels of violence, street gangs are unlikely to evolve into 'full-fledged organised crime groups' (ibid.). True as this may be in one place at one time, is it a prudent leap of faith to base criminal justice system responses on such suppositions? While there are, as Marcus Felson suggests, abundant 'misconceptions' about gangs, a discussion of 'crime and everyday life' which refers only to the misconceptions is surely deficient (Felson 1994).

The scholars who have contributed to this volume have approached both the academic literature and popular perceptions and misconceptions in a variety of ways. One of the leading American researchers Diego Vigil, and his associate Steven Yun, restate Vigil's influential 'multiple marginality' thesis and test its explanation of the origins of gangs against the evidence of the Vietnamese community in California. Subcultural theories are subjected to close scrutiny in several essays. Roger Burke and Ros Sunley place their own recent studies and 'post-modern' perspective in a British research tradition stretching over three decades. German and Australian phenomena are presented by Joachim Kersten and Judith Bessant and Rob Watts from similar standpoints, emphasising discourses on masculinity. The richness of their observations demonstrates the inadequacy of taxonomies that distinguish simplistically between 'delinquent' subcultures and gangs. These contributions also illustrate the range of disciplinary backgrounds and theoretical paradigms which have been brought to bear on gangs over the past half century.

In the first half of the twentieth century, for example, there was a good deal of research on gangs and delinquent groups by British psychologists and psychoanalysts (Scott: 1956). From the 1960s onwards sociologically oriented subcultural studies have held the field. In 1996 a report commissioned by the Home Office concluded that, in spite of a decade of violent incidents associated with gangs, there had been little research in the United Kingdom specifically on gangs. The police service have developed no collective view of what a gang is. A survey of fourteen police forces found that in one third of cases force commanders thought that there were gangs in their areas while local units reported that there were none! (Stelfox 1996: 2). Conceptual confusion abounds. The obtrusive subcultures discussed in this volume by Burke and Sunley may in some places be manifest in ganglike groups. The one gang to which Burke and Sunley specifically refer appears to have evolved from a group of football hooligans. Curiously, the British police are agreed that football hooligans (and terrorists) can be excluded from their otherwise very accommodating definition of gangs. Clearly there is much work to be done before we have an adequate picture of the prevalence of groups in Britain resembling either Klein's street gangs or other criminally oriented enterprises with comparable characteristics.

For Germany, Joachim Kersten takes us a step further with a preliminary analysis which categorises criminal youth groupings across several dimensions. Like Burke and Sunley in Britain, Kersten finds it most instructive to ground a discussion of gangs in Germany in a context of modern subcultural history. Unlike Klein, who says that there are American-style street gangs in Berlin, Kersten believes that there are no groups anywhere in Germany which meet Klein's gang criteria. Xenophobia and racism are critical impulses associated with German youth violence and an underclass ideal of hegemonic masculinity. Kersten's attention to what youth actually say is an important reminder of the need to understand the ideas which often serve to legitimate and motivate violent behaviour. Situational analyses must be complemented by accounts of ideologies, however crude or repugnant they may be.

In contrast to American evolutionary models of youth gang formation leading in some cases to more organised activity and links to adult criminal gangs (Taylor 1990), the contemporary Russian scene is described by Paddy Rawlinson as one in which the dominant organised criminal syndicates co-opt youth groups before they develop an autonomous existence. As in Sicily and other parts of Italy where the Cosa Nostra or Camorra hold sway (Gambetta 1993: 255), some of the more loutish youth gang behaviour is subdued by ruthless adult organisations with more lucrative criminal business operations. But this relatively trivial benefit counts for little in a society whose own leaders acknowledge that organised crime threatens the very existence of the state. Given that some observers had concluded by the early 1990s that in Russia 'the Mafia is the state' (Vitaliev 1991; Vaksberg 1991), the Russian outlook is indeed grim (Lloyd 1995).

The picture in South Africa is also bleak—an exemplar of the impact on youth of prolonged racial and ethnic conflict, alienation, and economic dislocation. Michael Cross has shown how three interrelated youth subcultural worlds can be distinguished in South Africa:

> lumpen and unemployed youth delinquent and semidelinquent subcultures; middle-class cultural rebellion and reformist movements; and working-class student and youth resistance culture, activism, and political militancy (Cross 1993: 380).

Cross's analysis provides a historical basis for understanding current gang activity and the new official efforts at prevention and rehabilitation foreshadowed in this volume by Donald Pinnock and Mara Douglas-Hamilton. The 1970s saw a melding of an emerging street gang culture with youth resistance in schools. In a resurgence of gangsterism in the 1980s, township gangs actually became accomplices of the police in targeting 'schoolchildren, mainly girls, and student and youth political leaders' (Cross 1993: 390). Whether modern South African gangs are better thought of as politically reactionary or criminally opportunist, Pinnock insists that we must recognise their role as the locus of essential ritual and adolescent rites of passage. This perception, in varying degrees, is also present in the historical account of Melbourne's bodgies and widgies by Judith Bessant and Rob Watts and in the work of Marianne Nielsen and her colleagues on the Navajo Nation.

Bessant and Watts have used an innovative form of retrospective ethnography, drawing on the memories of former gang members to reconstruct the texture and meaning of gang lives in the 1950s. Writing of suburban activity in a prosperous Australian city they contend that gang membership was 'essentially about the construction of situations in which awesome struggle and heroic loyalty were conjoined in violence'. There is a remarkable resonance between this insight and the Navajo Nation

Judicial Branch's view of what has happened to many Navajo youth who have 'lost their cultural bearings'. Young Navajo (and some Hopi, Sioux, and Apache) have adopted the baggy clothes, colours, graffiti, tattoos, and street talk of Los Angeles. A Navajo Nation judge reports local youth gang members being paid by established older Albuquerque gangs to undertake violent acts, steal, or destroy property (Judicial Branch of the Navajo Nation 1995: 4). To explain the origins and appeal of gangs among Navajo youth, members of the Judicial Branch have suggested that traditional 'war way thinking' has been appropriated and misdirected. 'War way thinking' it is argued must be refocused into socially constructive channels.

Until very recently Native American gangs had barely been noticed by either justice authorities or scholars. The sparse literature on American Indian criminality is summarised in Poupart (1995), Silverman (1996), and Armstrong et al. (1996). There was useful data in a report by the Arizona Criminal Justice Commision (1993). But the essay by Nielsen, Zion, and Hailer in this collection is a major step forward in this field. Similarly, as Robert Gordon shows, Canadian criminologists have been slow to investigate or even acknowledge the existence of gangs. But Gordon's synthesis of recent work by colleagues and students, complemented by his exposition of the findings of the Greater Vancouver Gang Study, provides a benchmark for more comprehensive research. He supplies soundly-based correctives to the exaggerations and misconceptions of the Canadian press.

The propensity of the media to promote moral panics is well known. (Cohen 1972; Kelsey and Young 1982; Zatz 1987; Goode and Ben-Yehuda 1994). However, it is one thing to discount media sensationalism but another to conclude, as Finn-Aage Esbensen (1996: 139) does for the United States, that the 'current youth gang problem is to a considerable extent a media creation'. As in Gordon's Vancouver, investigations in Melbourne by Ian Warren and Megan Aumair indicated that gangs in that city were indeed more transient and episodic in their activity than media depictions implied. What is evident from the Australian and Canadian press, and could no doubt be demonstrated elsewhere, is the considerable impact of the media both in disseminating gang imagery and provoking community fears.

In Australia, Canada, and Britain it is possible—though we are inclined to think otherwise—that gang realities are less fearsome than media headlines would suggest. In Papua New Guinea and New Zealand official or academic complacency certainly would be misplaced. In relation to the turbulent Papua New Guinea environment, Sinclair Dinnen describes a process of gang 'surrender' to authorities which may have potential for expansion if accompanied by provision of employment opportunities. However, there are good grounds for thinking that the most powerful gangs and older criminal elements will not be attracted to the surrender option. In other cases, the surrender may turn out to be merely a tactic preceding a regrouping of gang elements. There is as yet no evidence of improvement in public safety in Papua New Guinea's major urban areas. At the time of writing, the government has again had to impose curfews in the capital city to achieve minimal restraint of gang crime. Port Moresby's prisons are porous. And, the conclusion of another scholar Andrew Strathern (1993: 54) remains deeply troubling: 'Neither landowners nor raskal appear to recognise any superordinate right of the state to control their activities and demands'.

The New Zealand scene, as described by Pahmi Winter, exhibits a quite different gang strategy. Neither surrender (tactical or genuine) nor rejection of state authority characterises the stance of New Zealand's largest ethnic gangs. Both of the two dominant gangs, Black Power and the Mongrel Mob, have sought an accommodation with New Zealand authorities. The pursuit of recognition and legitimacy as agents of government employment and welfare schemes has gone hand in hand with continuing criminal activity on a large scale. Gang leaders and advisers have developed a rhetoric, demeanour, and negotiating style which convinces some observers that a policy of constructive engagement with gangs may lead to a gradual moderation of law-breaking behaviour. Police and many other political and civic figures remain sceptical of the benefits of dialogue and persuasion. For them, the more compelling concerns are accumulating examples of gang violence, links with international organised crime, intimidation of witnesses, police, and justice system professionals. Government departments and agencies continue to strive to reach a common view on how best to deal with gangs which have developed considerable skill in 'working the system'. At the same time, police, who are aware of the growing presence of the Hell's Angels and Bandidos in New Zealand and their links with smaller local gangs, are seen on television urging the public to press their MPs for tougher action.

Readers of these essays will be tantalised by echoes, resonances, and glimpses of comparable and alternative realities. It would be premature in our present state of knowledge to attempt to impose some universal taxonomy, theory of gang growth, or other explanatory framework on the diverse experiences reported here. There is a great deal more to do before we have even the empirical basis for confident theoretical reformulations.

As Klein (1995b: 232) rightly says about the United States: 'A decent typology of gangs in the 1990s could help us decide how best to approach them for both prevention and control. Know your gangs.' We need research on many parts of the globe not covered in this collection: much of Africa, south and central America, India, Japan, China, and elsewhere. We need also to draw together disparate theoretical and conceptual approaches to youth subcultures, organised crime, delinquency and ganging (Brake 1985; Esbensen 1996: 133; Gottfredson and Hirschi 1994; Wilson and Howell 1993).

In this volume we make no attempt at a comprehensive examination of gang suppression or prevention strategies. We may note at this stage the courage and optimism displayed by many front-line workers wherever gangs currently prevail. The ambitious restorative justice enterprise in South Africa, described by Don Pinnock and Mara Douglas-Hamilton, shows the potential for culturally relevant, and theoretically informed, preventive and rehabilitative programs. Pinnock blends intimate local knowledge with insights drawn from a wide range of anthropological and criminological inquiry. What he says about the role of ritual processes and rites of passage to adulthood fits well with observations elsewhere about ambiguous masculinities. And there is much international interest in programs of the kind he is fostering. By contrast, allusions by Huff (1992: 35-6) and others to the different consequences of American 'malignant neglect' and European social planning appear to bemuse American authorities rather than stimulate fresh lines of investigation or policy innovation.

A comparative project does not entail facile assumptions that advances in understanding can readily be translated into trans-cultural policies and practices. There are many traps for the unwary (Schneider 1994) in what Patricia Steinhoff (1993: 828) has dubbed 'answers for America research'. In a penetrating review essay on Japanese policing, Steinhoff warns against black box cultural explanations. 'How and why', she asks, 'does a society with extremely low crime rates also support over 3,000 organised crime groups with more than 85,000 members?' (Steinhoff 1993: 849 cf Head 1995). To understand the role of culture in accounting for this kind of reality, Steinoff insists that there is little value in 'positing abstract cultural mindsets that systematically polarise societies on the basis of their differences'. The more productive approach is to try to understand the ways in which the 'everyday institutional context of life' constrains and is progressively shaped by individual choices in particular societies. Assessments of the role and impact of gangs in diverse social and cultural environments remind us that time and place make a difference. Gang phenomena need to be understood both in historical and prospective contexts. The policy-maker needs guidance on future possibilities as well as an understanding of the past. We believe that the essays that follow make the case for further, more systematic, comparative study. They certainly provide a choice of promising starting-points in a still under-developed field.

REFERENCES

Arizona Criminal Justice Commission (1993) *Street Gangs in Arizona 1992: A Report from the Arizona Statistical Analysis Center.*

Arlacchi, Pino (1991) 'Organized Crime and Criminal Gangs', in Susan Flood (ed.), *Illicit Drugs and Organized Crime: Issues for a Unified Europe*, Chicago: Office of International Criminal Justice, University of Illinois at Chicago.

Armstrong, Troy L., Guilfoyle, Michael H., and Melton, Ada Pecos (1996) 'Native American Delinquency: An Overview of Prevalence, Causes, and Correlates', in Marianne O. Neilsen and Robert A. Silverman (eds), *Native Americans, Crime, and Justice,* Boulder: Westview Press, 75-88.

Ball, Richard A. and Curry, G. David (1995) 'The Logic of Definition in Criminology: Purposes and Methods for Defining "Gangs"', *Criminology* 33(2): 225-45.

Baur, E. Jackson (1964) 'The trend of juvenile offences in the Netherlands and the United States', *Journal of Criminal Law, Criminology, and Police Science* 55(3): 359-69.

Becker, Carl B. (1988) 'Report From Japan: Causes and Controls of Crime in Japan', *Journal of Criminal Justice* 16(5): 425-35.

Beinart, William (1987) 'Worker Consciousness, Ethnic Particularism and Nationalism: the Experiences of a South African Migrant, 1930-1960', in Shula Marks and Stanley Trapido (eds), *The Politics of Race, Class and Nationalism in Twentieth Century South Africa,* New York: Longman.

Beresford, David (1996) 'S. African police helpless before torrent of crime', *Guardian Weekly*, June 16.

Bloch, H.A. and Niederhoffer, A. (1957) 'Adolescent Behavior and the Gang: A Cross-Cultural Analysis', *Journal of Social Therapy* 3: 174-9.

Bojin, Lai (1992) 'Gang Crimes in Shenzhen', in Ann Lodl and Zhang

Longguan (eds), *Enterprise Crime: Asian and Global Perspectives*, Chicago: Office of International Criminal Justice with the Shanghai Bureau of Justice and the East China Institute of Politics and Law, 52-60.

Borodin, Stanislav B. (1990) 'Crime trends and directions in the criminal policy of the USSR', in Vladimir N. Kudriavtzev (ed.), *Soviet Criminology Update*, Papers collected by the Institute of State and Law of the USSR Academy of Sciences, Rome: United Nations Interregional Crime and Justice Research Institute, Publication No. 38, July: 1-15.

Braithwaite, John (1989) *Crime, Shame and Reintegration*, Sydney and Cambridge: Cambridge University Press.

Brake, Michael (1985) *Comparative Culture: The Sociology of Youth Cultures and Youth Subcultures in America, Britain and Canada*, London: Routledge and Kegan Paul.

Breckenridge, Keith (1990) 'Migrancy, Crime and Faction Fighting: the Role of the Isitshozi in the Development of Ethnic Organisations in the Compounds', *Journal of Southern African Studies* 16(1): 55-78.

Buckwalter, Jane Rae (ed.) (1990) *International Perspectives on Organized Crime*, Chicago: Office of International Criminal Justice, the University of Illinois at Chicago.

Campbell, A. and Muncer, S. (1989) 'Them and us: a comparison of the cultural context of American gangs and British subcultures', *Deviant Behavior* 10(3): 271-88.

Campbell, Anne, Muncer, Steven and Galea, John (1982) 'American Gangs and British Subcultures: A Comparison', *International Journal of Offender Therapy and Comparative Criminology* 26(1): 76-89.

Campbell, Duncan (1993) 'East Europe "poses crime threat"', *Guardian Weekly* June 6: 5.

Chebotarev, Gennady (1990) 'Organised Crime in an International Dimension', in Jane Rae Buckwalter (ed.), *International Perspectives on Organized Crime,* Chicago: Office of International Criminal Justice, The University of Illinois at Chicago, 95-9.

Clinard, Marshall B. and Abbott, Daniel J. (1976) 'Community Organisation and Property Crime: A Comparative Study of Social Control in the Slums of an African City', in James F. Short (ed.), *Delinquency, Crime and Society,* Chicago: University of Chicago Press, 186-206.

Cloward, Richard A. and Ohlin, Lloyd E. (1960) *Delinquency and Opportunity: A theory of delinquent gangs,* New York: Free Press.

Cohen, Stanley (1972) *Folk Devils and Moral Panics: The Creation of the*

Mods and Rockers, London: McGibbon and Kee,

Conly, Catherine H., with Kelly, Patricia, Mahanna, Paul, and Warner, Lynn (1993) *Street Gangs: Current Knowledge and Strategies*,Washington DC: National Institute of Justice.

Cooper, Paul (1993) 'Violent tide rising in townships', *The Times Higher Education Supplement* No. 1100, December 3: 13.

Cross, Michael (1993) 'Youths, Culture, and Politics in South African Education: The Past, Present, and Future', *Youth and Society* 24(4), June: 377-98.

Cummings, Scott and Monti, Daniel J. (eds) (1993) *Gangs: The Origins and Impact of Contemporary Youth Gangs in the United States*, Albany: State University of New York Press.

Curry, G. David, Ball, Richard A., and Decker, Scott H. (1996) 'Estimating the National Scope of Gang Crime from Law Enforcement Data', National Institute of Justice Research in Brief, August.

Davis, Mike (1992) *City of Quartz*, New York: Vintage Books (1st ed. London: Verso 1990).

Devlin, Bruce (1992) 'Outlaw Bikies New Threat to Europe', *Reader's Digest* (Australian edition), July: 81-8.

Epstein, Irving I. (ed.) (1986) 'Juvenile Delinquency in China', *Chinese Education* 19(2).

Esbensen, Finn-Aage (1996) 'A National Gang Strategy', in J. Mitchell Miller and Jeffrey P. Rush (eds), *Gangs: A Criminal Justice Approach*, Cincinnati, OH: Anderson Publishing, 131-41.

Felson, Marcus (1994) *Crime and Everyday Life: Insights and Implications for Society*, Thousand Oaks: Pine Forge Press.

Finckenauer, J.O. and Kelly, L. (1992) 'Juvenile delinquency and youth sub-cultures in the former Soviet Union', *International Journal of Comparative and Applied Criminal Justice* 16(2): 247-62.

Friedland, Jonathan (1993) 'Underworld Mergers: Hard times force yakuza gangs to pool resources', *Far Eastern Economic Review* 156(32) August 12: 19.

Gambetta, Diego (1993) *The Sicilian Mafia: The Business of Private Protection*, Cambridge MA: Harvard University Press.

Gay, Bruce W. and Marquart, James W. (1993) 'Jamaican Posses: A New Form of Organised Crime', *Journal of Crime and Justice* XVI(2): 139-70.

Gottfredson, Michael R. and Hirschi, Travis (1994) 'A General Theory of Adolescent Problem Behavior: Problems and Prospects', in Robert D. Ketterlinus and Michael E. Lamb (eds), *Adolescent Problem Behaviors*:

Issues and Research, Hillsdale NJ and Hove UK: Lawrence Erlbaum Associates, 41-56.

Hamm, Mark S. (1996) 'Doing Gang Research in the 1990s: Pedagogical Implications of the Literature' in J. Mitchell Miller and Jeffrey P. Rush (eds), *Gangs: A Criminal Justice Approach*, Cincinnati OH: Anderson Publishing, 17-31.

Handelman, Stephen (1994) *Comrade Criminal: The Theft of the Second Russian Revolution*, London: Michael Joseph.

Hardman, Dale G. (1967) 'Historical Perspectives of Gang Research', *Journal of Research in Crime and Delinquency* 4(1): 5-27.

Hagedorn John M. with Macon, Perry (1988) *People and Folks: Gangs, Crime and Underclass in a Rustbelt City*, Chicago: Lakeview Press.

Harrison, Faye V. (1988) 'The Politics of Social Outlawry in Urban Jamaica', *Urban Anthropology and Studies of Cultural Systems and World Economic Development* 17(2-3): 259-77.

Hazlehurst, Kayleen M. (1993) *Political Expression and Ethnicity: Statecraft and Mobilisation in the Maori World*, Westport and London: Praeger.

Head, Anthony (1995) 'Japan and the Safe Society', *Japan Quarterly* 42(2): 146-54.

Hills, Ben (1993) 'Yakuza under siege', *Courier Mail* May 28: 9.

Horowitz, Ruth (1990) 'Sociological Perspectives on Gangs: Conflicting Definitions and Concepts', in C. Ronald Huff (ed.), *Gangs in America,* Newbury Park CA: Sage, 37-54.

Howell, James C. (1994) 'Recent Gang Research: Program and Policy Implications', *Crime and Delinquency* 40(4): 495-515.

Huff, C. Ronald (ed.) (1990) *Gangs in America*, Newbury Park: Sage.

Huff, C. Ronald (1992) 'The New Youth Gangs: Social Policy and Malignant Neglect', in Ira M. Schwartz (ed.), *Juvenile Justice and Public Policy: Towards a National Agenda,* New York: Lexington Books, 20-44.

Italian Society of Criminology (1977) *Sixth Congress: Pre-Congress Acts,* Adriatica Editrice, Bari (English summary, National Criminal Justice Reference Service Document Database, Accession No. 051402).

Interpol (1967) *Juvenile Gangs: Anti-Social Behaviour and Delinquency,* Paris: International Criminal Police Organisation.

Jackson, Pamela Irving (1991) 'Crime, Youth Gangs, and Urban Transition: The Social Dislocations of Postindustrial Economic Development', *Justice Quarterly* 8(3): 379-97.

Jackson, Patrick G. (1989) 'Theories and findings about youth gangs',

Criminal Justice Abstracts 21(2): 313-29.

Jamieson, Alison (1994) 'Mafia and Institutional Power in Italy', *International Relations* 12(1): 1-24.

Jan, Lee-jan (1993) 'Asian Gang Problems and Social Policy Solutions: A Discussion and Review', *The Gang Journal* 1(4): 37-44.

Joe, Karen (1993) 'Issues in Accessing and Studying Ethnic Youth Gangs', *The Gang Journal* 1(2): 9-23.

Joe, Delbert and Robinson, Norman (1980) 'Chinatown's Immigrant Gangs: The New Young Warrior Class', *Criminology* 18(3): 337-45.

Johnson, Elmer H. (1996) 'Guided Change in Japan: The Correctional Association Prison Industrial Co-operative (CAPIC) and Prison Industry', in Obi N. Ignatius Ebbe (ed.), *Comparative and International Criminal Justice Systems: Policing, Judiciary and Corrections*, Boston: Butterworth-Heinemann.

Johnson, R.W. (1989) 'Terror in the townships', *New Statesman and Society* 2, September 8: 14-16.

Judicial Branch of the Navajo Nation (1995) *Field Initiated Gang Research: Finding and Knowing the Gang Nayéé in the Navajo Nation*, A Proposal to the Office of Juvenile Justice and Delinquency Prevention, Office of Justice Programs, United States Department of Justice, June 20.

Junger-Tas, J. (1974) 'La Rencontre Du Citoyen et de la Justice Penale [Violent Crime by Juveniles: Sociological Perspectives]', *Revue de Droit Penal et de Criminologie* 54(1) April: 661-82.

Justice and Law Reform Committee (1996) *Report: 1993/606 Petition of D.F.E. Harrington as Mayor and the Councillors of Invercargill City Council and others,* Wellington: New Zealand House of Representatives, First Session, Forty-Fourth Parliament.

Kelsey, Jane and Young, Warren (1982) *The Gangs: Moral Panic as Social Control*, Wellington: Insittute of Criminology, Victoria University of Wellington.

Klein, Malcolm W. (1995a) 'Foreword to the First Edition (1991)', in George W. Knox, *An Introduction to Gangs,* New Revised Edition, Bristol IN: Wyndham Hall Press, i-iv.

Klein, Malcolm W. (1995b) *The American Street Gang*, New York: Oxford University Press.

Knox, George W. (1995) *An Introduction to Gangs,* New Revised Edition, Bristol IN: Wyndham Hall Press.

Lasley, James R. (1992) 'Age, Social Context and Street Gang Membership: Are "Youth" Gangs Becoming "Adult" Gangs?', *Youth*

& Society 23(40): 434-51.

Lavey, Donald (1990) 'Interpol's Role in Combating Organised Crime', in Jane Rae Buckwalter (ed.), *International Perspectives on Organized Crime,* Chicago: Office of International Criminal Justice, The University of Illinois at Chicago, 87-93.

Lloyd, John (1995) 'The Russians are Coming', *London Review of Books,* May 11: 24-5.

Lynn, U.N. (1978) *Backgrounds of Crime and Delinquency,* Tokyo: United Nations Asia and Far East Institute for the Prevention of Crime and Treatment of Offenders, Resource Materials Series No. 14.

McDonald, William F. (1995) 'The Globalization of Criminology: The New Frontier is the Frontier', *Transnational Organized Crime* 1(1): 1-22.

McGregor, Richard (1996) 'Executions curb crime wave', *The Weekend Australian,* June 8-9.

Martens, Frederick T. (1990) 'African-American Organized Crime: An Ignored Phenomenon' in Jane Rae Buckwalter (ed.), *International Perspectives on Organized Crime,* Chicago: Office of International Criminal Justice,University of Illinois at Chicago, 101-18.

Massing, Michael (1996) 'Crime and Drugs: The New Myths', *The New York Review of Books* XLIII(2), February 1, 16-20.

Miller, J. Mitchell and Cohen, Albert (1996) 'Gang Theories and their Policy Implications', in J. Mitchell Miller and Jeffrey P. Rush (eds), *Gangs: A Criminal Justice Approach*, Cincinnati OH: Anderson Publishing, 3-16.

Miller, Walter B. (1983) 'Youth Gangs and Groups', in Sanford H. Kadish (ed.), *Encyclopedia of Crime and Justice,* New York: Free Press, 1671-9.

Miller, Walter B. (1990) 'Why the United States Has Failed to Solve Its Youth Gang Problem', in C. Ronald Huff (ed.), *Gangs in America*, Newbury Park CA: Sage, 263-87.

Monti, Daniel J. (1994) *Wannabe: Gangs in Suburbs and Schools,* Oxford and Cambridge MA: Blackwell.

Moodie, T. Dunbar (1988) 'Migrancy and Male Sexuality on the South African Gold Mines', *Journal of Southern African Studies* 14(1): 228-56.

Moore, Joan (1993) 'Gangs, Drugs, and Violence', in Scott Cummings and Daniel J. Monti (eds), *Gangs: The Origins and Impact of Contemporary Youth Gangs in the United States,* Albany: State University of New York Press, 27-46.

OJJDP Office of Juvenile Justice and Delinquency Prevention (1995) Juvenile Gangs, Rockville MD: Juvenile Justice Clearinghouse.

Pilkington, Hilary (1994) *Russia's Youth and its Culture: A Nation's Constructors and Constructed*, London and New York: Routledge.

Poupart, Lisa M. (1995) 'Juvenile Justice Processing of American Indian Youths: Disparity in One Rural County', in Kimberly Kempf Leonard,Carl E. Pope, and William H. Teyerherm (eds), *Minorities in Juvenile Justice*, Thousand Oaks; Sage: 179-200.

Rand, Alicia (1987) 'Transitional Life Events and Desistance from Delinquency and Crime', in M.E. Wolfgang, T.P. Thornberry and R.F. Figlio (eds), *From boy to man: from delinquency to crime*, Chicago: University of Chicago Press, 134-62.

Ruggiero, Vincenzo (1990) 'The Camorra: "Clean" Capital and Organised Crime', in Frank Pearce and Michael Woodiwiss (eds), *Global Crime Connections: Dynamics and Control*, London: Macmillan, 141-61.

Sanchez-Jankowski, Martin (1991) *Islands in the Street: Gangs and American Urban Society,* Berkeley CA: University of California Press.

Sanders, William B. (1994) *Gangbangs and Drive-Bys: Grounded Culture and Juvenile Gang Violence*, Nw York: Aldine de Gruyter.

Sarnecki, Jerzy (1986) *Delinquent Networks*, Stockholm: National Council for Crime Prevention Sweden.

Schneider, Hans Joachim (1994) Review of Robert Y. Thornton with Katsuya Endo, *Preventing Crime in America and Japan: A Comparative Study (1992)* in *International Journal of Offender Therapy and Comparative Criminology* 38(3): 272-5.

Schneider, Jane and Schneider, Peter (1994) 'Mafia, Antimafia, and the Question of Sicilian Culture', *Politics and Society* 22(2), June: 237-58.

Scott, Peter (1956) 'Gangs and Delinquent Groups in London', *British Journal of Delinquency* 7(1): 4-26.

Serio, Joseph (trs) (1992) *USSR Crime Statistics and Summaries: 1989 and 1990,* Chicago: The Office of International Criminal Justice, University of Illinois at Chicago.

Shelden, Randall, G., Tracy, Sharon K., and Brown, William B. (1997) *Youth Gangs in American Society*, Belmont CA: Wadsworth.

Shikita, Minoru and Tsuchiya, Shinichi (1992) *Crime and Criminal Policy in Japan: Analysis and Evaluation of the Showa Era, 1926-1988,* New York: Springer-Verlag.

Shipler, David (1978) 'Youth Problems in Russia: I Juvenile Crime Wave', *Reader's Digest* (Australian edition), September, 42-5.

Short, James F. (1975) 'Gangs, Violence, and Politics', in Duncan

Chappell and John Monahan (eds), *Violence and Criminal Justice*, Lexington MA: Lexington Books, 101-12.

Silverman, Robert A. (1996) 'Patterns of Native American Crime', in Marianne O. Nielsen and Robert A. Silverman (eds), *Native Americans, Crime, and Justice*, Boulder: Westview Press, 58-74.

Spergel, Irving A. (1990) 'Youth Gangs: Continuity and Change', in Michael Tonry and Norval Morris (eds), *Crime and Justice: A Review of Research*, 12, Chicago: University of Chicago Press, 171-275.

Spergel, Irving, Curry, D., Chance,R., Kane, C., Ross, R., Alexander, A., Simmons, E., and Oh, S. (1994) *Gang Suppression and Intervention: Problem and Response, Research Summary*, Washington DC: Office of Juvenile Justice and Delinquency Prevention.

Spergel, Irving A. (1995) *The Youth Gang Problem: A Community Approach*, New York: Oxford University Press.

Steinhoff, Patricia G. (1993) 'Pursuing the Japanese Police', *Law and Society Review*, 27(4): 827-50.

Stelfox, Peter (1996) *Gang Violence—Strategic and Tactical Options*, London: Home Office Police Department.

Stelling, W. (1972) *A Generation without Allegiances,* National-Verlag, Gmbh, Hannover (title translation and English language abstract in NCJRS Document Data base, Accession No. 031204).

Straker, Gill with Moosa, Fathima, Becker, Risé, and Nkivale, Madiyoyo (1992) *Faces in the Revolution: The Psychological Effects of Violence on Township Youth in South Africa*, Cape Town: David Philip; Athens: Ohio University Press.

Strathern, Andrew (1993) 'Violence and Political Change in Papua New Guinea', *Pacific Studies* 16(4): 41-60.

Sullivan, John P. and Silverstein, Martin E. (1995) 'The Disaster Within Us: Urban Conflict and Street Gang Violence in Los Angeles', *Journal of Gang Research* 2(4): 11-30.

Takagi, Paul and Platt, Tony (1978) 'Behind the Gilded Ghetto: An Analysis of Race, Class and Crime in Chinatown', *Crime and Social Justice* 9 (Spring-Summer) 2-25.

Tanioka, Ichiro and Glaser, Daniel (1991) 'School Uniforms, Routine Activities, and the Social Control of Delinquency in Japan', *Youth and Society* 23(1): 50-75.

Taylor, Carl S. (1990) *Dangerous Society,* East Lansing MI: Michigan State University Press.

Tonry, Michael (1995) *Malign Neglect—Race,Crime, and Punishment in America*, New York: Oxford University Press.

Toy, Calvin (1992a) 'Coming out to Play: Reasons to Join and Participate in Asian Gangs', *The Gang Journal* 1(1): 13-29.

Toy, Calvin (1992b) 'A Short History of Asian Gangs in San Francisco', *Justice Quarterly* 9(4): 647-65.

United Nations (1995) *Crime Prevention Strategies, in Particular as Related to Crimes in Urban Areas and Juvenile and Violent Criminality, Including the Question of Victims: Assessment and New Perspectives*, Cairo: Secretariat Working Paper, Ninth United Nations Congress on the Prevention of Crime and the Treatment of Offenders, 29 April-May 8.

United Nations Expert Group Meeting (1994) *Children and Juveniles in Detention: Application of Human Rights Standards*, Vienna, October 30 to November 4.

Vaksberg, Arkady (1991) *The Soviet Mafia*, London: Weidenfeld and Nicolson.

Vesselinovitch, Alexander S. (1996) 'Organized Crime in Russia: An Overview,' paper presented at 10th International Conference, Society for the Reform of Criminal Law, Whistler BC, Canada, August 23.

Vitaliev, Vitali (1991) 'For system, read mafia', *The Times Literary Supplement,* Vol. No. October 4: 12.

Volobuev, Anatoli (1990) 'Combating Organised Crime in the U.S.S.R.: Problems and Perspectives', in Jane Rae Buckwalter (ed.), *International Perspectives on Organised Crime,* Chicago: Office of International Criminal Justice, University of Illinois at Chicago, 75-82.

Weinberg, S. Kirson (1976) 'Shaw-McKay Theories of Delinquency in Cross-Cultural Context' in James F. Short (ed.), *Delinquency, Crime and Society,* Chicago: University of Chicago Press, 167-85.

Westermann, Ted D. and Burfeind, James W. (1991) *Crime and Justice in Two Societies: Japan and the United States,* Pacific Grove CA: Brooks/Cole Publishing.

Whitfield, R.G. (1982)'American gangs and British sub-cultures: a commentary', *International Journal of Offender Therapy and Comparative Criminology* 26(1): 90-92.

Wikström, Per-Olaf H. (1991) *Urban Crime, Criminals and Victims: The Swedish Experience in Anglo-American Comparative Perspective,* New York: Springer-Verlag.

Wilson, John J. and Howell, James C. (1993) *A Comprehensive Strategy for Serious, Violent, and Chronic Juvenile Offenders*, [Washington DC]: Office of Juvenile Justice and Delinquency Prevention, U.S. Department of Justice.

Wilson-Smith, Anthony (1989) 'Gang Warfare, Soviet-Style', *Maclean's* 102(21) May 22: 44.

Wolter, H. (1975) "West Deutschland—Rockers—Eine besondere Form der Bandenkriminalität" [West Germany—Rockers—A Special Form of Gang Criminality], *Kriminalistik* 29(1): 13-17.

Zatz, Marjorie S. (1987) 'Chicano Youth Gangs and Crime: The Creation of a Moral Panic', *Contemporary Crises* 11(2): 129-58.

Zoglin, Richard (1996) 'Now for the Bad News: A Teenage Time Bomb', *Time* January 15: 46-7.

2 Post-Modernism and Youth Subcultures in Britain in the 1990s

Roger Burke and Ros Sunley

INTRODUCTION

There is an extensive literature in the USA which discusses the issue of criminal youth gangs. Such gangs tend to be defined as problematic when they engage in violent activities and there is a recognition that these are often connected to the consumption and sale of illicit drugs (Spergel 1995). Explanations for the existence and behaviour of these groups of young people are part of a long and established tradition with their roots in the Chicago School of the 1920s and 1930s.

Shaw and McKay (1972) argued that crime and delinquency are transmitted by frequent contact with criminal traditions that have developed over time in disorganised areas of the city. Sutherland (1937) developed this idea by arguing that the necessary preconditions for criminal behaviour are a set of motivations, attitudes and techniques which have to be learned. Merton (1938) provided a motive by proposing that all societies establish certain common success goals which all individuals are expected to pursue (e.g. wealth), establish certain approved ways of achieving these goals (e.g. hard work), yet fail to provide equal access to the opportunity structure which will allow success. Consequently, individuals are forced to use illegitimate means of achieving material goals. Merton's scheme was extremely influential in the development of the first wave of subcultural theories to emerge in the USA in the 1950s and 1960s.

Albert Cohen (1955) replaced Merton's emphasis on the acquisition of financial rewards as the motivation for delinquent behaviour, with the notion of the attainment of status. Cohen recognised that society is stratified into socioeconomic classes but noted that it is the values and norms of the middle class which are dominant and are used to judge the success and status of *everybody* in society. Cohen argued that the young working class male, exposed to a different pattern of socialisation, is unlikely to internalise middle class norms, but is thrust into a competitive system which is governed by alien and incomprehensible middle class norms and values. In this way, the young working class male undergoes 'status frustration'. Several young males interacting in conjunction form a delinquent subculture.

Cloward and Ohlin (1960) argued that there are *two* opportunity structures in society, one legitimate (as in Merton's conception of anomie theory) and one illegitimate (as in Sutherland's conception of differential association theory). Because of the unequal nature of society, people do not have equal access to the means of achieving legitimate success. On the other hand, people have differential access to deviant or criminal opportunities: *criminal* subcultures arise where an illegitimate opportunity structure is available; *conflict* subcultures occur where there are no visible and successful criminal systems in existence; while *retreatist* subcultures exist where both legitimate and illegitimate opportunity structures are closed off.

Miller (1958) argued that delinquency is a 'natural' product of lower class culture whose values, or 'focal concerns' are to some extent in conflict with those of the dominant middle class. Lower class 'focal concerns' of autonomy, fate, excitement, smartness, toughness, and trouble are transmitted from generation to generation via the lower class youthful peer group which performs the same emotional function as the middle class family. *Delinquent* activity is a convenient way of achieving most, if not all, of these values.

Analysis of youth subcultures in the USA since the 1970s has predominantly focused on issues of violence, ethnicity and poverty. For example, Wolfgang and Ferracuti (1967), identify a 'subculture of violence' where trivial insults are expected to be met with violence, and failure to respond in this way is met with social censure from the peer group (ibid 1975) adapted this theory to explain violence among American Blacks. Maintenance of a manly image is important in the subculture, and individuals who are unable to resolve conflicts verbally are more likely to resort to violence in order to assert their masculinity. Behaviour is partly a response to social conditions, and partly the result of an individual's acceptance of the ideas and values which he has absorbed from the subculture of violence. Maxson and Klein (1990) have more recently recognised that certain youth groups, for example, racist 'Skinheads' and neo-Nazi organisations, engage in group related violent behaviour for ideological—including political and religious—ends.

Recent American analysts have argued that poverty is simply the root cause of gangs and the violence they produce. Miller (1958) had argued that lower class delinquency was a normal response to sociocultural demands; in his later writings he essentially adopts a 'culture of poverty' view to explain the self-perpetuation of gang life, a view that emphasises the adaptational aspects of the gang to changing socioeconomic circumstances (Miller 1990). However, the most popular current theory to explain criminal behaviour among poor young people in the American inner-city is Wilson's 'underclass theory' where it is suggested that groups in socially isolated neighbourhoods have:

> few legitimate employment opportunities, inadequate job information networks and poor schools not only give rise to weak labour force attachment but also raise the likelihood that people will turn to illegal or deviant activities for income (Wilson 1991: 462).

Wilson fails to address the issues of gang formation and explain the development of specific types of gang problems (Hagedorn 1992). Nevertheless, a number of observers assume a close correlation between gangs, gang violence and the development of an underclass or the degree of limitation on available social and economic resources (Krisberg 1974; Anderson 1990; Taylor 1990). Poverty is central to the underclass thesis—and various writers recognise that the absence of economic resources leads to compensatory efforts to achieve some form of economic and successful social adjustment (William 1989; Moore 1991). It is in this context that Spergel (1995: 149) argues that, 'a subculture arises out of efforts of people to solve social, economic, psychological, developmental, and even political problems'. It is a thesis entirely compatible with the theoretical perspective we develop later in this paper to explain the existence of various youth subcultures in Britain in the 1990s.

American subcultural theories influenced a series of studies that were conducted in Britain during the 1960s. The most important of these was conducted by Downes (1966) who showed that there no evidence of the existence of organised delinquent gang subcultures (Cloward and Ohlin) or a 'counter culture' in the British context. He found that young delinquents were alienated from middle class institutions such as the school or the work place. They had a considerable amount of free time but, because of their relatively deprived social and economic position, had no access to the goals of 'teenage culture'—consumer products such as transistor radios, record players, motorbikes, and clothes. Downes argues that these young people turned to delinquency as the only way of filling up their spare time and gaining some form of excitement.

Parker (1974) conducted a survey of young people in an area of Liverpool which official statistics suggested had a high rate of offending. He found there was a pattern of loosely knit peer groups, not one of tightly structured gangs. Offending was not a central activity. Young people shared common problems, such as unemployment and limited leisure opportunities. Some had developed a temporary solution in the form of stealing car radios. Parker found that the community in which the youngsters lived was one which largely condoned theft, provided the victims were from outside of the area.

Pryce (1979) studied African-Caribbean youngsters in the St Paul's area of Bristol. He suggests that the first African-Caribbeans to arrive in the 1950s came to Britain with high aspirations, but found that they were relegated to a force of cheap labour. They and their children were subject to racism and discrimination, which contributed to a pattern of 'endless pressure'. Pryce suggested there were two types of adaptation to this pressure. One was to be stable and law abiding, the other was to adopt an expressive, disreputable attitude. Second and third generation African-Caribbeans were more likely (but not bound) to adopt the second response. Pryce suggested two further divisions within this second category. The first, 'hustlers', would reject low status work if it was possible. Instead they would take part in robberies, deception, drug-dealing or pimping. Such activities would support a lifestyle which gave a feeling of mastery and autonomy. The second subcategory contained 'teeny-boppers'. They were typically school-leavers with few qualifications, for whom any available work would be unrewarding. The typical pattern was to lose jobs quickly, to fall out with parents, then to drift into petty crime.

These studies were important because they explicitly alerted our attention to specific historical factors, in particular the level of economic activity, and to the importance of a structural class analysis in the explanation of subcultural delinquency. They also demonstrated that different groups within the objective working class, had identified distinct problems in terms of negative status and their relationship to the economic mode of production. Furthermore, these different groups had chosen their own distinct solutions to their perceived problems. It was these themes that were developed by a group of sociologists centered on the Centre for Contemporary Cultural Studies (CCCS) at the University of Birmingham in the 1970s who sought to explain the rise of what have been termed 'spectacular' youth cultures such as Teddy Boys, Mods, Skinheads, and Punks.

We are of the opinion that British youth gang activity can only be understood in the context of the wider subculture to which the particular young people subscribe. It is our aim therefore to use and develop the approach of the Birmingham CCCS to outline some of the youth cultures that exist in Britain in the 1990s, and to discuss the criminal and public order implications of their existence. Our objectives are to:

- briefly outline the subcultural theory developed by the Birmingham CCCS in the 1970s;
- explain how post-modernist theories help us to develop the CCCS analysis in order to make sense of the fragmented social world inhabited by young people in the 1990s;
- provide a brief discussion of how young people become members of subcultural groups;
- outline some of the most significant youth subcultures, their interests and values, that existed in Britain in the mid-1990s;
- describe the points of intersection between the various subcultural groupings.

'RESISTANCE THROUGH RITUALS'--THE WORK OF THE BIRMINGHAM CCCS

Professor Stuart Hall and his associates at the Birmingham CCCS provide the following definition of group culture:

> the peculiar and distinctive 'way of life' of the group or class, the meanings, values and ideas embodied in institutions, in social relations, in systems of beliefs, in mores and customs, in the uses of objects and material life (Hall and Jefferson 1975: 10).

In terms of this definition individuals are born into particular cultures, *shaped* by them and *constrained* by them. Different groups coexisting in the same society will have their own distinctive cultures which set them apart from other groups. At the same time these groups will accept and share certain aspects of each other's culture. Nevertheless, these distinct cultures do not share the same status in society. Cultures are *ranked* and stand in opposition to one another in relationships of domination and subordination. This is a neo-Marxist argument which proposes that the most powerful group in society will also possess the dominant culture which will be presented as *the* culture.

Hall and Jefferson argue that in modern societies the major cultural configurations are cultures based on social class, but within these are subcultures which are defined as:

> smaller, more localised and differentiated structures, within one or other of the larger cultural networks (Hall and Jefferson 1975: 13).

The larger cultural configuration is referred to as the 'parent culture'. *Subcultures*, while having different focal concerns from the parent culture, will share some common aspects with the culture from which they were derived. In order to explain the existence of a particular subculture it is necessary to analyse it in terms of its relationship to the dominant culture. Subcultures coalesce around certain activities, values, uses of material artefacts, and territorial space. When these are distinguished by age and generation they are called 'youth subcultures'. Some, like delinquent subcultures, are persistent features of the parent culture, but others appear only at certain historical moments then fade away. These latter subcultures are highly visible and, indeed, 'spectacular'.

Hall and his associates argue that, although members of 'spectacular' subcultures may well look very 'different' from their parents or peers, they will still share the same class position, the same life experiences, and generally the same outlook as the parent culture. All they are doing, through their distinctive dress, life style, music etc., is producing a different cultural 'solution' to the problems posed for them by their material and social class position and experience.

These later British subcultural studies shared a common Marxist perspective which proposed that spectacular youth cultures arise at particular historical 'moments' as cultural solutions to structural problems. Writers in this tradition distinguish *three* levels of analysis: *structural, cultural,* and *biographical.*

Structure refers to that aspect of society which is beyond the control of the individual, the 'constraints', 'conditions', 'contingencies' or 'imperatives' derived from the class system and the distribution of wealth. These are the 'problem' to which 'culture' is the solution.

Culture focuses on the traditions, meanings, and ideologies which are patterned responses to structural conditions. Subcultures are the specific form through which the subordinate group resists the dominant culture.

Biography refers to the pattern of personal circumstance through which the culture and structure are experienced by the members of the subcultural group.

This new wave of subcultural theorists were concerned with the historical and environmental context in which particular youth subcultures arise and the details of 'style' (symbols and coded meanings) adopted by these. They argued that style is a form of resistance to subordination which is essentially a *ritualistic*, *symbolic* or *magical* resistance since it is not, actually, a *successful* solution to the problem of subordination. For these writers, resistance is not seen as a desperate 'lashing out' or a passive adaptation to an anomic situation of disjunction, but a collective response designed to resist or transform dominant values and defend or recapture working class values—to *win space,* to reclaim community, and reassert traditional values. This resistance is symbolic rather than real.

Stan Cohen (1973) notes three contexts in which concepts of ritual, myth, metaphor, magic, and allegory are invoked by these writers:

- The target for attack is inappropriate or irrational in the sense of not being logically connected with the source of the problem, for example, Skinheads beating up young Asians or gay people, or football hooligans vandalising trains, are in reality reacting to other things—threats to community, homogeneity, or traditional stereotypes of masculinity.

- When the solution does not confront the real material basis of subordination and is not a genuinely political response; the activities are seen as merely gestures, like sticking pins in a doll—a very bad case of false consciousness.

- When the subcultural style denotes something beyond its surface appearance, for example, the boots worn by Skinheads are making oblique coded statements about relationships to a particular past or present.

This group of writers concentrated on two broad but overlapping areas: mainstream youth and delinquency, especially the transition from school to work (or to unemployment), and expressive or spectacular youth cultures.

MAINSTREAM YOUTH SUBCULTURES

The two major studies of mainstream youth subcultures are those of Willis (1977) and Corrigan (1979). Both studies are concerned with the transition from school to work among urban lower working class adolescent boys.

Paul Willis conducted a study of adolescent males in a Midlands' Comprehensive School of how working class kids get working class jobs. He found that the boys were involved in a 'counter-school culture' which has many profound similarities with the culture its members are destined for—shop floor culture. The youngsters resisted school which they considered to be an irrelevance and subverted the institution by developing their own hidden curriculum of 'skiving' and 'having a laff'. Willis notes that their techniques of insubordination provide an unofficial preparation for labour within a capitalist system. Their culture of insubordination in school is thus a ritual (or magical or symbolic) solution in that it does not address itself to the problem with which they are faced—a knowledge of the inevitability of a dead end job—and cannot therefore actually solve it.

Paul Corrigan conducted a study among fourteen and fifteen year old males in two working class schools in Sunderland and was concerned with the distribution of power and subordination in the schooling system. He argues that school has been *imposed* on working class children and the system attempts to *change* them, to control them and mould them in terms of middle class morality and values. Their misbehaviour becomes a resistance movement or guerrilla warfare against the school's discipline and attempts by the teachers to assert authority. Hence, their chosen strategies involved playing truant from school, 'mucking about', and getting into trouble. Corrigan argues that much of the activity engaged in by working class adolescents is simply 'passing the time' or 'doing nothing'.

Neither Willis nor Corrigan are discussing spectacular cultures with highly visible styles of dress or music, or even values and behaviour patterns, but normal 'mainstream' working class adolescent culture derived from and/or conditioned by the parent culture. The 'problem' is an alien or irrelevant education system followed by the prospect of a boring and dead end job (or, nowadays, the dole queue) and the 'solution' is a 'culture of resistance' manifested in truancy and petty offending. Actions are ritualistic (or magical) but they can never solve the problem.

Research on the subcultural contexts of the lives of young women has benefited from more generalised studies of how the experiences of family, school, and work are negotiated by young women (Griffin 1985; Mirza 1992) and how they cope with issues of femininity and sexuality (McRobbie 1991; Lees 1986; Hudson and Ineichen 1991), and from feminist studies which are more frequently focused on the involvement of young women in crime (Carlen 1988; Campbell 1981; Cain 1989).

The above authors all agree that young women are less visible in the public sphere than young men. They are divided, however, as to whether young women form themselves into gangs, or whether their friendship networks are more likely to take the form of a 'best friend' relationship (Campbell 1981; McRobbie and Garber 1976). Angela McRobbie argues that the 'culture of femininity' operates in ways that are similar to the masculine 'delinquent subculture', as a means by which working class girls develop an 'anti-school' culture of resistance (McRobbie 1991).

The early work examining female culture consigned young women to a 'bedroom culture' (McRobbie and Garber 1976). When young women enter the territory of the street or subculture, they are, it is argued, perceived to be acting on male terms as girlfriends, appendages, whores, and sluts (Lees 1986) The 'culture of femininity' concept undoubtedly provided a partial, but limited, explanation of the low rate of recorded female juvenile criminality. The post-war period of youth culture with its emphasis on music, fashion, and style has increasingly become a consumerist culture. Like young men, young women gain access to at least the periphery of subcultural groups through the acquisition of artefacts associated with those groups. Although clearly an examination of the objectification of young women by their male peers is an important debate, it fails to fully represent the relationship between young men and women as they hang out in their friendship groups together. If we start from the supposition that young women are merely the passive observers and hangers-on of their male peers' youth subcultures, and focus only on the negative aspects of these relationships, we are unlikely to recognise the active role young women play within their involvement in youth subcultures.

SPECTACULAR YOUTH SUBCULTURES

'Spectacular' youth subcultures involve the adoption, by young people of both sexes (generally working class young people), of a distinctive style of dress and way of using material artefacts combined usually with distinctive life-styles, behaviour patterns, and musical preferences. Our brief review will focus on four examples: Teddy Boys, *Mods*, *Rockers* and *Punks*.

Teddy Boys

The Teddy Boys emerged in the early 1950s. Tony Jefferson (1976) argues that they adopted their particular cultural response in an attempt to defend, symbolically, a constantly threatened space and a declining status. Their response to the growing structural inequalities of post-war Britain consisted of attempts to reaffirm traditional working class values and sense of territory both of which were under attack from the expropriation of land by developers.

These young males lacked status and were being further deprived, for various structural reasons, of what little they possessed so there remained only the self and its cultural extension through dress and appearance, and its social extension through the group. Jefferson argues that attacks on Black and Cypriot people were simply a matter of self-defence. The *coincidental* influx of immigrants in the 1950s was wrongly perceived as a *cause* of the relatively worsening position of the lower working class in an age of increasing affluence.

Mods

The Mods emerged in the early 1960s. Brake (1980) distinguishes three categories of this subcultural grouping: a high camp art school version—with boys in make-up—the fore-runners of the later New Romantics; mainstream or 'smooth' Mods—sharply dressed in suits with neat, narrow trousers and painted shoes, their girl friends with short hair and 'classic' shirts or dresses; and Scooter Boys—riding Italian motor scooters (a 'working class sports car') covered in chrome accessories, with many headlights and mirrors, wearing jeans and industrial work boots (they would later mutate into Skinheads).

Hebdige (1979) argues that the principal focus of the Mod's life was the pursuit of leisure. The Mod was attempting to compensate for his lowly position in the day-time, working world, status hierarchy, by living solely for the night-time leisure world of night clubs. This led to the adoption of amphetamines ('speed') as the drug of choice—they needed to keep mind and body synchronised—to keep going and make the most of the precious night.

Rockers

At the same time as the Mods there were the Rockers. Like the Mods they were working class and had left school early. They were not part of the new embourgeoisified working class of teenage consumerism and fashion, however, but stuck in the more unskilled and routinised manual jobs. Brake (1980) distinguishes two groups: 'Bikers'—organised around the cult of the motor bike and distinguished in clothing by black leather jackets, and in life-style by their anti-domesticity and violence, identifying with the American Hell's Angels; and 'Greasers'—who came a bit later and, although they adopted a similar scruffy working class masculine image, were less committed to motor bikes and could well be non-riders.

All Rockers saw themselves as aggressive and masculine and saw the Mods as contemptibly feminine. Young women members of this culture were equally aggressive and much like the young males. Hard rock music and the motor bike were linked into macho values of violence, sexuality, and masculinity, the idea of the 'real man', contemptuous of the ever present threat of death from a bike crash. Their 'problem' was in many ways the same as that of the Mods and later the Skins and before them the Teds but their solution was the affirmation of pure male, macho values. Unlike the Skins they rejected the values of 'traditional' working class culture.

Skinheads

Skinheads emerged in the late 1960s and had their origins among the 'hard Mods'. They wore a very distinctive uniform of Dr Martin industrial boots, very close cropped hair, short wide Levi jeans and braces over button-down Ben Sherman shirts. Female Skins wore a very similar uniform. Like the Rockers they cultivated an image of being hard, macho, very sexist, masculine, racist and conservative. They went around in groups and were much addicted to football. Their music was Ska, Blue Beat, and later Reggae. Their drugs were for the most part alcohol and some 'speed'. They were preoccupied with territory and were rather violent, their principal victims being immigrants, especially Asians ('Paki-bashing') who were perceived to be dirty and considered to lower the respectability of the district; homosexuals (who were seen to be corrupt and vicious); and Hippies (unwashed and lazy). Hebdige (1979) argues that Skins borrowed much of their style from the Caribbean community which, considering the Skins dislike of immigrants, was rather ironic.

However, what the Skins were really trying to do was to recover the traditional working class culture which had been eroded but, at the same time, had borrowed liberally from Black Caribbean culture so:

> its rituals, language and style provided models for those white youths alienated from the parent culture by the imagined compromises of the post-war years (Hebdige 1979: 18).

This notion that the Skins were trying, not unlike their Ted predecessors, to recover traditional working class values and mores, underpins all accounts of this subcultural grouping.

Punks

Punks emerged in 1976. Brake (1980) sees Punk as developing, in part, out of new wave music and argues that it was the first genuine working class *bohemian* culture. Hebdige (1979) notes that it was consciously working class, scruffy, earthy, dirty in clothing and language, but at the same time with a sense of parody and steeped in irony.

Punk music was heavily influenced by Reggae simply because it was alien music that disavowed Britishness and the Punks openly identified with Black British and Caribbean culture, lifting some features from Rastafarian styles (dreadlocks, Ethiopian colours, and some Rastafarian rhetoric and even a hybrid 'Punk dub' appeared in Punk Rock), and Punk bands figured prominently in the anti-National Front, Rock against Racism campaign. But at the same time Reggae and Punk Rock were different, and developed in separate directions. Punk cynics (described as dole queue rock) sang of dole queues, high rise flats, white riots, anti-royalist sentiments, exile, alienation, anarchy, and hopelessness. The whole style was embedded with anarchy and nihilism—it was a celebration of chaos. The clothing and hair styles were homologous with the swearing, spitting, vomiting, amphetamines, and 'soulless' frantic (crude and chaotic) music.

Punk was a culture that reflected a consumer-based society moving out of affluence into real economic, social, and political crisis. However, unlike any previous music-based youth culture, the punks attempted to break down the barriers between performers and audiences and, unlike any previous working class youth culture, they produced their own literature—cheap barely literate badly produced fanzines like 'Sniffing Glue'. But, as Hebdige (1979) says, although the style signified chaos at every level it was thoroughly ordered all the same. It was homologous precisely *because* of its lack of fit, its deliberate contradiction. Thus, spitting: applause; bin-liner: garment; anarchy: order. Unlike the Skins who were attempting a magical return to an imagined past of working class community, the punks deliberately cut themselves off from the parent culture and portrayed themselves as aliens, inscrutable, wholly other. Their rituals, accents, and objects were used to signify 'working-classness', but an abstract, disembodied working-classness which refused to make sense.

Hebdige argues that by breaking both with the working class parent, culture and with their own experience, the punks reflected the pre-categorical realities of modern bourgeois society—inequity, powerlessness, alienation, lack of any reasonable future. Their style did not magically *resolve* contradictions but *represented* them in the form of visual puns like torn tee shirts and bondage trousers.

These studies of the Birmingham School represent an important development of earlier subcultural theory. The early American studies and the work of Downes, Parker and Pryce, in the British context, had recognised that working class youth offending was in response to economic or status deprivation. The Birmingham studies more clearly linked these two forms of deprivation. Particular youth subcultures or status groups arise in response to the perceived economic problems of distinct groups of young people. These studies appear to presume, however, a linear development of history where different subcultures arise, coalesce, fade and are replaced as economic circumstances change. For example, the Mods were a product of the dole queue despondency of the late-1970s. The 1990s have been characterised, however, by the coexistence of a number of different subcultures.

We shall argue later in this essay that this coexistence of different subcultures is the outcome of a fragmented society where specific groups of young people, not necessarily with their origins in the traditional working class, have coalesced to create solutions to their specific socioeconomic problems. Central to our account is the possibility of choice. The simultaneous existence of different subcultures enables some young people to *choose* the solution to their problem from the various subcultures available.

The early subcultural studies, and indeed the work of the Birmingham School tended to suggest that young people had limited choices, if any, between *the* subculture in existence at a particular time and in that geographical space, and a life of conventionality. Our analysis suggests that many contemporary young people are able to choose from a wider range of concurrent subcultures which offer different solutions to their particular subjective socioeconomic problem. Furthermore, it is proposed that entry into a youth subculture is a part of the normal transition from childhood to adult status for the contemporary young person in Britain. The following two sections are based on a study conducted by Sunley and Garrett (1995) in a Midlands city in England and examines the processes which young people undergo during their adolescent years which lead to them becoming members of youth subcultures.

GROUP IDENTITY AND YOUTH CULTURE: THE TRANSITIONAL PERIOD OF ADOLESCENCE

The transitional period of adolescence occurs between the ages of thirteen and sixteen. Young people of this age group are moving from the adult controlled leisure facilities such as youth clubs and sport towards adult commercialised leisure (Hendry 1993: 114). It is during this stage that young people spend time 'hanging out' in the neighbourhood—visible to the public eye, with peer led internal control and limited formal external controls. The relationships between the young people and the community around them can become strained, and often problematised. They are seen to be doing nothing, with little recognition of the importance and normality of such behaviour. However, three stages of adolescent leisure use are associated with the development of social competency (Hendry 1983). The phases provide the young people with the opportunity to: observe peer behaviour in a controlled setting; rehearse the behaviours and roles associated to adult status; test out their competence in a commercial setting.

For young people there are several different symbols of adult status that can be used during the transitional stage to indicate movement along the pathway from childhood to adulthood. Some symbols are legitimated but may still be inaccessible to the young people: work, commercialised leisure, clothes, music. Others may not be considered legitimate but may be more easily accessible: drugs, drink, sex. Other parental expectations such as the fulfilment of particular domestic roles may not be considered as valid symbols and are not necessarily given the same emphasis for male or female children.

The safety issue is important in the context of this transitional period of adolescence. The groups observed in a recent ethnographic study carried out in an affluent but inner city area of a Midlands city in England break the assumed formation of single sex groups and predominantly mix together (Sunley and Garrett 1995). If we accept the hanging out behaviour of young people as an important aspect of social development for both young men and young women then some social acceptance of this behaviour is important. While young people are not accepted in groups on the street or in public place, and are perceived by others as a threat, they may be forced to gather in less safe environments or risk being identified by authority figures as a problem. The young men in the Midlands group were regarded as a greater problem than the young women, even though the groups are often mixed. The 'bad' behaviour, other than teenage sex, was presumed to be carried out by the young men (Sunley and Garrett 1995).

Until Angela McRobbie's analysis of female youth culture in the late 1970s, British analysis of youth culture was concentrated in the male sphere (McRobbie 1991). Writers such as Howard Parker and Paul Willis looked at how working class boys resisted their material situation through youth culture. These studies largely ignored the young women in the environments they looked at, implying that they played a passive role (Parker 1974; Willis 1977). McRobbie identified distinctive female youth subcultures separate from that of males. Therefore the issue of whether girls were present or absent in male subcultures became less significant. Female subculture was less public, a culture of the bedroom or disco. This partially explained why the young males are seen as more of a problem (McRobbie 1991). Studies on both gender cultures though point to the idea that, as well as resistance, the cultures are a way of preparing for likely roles in the future. The lads for unskilled manual labour; the girls for domestic work (Frith 1984).

A decade later a different picture is discernible. The groups observed in the Midlands study, especially when they met as a whole, were mixed and the young women took an active role. They participated in all the social activities of the group including drinking and drug taking, as well as sexual experimentation. This mixed gendered group presumed that the young women would participate and even dictate on occasion the terms of group activity, thereby perhaps reflecting changing gender roles in society (Sunley and Garrett 1995). Young women especially are rejecting the traditional roles of housework and domestic labour. The rejection of this role may therefore be reflected in the role observed in the groups studied. This is not to say that the young women's active role was always accepted without challenge by the young men in the groups. Much of the young women's power appeared to come from their ability to access adult leisure space. Group members revealed that many of the young women are more likely to gain access to an '18' certificate film at the cinema, or entrance to pubs or night-clubs in the city. Many of the young women are also more likely to be served alcohol and cigarettes in shops. This may lead to increased status within the group (Sunley and Garrett 1995).

Other actors who encountered the groups in the Midlands study were less likely to see the divides in these terms. The attitude of the local police in terms of delinquency, was similar to that of male sociologists in the past. To them, the 'trouble' was seen to come from the young men. The young women were seen in a paradoxical light. The youngest women in the group were viewed as 'at risk', by hanging out with the group they would become 'bad' women. The older young women in the group appeared to be already labelled as 'bad' therefore a danger to the young women in terms of their influence, and a danger to the group as a whole with their purchasing power in terms of alcohol (Sunley and Garrett 1995). Female deviance or potential deviance remains sexualised in a way that male deviance is not. The young people observed in the Midlands study spent long periods of time in mixed groups particularly at weekends, some segregation occurring on weekday evenings when the young women spend time in each others homes.

The appearance of a mixed group did concern the local beat officer of the area, who suggested that in such a group the males and females would 'show off to each other'. He also suggested that it was the older females who were more of a problem as they could more easily buy drinks for the rest of the group. The wide age range of the larger group (twelve to eighteen) was, he felt a major issue, the younger ones potentially influenced by the older members. His perception was of a cohesive group. This, however, has not been our experience of observing and talking to the group. It appears more likely that this particular group was made up of several subgroups who met together because of the convenience of the location and the seeming attraction of a larger peer group (Sunley and Garrett 1995).

During a period of economic recession the availability of paid work for adolescents is more likely to be restricted. Parents may also have limited funds available to provide the resources required by young people to access the legitimate symbols of adult status. Failure to access the legitimate symbols may be a factor in the experimentation by young people in drug use, drinking, and sex and their association to youth culture and subcultural groups.

The visits to the local town centre were a regular event for the older group members. It was the young women in the groups who gained access to commercialised leisure at an earlier age and on a more regular basis. The young men were often left behind, and it is on those nights when the young women have left the groups together that the young males are to be found together messing about and drinking (Sunley and Garrett 1995). The potential imbalance in leisure opportunity does offer some status to young women, contradicting the view that young women have less social outlets than the males. Young people in an earlier survey felt strongly that young women should have the same freedoms as young men, the females (76%) holding such an opinion more often than the males (62%) (Furnham and Gunter 1989: 97-8). This seemed to be the view of the young people in the Midlands study. The importance of the central phase for the development of social and interpersonal skills in the company of close friends should not be underestimated. The intimacy of the personal relationships is also a mark of the gradual detachment from the security of the family (Youniss and Smollar 1985, Lloyd 1985).

ADOLESCENCE AND IDENTITY THROUGH SUBCULTURAL GROUPS

The transitional stage of adolescence in which young people within their peer groups develop intimate friendships and practise social skills required for adult life is a neglected area of research. Many assumptions of gender differences in this experience of adolescence underestimate changes in the social relationships within many mixed gender friendship groups. 'Hanging out' is viewed as a social problem, there is a desire expressed by many adults involved with young people to enforce upon them constant activities as a prevention to boredom, which is presumed to lead to social nuisances. This view does not recognise the importance of space for young people to discover themselves. Much adolescent leisure is about 'not doing', about 'hanging out', about 'talking to friends', about 'being alone to think', and this is the harder dimension to explore (Hendry *et al* 1993: 2-3). The provision of legitimate public space in which young people can 'hang out' together, with limited formal control or supervision could provide an arena for these activities.

The use of outworkers in some areas has been successful, but restrictions on resourcing for youth services particularly for the thirteen to sixteen age range, will mean that funding for these service areas is unlikely. The 'problem' of youth is unlikely to disappear, while young people, increasingly females as well as males, are perceived within communities as an unwelcome subgroup. The examination of youth subcultures has been criticised for its emphasis on 'exotic subcultures'—providing, it has been argued, a poor reflection of the transitory phase of young peoples lives (Wallace and Cross 1990: 1). We would argue that an examination of broader youth culture must remain part of our examination of the lives of young people in this transitory phase. Many of these cultural groups have been and currently are the focus of moral panics. Although the majority of young people may themselves not directly identify themselves as members of any particular subcultural group, many form peer group allegiances around the artefacts of such groups and will, through their identification with particular musical styles, fashions, drugs etc., be identified and classified by others in terms of those allegiances.

Group identity through the trappings of subcultural groups is an important aspect of the transitional phase of adolescence. It is arguably through the association with particular music tastes, and styles of clothes, that young people can forge group identity. Structural changes in British society encourage greater reliance on such associations for longer periods of young people's lives. Where the opportunity for identity development through work, family, or commercialised leisure becomes more difficult to attain, then the group identity associated to wider subcultural groups may become all the more important.

REFLECTIONS ON SPECTACULAR YOUTH SUBCULTURES

The Birmingham School sought connections between the structural contradictions of capitalist society and the forms assumed by youth subcultures. The succession of subcultural styles is intended (unconsciously) to resolve (magically) the contradictions hidden in the parent culture. Thus, the Mods attempted to realise the conditions of existence of the mobile white collar worker, while Skinheads attempted to recover the traits associated with hard manual labour. This Marxist analysis argues that these 'revolts into style' cannot possibly *resolve* the contradictions, only express them or symbolically re-transcribe them. Successive patterns therefore tend to repeat themselves—the same problems generate the same solutions.

The early US subcultural studies had portrayed young delinquents as frustrated social climbers. This later British version was proposing that these young people were cultural innovators and social critics. Both versions are underpinned by the implication that youthful deviance is some form of defiance or rejection of conventional society. The neo-Marxists are inclined to argue that deviance is a form of mass proletarian resistance—a sort of pre-political revolutionary consciousness, which ignores the simple fact that much youthful disaffection and disorder is racist, sexist, conservative, irrational, and vicious. Such criticisms are embarrassing for writers encumbered by the intellectual baggage of Marxism who find themselves explaining such working class deviations in terms of historicist notions of 'false-consciousness'. Those of us who recognise a heterogeneous proletariat divided by the extensive free-market economic revolution of the past twenty years have no such problem. We recognise that separate groups within the traditional working class have had different experiences of economic change: the *problems* experienced by different groups are diverse and the *solutions* devised similarly disparate.

In order to make sense of contemporary British youth subcultures it will be useful adapt the analysis of the Birmingham CCCS in the context of debates about post-modernist society.

POST-MODERNISM AND YOUTH CULTURES

Post-modernism rejects the idea of grand theories or meta-narratives that seek totalising explanations of human behaviour which are the basis of modernity. Culturally, post-modernism stresses the ephemeral in preference to the fixed and absolute. Fashion, image, and popular culture are all important. Contemporary Britain is characterised by increasingly diverse and fragmented social groups which have different values and experiences of life. This diversity of interests has placed strains on conventional representative democratic systems. Many young people express total contempt for traditional political parties which are perceived as not representing their interests. Some commentators have despaired of these young people as being only concerned with what they regard as peripheral political issues such as animal rights or environmentalism, and being obsessed with style and images instead of commitment and substance.

The cultural impact of post-modernity has become the basis of a whole school of social theory. Whereas many writers had attempted to develop large scale theories to explain society in terms of enduring, identifiable social structures, post-modernists tended to also see themselves as post-structuralists, emphasising the redundancy and futility of such efforts. Post-modern writers celebrate the failure of the modern project to establish rational foundations for knowledge, and embrace the trend towards human diversity and social fragmentation. They argue that there is no objective reality behind the plethora of social meanings. Accounts and definitions have no objective or external reference. They are elements in a free floating system of images which are produced and reproduced through the medium of popular mass communication which comes to define reality to consumers. These trends allow the expression of the diversity of human needs and interests. They challenge the validity of modern claims to privileged forms of knowledge for the powerful. Post-modernism gives voice to the less powerful and oppressed. In particular, a post-modernist interpretation of youth subcultures enables us to recognise that individuals, and different groups of young people, living in a fragmented society, have different life-experiences, different *problems,* and are able to choose a *solution* offered by different subcultures.

In choosing to adopt a broadly post-modern theoretical position we have *adapted* rather than rejected the position of the Birmingham CCCS. We recognise that separate groups of young people, not all members of the traditional working class but in existence concurrently at the same historical moment, have had very different experiences of the radical economic change that has engulfed British society since the late 1970s. These very different groups have developed their own subcultural solutions for coping with this transformation. It is an analysis which recognises the relationship of these disparate groups to the contemporary mode of production and will be developed in the following sections to enable us to make sense of some of the key youth subcultures that have emerged in Britain in the late 1980s, the 1990s, and their points of intersection.

BRITISH YOUTH SUBCULTURES IN THE 1990s

There have been a wide variety of youth subcultures in existence in Britain during the 1990s and it will be necessary to be selective in our discussion. It will be observed that the members of each group has consciously (or unconsciously) identified a *problem* which can be located in terms of their differential relationship to the contemporary mode of production. Each group has developed a very different subcultural *solution* to deal with their problem. Nevertheless, these apparently very different solutions can be categorised in two broad distinctive strands. The first strand involves a nostalgic backward look to times past when a romanticised and caricatured white working class took pride in its place in a GREAT Britain and follows in the tradition established by Teddy Boys in the 1950s and Skinheads in the 1970s. The second strand involves a forward look and discussions of environmental issues and gender politics. Many interesting coalitions have developed between different subcultural groupings but in general these can be located in the context of one of the two broader strands.

Lager Louts

The term 'lager lout' was commonly used in the late 1980s to refer to groups of young males said to be terrorising small towns in southern Britain after drinking copious quantities of strong alcohol. It appears that many of these youngsters were not part of the traditional working class or unemployed—those groups usually associated with such activities. It seems that many had quite well paid jobs and came from 'respectable' middle class backgrounds or from upwardly mobile working class backgrounds. Interestingly, the moral panic about 'lager louts' coincided with a rapid increase in house prices in southern Britain which had the unintended consequence of destabilising the traditional aspirations of many 'respectable' young people who have sought security in terms of marriage, family life, and home ownership.

Ironically, this phenomenon had arisen at a time when government policy was to encourage home ownership as part of a strategy of developing a property owning democracy, with inherently conservative social values. The escalation in house prices that occurred in the late 1980s made marriage and home ownership an economically non-viable proposition for many young people. It could be argued that their *problem* was the inaccessibility of the traditional informal restraints on behaviour recognised by control theorists and unrestrained by marriage, mortgage and children. Their *solution* was mindless hedonism. The term 'lager lout' is no longer in common usage and there are several possible consequences of the short-lived phenomenon. First, there is evidence that increasingly more young people are choosing to live on their own and not become involved in relationships with others. Second, groups of young people who would previously have been absorbed into 'respectable' forms of social relations based on home ownership and marriage are being placed at risk of being recruited into other deviant subcultural groupings such as 'Ravers' and 'Slackers' discussed below.

Football Hooligans

Football hooliganism has been a serious issue since the 1970s when virtually every professional football match played in Britain was marred by crowd disorder and violence. There has been recent evidence, however, of both a substantial reduction in the size, and the changing nature, of this phenomenon. The implementation of the Taylor Report following the Hillsborough Stadium football disaster, where over 90 Liverpool football fans were crushed to death, has had important implications for what has always been a mass, predominantly male working class, spectator sport in Britain. First, all major football clubs have been forced to introduce all-seater stadiums. The consequence of this development has been a substantial increase in the price of admission charged by all clubs. Interestingly, while attendance levels have risen since the implementation of the Taylor Report (reversing the long-term trend of spiralling decline) there is evidence of a change in the socioeconomic and gender composition of those attending matches. It seems highly likely that the long-term future of professional football in Britain will consist of a predominantly affluent middle class, family-based spectatorate watching working class gladiators, mirroring developments in professional sport in the USA in recent years.

In the meantime it appears that football hooliganism as a mass activity is in serious decline. Sporadic acts of violence continue at professional football matches, and rather more incidents occur away from the actual stadia where the policing of large numbers of people is far more problematic. Nevertheless, all the evidence points to a substantial decrease in the numbers involved. Indeed, it might be appropriate to announce the death of the football hooligan as a distinct youth subculture. At the same time that there has been a quantitative decline there has been an increase in the qualitative seriousness of the phenomenon. Football grounds have become recruiting grounds for far-right political groups such as the British National Party who have been popular with disaffected working class youngsters who have clung tenaciously to their traditions in the face of spiralling costs. It is ironic that the gentrification of professional football has alienated many of its traditional fan-base, who have become attracted to the simplistic political solutions of the far-right.

Linked to the infiltration of football crowds by the political far-right has been the development of football related violence on an international scale. There is considerable evidence that a serious outbreak of violence at an Ireland v England international football match in early 1995, which led to the abandonment of the game, was organised and planned by right-wing political groups. There have also been close links between right-wing hooligans throughout Europe. There is a distinct irony in the fact that British Skinheads and football hooligans are admired, respected, and imitated throughout Europe.

There is also evidence that some groups of football hooligans have coalesced into the more traditional youth criminal gangs to be found in the USA. It has been alleged that a particularly notorious group of London football hooligans has become central to the control and distribution of drugs such as ecstasy and LSD which have become associated with the 'Rave' culture. This finding is apparently significant in two ways. First, it appears that a group of young males brought together with a shared interest in the football hooliganism subculture have branched out into the more traditional criminal world. Second, these young males more traditionally associated with alcohol consumption, macho values, and physical violence have moved into subcultural areas associated with the 'peace and love' ethos of the 'Rave' culture. Nevertheless, we need to be careful here. These young men originate from areas with a tradition of organised criminal activity and their interests in this way of life probably pre-date and are inherently more significant to their lives than their involvement in the 'football hooligan' subculture. It is probably the case that they are merely adapting their criminal potential to changing social conditions. In terms of Cloward and Ohlin (1960) these young men are a focal point to the coming together of criminal, conflict, and retreatist subcultures.

The New Fascists

In recent years there has been a revival of interest in extreme right-wing political parties among many young working class males in poor inner-city areas. Racism has long been a salient ingredient of particular youth subcultures, for example, Teddy Boys and Skinheads. Indeed, many would say that the 'new racists' are merely a contemporary political manifestation of these groups. The success of the ultra-right British National Party in 1993 in winning a seat on Tower Hamlets Council, an area of extreme social deprivation with a large ethnic minority population, provides an interesting example. Evidence suggests that many young people in the area saw their problem as being unable to gain access to local authority housing in an area where their families had been housed for generations. Perceiving groups of relatively recent immigrants from ethnic minority backgrounds to be favoured by the local Labour controlled council, they considered the solution to their problem to be support for a political party which would put the interests of indigenous white people first.

The 'new fascists' are, however, a widespread phenomenon not merely restricted to run-down inner city areas with large influxes of non-white immigrants. We have noted above the close links with the football hooliganism subculture and this pattern of recruitment is widespread both internally to Britain and also on a national level. There is also evidence, however, that the new fascism is gaining recruits from areas not normally associated with overt and organised racism. For example, the British National Party has moved the centre of its operations to rural central England and has been particularly successful in recruiting among young males traditionally associated with the highly organised left-wing, trade union dominated, coal mining industry damaged to the point of non-existence as the result of government policies since 1979.

New Age Travellers

'New Age travellers' is a generic term which has been widely used in the media, but rarely among participants, to describe groups of 'scruffy' young people who have apparently 'dropped out' of 'normal' society and have chosen to take to the road in convoys of battered old vehicles. There appears to be an urban variation on this grouping who are commonly involved in squatting in previously unoccupied housing. Eschewing traditional forms of employment, many (by no means all) live off welfare benefits, begging, and petty crime. Many of these young people perceive their *problem* to be a Britain in terminal economic decline which has failed to deliver the consumer affluence promised by post-war capitalism, while many others have chosen to reject the values of materialism. For these people (not all New Age travellers are young), the *solution* to their problem is to establish an alternative life-style outside of 'straight' society. Many among their number consider themselves to be anarchists and belong to overtly anti-capitalist groups such as 'Class War'.

It would be inappropriate, however, to consider all those young people labelled as 'New Age travellers' to be a close-knit politicised homogenous grouping. The level of commitment to anarchist politics is undoubtedly variable, but there does seem to be some general commitment towards anti-authoritarianism, a rejection of the traditional party political system which is considered irrelevant, and an enthusiasm for predominantly green politics centring on single issues such as animal rights and the fast-expanding anti-roads movement (a group of protesters who physically challenge and obstruct the road building program in Britain).

It will be the case, however, that some adherents to this life-style have little enthusiasm for more overt political manifestations of this subculture but quite simply enjoy the freedom from the 'rat-race' of conventional society and the pleasures of copious quantities of alcohol and drugs. There have been some quite close links between 'New Age travellers' and the 'Rave' culture and there are some apparent crossovers between the two groups. Some students and other groups of young people share serious political concerns for environmental and animal rights politics and many of these are on the fringes of New Age culture if only on a weekender basis. Some groups of young people seem to have affinities with more than one contemporary subculture and are not easy to categorise.

Gangsta Rap and Dancehall

'Gangsta Rap' originated in the USA as a form of Black musical protest and has a close relation in 'Dancehall', a mutant variation of Jamaican Reggae which uses sexually explicit and often highly charged political lyrics. This youth subculture has been extremely popular in Britain among disaffected black youth with its adherents identifying their *problem* to be the dominant white culture and see their *solution* to be criminal activity including burglary, street robbery, and drug-dealing (particularly 'crack' cocaine). While adherence to the more extreme manifestations of this culture is a minority interest, there does appear to be much popular support among many Black youngsters for milder variations of this subculture. It also has a growing support among groups of disaffected young whites and Asians who have adopted its style of dress. The widespread wearing of 'L.A. Raiders' (an American Football team) caps is a conscious celebration of the 'resistance' of the participants in the Los Angeles riots of a few years ago. This subcultural grouping cannot be categorised into either of the two broad strands identified above. Obviously, alienated young Black people will find no common ground with white racists, but there have undoubtedly been crossover links on the margins with young people involved in the 'Rave' culture discussed below.

Raves

A rave is an often illegal all night (and often longer) dance where participants dance frenetically to extremely loud repetitive music usually under the influence of amphetamine based drugs called 'ecstasy', or more recently in its purer form known as 'whiz' or 'speed'. Links between music, dancing, and amphetamines are not new. 'Speed' was an important part of the 'Mod', and later northern soul, scenes. The latter involved all night and all weekend dances.

The modern contemporary raves emerged out of the London warehouse party scene of the early 1980s which developed into an influential youth subculture. The music was a combination of 'funk', 'hip hop' (from New York), and 'house' (from Chicago and Detroit). By the end of the 1980s 'Warehouse' culture had become increasingly commercialised with a radical mutation taking the opposite direction and developing into 'Acid House'. The new venues were sited outside of the large urban conurbations, often sited in fields and disused airfields close to the essential motorway network.

Raves are interesting because they attract members of different youth subcultures including New Age travellers, many of those who were once termed 'lager louts' and their contemporary equivalent the 'townie' along with middle class students. The coming together of such diverse subcultures in usually peaceful circumstances (sometimes fighting together against police officers seeking to restrain their activities) is fascinating phenomenon which can only really be explained by the chemical properties of their chosen drug which synthesises the dance inspiring activities of 'speed' with the psychedelic properties of LSD and encourages a feeling of well-being and 'love' for all human beings. It would seem that ravers of different types all share a common problem with a 'meaningless' existence and seek a 'solution' in unbridled hedonism.

The Rave scene was still extremely popular in 1995 but was nevertheless under threat from two separate sources. First, the *Criminal Justice Bill* 1994 has given the police powers to control large gatherings of people who gather for Raves. There is little evidence to date that the police have used these powers. Second, there is evidence that pure 'ecstasy' has become virtually impossible to obtain and Raves are no-longer about peace and love.

SUMMARY AND CONCLUSION

In this chapter we have provided a brief overview of previous explanations of the existence of youth subcultures. The pioneering and enduring work of the Chicago School of sociology in the 1920s and 1930s, and the US subcultural theorists in the 1940s and 1950s has been noted, and we have identified how the Birmingham Centre for Contemporary Cultural Studies developed a neo-Marxist version of subcultural theory in the 1970s to explain how successive groups of British working class youth have consciously or subconsciously identified problems in relation to a changing economy and sought their own solutions.

It has been shown that the analysis favoured by the Birmingham CCCS is still a useful explanatory tool when it is adapted to take account of the recognition that a whole range of competing subcultural groups are in concurrent existence in what might be termed post-modern society. These separate groups of young people have had very different experiences of the radical economic change that has occurred in Britain in the last twenty years. These very different groups have developed their own subcultural solutions for coping with this transformation. It has been further suggested that many contemporary young people are able to choose a subcultural solution to their subjective socioeconomic problem from some of the alternatives available. Significantly, membership of subcultural groups is an important and normal aspect of the transitional phase of adolescence which enables both young males *and* females to develop a sense of individual and group identity.

We have identified some of the key youth subcultures in existence in Britain in the 1990s, discussed their chosen subcultural *solution* to their predicament, and located some of the points of intersection between different groupings. It is impossible to predict whether or not these coalitions will coalesce into more permanent alliances or disintegrate and reform in other directions. We can only reiterate that deviant behaviour conducted in a group or gang context in Britain can only be understood in the context of the youth subculture to which the young people belong.

It is not readily apparent whether our theoretical perspective could be successfully applied to the study of youth subcultures and gangs in other advanced industrial societies. Certainly, our brief review of the contemporary US literature suggests that our approach might be usefully applied to the study of American gang behaviour. Spergel (1995) observes that subcultures arise because people group together to create group solutions to shared socioeconomic problems and there is the possibility that our analysis could help to describe and explain different groups within the larger configuration of the underclass.

There will inevitably be differences in subcultural manifestations within different societies, although there will be some degree of crossover. For example, the Gangsta Rap and Dancehall subcultures in contemporary Britain have their origins in America and Jamaica, while the Skinhead subculture with its origins in late-1960s London has been successfully adopted by racists and white supremacists throughout Europe and America. There is some suggestion that colourful, flamboyant, status-based 'spectacular' youth subcultures have been more common in Britain than in America, although this may have something to do with the rather different experience of poverty among young people in the two societies. Unemployed British young people have in the past had their subcultural experimentation subsidised by a welfare system generous by American standards. It is extremely likely, however, that the British youth subcultural profile will become more austere as a reflection of the current retreat from welfarism in this society. Only further empirical investigation will provide answers to these questions.

REFERENCES

Althusser, L. (1969) *For Marx* (trans. B. Brewster), London: Allen Lane.

Anderson, E. (1990) *Street Wise*, Chicago: University of Chicago.

Becker, H.S. (1963) *Outsiders: Studies in the Sociology of Deviance*, New York: Free Press.

Brake, M. (1980) *The Sociology of Youth Cultures and Youth Subcultures*, London: Routledge and Kegan Paul.

Brake, M. (1985) *Comparative Youth Culture*, London: Routledge

Cain, M. (ed.) (1989) *Growing Up Good: Policing the Behaviour of Girls in Europe*, London: Sage.

Campbell, A. (1981) *Girl Delinquents*, Oxford: Blackwell.

Carlen, P. (1988) *Women, Crime and Poverty*, Milton Keynes: Open University.

Clarke, J. (1975) *Ideologies of Control of Working Class Youth*, University of Birmingham: Centre for Contemporary Cultural Studies.

Cloward, R.A. and Ohlin, L.E. (1960) *Delinquency and Opportunity: A Theory of Delinquent Gangs,* New York: Free Press.

Cohen, A.K. (1955) *Delinquent Boys: The Culture of the Gang*, New York: Free Press.

Cohen, P. (1986) 'Rethinking the Youth Question', in *Youth and Policy: The Journal of Critical Analysis working paper series,* Institute of Education,

University of London.

Cohen, P. (1972) 'Sub-Cultural Conflict and Working Class Community', *Working Papers in Cultural Studies*, No.2, Birmingham: CCCS, University of Birmingham.

Cohen, S. (1973) *Folk Devils and Moral Panics*, London: Paladin.

Corrigan, P. (1979) *The Smash Street Kids*, London: Paladin.

Curtis, L.A. (1975) *Violence, Race and Culture*, Lexington, Massachusetts: Health.

Downes, D. (1966) *The Delinquent Solution*, London: Routledge and Kegan Paul.

Frith, S. (1984) *The Sociology of Youth*, Ormskirk, Lancs: Causeway Press.

Furnham, A. and Gunter, B. (1989) *The Anatomy of Adolescence*, London and New York: Routledge.

Gramsci, A. (1971) *Selections from the Prison Notebooks of Antonio Gramsci* (translated from *Quaderini del Carcere*), Q. Hoare and G.N. Smith (eds), New York: International Publishers.

Griffin, C. (1985) *Typical Girls? Young Women from School to the Job Market*, London: Routledge and Kegan Paul.

Hagerdorn, J. (1992) 'Gangs, Neighbourhoods, and Public Policy', *Social Problems* 38 (4): 529-42.

Hall, S. and Jefferson, T. (eds) (1976) *Resistance Through Rituals: Youth subcultures in post-war Britain,* London: Hutchinson.

Hebdige, D. (1976) 'The Meaning of Mod,' in S. Hall and T. Jefferson (eds), *Resistance Through Rituals: Youth Subcultures in post-war Britain,* London: Hutchinson.

Hebdige, D. (1979) *Subculture: The Meaning Of Style*, London: Methuen.

Hendry, L.B. (1983) *Growing Up and Going Out,* Aberdeen: Aberdeen University Press.

Hendry, L.B., Shucksmith, J., Love, J.G. and Glendinning, A. (1993) *Young People's Leisure and Lifestyles,* London and New York: Routledge.

Hoyles, M. (1994) 'Lost Connections and New Directions', *Working Paper No.6,* London: Comedia and Demos.

Hudson, F. and Ineichen, B. (1991) *Taking it Lying Down: Sexuality and Teenage Motherhood*, London: Macmillan.

Jefferson, T. (1976) 'The Cultural Meaning of the Teds', in S. Hall and T. Jefferson (eds), *Resistance through Rituals: Youth Subcultures in Post-war Britain,* London: Hutchinson.

Jones, G., Wallace, C. (1992) *Youth, Family and Citizenship,* Buckingham: Open University Press.

Krisberg (1974) 'Gang Youth and Hustling: The Psychology of Survival', *Issues in Criminology* 9 (Spring 1) : 115-31.

Lees, S. (1986) *Losing Out: Sexuality and Adolescent Girls*, London: Hutchinson.

Lemert, E. (1967) *Human Deviance, Social Problems and Social Control*, Englewood Cliffs: Prentice Hall.

Lloyd, M.A. (1985) *Adolescence*, London: Harper and Row.

Marx, K. (1970) *The German Ideology,* London: Lawrence and Wishart.

Matza, D.M. (1964) *Delinquency and Drift*, New York: Wiley.

Maxson, C.L. and Klein, M.W. (1990) 'Street Gang Violence: Twice as great or half as great?', in C.R. Huff (ed.), *Gangs in America*, Newbury Park, CA: Sage.

McRobbie, A. (1978) 'Working Class Girls and the Culture of Femininity', in Women's Study Group, *Women Take Issue*, Centre for Contemporary Cultural Studies, University of Birmingham, London: Hutchinson.

McRobbie, A. (1991) *Feminism and Youth Culture: From 'Jackie' to 'Just Seventeen'*, London: Macmillan.

McRobbie, A. and Nava, M. (1984) *Gender and Generation,* London Macmillan.

McRobbie, A. and Garber, J. (1975) 'Girls and Subcultures—An Exploration' in S. Hall and T. Jefferson (eds), *Resistance Through Rituals: Youth subcultures in post-war Britain*, London: Hutchinson.

Merton, R.K. (1938) 'Social Structure and Anomie', *American Sociological Review 3* (October): 672-82.

Miller, W.R. (1958) 'Lower Class Culture as a Generating Milieu of Gang Delinquency', *Journal of Social Issues* 14: 5-19.

Miller, W.R. (1990) 'Why the United States has Failed to Solve its Youth Gang Problem', in C.R. Huff (ed.) *Gangs in America*, Newbury Park, CA: Sage, 263-87.

Mirza, H.S. (1992) *Young, Female and Black*, London: Routledge.

Moore, J.W. (1991) *Going Down to the Barrio*, Philadelphia: Temple University Press.

Mungham, G. and Pearson, G. (eds) (1976) *Working Class Youth Culture*, London: Routledge and Kegan Paul.

Nava, M. (1992) *Changing Cultures: Feminism, Youth and Consumerism*, London: Sage.

Parker, H. (1974) *View From the Boys*, Newton Abbot: David and Charles.

Poulantzas, N. (1975) *Classes in Contemporary Capitalism*, London: New Left Books.

Pryce, K. (1979) *Endless Pressure: A Study of West Indian Life-Styles in Bristol,* Harmondsworth: Penguin.

Shaw, C.R. and McKay, H.D. (1972) *Juvenile Delinquency and Urban Areas*, Chicago: University of Chicago Press.

Spergel, I.A. (1995) *The Youth Gang Problem: A Community Approach*, Oxford: Oxford University Press.

Sunley, R. and Garrett, S. (1995) *Young People 'On the Park': Politics, Place and Gendered Space*, unpublished paper delivered to the British Sociological Association Annual Conference, Contested Cities: Social Process and Spatial Forms, 10-13 April 1995, University of Leicester.

Sutherland, E.H. (1937) *The Professional Thief: By a Professional Thief*, Chicago:

University of Chicago Press.

Taylor, C.S. (1990) *Dangerous Society*, East Lansing, MI: Michigan State University Press.

Taylor, I. and Wall, D. (1976) 'Beyond the Skinheads—comment on the Emergence and Significance of Glamrock', in G. Mungham and G. Pearson (eds), *Working Class Youth Culture*, London: Routledge and Kegan Paul.

Wallace, C. and Cross, M. (eds) (1990) *Youth in Transition: The Sociology of Youth and Youth Policy*, Basingstoke: Falmer.

Willis, P. (1977) *Learning to Labour*, London: Saxon House.

Wilson, W.J. (1991) 'Public Policy Research and the Truly Disadvantaged', in C. Jencks and P.E. Petersen (eds), *The Urban Underclass*, Washington, DC: the Brookings Institution.

Wolfgang, M.E. and Ferracuti, F. (1967) *The Sub-culture of Violence: Towards an Integrated Theory in Criminology*, Beverley Hills: Sage.

Youniss, J. and Smollar, J. (1985) *Adolescent Relations with Mothers, Fathers and Friends,* Chicago: University of Chicago Press.

3 German Youth Subcultures: History, Typology and Gender-Orientations

Joachim Kersten

INTRODUCTION

Historical accounts of postwar German youth subcultures usually begin with the rebellious *Halbstarke*—the white, rock'n'roll-loving teenage crowds and neighbourhood groupings of the 1950s and 60s. Class and gender aspects of youth subcultures, and the provocative potential of subcultural styles, can be observed in numerous German postwar youth phenomena. These dimensions first become apparent in two extremely different groupings of the early 1940s: *Edelweißpiraten* and *Swing-Jugend*. Both youth subcultures were regarded as 'criminal' and were exposed to the full rage of the Nazi control apparatus. The lower working class neighbourhood cliques with the *Edelweiß* image (the romantic name was actually given to them by the Gestapo) and the middle/upper class high school student members of *Swing* groups revealed patterns of class origin, gender representation, and provocative style that were to re-emerge in most postwar subcultures. Lower class groupings tended to be risk-oriented while those of the middle class put much less emphasis on risk and masculinity. Both types of youth subcultures tended to antagonise the mainstream, or to irritate both the formal and informal control systems of the dominant culture.

Edelweißpiraten were neighbourhood groups. Their members were involved in self-organised action like weekend outings or spontaneous meetings. 'Uncontrolled' youthful activity was strictly prohibited under Nazi rule. The police of the Third Reich used a special anti-loitering law (*Eckensteherverordnung*) to control and sanction any form of youth assembly outside the official Hitler Youth organisations. *Edelweiß* groups represented a kind of 'boy scout' style. Members wore edelweiss flowers under the lapels of their jackets. In the tradition of free German youth movements, NGO youth so to speak, they wore 'bloomers' or *lederhosen* and white socks. During weekend trips they camped, lit fires and sang forbidden songs. Like all neighbourhood groupings they were involved in petty crime and in turf fights. The cliques were particularly strong in working class industrial cities like Cologne. Confrontational routines of these cliques included attacks on Hitler Youth members. The Nazi police saw *Edelweißpiraten* as a serious form of youth crime. Members were arrested, held in prison and, in some cases killed by the Nazi criminal justice system.[1]

Swing-Jugend were groups that came to the attention of the Nazi authorities at approximately the same time as *Edelweißpiraten*. From the perspective of the 1990s *Swing* kids appear to have been engaged in perfectly harmless leisure activities. Quite different to the 'youth movement' style of *Edelweißpiraten*, *Swing* kids wore upper class clothes, they drank, danced and listened to their favourite music: swing or jazz. Their suits were fashionable: English-style civilian, not military, suits. However, 'English style' was considered deeply decadent by the Nazis. England was the enemy, swing and jazz were labelled *Negermusik* and seen as proof of the inferiority of non-Aryan 'races'. Having a good time (which the Nazi elites frequently did themselves) while Germany was fighting a war of life and death, was not allowed, especially for high school students from privileged social backgrounds.

When SS and police-chief Heinrich Himmler heard about *Swing-Jugend* he sent a cable to all security forces. He ordered the arrest of the members of *Swing* groups. They and their parents were to be sent to concentration camps. There they should be exposed to hard work and regular floggings. Himmler equated the decadence and impertinence of these privileged youths to treason. Although this subculture had very few members and caused no damage, did not steal or attack anyone, their 'crime' of 'English style' clothing provoked the Nazis probably more than the more numerous cliques of *Edelweißpiraten*.

In the immediate aftermath of the war and the collapse of the Nazi regime, the circumstances of the generation of young persons received little attention in youth sociology. They were called *Trümmerjugend*—'youths in ruins'. In large part their cliques consisted of young survival specialists, many of them without families or homes. Their cliques were their families on which they had to rely. In cases where they had families and younger brothers and sisters, more often than not these youths were the main breadwinners. Tens of thousands of them lived in the ruins or in former air-raid shelters. They were involved in black market operations and in crime which partly resulted from need and difficult circumstances, and partly served as an accomplishment of self-esteem.

In the early 50s there was some concern on the part of the Western allies about anti-semitic and racist activities carried out by youth cliques, especially in the Western part of Berlin. But it was the 'non-political' *Halbstarke* which provoked the first postwar debate about youth crime in Germany. In retrospect, it was not youthful crimes, the screening of 'Rock around the Clock', or rock-inspired riots, which explained the heavy-handed reaction of the public, the media, social workers and the authorities. The press photographs of the 50s and 60s 'riots' show well-groomed youngsters in blue jeans who look like American high school students. For some obscure reason they seem to be screaming their lungs out. The provocation was *Halbstarken* style. On the other hand, the teenagers themselves were outraged by baton-policing action, and by discrimination campaigns run by the media, politicians, and teachers. All this led to an escalation, a youth rebellion, largely expressed as vandalism throughout the Western part of the country, but also, in less spectacular forms, in the East.

Screaming to what the main stream still considered '*Negermusik*', hanging out on street corners, smoking in public, wearing the hair and dress style of those who won the war, these youths reminded their parents and teachers of the fact that Germany had lost the war. The industrious, quiet and very grey *Wiederaufbau* Germans drew their legitimacy from hard work. They saw themselves as reconstructing Germany out of ruins. The style and public appearance of *Halbstarke* confronted whatever was left of German culture with the fact that nothing could stop the advance of American popular culture. At that particular stage of West-German postwar development it was not the privileged middle or upper class youths[2] who could provoke the main culture but the noisy working class teenagers.

Blue jeans, greasy hair, and music soon entered the main stream through the department stores, and the developing fashion, music and entertainment industries. *Halbstarke* were succeeded by the rebellious lower class style of the biker culture (called 'Rocker' groups in Germany) with their homophobia, misogyny, xenophobia and admiration for what they thought was U.S. culture.[3] In the 60s and 70s the term 'Rocker' became a symbol for violent youth crime. As such these groupings were always good for a headline in the tabloid press ('"Rocker" gang attacks beer-garden—Police helpless and of no use'). 'Rockers' were over-represented in violent youth crime like serious assault. In major cities such groupings could develop into small size imitations of U.S. motorcycle gangs with links to organised crime, drug trading, gambling and prostitution.

In the late 60s it was again privileged youth that shook postwar Germany's public and political system deep into the 1970s. The nasty image of the 'Rocker' subculture was used by the tabloid press in commenting on the first confrontations between police and students in Berlin. West Berlin's media and politicians labelled the students of 1967/68 'Polit-Rocker'. Again, a look at the press photographs and documentary films leaves a different impression. These images are of orderly young men (few females) predominantly dressed in dark suits and ties (like the Blues Brothers but without hats and shades), sitting on university lawns and listening to political arguments. They may cast votes on declarations against university politics or U.S. involvement in the Vietnam War. When they took to the streets the outrage caused by the visibility of a student (elite) rebellion affected the whole culture. As in the Nazi era, quite a number of ordinary citizens, and law and order representatives, suggested sending the students 'to the camps'.

Aside from intellectual and semi-orderly *Exi* style there was an element of provocative 'unkemptness' in the youth rebellion of the 60s and 70s. In the mid-60s, public resentment was directed against high school kids called *Gammler*. This was another label used by the irritated mainstream, not by the members of the subculture themselves.[4] On this occasion they were hanging around street corners and parks; as far as music was concerned they preferred the Beatles or the Rolling Stones. They transformed a piece of military uniform, the parka, into a garment of love and peace, and a billboard for other philosophies considered deviant in their time. *Gammler* were the early German hippies, and their program was interpreted as being against the values of the working class especially the notion of work giving meaning to life.[5] Again, like *Swing* youths, *Gammler* were an example of 'crimeless crime': a provocation through style. In what is romanticised as the '68 movement' (or still hated and held responsible for the 'German disease'), new expressions of intellectual, academic and political criticism became associated with Hippie style and Third World revolutionary symbolism (Che Guevara). Activities and style were mostly oriented toward protest or the expression of youthful 'political' identity. Sometimes the student movement had elements of a rebellion, but only a very small segment of it turned into violent armed opposition (e.g. Baader-Meinhoff or Red Army Faction, or related terrorist gangs). For parts of the conservative mainstream, 'youth violence' and 'student unrest' became the synonym for the years following 1967/68.[6]

Space prevents a detailed description of later youth cultures. Suffice to say that, in their provocative elements, similar patterns of class background and gender representation reappear. In relation to youth crime and public order problems the squatters's movement, 'Punks', hooligans and 'Skinheads' were the most visible and provocative subcultures. 'Skinheads' will be one focus of the subsequent analysis. After 1989 in reunited Germany they caused trouble, resentment, and massive fear as representations of Nazi symbolism. In terms of style history, however, they are not so much successors of Nazi (S.A. or *Landser*) style but follow the tradition of 'Rocker' groupings.

YOUTH GROUPINGS IN THE CONTEXT OF YOUTH CRIME

Underclass/Marginalised Groupings

The most visible subcultural groupings, their involvement in criminal activities, their gender representation, and their main opponents can be represented schematically (Table 1). As far as the first two scenarios (homelessness and drugs) are concerned, German cities display as many of the various elements of homelessness in combination with social decay and young/middle age marginalised drug addicts as those in other industrialised countries. Numerically speaking the visibility of members of the drug subculture is high in all categories of registered crime. However, German heroin addicts (crack is far less widespread than in the U.S.) seem much less involved in property offences (like break and enter) or interpersonal crime (street robbery) than their counterparts in the inner city neighbourhoods of North American cities, or in Melbourne and Sydney, for instance.

By their very nature, neighbourhood cliques are, major protagonists in the commitment of 'bread and butter' youth crime—be it assault or against property. As in other industrialised societies the German groupings tend to be male-dominated and of lower class social background. Groups or cliques (with a higher form of organisational structure) give themselves names, very often copies of American gang names. Names can also have a reference to the suburb, although nowhere are there any 'postcode' names as in the suburbs of Melbourne. Members may wear uniform-like dress. Bandannas are rare, and—to the best of my knowledge—nowhere in Germany do groupings fulfil the criteria of Klein's U.S. youth gang definition (Klein 1995). In the case of children of migrants, names may have an ethnic connotation (e.g. 'Turkish Power Boys'). In cities with ethnically segregated areas (e.g. Berlin Kreuzberg), groupings can be predominantly of non-German background. Their 'Ausländer' ('non-German') status can be partly a stigmatising label attached to these groupings and their members (most obvious in the compilation of crime statistics).[7] It can be also a matter of group identity and self-esteem.

Table 3.1: A Typology of Marginalised Youth Groupings in the Context of Youth Crime, Germany

Groupings/cliques/ gangs	Involve-ment	Criminal activities	Gender	'Enemy'/ opponents
'Punks'/ alcohol/ homeless	full time	property	♂/♀	police, shopkeepers, 'Skinheads'
Drug-scene (Heroin)	full time	narcotics law/ property	♂/♀	police
Neighbourhood gangs/ cliques of young underclass Germans	full time	property/ against person	♂	other gangs/ cliques
Immigrant youths	full time	property/ against person	♂	other gangs/ cliques, right wing youths, 'Skinheads'
Aussiedlerjugendliche (see p.7)	full- and part time	against person	♂	immigrants, other youths, police
East German city- and small town groupings/ cliques/gangs	full- and part time	property/ against person, motor vehicle theft	♂	individual persons, other groupings/ cliques

Groupings, cliques, and occasionally gang-like formations of *Aussiedlerjugendliche* are a relatively new phenomenon in Germany. The influx of families of German expatriates from Eastern Europe and from parts of the former Soviet Union has been high in the last decade. Although of German 'blood' many *Aussiedler* do not speak German, and because of the ghettoisation of *Aussiedler* in German cities their male adolescent offspring have become quite visible in confrontational groupings and the related areas of interpersonal youth crime. Groups of adolescents and young men in the Eastern cities of Germany are heavily involved in motor vehicle theft and related crime areas (reckless driving, drink-driving, driving without a license). Some aspects of the situation there appear similar to Beatrix Campbell's (1993) account of youth riots in Great Britain.

Non-Marginalised Groupings

As research into German racist/antisemitic youth violence (Willems 1993; Erb 1993, 1996) has shown, most offenders of crimes with racist and antisemitic dimensions come from non-marginalised social backgrounds: they go to school or have a job/apprenticeship, and their family background is *not* predominantly from single parent families/ broken homes etc. Similarly, soccer hooligans take part in 'weekend wars' with hooligans from other clubs, but live an ordinary and disciplined working life during the week. 'Skinheads' tend to be of lower middle class/working class origin. Their fathers were and are among those affected by structural unemployment in the secondary sector. As in England, the Netherlands and Belgium, the potential for violence on the part of soccer fans requires major police attention at every National League weekend.

Soccer fans do wear the 'colours' of their clubs, and their violence is less premeditated than that of the hooligans. Interpersonal crime in the context of kick-boxing clubs and other 'martial arts' scenarios has come into focus after the events in Solingen. There the alleged arsonists who burnt down a house of Turkish migrants, killing seven women and children, were members of a martial arts school. In Germany, just as in Japan, some of these organisations tend to attract violent right wing persons and other thugs. The organised Right in Germany sports an 'orderly' and 'disciplined' image and officially rejects violence. Aside from blatant antisemitism and racism, some members do condone violence against minorities or political 'enemies' and have been involved in interpersonal crime.

Table 3.2: A Typology of Non-marginalised Youth Groupings in the Context of Youth Crime, Germany

Groupings	Involvement	Criminal activities	Gender	'Enemy', opponents, victims
right wing youths	part time	against person/ arson/ racist antisemitic propaganda	♂ ♀	'leftists', disabled persons, immigrants, other persons
hooligans	part time	against person/ arson/ vandalism	♂	other hooligans, police, shop owners
'Skinheads'	mostly part time	against person/ hands-on violence/ racist antisemitic propaganda	♂ ♀	other groupings, 'Punks' and individual persons, immigrants, police, 'leftists'
soccer fans	part time	against person/ hands-on violence	♂	other soccer fans
martial arts scenes	part time	against person/ hands-on violence	♂	other martial artists, individual 'opponents'
Organised right wing parties/ Neo-Nazi groups	mostly part time	racist antisemitic propaganda	♂ ♀	'the system', 'the left', 'the Jews'

NEIGHBOURHOOD CLIQUE, HOOLIGAN AND 'SKINHEAD' ORIENTATIONS

The groupings discussed above can be divided into three main categories: neighbourhood/ turf 'gangs', violent hooligans, and members of the 'Skinhead' subculture. Neighbourhood groupings outnumber the other two forms. Among violence prone hooligans the dividing line between them and soccer fans is not very clear, so they probably outnumber the 'Skinheads' which are estimated at 8000 Germany-wide. Out of these approximately 2000 are hands-on violent offenders. In regards to all registered hate crimes 'Skinheads' account for less than 10% of the total.

It is evident that despite these differences, it is a combination of masculinist style, role models and action which influences a substantial part of the groupings' culture and identity. While neighbourhood clique members stick to their turf as members of U.S. inner city gangs do, hooligans follow the principle: 'have baseball bat will travel'. Celebrations of Hitler's birthday, or 'Rudolf Hess' memorial days are 'Festtage' that attract 'Skinheads' and right wing youths. Using e-mail and other modern communications technology, these groupings have managed to outsmart police and intelligence. With support from a local right-wing infrastructure, for a day 'Aufmärsche' (marches in military formation) of 'Skinheads', hooligans and other right wing youths could turn smaller cities into Nazi turf. The image of being 'in the hands of Neo-Nazis' or 'Skinheads' is deeply embarrassing to most locals and their city government. However, it has become public, particularly in the Eastern part of Germany, that some smaller towns have threatened 'to get in the Skins' to deter the erection of homes for asylum seekers in their particular region.

Neighbourhood clique members fight in groups. Their 'philosophy' is closer to that of a young initiated village warrior than to the individual 'Rambo' fighter the hooligan represents. 'Skinheads', particularly from right wing/racist/nationalist factions, view themselves as soldiers for a white Germany. Their violence is similar to that of hooligans. It includes unmitigated attacks on people of colour, disabled persons, and 'enemies' of all sorts, and the assaults frequently involve a dehumanisation of the victim. Only cliques have material territory to protect. Very few 'Skinhead' groupings are neighbourhood groupings. Their definition of territory is even more abstract than that of hooligans (where the defence of the soccer club, the city, or in the case of European or World Cup games, the country, serve as the legitimation for an attack on others). Hooligans and 'Skinheads' consume high amounts of alcohol on a routine basis, so their inhibition to use and enjoy confrontations and hands-on violence is lowered. Violence does not happen because these youths have been drinking too much. They drink continuously so violence can happen at any time.

Table 3.3: Orientations of Neighbourhood Cliques, Hooligans and 'Skinheads', Germany

Orientations, ***focal concerns,*** **activities**	**Neighbourhood cliques/ gangs**	**Hooligans**	**'Skinheads'**
visibility	neighbourhood	before, during and after soccer games	soccer, right wing scene, 'Festtage', concerts
style	warrior	fighter	*Landser* (WW II German soldier) or working class
territory/ turf	most important	soccer club 'City'	abstract notion of race and nation/ working class culture
drugs	dope/ alcohol	mostly alcohol	public drinking of canned beer/ 'Kampftrinken'
masculinity	important, loyalty to one's group and turf;	important, army of soccer mercenaries	important, *Kameradschaft* (mateship)
'honour', 'mateship', 'respect'	important	less important	*Stolz* (proud to be German, SHARP, Redskin, working class and so on)
focal concern	control and protection of hood and honour	combat, dehumanisation of victim	*Deutschland* as the hood, combat, dehumanisation of victim

The confrontations that lead to violence and victimisation can be attributed to three main focal concerns of 'warrior/fighter' masculinities: territory (in material or abstract terms, also as fights over 'honour/respect', 'race' etc.), women and their protection or—again in more abstract terms—heterosexual prowess, homophobia etc.), and as a display of masculine skills or rather ersatz skills (theft, reckless driving, motor vehicle theft, street robberies). The related gender orientations are discussed in the next sections.

A THEORY OUTLINE

In this section I approach current outbreaks of xenophobia and racism in Germany in the context of prevailing discourses of masculinities. The theory framework for the following discussion of confrontational orientations and practices among members of cliques and groupings is based on Connell's (1987, 1994) contribution to the sociology of gender and Messerschmidt's (1993) application of the notion of 'hegemonic masculinity' to crime. Furthermore, public displays of confrontational practices have been described in Gilmore's (1991) comparative work on rituals of masculinity. Without explicit reference this part also draws on feminist theorising on gender/ social control (Cain 1989/1999; Walklate 1995) and gendered forms of crime and victimisation (Stanko 1994). The next section looks at practices of young males in subcultures which express xenophobic and racist orientations within a framework of masculinist norms.

Confrontational attitudes need to be distinguished from racist and xenophobic practices which constitute violent assaults carried out by groupings or individual males (Lau and Soeffner 1994). The *auteurs* of explicit xenophobia and racism reveal masculinist orientations as discursive strategies, as a struggle towards hegemonic masculinity. Offenders of spontaneous hands-on violence, or of arson attacks, or as participants in fights between groupings, or as perpetrators of attacks against individuals of foreign origin/ different colour of skin/ homosexuals/ handicapped persons, do not necessarily belong to the same groupings, nor even to the same subcultures (Willems 1994). Youths who have killed (mostly women and children) by setting fire to houses and institutions for *Asylanten/Asylbewerber* (non-Germans who have been granted political asylum status, or who have applied for it) are not identical with those who have publicly assaulted non-Germans, and those who desecrate Jewish cemeteries or concentration camp memorials. These may belong to yet another subcultural context (Erb 1994). Still, they all rely on norms which see confrontation as a masculine enterprise, and therefore as legitimate.

While in other works I have looked at gendered practices as the social action of masculinities (Kersten 1993, 1996), this essay looks mainly at discursive strategies. The most prominent German contributions to the debate on youth violence support a general notion of 'social disintegration' (Heitmeyer 1991) as the underlying cause of youth problems. This theorising has been criticised for its vagueness and methodological flaws, for its mythological reference to a 'golden past', and for its gender-blindness. Most obviously, the 'Bielefeld School' fails to acknowledge the diverse range of phenomena in the area of youth violence (v.Trotha 1995).

In contrast, the empirical section of this paper looks at masculinities from different periods (young male inmates of the early 1980s; German 'Skinheads' in the 1990s) and compares constructs of foreigners as 'enemies'. These constructs are examined as a situational accomplishment of gender in terms of Messerschmidt's conception of crime as a situational accomplishment of hegemonic masculinity (Messerschmidt 1993). The data indicate that confrontational practices in the form of racist attitudes are a characteristic feature of the behaviour of marginalised young males even when actual outbreaks of such violence do not occur. The final section of this essay discusses recent confrontational practices of xenophobia and racism in the context of German post-reunification politics.

Marginality, Confrontation and Ideals of Masculinity

Obviously in view of cross-cultural data on crime and victimisation there is a gender-confrontation-social control nexus. But these separate elements cannot be considered to constitute a general theory of causes. It is misleading (although sometimes understandable from a victim's or activists' standpoint) simply to equate maleness with crime and violence. Such a view ignores significant variations in masculinity as 'a configuration of practice around the position of men in the structure of gender relations' (Connell 1994: 3). Ethnographies have described the significance of different ideals of masculinity. There are cultures in which the dominant type of masculinity is more or less openly directed towards violent confrontation, domination, and control (Gilmore 1991). In other cultures the socialisation of young males towards hegemonic masculinity is not attached to norms of physical prowess, hard work, and the readiness to fight.

In some cultures proof of scholarly aptitude (*Bildung*) is regarded as a much more significant demonstration of masculinity than prowess of the machismo type. Competitive displays of skills in public arenas, such as good public speaking ability, are another recognised area of achievement. However, many male-dominated cultures require their young males to defend their community/ country by learning skills of 'protection': frightening, attacking and killing enemies. Trained by older men—younger men are forced, sometimes by means of rather distasteful rituals, to enter into a collective of disciplined young warriors and not to become an individual hero (of the 'Rambo-type'). Mental and physical strength on the part of male members of the tribe/ village etc. are regarded as a guarantee of a community's safety from outside attacks. As such these skills serve as a measure of masculinity. Young men are expected to be reliable in the general task of protecting the community's members, its name and honour, and its achievements.

'To be a man' in these terms means to demonstrate the capacity and determination to endure physical and psychological hardship for the community's safety and well-being. For young males this status of respected masculinity has to be learned and earned. It can be taken away if the individual fails to meet the community's expectations. The public and private control of such culture-specific ideals of masculinity is not restricted to men alone. In some cultures females young and old, participate in, or even determine, appropriate public behaviour of young men. For young males public displays of proper masculinity are obligatory. A failure to live up to this endangers the status of the individual young man in terms his of marriageability, respect and status. Masculinity as a configuration of certain orientations and practices is not an anthropological constant because ideals of masculinity as a range of specific skills differ from culture to culture.

Modernisation and Ideals of Masculinity

Modernisation, and especially the rise of the tertiary sector of the labour market, have eroded the notion of physical work as the only form of 'real men's' work. Also, the exclusively masculine character of work outside the home has not been maintained. Still, work in the house, child-rearing, and care-related work remain as domains of unpaid or poorly paid activity. In most industrialised societies care for other humans and housework are left to females and/ or people of minority status. Such activities are in the main still regarded as substantially 'unmanly' by most males in society, particularly among young males with low educational status.

At the same time, labour markets in Western societies 'release' vast sections of the working-age population, and access to professional status and an average income is restricted to fewer and fewer members of the work force. Young males of working class origin or from marginal social backgrounds suffer a loss of that class status that used to be guaranteed by steady paid work. In the traditional industrial regions of Europe and North America (as well as Australia) paid work in the secondary sector, as an exclusively male-dominated domain, formed the core of masculinist working class culture. The basis of this culture has been severely eroded over time. However, ideals of masculinity related to factory work have survived in subcultural styles, rituals and practices of exclusion, among them mysogynistic, homophobic and xenophobic orientations. 'Skinheadism' is a celebration of the inimical elements of a white masculinist working class mentality: nationalism, territorial control, collective euphoria related to sports, alcoholism, sexism and racism.

Subcultural maintenance of styles and phobias of the 19th century is an indication of the ideological and artificial state of present masculinities. Such masculinities require permanent peer monitoring, demonstrative shows of 'manhood', and the creation of constructs of 'others' as enemies.

Men are perhaps less necessary for the long term survival of communities than women (Gilmore 1991, Badinter 1993). The fear of being dispensable is inevitably at the base of social, psychological and cultural practices which create the appearance that masculinity and male-dominated domains are both necessary and exclusive.

IDEALS OF MASCULINITY AND SOCIAL MARGINALITY

The struggle for hegemonic masculinity does not only exclude women from the domain of public power, of cultural domination, and the use of force. Access to these domains is also restricted to a minority of males. In male-dominated cultures most males share certain privileges over women and children. But colour of skin, minority/ majority status, education and class origin, age, and sexual preference, form the main parameters that regulate access to domains of male domination and thus, regulate the relation between hegemonic and subordinated masculinities. 'A hegemonic form of masculinity is likely to exist, with other masculinities arrayed around it' (Connell 1994: 5).

Hegemonic and subordinated masculinities form hierarchies. In the lower echelons public or private forms of crime can offer a final opportunity to participate in hegemonic masculinity or at least to organise a situational display of hegemonic masculinity by denigrating and dehumanising victims in the home or on the streets (Messerschmidt 1993). Routine enactments of private violence as assaults in the home against females and children are open to adult males of all ages, social and ethnic/racial backgrounds. Public displays of hegemonic status often occur as risk-taking behaviour. The fact that marginalised young males resort to such risky demonstrations of gender is one of the factors that explain the link between class and race discrimination, gender and crime visibility.

Proof of masculinity, as a particular participation in hegemonic masculinity (Messerschmidt 1993), takes the form of street crimes and rape of the type that is most likely to be reported by victims to police, or to crime survey researchers (Kersten 1993a). In other words: marginalised segments of the population frequently experience some of the most visible displays of masculinity, either as offenders, or as victims, or both. Underclass young males have no capacity to challenge the control of domains of hegemonic masculinity. They have to stick to their guns and to the places they come from. This leads to crime resulting from the desire to defend territorial domains, to high rates of inter-class victimisation, and criminalisation in underclass sections of society.

Gendered mechanisms of marginalisation reproduce themselves in a self-perpetuating spiral of crime and violence. This is fed by a continuous urge to perform contextual, situational, unstable, dangerous and destructive displays of domination through the use of force and crime: stealing cars and driving dangerously, displays of heterosexual prowess and other practices which put these young men at extreme risk of being killed, being apprehended, becoming addicted to illegal substances and living a life of crime. This also puts women, children and men in their social and physical surroundings at higher risk than is the case in the non-marginalised sections of the community. One way in which subordinated masculinities can participate in hegemonic masculinities is by creating sub-masculinities. This is a key to an understanding of xenophobic and racist orientations among working-class and underclass youths.

Constructs of the Enemy in Underclass Subcultures

G. Pearson (1976) has examined the category of racist stereotyping propagated by members of the original 'Skinhead' groups in England. The racist construct of 'the Paki' combines contradictory qualities of anti-social behaviour and attitudes: 'the Paki' is lazy and draws the dole, but works day and night to take away jobs from white men; he is impertinent but keeps to himself; he is gay but still obsessed with seducing white women, and so forth (1976: 65). These images foreground the negative characteristics of social behaviour associated with male work, male sexuality and male bodies as the bodies of 'others', and generate consensus-based constructs of dangerous male 'others'. Similar constructs of the male 'enemy' were employed by inmates of correctional institutions in a German study carried out in the late 1970s and early 1980s. When young male inmates voiced their resentment against foreigners ('Kanacken': a term of abuse traditionally directed against southern European migrant workers in Germany) they accused foreigners of being the perpetrators of the following categories of crime and 'maladjusted behaviour':

- property crime, as opposed to breadwinning through hard work;
- violent crime, as a threat to the safety of German society;
- sexual assault, as the 'other' of 'decent heterosexuality';
- lack of hygiene, as the 'other' of cleanliness;
- and arrogance as a failure to adjust to one's 'proper place' in German culture.

The answer to the question 'Why are you against foreigners?' contains a synthesis of negative character traits attributed to migrant workers (Kersten and von Wolffersdorff-Ehlert 1980; Kersten 1994).

G1: What is it they want around here [in Germany]? Fuck our women, that's all they are here for, right?

I1: They want to work, and that's to our benefit (interviewer).

G1: There are enough people around who can do the dirty work.

G2: There are more Canucks around than Germans; Germans don't get work. They [the Germans] would sweep the streets, sure.

I2: For a long time they carried out the work the Germans didn't want to do any more, like construction work, dirty work (interviewer).

G3: Because they *are* dirty swine, aren't they ...

G2: Look at their homes, there's a cloud of garlic above them.

G1: Cut-throats and child molesters, that's what they are, and that's why they are in here [in prison].[8]

Procreation and provision as domains of male domination and control (Gilmore 1991) are focal concerns of hegemonic masculinity. The foreign 'other' is portrayed as a rapist and a pimp. To devalue their masculinity foreigners are also depicted as homosexuals and dirty. Their gayness and their supposedly unkempt appearance put migrants into non-marriageable categories, i.e. they become anti-social masculinities. Constructs of hegemonic masculinity depict men as providers for women and children. Foreigners are depicted as thieves and misers who loiter around city squares and railway stations. Foreign men are regarded as a threat to the well-being of German society. Back home, they would procreate without being troubled to provide for their children and families. A repeated accusation against migrant workers and foreign-born fellow inmates was directed against their supposed impertinence. The non-Germans and their cultural background were considered inferior according to the standards of German culture. Even the correctional institution, not exactly a chosen place by the German inmates either, was regarded as 'too luxurious' for foreign fellow inmates.

Taken together, these constructs portray the foreigner as a member of subordinated masculinities. The image serves as a blueprint for the very antithesis of the domains that produce and reproduce claims to hegemonic masculinity: procreation, protection and provision. As the 'other' of hegemonic masculinity, such constructs of 'evil' men are identical with 'stranger danger' masculinities at the core of the fear of crime, and represent antisocial, uncontrolled, and therefore dangerous masculinities that should be kept at bay—or eliminated altogether.

Messerschmidt has described the strategies that, from an underclass position, render possible the achievement of a 'particular form of hegemonic masculinity' (1993: 109). The situational subordination of weaker objects like other underclass males during territorial wars or street robberies, and of females, children, and sometimes of other males (e.g. in the prison environment) during rape and assault, accounts for the extreme visibility of interpersonal street crime involving marginalised males (ibid.: 113ff). Inmate status narrows the options. An investment in strategies that dehumanise 'enemy' males serves to boost one's own sense of belonging to a local, culturally legitimate, force of protection. As odd as it appears, German women, German workers, and the German culture are 'protected' according to these views by incarcerated violent young prison inmates. The inmates construct a typology of positive masculinities (the caring father, the man who does not rape, the working man as a provider) which includes themselves in a discourse of hegemonic masculinity (see Silverstein 1993 for similar strategies in the prison context) and excludes 'Canucks' as parasitical enemy masculinities.

Constructions of the Enemy in the 'Skinhead' Subculture

In recent interviews with German 'Skinheads' (Farin and Siedel-Pielen 1993; Farin 1996) similar reference is made to ideals of hegemonic masculinity. The new study (Farin 1996) uses material from 405 questionnaires filled out by members of the subculture. The most frequent answers to the question 'What does it mean to be a 'Skinhead'?' appertain to ideals of hegemonic masculinity:

- readiness to fight;
- emphasis on one's own cultural superiority or the superiority of the male working class culture;
- visibility as a force and significance of 'Skinhead style' as a symbol of masculinity;
- collective drunkenness.

These and other less frequent replies of 'national pride'; 'honour'; 'mateship' are equally to be found among street gangs and other visible groupings of young underclass males.

The earlier German 'Skinhead' study (Farin and Siedel-Pielen 1993) contains eight full-length interviews with members of German 'Skinhead' groups. Included are group conversations with 'Skinhead' girls. More than half of those interviewed were female. Despite this female element, frequent reference is made (ten times on each occasion) to combat-readiness and to the actual experience of violent confrontations. In nearly the same dimension, statements reveal antagonistic orientations towards 'enemies' (left wing *autonome*; *nazibräute*, i.e. Eva Braun girls; *dumme fickhennen*, i.e. 'dumb fuckbirds'; gays; Russians; the 'dirty'). To female 'Skinhead' members this specific subcultural style entails the ultimate display of antagonism, and, as they put it, the 'absolute refinement of one's own existence'.

Skin girls act out orientations that devalue particular femininities. There is also a clear reference to 'purity' and to violent confrontation. The public apprehension that springs from 'Skinheads' characteristic style of dress and behaviour creates at the same time an extremely visible form of public masculinity and, among members of the subculture, feelings of being the victims of a conspiracy. They frequently feel that their appearance is intentionally misinterpreted and that they are being discriminated against. This, in turn, provides legitimacy for the type of aggression directed at bystanders or critics.

Notwithstanding their belief that they are victims, female 'Skinheads' love 'toughness', the military and soldiers. Their male counterparts express misogyny, homophobia and a rhetoric of dehumanisation which fits into Gilmore's schematic representation of 'tough' masculinities. The destructive ideas of 'Skinheads' are directed against migrants, people with different skin colour, homosexuals and the homeless. They serve as a blueprint for white male superiority. Black men are distrusted because 'they take away our women'. Asians should not be beaten up 'without a cause'. The young men quoted in the study promote 'clean and effective' ways of getting rid of refugees. This is an obvious reference to Nazi methods of elimination and genocide.

With no job, no educational background, and a criminal record, the marriageability of these young men is at stake. Therefore, they fancy themselves as members of a masculine force of protection (*Deutschlands Rechte Polizei*, i.e. 'Germany's Right Wing Police', a song of the 'Skinhead' band *Störkraft*) against what they see as 'waves of foreigners invading the country'. Because they view themselves as the only ones capable of saving the 'German race', the women and the purity of the *Vaterland*, they will finally achieve the status that good and respected masculinities command. Accordingly, their attacks on housing facilities for refugees (events in Hoyerswerda, Rostock etc.) are perceived as having the support of the local population—skins see themselves as the 'people's right wing resistance'.

'Skinhead' Song Texts

Texts of 'Skinhead' songs are evidence for Loewenstein's observation about contradictions in racist stereotypes (1951, quoted in Gabel 1967). At the extreme edges of the social spectrum sentiments seesaw between hatred of 'others' and self-pity, the construct of the enemy ranges from being the image of parasites to that of powerful opponents. Again, issues of particular hegemonic masculinity like mateship and fighting, and the dualism of US (skins) vs THEM ('normal people'), are at the forefront. The most popular band *Böhse Onkelz* (misspelled *Böse Onkels*, i.e. 'Nasty Uncles') promote a readiness to fight foreigners. Other *onkelz* hooligan songs like the infamous (and never officially released) '*Türken raus!*' ('Turks out') became part of the soccer cult. All of them stress the significance of territory, mateship and drinking ('One for all, all for one'). 'Skinheads' are portrayed as victims ('Lies about you') and as patriots ('Love of Germany, German women and German beer').

Some of the more 'philosophical' texts of the *Onkelz* attempt a sort of amateur sociology, not too different from the quintessence of parts of the most prominent authors dealing with violent youths ('Bielefeld School'). Such texts 'theorise' violence in terms of social disintegration:

> The rule of the street is the law of violence.
> The rule of the street means blood on the ground.
> War in the (soccer) stadium, war in the streets.
> Never-ending violence is the outcome of poverty and unemployment.

Onkelz song material celebrates exclusive feelings of a men's world beyond the everyday constraints of work and family: they could be the hymns of any association of 'real' males in any male dominated society. *Störkraft* is listed among the more important right wing bands and some texts emphasise the victim/unappreciated hero image ('He has no friends'). At the same time, the annihilation of human life is seen as an imperative of male toughness ('He does not care about a human life, he has no moral standards, owns no heart'), and the joys of being violent are underscored ('He loves war, he loves violence. If you are his foe, he'll bump you off': '*Störkraft, Mann für Mann*').

'Skinhead' song texts openly call for the dehumanisation of the non-German population. The reference points of accusations against non-Germans that legitimise exclusion and violence are identical with those employed in the statements of prison inmates referred to earlier. For example, a text (‘*Muselmann, oh Muselmann*’) by the group *Volkszorn* (‘People’s Rage’) alludes to dirt, odour, seduction of German women, criminality and fraud, in its depiction of the anti-social properties of foreign male ‘others’. The self-stylisation of the group points to:

- protection (‘We are going to save Germany in its darkest hour’), and
- fighting a powerful enemy (‘*Rotfront verrecke* [socialist front], to hell with you. You are to die so Germany can live. *Autonome*—vandalise the city, destroy everything. The tables are turned (on the Reds) before our *Vaterland* goes down the gurgler’).

The band *Endsieg* proclaims the eradication of foreign dirt, smell and fraud in the terminology of *Endlösung* (‘Final Solution’). Other texts herald the protection of the honour of German women in order to uphold the purity of the German race. Turkish boyfriends of German girls should be castrated.

> You meet a Turkish man
> with a German wife.
> You know it’s *Rassenschande* [Nazi terminology for inter-racial sexuality]
> ... cut off his dick,
> so he’ll kick the bucket.

RACIST YOUTHS IN POST-REUNIFICATION GERMANY

Xenophobia and racism have a gendered quality. They are to a very great extent the result of the construction of subordinated masculinities as ‘others’. They form the male *gestalt* that legitimises feelings of hate and practices of hate-crimes in terms of ‘protection’. The common denominator of most youths who participate in provocative xenophobic/ antisemitic/ homophobic activities is their desire to fulfil the claims of gender by acting within the parameters of a ‘protection masculinity’. Psychological studies usually hold to the view that the xenophobia and racism that occurs among Neo-Nazis, ‘Skinheads’ etc. operates by projecting hated qualities of the self onto dehumanised objects. This may or may not be true. What it does not do, however, is answer the question as to:

a) why confrontational xenophobic or racist attitudes and practices are gender specific across all times and cultures, and
b) what circumstances turn such attitudes into manifest violence and victimisation.

The 1980s inmates were part of a 'Rocker'/neighbourhood cliques subculture. Their xenophobic attitudes did not lead to violent practices. The identical constructs of the foreigner as 'enemy' in youth subcultures of the 1990s caused outbreaks of violence and left behind victims who were burnt, stabbed, beaten or virtually frightened to death.

After reunification, racist orientations on the part of subordinated youth coincided with changes in the German political and social climate. This has facilitated, if not promoted, xenophobia and racism as a confrontational practice for a number of reasons. Economic problems caused by a delayed recession (there was a boom immediately following reunification), and by the immense financial, social and psychological costs of turning the inefficient East German system into a capitalist market economy, have had an impact upon a vast number of young men. The collapse of the Berlin Wall had the effect of suspending all operative categories of hegemonic masculinity in the former East German state: The Party (SED), the State Security Police (Stasi) and the armed forces all suffered a loss of power and prestige. Only a secondhand version of the new (West German) ideals of masculinity was available for men in the East for which the used car market may serve as a fitting paradigm. West Germans took the initiative, they took the high status jobs in what was left of the East German industry, they took over the universities, the police and the media. They were also said to be more attractive to East German women.

The euphoria which caused fear and apprehension among Germany's European neighbours was short lived for many in the East because it turned out to be a devaluation of many aspects of everyday life: loss of esteem among employees/workers, partners in relationships, party members, and members of old elites, hit East Germans of all ages and of both sexes. The consequences affected young males differently from females. The latter experienced the wholesale demolition of child care services and equal opportunity in the labour market, the former were denied access to hitherto uncontested domains of masculinity. Furthermore, integration paths into the life-worlds of family, school and work were radically changed. As a multi-dimensional cultural crisis, the post-reunification experience created fertile ground for nationalism, Neo-Nazism, and chauvinism in general. Neo-Nazism was imported by Western activists who had long suffered under a marginal political status in the West. They suddenly gained importance and new respect in the East.

The second wave of right wing sentiment moved back from the eastern parts of the country to the west at a time when the costs of reunification and the recession had hit the whole country. Bergmann and Erb (1991: 9ff) called this a 'transfer of violence': West German political organisations of the extreme political right began to fill the political vacuum in the East but soon lost organisational structure and became a subcultural form. Loose groupings, viewing themselves as 'forces protecting Germany', then emerged in the Western part where the proportion of foreigners, particularly of Turkish origin, was much higher.

During this period politicians of the leading parties took comfortable rides on tidal waves of hidden and open resentment against foreigners, *Asylanten* and the politics of the (disorganised) Left. Conservative politicians began to formulate a vocabulary of dehumanisation. The terms *Asylbetrug/Asylmißbrauch* (asylum fraud/ abuse of the constitutional right to apply for asylum status) were officially coined and provided legitimacy for constructs of the foreigner as a criminal outcast.

The post-reunification hangover was accompanied by *Wohlstandschauvinismus*, the chauvinism of the well-to-do in the West. It coincided with wide-spread xenophobia in the formerly secluded East where Vietnamese and African guest workers from other 'socialist' nations had enjoyed more freedom and access to consumer goods than the East German working population in general. The entire society was enveloped by a climate of insecurity, by fear of imminent change, fear of crime and by open aggression and xenophobia as the reverse side of such fears. The established forces of hegemonic masculinity (politicians, police, the criminal justice system) suffered a loss of credibility. They were seen as 'too soft' and lenient on the question of immigration. The political terms *Durchrassung der Gesellschaft* ('racial hotchpotch') and *Ausländer und Asylbetrüger* ('foreigner and asylum fraud') were aimed at demonstrating firmness and determination on the part of the political Right but in fact fostered a climate of dehumanisation which stigmatised those non-Germans with asylum, refugee or resident foreign worker status (e.g. Turks).

Frightening, chasing and killing dehumanised 'others' is men's work. This has been demonstrated in historical studies on war crimes (Dower 1986; Browning 1991). In the aftermath of German reunification a prevailing climate of opinion in the political mainstream, sanctioning the dehumanisation of immigrants, has legitimised subcultural and subordinated masculinities and allowed them to take over as the 'forces of protection' of the fatherland. In these scenarios the devaluation of 'others' can be a mechanism to accomplish gender goals. Hateful attitudes are transformed into brutal action. Brutality as men's work is conformity combined with sadism, euphoria and the collective feeling of masculine superiority.

The norms of masculine mateship require individuals to suppress autonomous feelings of guilt and empathy with the victims. An individual's failure to conform to the norm of loyalty in doing dirty men's work is seen as weakness and lack of manliness among the following masculinities: soldiers on both sides in the Pacific War (Dower 1986); 'ordinary men' of the German Reserve Police Force during the mass murder of unarmed Jewish men, women and children in Poland (Browning 1991); British soccer hooligans during 'excursions' at home and abroad (Buford 1992); underclass youths during the British riots of the 1990s (Campbell 1993); and finally among members of 'Skinhead' and right wing subcultures during the racist attacks in reunified Germany.[9]

REFERENCES

Badinter, Elisabeth (1992) *XY: de'l Identité Masculine*, Paris: Odile Jacob.

Bergmann, Werner and Erb, Rainer (eds) (1994) *Neonazismus und rechte Subkultur*, Berlin: Metropol.

Bjorgo, Tore (Hrsg.) (1995) *Terror from the Extreme Right*, London: Frank Cass.

Browning, Christopher (1991) *Ordinary Men: Reserve police battalion 101 and the Final Solution in Poland*, New York: Pantheon.

Buford, David (1992) *Geil auf Gewalt—Unter Hooligans*, Munich: Carl Hanser.

Cain, Maureen (1990) 'Towards Transgression: New directions in feminist criminology', *International Journal of the Sociology of Law* 18: 1-12.

Cain, Maureen (ed.) (1986) *Growing Up Good: Policing the behaviour of girls in Europe*, London: Sage.

Campbell, Beatrix (1993) *Goliath: Britain's dangerous places*, London: Methuen.

Carrigan, Tim, Connell, Bob, and Lee, John (1985) 'Toward a New Sociology of Masculinity', *Theory and Society* 14: 551 - 603.

Connell, Robert W. (1987) *Gender and Power*, Sydney: Allen and Unwin.

Connell, Robert W. (1994) 'The Making and Remaking of Masculinities in Contemporary Societies', Vortrag, 'Reproduktion und Wandel von Männlichkeit' Ludwig-Maximilians-Universität, 27-28 September. Munich.

Connell, Robert W. (1995) *Masculinities*, Cambridge: Polity Press.

Dower, John (1986) *War Without Mercy: Race and Power in the Pacific War*, New York: Pantheon.

Erb, Rainer (1994) 'Antisemitismus in der rechten Jugendszene', in W. Bergmann and R. Erb (eds), *Neonazismus und rechte Subkultur*, Berlin: Metropol, 31-76.

Farin, Klaus (eds) (1996) *Skinhead—A Way of Life: Eine Jugendbewegung stellt sich selbst dar, Hamburg: Europäische*, Verlagsanstalt/Syndikat.

Farin, Klaus and Siedel-Pielen, Eberhard (1993) *Skinheads*, Munich: Beck.

Gabel, Joseph (1967) *Ideologie und Schizophrenie*, Frankfurt: Suhrkamp.

Gilmore, David (1990) *Manhood in the Making: Cultural concepts of masculinity*, London: Yale University Press.

Heitmeyer, Wilhelm (1991) 'Desintegration und Gewalt', *DVJJ-Journal* 3 (1/2): 76-84.

Karazman-Morawetz, Inge and Steinert, Heinz (1993) *Jugend und Gewalt*, Wien: Forschungsbericht des Instituts für Rechts und Kriminalsoziologie.

Katz, Jack (1988) *Seductions of crime: Moral and sensual attractions in doing evil*, New York: Basic Books.

Kersten, Joachim (1993a) 'Street Youths, *Bosozoku*, and *Yakuza*: Subculture Formation and Societal Reactions in Japan', *Crime and Delinquency* 39 (3): 277-95.

Kersten, Joachim and Steinert, Heinz (eds) (1996) *Jahrbuch für Rechts- und Kriminalsoziologie, '96*, Baden Baden: Nomos.

Kersten, Joachim (1996) 'Culture, masculinities, and violence against women', *British Journal of Criminology* 36 (3) (in press).

Kersten, Joachim (1994b) 'Feindbildkonstruktionen und Gewalthandlungen bei Gruppierungen junger Männer', in W. Bergmann and R. Erb (eds), *Neonazismus und rechte Subkultur*, Berlin: Metropol, 125-42.

Kersten, Joachim (1993b) 'Crime and Masculinities in Australia, Germany, and Japan', *International Sociology* 4: 461-78.

Klein, Malcolm (1996) 'Gangs in the U.S. and in Europe', European Journal on Criminal Policy and Research', (in press).

Landesamt für Verfassungsschutz Baden-Württemberg (1991) *Skinheads*, Stuttgart.

Lau, Thomas and Soeffner, Hans-Georg (1993) 'Fremdenfeindlichkeit und Rechtsradikalismus', in W. Bergmann and R. Erb (eds), *Neonazismus und rechte Subkultur*, Berlin: Metropol, 15-30.

Messerschmidt, James W. (1993) *Masculinities and Crime—Critique and reconceptualisation of theory*, Lanham, Maryland: Rowman and Littlefield.

Messerschmidt, James W. (1996) 'Von der Analyse der Männerherrschaft zur Forschung über Geschlechterverhältnisse', in J. Kersten and H. Steinert (eds), *Starke Männer—Jahrbuch für Rechts- und Kriminalsoziologie*, Baden Baden (im Druck): Nomos.

Messerschmidt, James W. (1994) 'Schooling, masculinities, and youth crime by white boys', in T. Newburn and E. Stanko (eds), *Just boys doing business? Men, masculinities and crime*, London: Routledge and Kegan Paul, 81-99.

Newburn, Tim and Stanko, Elizabeth (eds) (1994) *Just boys doing business? Men, masculinities and crime*, London: Routledge and Kegan Paul.

Newburn, Tim and Stanko, Elizabeth A. (1994) 'When men are victims: the failure of victimology', in T. Newburn and E. Stanko (eds), *Just boys doing business? Men, masculinities and crime*, London: Routledge and Kegan Paul, 153-65.

Pearson, Geoff (1976) '"Paki-Bashing" in a North East Lancashire Cotton Town: A case study and its history' in G. Mungham and G. Pearson (eds), *Working Class Youth Culture*, London: Routledge and Kegan Paul.

Rodriguez, Luis J. (1994) *Always running*, New York: Simon and Schuster.

Silverstein, Martin (1993) 'Parole—"Good Guys" and "Bad Guys" Struggle for Freedom', paper presented to American Society of Criminology Annual Meeting, Pheonix, 27 October.

Stanko, Elizabeth A. (1994) 'Challenging the problem of men's individual violence', in T. Newburn and E. Stanko (eds), *Just boys doing business? Men, masculinities and crime*, London: Routledge and Kegan Paul, 32-45.

Trotha von, Trutz (1995) Review of W. Heitmeyer et al. Gewalt, Schattenseiten der Individualisierung bei Jugendlichen aus unterschiedlichen Milieus, *Kölner Zeitschrift für Soziologie und Sozialpsychologie* 4: 781-84.

Walklate, Sandra (1995) *Gender and crime: An introduction*, Hemel Hempstead: Prentice Hall.

Willems, Helmut (1994) 'Kollektive Gewalt gegen Fremde: historische Episode oder Genese einer sozialen Bewegung von rechts?', in W. Bergmann and R. Erb (eds), *Neonazismus und rechte Subkultur*, Berlin: Metropol, 209-26.

NOTES

1. After 1945 *Edelweißpiraten* sought 'co-operation' with the occupying forces but were turned down. Allied authorities did not see them as youthful resistance against the Nazi regime (as some youth sociologists of the 70s and 80s tended to do, ignoring the historical facts) but rather as *Werewolf* organisations, or as dangerous young criminals and racist thugs. *Edelweißpiraten* have carried out attacks against displaced persons of Polish origin. Some members were caught and sentenced to death, particularly for violent crimes.

2. For example the intellectual *Exi* (from existentialism) youths who were into Sartre, Hemingway, Cool Jazz, black coffee and Turkish smokes in city pubs.

3. Likewise many Skinheads in present Germany admire a (fictitious) white, male British working class as their culture of reference.

4. *Gammelig* or *vergammelt* is German 'slang' for old, greasy and rotten, a connotation of rebellious youth style that was later adopted by the original 'Punk' subculture.

5. Skinhead 'philosophy' emphasises the exact anathema of the *Gammler* style.

6. Academics who later joined the RAF terrorist groups like Meinhoff, Mahler, Ensslin were elite intellectuals. They were never really student leaders, but rather do-gooders and 'violent pacifists'. Some had the charisma of accountants, not of subcultural heroes of any sort. Whatever became of the

'revolutionaries' of 1968 (ministers of justice, managers, professors of sociology at universities, designers, or old hippies) their movement was the most pervasive and most fundamental challenge to postwar German culture and its political system.

7. The migrant kids' command of spoken, sometimes even written German may be much better than that of marginalised German children of equal age and equally poor school background.

8. G1, G2 and G3 were neighbourhood clique members in a juvenile institution. I1 and I2 were interviewers.

9. Parts of this paper were presented at the Goethe Institute Chicago symposium 'Youth Subcultures in Complex Societies' (October 1995) while other sections are a revised version of a paper presented to panel A0601: 'Class, Race, Masculinities and Crime', American Society of Criminology Annual Meeting: Challenges of Crime and Social Control, Miami 9-12 November, 1994. Thanks to Tim Mehigan (University of Melbourne), Rainer Erb (University of Potsdam) and Klaus Farin (Berlin) for comments and criticism.

4 Criminal Heirs—Organised Crime and Russia's Youth

Paddy Rawlinson

INTRODUCTION

In his introduction to the first comprehensive sociological study of crime and its effects on Russian society, published in 1993, the then Vice President Alexander Rutskoi commented: 'The present sweep of crime already poses a threat to the existence of the state, its institutions, and more so, to the people (*narod*) itself' (RAU Corporation 1993: 13). Implicit in his statement was the danger of organised crime, one of the most feared and influential forms of criminal activity in contemporary Russia. Recent statistics support the concern that within the economic life of the country the presence of the Russian 'mafia', as it is most commonly known,[1] is systemic (40% of all companies and 66% of all commerce, according to unofficial MVD figures for the first two thirds of 1995, have involvement with organised crime).[2] Fears that it has also infiltrated politics have been borne out by the increase in corruption amongst bureaucrats. But for many criminologists it is the effect of organised crime on society as a whole, and on its most vulnerable and impressionable members—the youth, in particular—that is proving the greatest area of concern.

This essay examines the influence of organised crime on the younger generation in the light of changing patterns within Russia's social and economic life over the past decade. It looks at the complex and ethical dilemmas thrown up by legal ambiguities in business, changing ideological values, and the onslaught of consumerism at a time when Russia's youth face the prospect of unemployment, poverty, and deep social crisis as the country limps towards a controversial and unconventional democratic political system and market economy heavily influenced by criminal syndicates.

Reconstruction to Deconstruction

Gorbachev's economic reforms, known as *perestroika* (reconstruction) were designed to address and rectify some of the major problems in a seriously ailing administer-command economy which, by 1981, some Western observers estimated to be operating in reverse (Hanson 1992: 12). Shortages of consumer goods were a constant feature of Soviet life forcing the frustrated population to seek other means of supply. Not surprisingly a burgeoning shadow economy and black market filled the space vacated by its legitimate counterpart. As Moscow academic Yuri Kozlov admitted: 'We were accustomed to the shadow economy and it was barely possible to live a normal life without black market goods and services' (Dolgova and Dyakov 1989: 144). It was this structure that acted as 'the breeding ground for organised crime'.

In a series of laws designed to encourage business initiatives and economic self-accountability—the Law on Individual Labour Activity (1987) and the Law on Cooperatives (1988)—Gorbachev inadvertently provided the ideal framework for expansion of organised criminal activity by creating opportunities for laundering vast amounts of capital accrued through illegal economic activity. It was this sector of society, already *au fait* with the rudimentary mechanisms of the market, albeit its illegal form, that would initially appeal to foreign business and thereby create the present 'grey area' of commercial activity which has stymied healthy economic growth. Further, in the new business conditions created by *perestroika*, which allowed for unrestricted profits and self-made rouble millionaires there appeared another fast-growing industry—that of extortion, or protection rackets.

A Brief History of Crime

The emergence of organised crime was not, as many opponents of *perestroika* believed, a consequence of Gorbachev's reforms, though there is little doubt that these reforms exacerbated an already extant problem. Dixelius and Konstantinov (1995) and Gurov (1995) trace organised criminal activity in Russia as far back as the nineteenth and early twentieth centuries when it tended to operate *outside* the legitimate framework. Bound by codes of behaviour and 'thieves' honour', collusion with the authorities was seen as the height of treachery and punishable by death

(Dixelius and Konstantinov 1995: 68). In the early twentieth century criminals who operated according to these codes were known as *vory v zakone*, literally thieves-in-law. But the criminal underworld underwent a number of metamorphoses determined, in the main, by the political and economic changes within the country. Organised crime in its present syndicate form emerged in the late 1960s and 70s as a response to economic stagnation *(zastoi)* and widespread political corruption under Brezhnev. Many of the 'old' criminals felt betrayed by the new *vory* who were prepared to operate within the legitimate structures:

> Now it seems in this case a 'thief-in-law' is the boss of a cooperative, a businessman, acting legally. For us to be 'in-law' meant working in the thieves' trade, and only in that (Gurov 1991: 8).

The collusion between entrepreneurial criminals or *tsekhoviki*[3] and members of the political *nomenklatura* provided the foundations for indigenous organised crime as it materialised during *perestroika*. Despite the anti-corruption campaigns led by Yuri Andropov (General Secretary of the CPSU 1982-84) and Gorbachev, little real progress was made in rooting out a problem that, by the mid 1980s, had become an integral part of the shadow economy, the foundation upon which the precarious legitimate economy then rested.

Of all the 'revelations' which found their way on to the pages of the Soviet press by investigative journalists, enthusiastically exploiting their new found freedoms, it was the exposure of widespread organised crime within a socialist society that threatened to wreck the faith of even the most hardened believers in communism. Organised crime had epitomised the inherently corrupting nature of bourgeois governments in whose interest it was to preserve such forms of criminal activity (Kuznetsova 1968: 215). Hence, its very presence in the Soviet Union undermined the ideological base upon which Marxist-Leninism claimed its moral superiority over other systems. Even criminologists had to admit that the irrefutable existence of organised crime in the USSR was a difficult concept to hold: 'When it finally did come out, it caught us psychologically unawares, fumbling even for words to describe it', (Khokhryakov 1989).

Media coverage of this new social threat helped to turn *glasnost* into *perestroika*'s nemesis. In the minds of the people organised crime and business had, as a result of Marxist-Leninist doctrine, become inextricably linked. In his attempt to build genuine socialism through economic reform Gorbachev ironically corroborated this linkage. His appeal to economic self-initiative, as a means of alleviating the burden of government subsidy and creating a correlation between labour, productivity, and profit (in contrast to the well-known maxim: 'They pretend to pay us, and we pretend to work') attracted those who had developed the expertise and accumulated the capital and connections needed to set up these individual initiatives—that is, black marketeers and organised crime. Subsequently Yeltsin's push towards rapid marketisation after the 1991 August coup further legitimised the hitherto illegal economic structures. Confused signals and mixed messages were transmitted to a society already in the throes of identity loss: the economic, political, and social health of Russia depends on money and markets. But money and markets equalled 'mafia'. What, therefore, was the younger generation to make of all this?

THE 'LOST' GENERATION

The call for openness and economic change fell on particularly fertile soil in the younger generation. For the majority of Soviet youth 'reconstruction' was a fait accompli. Three generations removed from the Revolution, few believed in a future for Soviet socialism. Cynicism lay where idealism had spurred-on their parents and grandparents. That their children refused to espouse even the fundamentals of socialism encouraged the older generations to regard the newly emerging youth movements as harbingers of doom, an ineluctable step towards complete social decay. As Hilary Pilkington concludes:

> In the Soviet Union, the crisis of youth symbolised the end of the bright future, it presaged the much grander civil war which so many expected to engulf the whole country and the return to a pre-modern and pre-moral society under the rule of local war-lords (Pilkington 1994: 160).

From 1986 unofficial youth organisations, known as *neformaly,* broke out all over the country in a multitude of social guises, a vociferous defiance of the cultural strait-jacket imposed by communism. Many of these groups had been fermenting during the pre-Gorbachev era. Technology, the gradual opening up of relations with the West under Brezhnev and, in particular, the development of foreign student language programs, had imported a limited but puissant experience of Western youth culture. Jeans and rock music replaced medals and anthems as symbols of prestige and 'belonging'. Gorbachev's appeal during the January 1987 Plenum of the Central Committee for a renewal of the 'spiritual /intellectual mood of Soviet society' (Klepach 1988) for the most part fell on deaf ears among the youth, drowned out by the strains of Led Zeppelin and the numerous Soviet bands which began to preach a new creed of desolation, destruction, and decadence.

Youth and the Party

Lenin's creation of the Komsomol, the official youth wing of the Communist Party, in 1918, defined the ideal role of Soviet youth for the next six or seven decades. But since the mid eighties, the Komsomol—which had earlier claimed 'We are the Party of the future, and the future belongs to youth' (Fisher 1959: 1)—had seen a consistent drop in its membership, down by four million in one year alone (Solnick 1990: 9). No longer a representative body of the majority it attempted to adapt its aims to accommodate the myriad of unofficial groups by funding clubs and centres for those willing to take on official sponsorship. But despite the small successes of integration there remained a section of the *neformaly* which displayed 'anti-social' or deviant tendencies. There was no question of integration with such groups and, as had been the case in the early days of the Soviet Union, the Komsomol was encouraged to engage in 'an ideological struggle' and win over the lost souls. The struggle was a decisive failure.

Youth Anti-Social Groups

> Do you know what's happening right before our eyes? A cult of violence is becoming the norm for teenagers (Shchekochikin 1987).

For hippies, punks, *rokery* (bikers) and *metallisty* (heavy metal fans) emulation of their Western counterparts was in itself rebellion. Their respective accoutrement, music, and argot symbolised new allegiances and ideals, a rejection of the status quo externalised. But as some turned West, others rejected alien cultures seeking instead to establish their own brand of patriotism and implement their own form of justice. Neo-fascism had found a place in Russia's *neformaly*.

The *Lyubery* became the byword for neo-fascist youth in the 1980s. Named after the Moscow micro-region Lyubertsy,[4] their place of origin, the 'Rambo-style youth cult' (Riordan 1989: 124) were renowned for a violent distaste of imported Western trends. Members of those peer groups which did not fit into the *Lyubery* perception of 'normality', including hippies and punks, were vulnerable to brutal and thuggish victimisation. The *Lyubery* possessed a black and white interpretation of the world, a reiteration of the values and violence that had dominated Soviet society throughout Stalinism and beyond. Their obsession with physical fitness and a predilection towards the martial arts made them formidable adversaries. But the attitude of the authorities to *Lyubery* 'social cleansing' was awkwardly ambivalent in much the same way that in post-Soviet Russia Zhirinovsky's ultra-nationalist ravings are tolerated by some so-called 'liberals' with a hint even of tacit approval. Suspicion and dislike of Westernisation, the resurgence of national pride in the midst of a barrage of media criticism against communism meant that the *Lyubery* found themselves protected by sympathisers in high places, to the point that the media had to curb their 'sensationalist' reporting of the group, and in one case even deny its existence (Riordan 1989: 129).

The *Afghantsy*, returnees from the war in Afghanistan, formed another of the major antisocial groups of the late 1980s. More amorphous in their structure and aims than the *Lyubery*, they nevertheless assumed a vigilante role, instigating order and reprisals where appropriate in an attempt to root out those who were exploiting the country they fought for. Targets included corrupt officials and speculators. The legitimacy of their cause, if not their tactics, meant that the militia often turned a blind eye to their actions, the nature of which many would interpret as a service to society.

Both groups initially operated from ideological stances. However as ideological values became superseded by materialism and the fight for survival rested more and more on wealth accumulation, able-bodied vigilantes turned to a more lucrative form of employment. In the growth industry of racketeering and other forms of organised crime, muscle became a highly prized commodity. For the *Afghantsy* their gun skills were to be highly marketable in a society that was to experience an unprecedented explosion of violence and murder in the war for economic supremacy that accompanied a commitment to full marketisation after the collapse of communism.

'Just give me money—that's what I want.'

> All is not well in the kingdom of children. Indeed, the youth economy has a speculative and shady tendency (Shchekochikin 1988: 13-14).

For decades a shadow economy had operated alongside the centrally planned system simultaneously sustaining it and exacerbating its failures. Speculation or profiteering had become as familiar a concept to the ordinary consumer as the Five Year Plan, and certainly offered more desirable commodities and services. The material aspirations of many Soviet youth, and the Western goods that symbolised rebellion and identity, could only be acquired through the black market. To maintain the desired lifestyle: 'We earn money "trafficking," and with sex—in one night you can earn 100 to 150 rubles' (Shchekochikin 1988: 9). Not surprisingly the conclusions of a survey conducted in 1987 amongst teenagers of 16 and 17 showed a high moral toleration for use of the illegal sector. Only 50% of the respondents condemned the notion of 'unearned income' that is, not derived from employment in state enterprises (Shchekochikin 1988). When asked: 'who, in your opinion, has a lot of money?' 'speculator' was mentioned 39 times, 'professor' only four.

In the midst of changing economic trends this mentality was obviously a cause for concern. Press coverage of the 'new rich'—the gangster-businessman hybrid—provided a new model of success for a section of society already comfortable with market values, albeit illegitimately realised. The ambiguities of legality and mixed messages on the question of economic and social morality, hotly debated in adult circles, left Soviet youth without the necessary consensus on 'right' and 'wrong' ambitions: comrade or criminal, *'biznessmeny'* or engineer? In a system which had previously held firmly onto the reins of moral pedagogy, youth was now left to decide its own direction in a society which had lost both identity and direction. The criminal path to material wealth became an attractive and, for a growing minority, the only viable alternative.

ORGANISED CRIME'S NEW RECRUITS

Until the draconian social changes of the 1980s organised criminal activity had been confined for the most part to the over-eighteens. Prisons, those 'universities of crime, maintained by the state' (Gurov 1995: 74), provided important contacts which could guarantee some form of security on the 'outside'. This was an important consideration for many offenders in a system which applied stringent rules of social re-integration hence frequently encouraging recidivism.[5] In return for guarantees of financial or legal security, favours would be carried out. Prison was the most fertile ground for recruitment of younger members to organised criminal groups.

Other doors to organised crime were provided by family contacts. Matrosyonok, the son of one of Ukraine's top bosses, was a typical example of this form of recruitment. At sixteen he was the leader of a Dnepropetrovsk gang (the youngest of the group) which became involved in 'mini-racketeering', or low level extortion (Vitaliev 1990: 117). It is interesting to note how 'criminal inheritance' is becoming unpopular with the new style gangster. Anton, a St Petersburg boss, explained how he wants his own children to find 'honest work' ('Rysk Maffiya' 1993) and regards his present career as an unavoidable rung on what Daniel Bell describes as the 'queer ladder of social mobility' (Bell 1963).

By 1990 organised crime had become a well-publicised and growing problem in the USSR encouraged by the breakdown of the old order and increasing evidence of the law enforcement agencies' inability to deal with the spread of crime. Criminologists were able to map those areas of Moscow controlled by specific organised crime gangs, many of whom comprised members in their late teens and early twenties (*Dispatches* 1990). The main groups operating in the capital were the *Dolgoprudny*, *Lyubertsy* (including former members of the *Lyubery*), *Solntsevo*, *Chechentsy,* and *Balashika*. Each worked their own turf and dealt more or less with specific areas of commerce, although there was some overlap. Yuzhny Port, the main (illegal) market for car spare parts was run by members of the Kopteva gang, a branch of the *Dolgoprudny* group.[6] The Chechen gang dealt in illegal narcotics and arms. Of the five groups, the *Balashika* was reputed to be the most violent (Romov 1990) and often defied the agreed boundaries of activity by carrying out raids in the centre of the city.

Heroes were created and martyrs buried. The *Solnstevo* gang, one of the strongest and most long-standing groups (recently the target of an unsuccessful police round-up known as 'Operation Sunset') erected an engraved headstone on the spot where Vladimir Solomatin, a popular boss, had been killed in a car accident in 1989. The authorities left the headstone untouched and it became a place of pilgrimage for young people from the Solntsevo region (*Dispatches* 1990). The 'mafia' alternative was becoming a commercially and morally attractive career move for increasing numbers of disillusioned youth.

New Times, New Crimes

> Things certainly haven't got any better for young people in the sense of having things to do, people have gotten involved with crime. Crime

has grown more than anything else around here. Speculation. That's what young people are getting involved with. Like my friends (Adelman 1994: 158).

The predicted fall in number of organised criminal groups during the early 1990s did not take place (Arshavskii and Vilks 1991: 91). The move to a market economy after the 1991 coup did little to improve the situation. Indeed Yeltsin's policy of rapid privatisation, like Gorbachev's *perestroika*, played into the hands of organised crime. A failure to understand the unique political and economic culture of Russia led many foreign investors and economic advisors to apply the same standards and modes of business behaviour in Russia as practised in liberal market societies. For example, the voucher scheme employed to redistribute state property gave dubious enterprises the opportunity to buy up shares from the public thereby transferring ownership from a corrupt state to an even more corrupt economic elite.

There has also been an increase in opportunities for legitimate employment. Many foreign firms have taken on countless Russians, paying them comparatively good wages, thus encouraging spending in a widening market of imported and high quality goods. Those who can afford to travel since visa restrictions were lifted, often return laden with merchandise purchased abroad. For the first time since the Revolution the disproportionate distribution of wealth is openly exhibited. Not surprisingly the politics of envy has affected those many members of society, in particular young people, who cannot aspire to the legitimate acquisition of a higher standard of living. As Yakhov Stakhov from the Chief Administration for Safeguarding Public Order (CASPO) stated:

> The most common reason why juveniles commit crimes is the high cost of the simplest goods and the impossibility of earning money for them legally ... Enterprises are reluctant to hire youngsters, even for the most menial jobs (Vetrov 1995: 5).

Robbery by juveniles between the ages of fourteen and seventeen accounted for 26.6% of that crime category in Moscow in 1991 (Alekseyeva and Patrignani 1994: 75).[7] Despite conflicting statistics—the Ministry of the Interior (MVD) claims a slight decrease in juvenile crime, whereas St Petersburg police indicate a small increase (from 4630 in 1994 to 4846 in 1995)[8]—there is sufficient evidence to show that the age of offending is falling. The anomic state of Russian society promises to drive more *nesovershennoletnye* (juveniles) into crime, and especially organised crime.

Social Fallout

The drop in living standards for the majority of Russian citizens as a result of the 'shock' tactics which introduced, among other 'reforms', the liberalisation of prices thereby pricing many commodities out of the reach of the low earner, has resulted in a sharp rise in alcoholism and drug addiction. To add to their distress many adults with families are finding themselves out of work and unemployable in the new competitive climate. Their children, some no more than toddlers accompanying other siblings, have become victims of abuse and are driven out of the home onto the streets. It has been estimated that there are 60,000 child vagrants in Russia (Vetrov 1995). Although little or no research has been done into the problem of child vagrancy and its recent growth, the sight of groups of young children begging on the metro and at main railway stations, formerly the preserve of Caucasian and Central Asian gypsies, is no longer uncommon.[9] Budgetary restrictions mean that local authorities are hard pressed to fund shelters for such groups. Funding that is provided is mostly charity based.

The problem of child vagrants in the large cities such as Moscow and St Petersburg has become more acute with the influx of refugees from regions of national conflict, particularly the southern regions. It has been estimated that half of the refugees in St Petersburg are children under the age of sixteen (Rafailov 1994: 173). By their mere existence such groups are highly vulnerable to the influence of organised crime.

> Every district has its mafia structure which uses the vagrants ... Each street child is taken in hand by a small criminal group—in essence a school for bandits, providing the next generation of organised criminals (Fayn 1994: 196).

Youth as drug consumers are also providing a widening market for organised criminal activity. Albin Saviliev from the International Association Against Drug Trafficking and Consumption warned that although his data shows little activity by organised crime in this area at present, it does provide cause for concern in the near future.[10] An official survey showed that the majority of teenagers who had taken drugs started between the ages of thirteen and sixteen (RAU 1993: 49). Registered drug users in St Petersburg in July 1993 stood at 2348 but according to Professor Borodkin, the city's leading specialist in illegal drug use, the actual figure is closer to 100-150,000 (Gilinsky, Podkolzin, and Kochetkov 1994: 220-21).

Until recently Russian organised crime's role in the narcotics trade consisted mainly of providing transit points through ports and across borders, usually moving drugs such as opium, coming from the Central Asian states and the occasional consignment of cocaine shipped from Columbia through St Petersburg and into Eastern and Central Europe. But the rise in narcotic and toxin abuse suggests that the market could soon be profitable enough to tempt criminal syndicates into direct sales.

A growing cause for concern is the proliferation of designer drugs. The demise of the military industrial sector after the end of the Cold War left many chemists facing redundancy and with little hope of a career relocation. Organised crime groups have offered alternative and comparatively well paid employment in underground laboratories in which a variety of synthetic drugs have been manufactured and, in some cases exported beyond the borders into Eastern and Central Europe.[11] In 1993 and 1994 the militia uncovered underground laboratories attached to universities in Moscow and St Petersburg (Dixelius and Konstantinov 1995: 246). The number of deaths from impure batches is hard to estimate owing to the nature of the clientele, many of whom are young vagrant users.[12]

Female prostitution is also on the increase and attracting an ever younger workforce. There is no shortage of willing teenagers attracted by the high earnings ($150 per foreign client as opposed to $80 which is the average monthly wage) and the ultimate enticement of finding a foreign husband. Prostitutes operated by Russian criminal gangs have been located as far away as the Netherlands and are a common feature of hotel life in Eastern Europe and Russia itself. The intense competition means that girls will work without using condoms thereby increasing the chances of contracting the HIV virus and other sexually transmitted diseases. Lena, a 23 year old prostitute admitted that she could not care less whether or not her clients demanded safe sex as her weekly earnings had to reach a certain limit or else she would be beaten by her pimp. Almost on cue her armed escort began his rounds amongst the girls in the bar.[13]

More directly, organised crime offers rapid career moves for its more successful members. It is not unusual to see millionaire *biznessmeny* in their early to mid twenties dressed in designer clothes and driving the ubiquitous American and Japanese four-wheel drives. Most youngsters are recruited through the popular sports clubs finding employment as young 'bulls' (*bychki, boitsy*) to the established gangs. The trainer in a Moscow boxing club estimated that an average of 50% of his lads ended up in criminal groups.[14]

Even though more young people are moving into 'mafia' linked crimes such as speculation and prostitution, it is almost impossible for them to operate as autonomous gangs in the main cities as they are immediately co-opted into more 'adult' organised criminal groups (at the bottom rung).[15] The former head of a regional police district gratefully commented that from a law enforcement perspective the territorial dominance of adult organised crime had helped to keep down the numbers of youth gangs where more obvious damage from hooliganism, drunkenness, etc. kept the militia busier than the less blatant crimes of money-laundering and extortion

LAW AND DISORDER

Despite its prominence in contemporary political debate—crime ranks as the country's second most pressing problem (Halligan and Mozdoukhov 1995: 30)—the government's response has been sluggish and generally ineffective. Clear up rates of organised criminal activity by the official agencies are dismally low, not surprisingly as technology and general resourcing is painfully inadequate. Obstruction of cases which eventually find their way to the courtroom, usually achieved by buying off or threatening judges and the prosecution, together with a lack of political will to tackle the problem vigorously, have added to the cynical attitude held by the public towards law enforcement. There is a worrying build-up of frustration amongst MVD employees, whose much maligned image is created mainly by the barrage of accusations about the levels of corruption amongst its members ('The first thing I'd do is sack 80% of the militia. The ones who aren't corrupt are useless'[16]), and threatens to push them into unorthodox means of law enforcement. Comparing the problem to that of Latin America Shchekochikhin explained:

> When just nine people per year are tried for gangsterism in a gangster society, the youngsters start talking of death squads ('Rysk Maffiya': 1993).

The legislative response to organised crime remains entrenched in the old system, defined in the Criminal Code (Article 77) of the RSFSR as Banditism: 'An organisation of armed gangs with the aim of attacking state or public enterprises and institutions, organisations or individual persons, and also the participation in such gangs and the carrying out of attacks' (Ugolovni Kodeks RSFSR 1987). The new Criminal Code to be implemented in 1996 aims to redress the deficiencies of definition but it seems unlikely that revised codification will make much difference as long as the criminal justice system continues to operate inefficiently and is susceptible to corruption at all levels. Further problems have been created by the issuing of a Presidential decree on Banditism which contradicts the ruling of the Constitution (Article 22) on the period of detention. The Constitution states that a person may not be detained 'for a period of more than 48 hours' before a judicial decision. The decree, however, allows for a suspect to be held in police custody and incommunicado for up to 30 days (*Rossiiskaia Gazeta* 1994).

Anomalies such as these in the Russian criminal justice system do little to create confidence in the country's path towards a legal state *(pravovoye gosurdarstvo)*. The nineteenth century defence lawyer Maklakov's criticism that 'the law is not honoured in Russia' remains as pertinent today as under the autocracy of the Tsar (Kucherov 1953: 237) and offers small incentive to a generation, encouraged to follow the path of liberal democracy, to believe in and adhere to an arbitrarily run criminal justice system. Who will protect their interests, economic or otherwise?

If the legal system fails to protect the innocent are they justified in seeking alternative avenues of redress? Protection rackets and security companies have become thriving industries in the state of lawlessness. Few businesses can operate without paying for cover (*krysha*). Organised crime has become the new arm of order, inextricably linked in the eyes of tomorrow's entrepreneurs with competitive business and the markets. It provides employment for many Russian youths in the capacity of bodyguards; and guarantees, within its own framework, the smooth running of business. This ability to function as surrogate law enforcement poses many ethical dangers for the future of Russian society which even now appears to be turning back to the preferred traditional system of authoritarianism. Whatever happens, over the next few years the majority of young people will, understandably, want to place themselves on the strongest side. The battle between the authorities and organised crime is in the eyes of Russian youth already decided. The fear that many will opt for the winning side is all too realistic.

CRISIS IN CRIMINOLOGY

The response by academics to the changing patterns of criminal activity and juvenile delinquency was tardy and confused. In 1989 a more enlightened group of criminologists, led by Azalea Dolgova, held the first round-table discussion on indigenous organised crime which gave a detailed analysis of the social and judicial problems created by organised crime as well as an honest appraisal of the inadequacies of contemporary criminology and law enforcement to deal with the problem. It concluded that the failure of the Soviet administer-command system, together with corruption at high levels, contributed significantly to creating those conditions conducive to the spread of organised crime—in particular the existence of a highly influential and extensive shadow economy.

Dolgova's definition of organised crime left little doubt as to its source and effect:

> Organised crime is a product of society and as such has its own specific characteristics and a strong reciprocal influence on public life (Dolgova and Dyakov 1989: 9).

Her thesis placed culpability for the emergence of organised crime in the USSR firmly on the shoulders of the system itself, breaking with the orthodox tradition both of the Soviet Union and the US that saw such a phenomenon as an 'alien conspiracy', borne out of 'external' (ethnic) rather than internal factors.

Juvenile crime specialists were also faced with the acknowledgment of uncomfortable home-truths which involved breaking away from the ideological constraints upon which a whole system of criminological thinking had been based. Soviet Marxist criminology regarded the causes of juvenile offending as an institutional rather than societal problem. Culpability was laid mainly with the offender's family, but also with the school and local Komsomol or Pioneer branch, all of which were deemed responsible for the moral education of their charges. It was simply the task of the state to 'regulate care, direct towards a specific end and offer whatever kind of help the parents needed to implement it' (Makhov 1970: 12). Most studies on delinquency pointed to a high incidence of offending with children from one parent families (Ribalskaia 1971: 11-14) or allowed for the fact that the adolescent was 'more morally pliable and susceptible to bad influences than a morally upright adult' (Connor 1972: 95), the assumption being that Soviet Marxism automatically produced 'morally upright' adults.

Studies of drug abuse in the mid 1980s began to contradict the Marxist paradigm of dysfunctional families—that is, those who in their behaviour rejected Soviet socialist ideological values. Gambiani's research into drug addiction found that one third of his respondents were under 25 and that although over 30% of his respondents' father were deceased, 23.6% of the remaining were members or candidates for membership of the Communist Party. Almost a quarter of the parents had a complete higher education (21% of mother and 29.1% of fathers) (Gambiani 1988). The failure to address problems of drug addiction amongst young people was vehemently attacked by criminologist Karpets as the following exchange during a round table on youth reveals:

> *Karpets*: Frankly speaking I am surprised that many ideological workers are only now suddenly aware of negative phenomena among youth, as if they arose only yesterday. This is the case, for example, with drug addiction ...
> *Reply*: But everything was alright in our country.
> *Karpets*: There was nothing 'all right' about drug addiction and there were some alarming statistics. We at that time were exploiting a theory that denied the social roots of crime under socialism (Karpets 1988: 32).

Recriminations were levelled against processes of denial. Youth was, after all, a reflection of the adult world following 'extremely attentively all the flaws in our ideological, political and educational work, and [who] consciously or unconsciously reproduce everything that is typical of adults' (Klepach 1988: 34). It was generally accepted that the continued denial of such problems could only serve to make them worse. But what was to be done? At the very time Soviet criminology accepted responsibility for its neglect of the growing problems of organised crime, juvenile offending, and an increasing relationship between the two, money from the state budget for research, provisions for centres to deal with 'victims' of these criminal allegiances,[17] and funding for educational programs as a prophylactic measure, began to dry up as the market increasingly dominated allocation of resources. The initial influx of Western aid to social programs has been cut back as reports of gross mismanagement of funds and the changing political climate in Russia discourage outside agencies from any long term financial commitment.

From a Western perspective how can we explain this increase in juvenile crime and the attraction for young people of organised crime? Merton's typology of anomie which includes an 'innovative' response to the strain between cultural demands and their legitimate achievement, in other words, the adoption of illegal activities as a means of achieving culturally prescribed goals, might offer an explanation for deviancy of this nature in the economically deprived sector of society (Merton 1949). But in Russia deviancy as innovation has not been confined to this sector. Indeed organised crime and its recruitment of youth is as attractive a proposition for high-ranking members of society and their offspring, as it is for those from the disadvantaged sectors. Peter Juviler offers Sutherland's theory of differential association as an explanation for deviancy within this group—that is, the adoption of 'anti-social values' in place of those dominant values which offer fewer advantages (Juviler 1976: 148). Subcultural theorists, including Cohen, Cloward and Ohlin, and Downes, account for deviancy within a relatively stable social environment where norms and ambitions are defined and longitudinal, which is hardly the case in the former USSR. The danger of applying Western-based theories to the problems of organised crime and youth in Russia lies in their inability to account for the persistent relationship between organised crime and the legitimate structures of the former USSR, and the extent to which this relationship has determined the nature of organised crime. Organised crime in Russia might display some similarities to that of America in the nineteenth century—the 'robber baron' scenario,[18] and Russian protection rackets might well operate along the same principle as those in Sicily (Gambetta 1993), but such similarities account only for fragmented activities and not a more general picture of the characteristics and influence of Russian organised crime. Centuries of economic centralism, isolationism and autocracy have shaped Russian culture as a unique and often confusing phenomenon. As the philosopher Alexander Zinoviev writes:

> What is the reason for such monstrous mistakes that Westerners make when they evaluate the phenomena of our life? The reason is that they measure our life too according to their own yardstick (Zinoviev 1986: 128).

The study of Russian organised crime is as much a comment on Russian society as it is on deviant elements. Russia's growing organised crime problem, its pervasive and dangerous influence on the future of the country, in particular on its youth, presents a challenge of self-reappraisal not just to Russian academics, educators, and law enforcers, but to those of us in non-Russian, capitalist states who have defined our own systems according to values which have gone unquestioned until the demise of the Communist bloc. Economic competition, the cult of the individual, and the dominance of materialistic values, have manifested in Russia in a grossly distorted form. But how far is this distortion actually an opportunity to glimpse Western values stripped naked of the layers of sophistication which over a period of time have been constructed to disguise their true nature: self-seeking, materially obsessive, and morally deprived? Herein lies the real challenge—does Russia's crimogenic condition and its effects on youth have lessons for us in the West and how should we deal with this both at home and abroad? In a study of what could be accorded the controversial soubriquet a 'mafia state', attention should also be paid to those who deviate from the criminal norm. These individuals operate independently of the dictates of politics and economics, are a positive driving force and a balance to the more familiar presence of the darker side of human nature. Such was the case of Dispacher, a Moscow sports teacher who refused to see his pupils enticed into organised crime without putting up some form of resistance. He trained and armed a group of teenagers from the ages of eighteen to 20 to resist the Orekho-Borisov gang and even managed to appeal to some of the gang members to 'do the right thing'. A backlash from those who resisted Dispacher's appeals resulted in his murder and those of his young crime busting team (Dixelius and Konstantinov 1995: 122). For the young people of a Moscow suburb he and his group were an antidote to the pervasive world of crime and no punishment. Dostoyevskian heroes were prepared to act for a better inheritance beyond that offered by organised crime. At the end of a chapter which paints a distinctly grim picture of Russia's future and that of its youth, it is perhaps appropriate to acknowledge the existence of positive moral motivations within that society. For, if nothing else, youth deserves a fuller picture of human behaviour. An acknowledgment of characters such as Dispacher, and there are many from different walks of life including the police, offers an alternative dimension in assessing the problems of organised crime in Russia and its influence on youth. Their ability to take on new ways of dealing with the 'mafia' threat to society presents a challenge to criminologists to find new ways of understanding this threat by altering the yardstick and preconceptions of what constitutes organised crime in any particular society.

REFERENCES

Adelman, D. (1994) *The 'Children of Perestroika' Come of Age*, New York: Armonk.

Alekseyeva, M. and Patrignani, A. (1994) *Crime and Crime Prevention in Moscow*, United Nations Interregional Crime and Justice Research Institute, Publication No. 52, Rome/Moscow.

Arshavskii, A. and Vilks, A. (1991) 'Antisocial Manifestations in the Youth Environment', Soviet Sociology 30 (2): 88-98.

Bell, D. (1963) 'Myth of the Cosa Nostra', *The New Leader* (46) December 23.

Connor, W. (1972) *Deviance in Soviet Society*, New York: Columbia University Press.

Dispatches (1990) 'Moscow's Mafia's Millions', London, Channel 4.

Dixelius, M. and Konstantinov, A. (1995) *Prestupni mir v Rossii*, St Petersburg: Bibliopolis.

Dolgova, A. and Dyakov, S. (1989) *Organizovannaia Prestupnost'*, Moscow Yuridicheskaia Literatura.

Fayn, A. (1994) 'Vagrant Children' in *Petersburg in the Early 90's: Cold, Cruel, Crazy,* Saint Petersburg Charitable Foundation 'Nochlezhka': 193-7.

Fisher, R. (1959) *Pattern for Soviet Youth: A Study of the Congresses of the Komsomol 1918-1954*, New York: Columbia University Press.

Gambetta, D. (1993) *The Sicilian Mafia*, Cambridge MA: Harvard University Press.

Gambiani, A. (1988) 'Drug Addiction', *Soviet Sociology* 26 (4): 50-7.

Gilinski, Y., Podkolzin, V. and Kochetkov, E. (1994) 'The Drug Problem in St Petersburg', in *Petersburg in the Early 90's: Cold, Cruel, Crazy,* Saint Petersburg Charitable Foundation 'Nochlezhka': 218-22.

Gurov, A. and Ryabin, V. (1991) *Ispoved' 'Vora v zakone'*, Moscow Rosargropromizdat.

Gurov, A. (1995) *Krasnaia Mafia*, Samotsvet MIKO Komercheskii Vestnik.

Halligan, L. and Mozdoukhov, B. (1995) *A Guide to Russia's Parliamentary Elections*, CTE Briefing No 1: December.

Hanson, P. (1992) *From Stagnation to Catastroika: Commentaries on the Soviet Economy 1983-1991*, New York: Praeger.

Juviler, P. (1976) *Revolutionary Law and Order*, New York: Free Press.

Karpets, I. (1988) 'Ideological and Political Development of Youth: Experience and Problem', *Soviet Sociology* 26(4): 29-49.

Khokhryakov, G. (1989) 'Mafia Leaves us Lost for Words', *Soviet Weekly,* July 22.

Klepach, N. (1988) 'Ideological and Political Development of Youth: Experience and Problem', Soviet Sociology, 26(4): 29-49.

Kucherov, S. (1953) *Courts, Lawyers and Trials*, New York: Praeger.

Kuznetsova, N.F. (1968) *Prestuplenie i Prestupnost*, Izdatel'stvo Moskovskogo

Universiteta.
Makhov, F. (1970) Leto v Lagere 'TOS', *Moscow Molodaia Gvardia*: 12.
Merton, Robert K. (1957) *Social Theory and Social Structure*, New York: Free Press.
Pilkington, H. (1994) *Russia's Youth and its Culture. A Nation's Constructors and Constructed,* London: Routledge.
Rafailov, G. (1994) 'Refugees' in *St Petersburg in the Early 90's: Cold, Cruel, Crazy*, Saint Petersburg Charitable Foundation 'Nochlezhka': 173-4.
RAU Corporation (1993) *Prestupnost'—Ugroza Rossii,* Moscow.
Ribalskaia, V. (1971) 'Kriminologicheskai Kharacterisitika Prestupnosti Nesovershennoletnikh' in S. Antipin and S. Narishkin (eds), *Nesovershennoletnie Pravonarushiteli*, Irkutsk, Irkutsk Oblastnoe Otdelenie Pedagogicheskogo Obshestva RSFSR: 11-14.
Riordan, J. (1989) 'Teenage gangs, "Afgantsy" and Neofascists' in J. Riordan (ed.), *Soviet Youth Culture,* London: Macmillan.
Romov, A. (1990) Interview for 'Moscow's Mafia's Millions', *Dispatches*, Channel 4.
Rossiiskaia Gazeta (1994) 'Ukaz—Banditism', June 17.
'Rysk Maffiya' (1993) Interview with Yuri Shchekhochikin, journalist on Literaturnaya Gazeta, Swedish TV1 Broadcast Spring 1993.
Shchekochikhin, Yu. (1987) 'Allo, My Vas Slyshim', *Literaturnaia Gazeta,* April 8.
Shchekochikhin, Yu. (1988) 'Before the Mirror', *Soviet Sociology* 26(4): 6-17.
Solnick, S. (1990) 'Does the Komsomol have a Future?' *Report on the USSR*, September 21: 9-13.
Stashkov, V. (1990) Interview for 'Moscow's Mafia's Millions', *Dispatches*, Channel 4.
Ugolovni Kodeks RSFRS (1987) Moscow: Yuridicheskaya Literatura.
Vetrov, A. (1995) 'The Ministry of Internal Affairs Requests Assistance in Combatting Teenage Crime', *The Current Digest of the Post-Soviet Press* 47(34): 5.
Vitaliev, V. (1990) *Special Correspondent,* London: Century Hutchinson: 117.
Zinoviev, Alexander (1986) *Homo Sovieticus*, London: Paladin Grafton Books.

NOTES

1. The author disputes the use of the term 'mafia' in relation to Russian organised crime. Organised crime in Russia operates as a syndicate, that is, a hierarchical organisation based entirely on business relations as opposed to the 'family' of nepotistic structures of the Sicilian mafia. Nor does syndicate crime in this sense operate according to codes of honour unless to protect the economic interests of the group. However certain organised criminal activity in the Central Asian Republics (e.g. the Uzbekistan 'Cotton Scandal' of the 1980s) does bear the

hallmark of more traditional forms of organised crime that might be termed 'mafia'.

2. Information supplied by Vladimir Osin from the Ministry of the Interior (MVD) research centre.

3. The *tsekhovik* was an underground factory owner producing black market goods and often acting under the protection of a government official.

4. These micro-regions are little more than dead-end suburbs on the outskirts of the major cities comprising tower-blocks and little in the way of amusement for teenage groups. They are notorious for their high crime rate.

5. All Soviet citizens needed a *propiska* or residency permit in order to rent accommodation and find employment. In an interview with an inmate of Lebedeva prison in St Petersburg, Olga described the problems of renewing her *propiska* which forced her to return to her life of crime in desperation rather than from choice (Interview, August 1991).

6. During filming of 'Moscow's Mafia's Millions' the local militia remained unperturbed by the fact that their presence and unwillingness to stop any of the gang selling spare parts was being recorded. From the official standpoint the *Kopteva* lads were fulfilling an important function by addressing the shortage of parts. Obviously the acquisition of parts for the black market through contacts at the relevant plants was an important exacerbatory factor vis a vis shortages. It also indicated that the official distributors profited through the inevitable palm greasing that occurred in such transactions (Rawlinson, Channel 4, 'Dispatches'—*Moscow's Mafia Millions* 1990).

7. Full criminal responsibility begins at the age of sixteen.

8. St Petersburg figures obtained by Malcolm Dixelius from unofficial estimates are more likely to be accurate than the official figures. A 'juvenile' is a young person between the age of 14 and 17 years old. Limited criminal responsibility begins at 14 years. Full responsibility begins at 16 years.

9. Observations made during a three month research trip to St Petersburg in 1994.

10. Interview with the author, December 1994.

11. Interview with member of the Regional Department to Combat Organised Crime, Narcotics Section. September 1994.

12. A report on the discovery of 'Chernobyl' heroin, allegedly manufactured from irradiated poppies growing near the site of the nuclear disaster was confirmed by the editor of the St Petersburg Press, Lloyd Donaldson, in a telephone interview in August 1995.

13. Interview conducted by the author in St Petersburg, June 1991.

14. Interview by Malcolm Dixelius, July 1993.

15. Information supplied by Andrei Konstantinov, crime correspondent for *Komsomol'skaya Pravda*.

16. Stashkov, former Colonel in Moscow MVD, interview with the author, September 1990.

17. Funding for the maintenance and education of female juvenile offenders in St Petersburg was still waiting for official approval in 1994. On the other hand financial backing for business is usually available, a sad reversal of former policy.

18. This argument has been put to me on various occasions by Western businessmen, police officers and members of criminal intelligence, as well as in numerous newspaper articles around the subject of Russian organised crime.

5 Vietnamese Youth Gangs in the Context of Multiple Marginality and the Los Angeles Youth Gang Phenomenon

James Diego Vigil and Steve Chong Yun

INTRODUCTION

In recent years Los Angeles has become known as the street gang capital of the United States, and of the world, as the number of US gangs dwarfs that of other industrialised nations. Los Angeles County has the most gangs in the nation, with 1,100 different street gangs and over 150,000 gang members (Hudson et al. 1995), numbers that have tripled over the past ten years. These gangs are responsible for a high proportion of drive-by shootings and violence in the streets, and gang-related homicides account for nearly 70% of all child and adolescent homicides in Los Angeles (Hudson et al. 1995).

Compounding the magnitude and the complexity of this problem is the ethnic diversity of the street gangs in Los Angeles. In addition to the well-known African American and Chicano (i.e. Mexican American) gangs, recent immigration patterns have resulted in the formation of street gangs in new ethnic communities, such as the Vietnamese. Ethnic gangs, and indeed individual gangs, vary widely in terms of typical characteristics, behavioural patterns, and sociocultural history. Our research has focused on exploring the utility of a model, which we refer to as multiple marginality, to delineate connecting strands between these different groups that explain the formation and persistence of the street gang phenomenon.

Multiple marginality was originally developed as a model to explain the Chicano gang phenomenon in Los Angeles (Vigil 1988). However, in analysing gangs in other ethnic groups, we have found that this framework provides insights into them as well. The purpose of this paper then is to briefly outline the multiple marginality theory and examine how it applies to the different ethnic gangs in Los Angeles. We will specifically focus on the Vietnamese experience, as the Vietnamese gangs are the most recent, and probably the least well understood, addition to the Los Angeles street phenomenon.

Multiple Marginality

Multiple marginality comprises a conceptual framework within which we can sequentially link events, times, places, thoughts, and people into an integrated understanding of the ecological, socioeconomic, cultural, and psychosocial factors that push (or pull) a youth into a gang. The notion of marginality is crucial in this framework, as the origins of youth gangs can be found in the 'margins', with both social and personal antecedents and consequences. For example, the gangs in Los Angeles have arisen in ecologically marginal areas of the city within marginal socioeconomic conditions which have fuelled the rise of gangs. African Americans and Chicanos have traditionally been channelled into ethnic enclaves (i.e. the ghettos and barrios), areas of the city that lacked the infrastructure of the more wealthy suburbs. When the Vietnamese first came to the US, they too first settled in such neighbourhoods, where rent was cheaper.

In terms of cultural orientation, youths are often on the 'margins' of two different ethnic spheres, betwixt and between cultures and identities, not quite belonging to either. This cultural stretch is particularly acute for the Chicanos and the Vietnamese, for part of their identity is tied to an immigrant language and to parents who still adhere strongly to the habits of their native country.

Linking all these elements of marginality under one framework allows us to generate a 'thick description' and broader assessment of this complex problem (Geertz 1973: 3). Such an analysis thus avoids the limitations of single-cause explanations of the gang problem, allowing us to follow over time the impact of macro (group history), meso (family history), and micro (individual life history) level factors. Such multiple forces working at various levels show how ecological and economic conditions foster the development of a subcultural mechanism of adjustment—the gang.

The multiple marginality framework must also include an intense focus on social control, or more precisely, the breakdown of social control in the community. Traditionally one of the strongest social control factors in the community has been the family. Marital stress, poverty, and culture conflict, however, have inflicted in some sectors of society a heavy toll on the family's ability to exert social control over youth. In the absence of fully functional families, social control has shifted to schools and law enforcement. However, as will be outlined, schools and law enforcement have also failed to exert adequate social control. The breakdown of parenting, schooling, and policing controls has allowed gang youths to adopt a lifestyle that, while fulfilling important needs for these youths, is detrimental to the community.

While ethnic minorities share some aspects of marginality within American society, the details of their development within the American context differ, as do their cultures. Thus, to see how multiple marginality applies to the Los Angeles street gang experience, we will briefly review the Chicano, African American, and Vietnamese communities and the street gangs that have developed within them.

Chicano Gangs

Los Angeles was originally a Mexican pueblo (Griswold del Castillo 1980), but the flood of Anglos in the late 19th century began the urbanization process. During the Anglo influx, Mexicans were forcibly separated from the rest of the city and pushed into barrios along the eastern margin of the town center (Camarillo 1979). The barrio was segregated, over-crowded, and lacked many of the amenities found in the Anglo residential areas. In many ways, it—and the other barrios that have come into being—remains in the same condition today.

Discrimination and repeated cycles of large-scale immigration, often resulting in low levels of education and high unemployment, have made it difficult to improve conditions in the barrio. 'Poverty, discrimination, and group choice helped to create the Mexican barrios, but urbanisation and the concomitant poor city planning and neglectful and uncaring authorities make the barrios an ecologically inferior place in which to raise a family' (Vigil 1988: 24). By the 1930s, these conditions had spawned street gangs in several of the older barrios of East Los Angeles. Some of these have persisted through many generations, while similar gang patterns have diffused into more recently established barrios.

Poverty not only degrades the ecological conditions of the barrio, but it has insidious impacts on the psychological well-being of barrio youth. Not surprisingly, most gang members come from the more impoverished families, which often are mother-centered (Vigil 1988).

The absence and/or inattentiveness of the father is a common theme in Chicano youth gang membership. In the Mexican family, the role of the father is traditionally that of the leader, and his stable presence exerts a large measure of social control over, and conformity among, children in the family. Additionally, as many gang members come from mother-centered households, with fathers absent or their roles attenuated, they may experience some role confusion as they try to resolve their self-identity. Thus, they may attempt to assuage their inner conflict through overemphasising their 'male' qualities by acting aggressively and modelling themselves after their 'street warrior' role models (Vigil 1988).

Moreover, both schools and law enforcement have also failed to exert control over gang recruitment and gang activities. Historical analysis lends us valuable insight into this problem. In the case of the education system, Mexican students were often subjected to the prejudices of their teachers and programs such as 'ability tracking' which placed African American and Mexican students on a substandard course of study (Bogardus 1934; Hill 1928). These problems persisted into the present era (US Commission of Civil Rights 1971). Language in particular has been a problem between teachers and Mexican students. Among the older generation in the barrio, many recall teachers punishing them for speaking Spanish. Today, despite the growing acceptance of ESL programs and the absence of such formal language discrimination, the predominance of Spanish speech at home and English at school can still cause significant problems (Vigil 1988).

Mexican American students, in the face of these problems, often found themselves falling behind in school, and their troubles were further compounded by their peers. Given the discrimination, their own lagging school performance, and a consequent natural desire to rebel against the educational system, many youths were pressured into not being a 'schoolboy'. To obtain respect from their peers, youths would ditch school with a group of friends to show that school (in which they were not doing well, anyway) '*no vale*' ('doesn't matter').

Chicano gang members have had particular difficulty in adjusting to school and by the age of sixteen most have dropped out of the educational system (Vigil 1988). Among the reasons cited for their 'turning-off' process were language problems, general malaise, and discrimination. It is important to note that school problems generally *precede* involvement in the gang. Thus, the educational system could potentially be a powerful factor in preventing students from joining gangs, if only we could find effective ways to turn students 'on' to the benefits and values of an education.

The last part of the social control triad is law enforcement. Mexican immigrants have traditionally been wary of law enforcement, an attitude that stems from their experiences with corruption in Mexico. Discriminatory attitudes and behaviour of the Los Angeles police and sheriffs reinforced this wariness. Moreover, barrio-police riots, although not common, are an integral part of the barrio's collective memory (Morales 1972; Mandel 1982). Barrio residents also feel that they are seen as being deviant and are ambivalent about the extra police attention that they receive just by living in the barrio (Gonzales 1981; US Civil Rights Commission 1970).

Culture conflict—that is, being betwixt-and-between two cultures—is also an important part of the multiple marginality framework. Chicano gang members are certainly acculturated, usually more so than their parents, and they have lost some of their 'Mexicanness'; but most are not completely integrated into the dominant culture as exemplified in the inability to speak fluent English. There is thus confusion over self-identity, and the youth are caught on the margins of two cultures. On the one hand, they will take pride in Chicano identity and will vehemently deny being *engabacheado* ('Anglicized'). They will speak with intense passion about the racism of gabachos. Yet at the same time, they will demean and separate themselves from the 'wetbacks' (Mexican nationals) and are embarrassed to be associated with them (Vigil 1988). Neither here nor there, Chicano youths who join gangs have created their own cultural interstice—a subcultural style dominated by the gang.

African American Gangs

African American gangs in Los Angeles, despite their much publicised existence, are relatively recent in origin, for the most part having begun to appear only after World War II. As California prospered in the post-war era, the African American population in South Central Los Angeles increased dramatically as people migrated from the southern parts of the United States. Old, established ghettos grew even larger, and new ghettos were created. For example, Watts, a well-known ghetto in South-Central Los Angeles, was originally home to two Mexican barrios—and only in the 1950s did it become predominantly African American. The expansion of the United States economy in the 1960s, in combination with the growth of federal programs aimed at eliminating or ameliorating the effects of poverty, led to continued growth of the local African American community.

However, the lingering effects of racial discrimination in combination with government cutbacks in social programs and a changing economic environment in the 1970s and 1980s, locked many African American men out of jobs. Between 1978-1982 alone, South Central Los Angeles lost more than 70,000 high wage jobs as over 200 manufacturing companies left the area (Soja et al. 1983; Johnson and Oliver 1991). As the job opportunities began to evaporate, more and more Latino immigrants entered the job market, thus providing employers with a cheaper pool of labor (Levy 1987). As a result, the unemployment rate of African American men reached as high as 50% in several areas of South Central Los Angeles (Oliver, Johnson, and Farrell 1993).

As unemployment levels have risen, so have the number of African American males in prison; today one out of four young African American men are part of America's penal system—incarcerated or on probation or parole. Lack of meaningful employment opportunities for many African American men has also undermined family stability (Fainstain 1986; Liebow 1967). As a consequence, large numbers of children in Los Angeles' ghettos are growing up in female-centered homes where a male presence is painfully absent (McLanahan and Sandefur 1994).

In addition to the widespread breakdown of families, the drug trade exploded in the ghetto with the arrival of cocaine, especially 'rock' or 'crack' cocaine. Although it is estimated that only one-third of African American gangs are actively involved in drug dealing (Klein, Maxson, and Cunningham 1988), the rise of the drug trade has contributed to the growth of African American drug gangs. In some cities, such as in Detroit, African American gangs have shifted their primary focus from a conflict orientation (i.e. fighting with other gangs) to drug dealing (Taylor 1990). However, in Los Angeles, most African American gangs remain loosely organised and oriented more towards conflict, than organised crime (Klein 1995).

Since the 1992 riots, a community-based truce has somewhat reduced such conflict. Nevertheless, gangs have become entrenched in certain parts of the African American community. For example, gang 'garb', i.e. a fashion style of wearing clothing or accessories of specific colours (blue for the 'Crips', red for the 'Bloods') is well known to both the police and the community. (Youths have been attacked and even killed for sporting the wrong colours.) The gangs have also become more complex, as they have branched out into confederacies that recruit members from more distant neighbourhoods, and subsets are now well-established in several Los Angeles suburbs. Crip and Blood gang sets have also appeared in Denver and other cities; although these gangs probably have little formal relationship to the gangs in Los Angeles (Klein 1995), it is clear that the

Los Angeles model of the African American gang has spread more widely.

THE VIETNAMESE EXPERIENCE

Having briefly examined some of the forces that make up the multiple marginality framework with respect to the Chicano and African American gangs, we now turn to a detailed analysis of the Vietnamese experience. In contrast to the Chicano and African American populations, who have a long history in America, the Vietnamese in America date back only to 1975.

The takeover of Saigon by communist forces in 1975 was the defining event that marked the beginning of mass Vietnamese immigration to America. In the aftermath of the fall of Saigon, tens of thousands of Vietnamese refugees were brought to the United States. At first they were housed in military camps as the American government struggled to find homes for these new arrivals. Within a short period of time, however, many of the Vietnamese refugees began migrating to a small area in Orange County, California, which would become known as Little Saigon.

When the first refugees came to suburban Orange County to reside in a politically conservative and predominantly Anglo area that lies just south of Los Angeles, Little Saigon was only a 1.5 mile strip of a few strawberry fields and several run-down shops.

In the last 20 years, however, the strawberry fields and shops have been transformed into a bustling commercial district that now generates over 60 million dollars annually in tax revenue and has a property value of over 70 million dollars (Cooper 1990). During this same period over 150,000 Vietnamese refugees have flocked to Orange County, making the area one of the largest Vietnamese enclaves in the world outside of Vietnam. The Vietnamese community is so large that, in some ways, it has become isolated from the mainstream community. Vietnamese refugees can find virtually any goods or service in Little Saigon, and there is little need to interact with the Anglo community. Indeed, a recent survey found that 55% of Vietnamese respondents spent half of their time or more in Little Saigon, and 13% spent all of their time only in the Vietnamese community (Masciola and Zielbauer 1995). Yet, while the Vietnamese have achieved remarkable economic success, there are still problems that lurk on the streets of Little Saigon. There remains a small but significant group of Vietnamese refugees who are still struggling with poverty, unemployment, and welfare dependency. In addition, Vietnamese parents struggle with culture conflict and change as their children become acculturated and integrated into American society. Perhaps related to both these problems are Vietnamese gangs, which have increasingly become more of a concern in the community. Polls conducted in the Little Saigon community in 1981 showed that 41% of the respondents believed that 'crime and gangs' were the 'worst problem' they faced. By contrast, a 1989 survey of the general Orange County population found that only 10% cited crime as their primary concern (Weikel 1990). These differences in perception and community concern were significant and pointed to an important underlying reality.

While the phenomenon of Vietnamese youth gangs has been subject to much media exaggeration and hyperbole, the gangs do exist and they are indeed a problem. However, the Vietnamese gangs are not part of an exotic Asian mafia, as they have often been portrayed in the media, but rather the creation of a complex network of psychological, socioeconomic, and cultural factors that unfortunately are found all too often in the lives of street youth of all ethnic backgrounds in southern California (Vigil 1993).

To understand this complex problem we have interviewed law enforcement officials, social workers, community leaders, teachers, and over 40 members of Vietnamese youth gangs. Clearly, more research is needed, but our investigation demonstrates that the Vietnamese youth gang problem must be understood in a context that goes beyond America's borders, and back to the time of the Vietnam War.

Early Arrivals

After the fall of Saigon in 1975, the first wave of refugees escaped from Vietnam and were brought into four refugee camps in the US, including one at Camp Pendleton, a military base near San Diego, California. Although these refugees had left behind virtually all of their possessions, they were fortunate in that they came to America relatively well-equipped for their new life. In general, they were well-educated, highly urbanised, of high socioeconomic status, and mostly young in age. Most importantly, most of them had come to America with their families intact (Liu 1979; Kelly 1977; Bach and Bach 1980; Nguyen and Henkin 1982; Stein 1979; Marsh 1980).

Despite the desirable characteristics of the refugees, American resentment of the Vietnam War was still high and many Americans opposed the Vietnamese influx. In a 1975 Gallup Poll 54% of the

American public opposed resettlement of the Vietnamese in the United States (*Time* 1975). The passage of time apparently has done little to alter those feelings, which were particularly intense in Orange County. In a 1981 poll of Orange County residents, for example, 60% favoured a moratorium on new refugee arrivals (Green 1981). Resentment became so intense that over one hundred residents of the Orange County city of Westminster demanded that the city council suspend the licences of Vietnamese-owned businesses. The mayor of Westminster at that time, commented:

> Our homeowners' association were very verbal and open about their feelings ... schools were screaming ... and the business community was extremely threatened. They were talking that because it was growing so fast, it was going to take over the whole city, that there would be no more Anglo people here (former mayor Kathy Buchoz, Westminster, July 1990).

This animosity is apparently still widespread. A recent poll showed that 59% of Vietnamese respondents in Orange County reported at least occasional discrimination or harassment because of their ethnicity (Kalfus 1995). Nevertheless, despite intense opposition, the Vietnamese continued to migrate to and settle in Orange County. The Vietnamese were attracted to southern California by the presence of Vietnamese communities that had sprung from Camp Pendleton, rumours of an abundance of jobs, and the favourable climate resembling that of their home country (Kelly 1977). As Little Saigon continued to grow and prosper, news of its success began to attract those who still were in Vietnam.

The 'Boat People'

While many Vietnamese were now prospering in California, many in Vietnam were planning their own migration. Thus, in the late 1970s, a second wave of refugees, the 'boat people', began fleeing Vietnam by the tens of thousands. By the middle of 1979 more than 290,000 Vietnamese had escaped (Grant 1979).

The impetus behind these refugees was the lure of prosperity in America, combined with the harsh reality of life in communist Vietnam. For example, many Vietnamese were forcibly relocated to 're-education camps' and the police were feared as they were known to torture civilians.

Life was particularly difficult for children, as one Vietnamese social worker explains:

> Survival was the most important thing and they had to make a living and live with the police ... These kids had to be prostitutes, robbers, sellers, and black marketeers in order to survive. They had to make every means to survive.

This theme of survival came up repeatedly in the stories of Vietnamese gang youths we interviewed. Thus the motives to leave Vietnam were strong, as one youth we interviewed explains:

> The communist way is messed up. And my dad dreamed of coming over here to America to make all our family go to school and do good ... They said it was rich and you could be free. You didn't have to do it the communist way.

This second mass flight of tens of thousands of Vietnamese escaped Vietnam primarily by sea on ramshackle ships and boats that were only minimally equipped for extensive sea travel. These vessels were typically extremely overcrowded and sanitary conditions were poor. Water and food were scarce and had to be rationed, and passengers were subject to typhoons, Thai pirates, and capture by government. Some estimate that as many as one-third of the boat people died at sea (Grant 1979). One youth we interviewed shared a particular horrid, but not uncommon, story:

> The pirates robbed us ... One girl with two earrings—they just cut off her ear ... She was taking too long with the earring so they just cut it off.

To make matters worse, many of the refugees, particularly the children, came without their families. The price of being smuggled out of the country was prohibitively high for many families, so Vietnamese parents would save enough money to send just their oldest child, in hopes that he or she would find success in America.

As a group, then, the boat people differed significantly from the first wave of refugees. The boat people were generally young (over half were children or teenagers) and poor, and they were less educated and less urbanised than the first wave of refugees (Grant 1979; Bach and Bach 1980; Skinner 1980; Nguyen and Henkin 1982). Nevertheless, like the first wave of refugees, they were also attracted to southern California and after having survived the ordeal of escaping from Vietnam, they looked forward to life in Little Saigon.

Disillusionment and Frustration

Many of the boat people sought to attain the American dream, and many have realised this goal. However, a small but significant number of refugees have not. They have been hampered by a number of factors, including their lack of English and lack of marketable job skills. While job training and English as a Second Language (ESL) programs should alleviate these deficits, the boat people came at a time of massive cutbacks in government aid and programs (Gold and Kibria 1989; Wilson 1987). Most importantly, many of the boat people who have struggled came without their most important resource: their family. The role of the family in the Vietnamese culture cannot be overemphasised, as it is the 'spirit of the family' that is the socioeconomic foundation for the Vietnamese:

> The family is the linchpin of economic adaptation strategies where individual members subordinate their short-term economic interest to the long-term economic self-sufficiency of the kin group (Desberats and Holland 1983: 28).

While many Vietnamese refugees, particularly first wave refugees, have prospered, many have not, particularly those who came in the second wave of refugees. This two-sided aspect of the Vietnamese community is reflected by a number of socioeconomic indices. For example, one report noted that:

> Less than 25% of 1981 arrivals were in the labor force and less than half of the 25% in the labor force had been able to find work. Refugees who arrived in the U.S.A. from 1975-1977 [in essence, the first wave of refugees] ... had rates of participation higher than the rate for the general population and had unemployment rates lower than the national figure of 7.5% (Office of Refugee Resettlement 1987: 18).

In 1982, 25% of first wave refugees were living in poverty, but among the 1980-82 arrivals the percentage was 90% (Efron 1990). These statistics help explain the fact that the unemployment rate in 1989 for refugees was twice the national average, despite the fact that first wave refugees had achieved income parity with the general population (Efron 1990).

Although many refugees have eventually found economic success in the 1990s, a significant number of them, especially when compared to Orange County as a whole, continue to have a difficult time finding employment—46% of Vietnamese respondents reported having a 'difficult' time finding employment, compared to the countywide response of only 16% who reported difficulty (Evans 1995). Moreover, the unemployment rate in the three Orange County cities with the largest concentration of Vietnamese refugees is higher (6.5% in Westminster, 7.1% in Garden Grove, and 9.7% in Santa Ana) than the countywide unemployment rate of 5.5% (Evans 1995). The Vietnamese make up only 5% of Orange County's population, but they accounted for 46% of the General Relief Program cases and 35% of AFDC (Aid to Families with Dependent Children) cases in 1994 (Evans 1995).

So marked is the condition of some refugees that W.J. Wilson, in a survey of refugees from all across the county, remarked, 'the influx of immigrants from Southeast Asia ... has been associated with ... problems that have traditionally plagued inner-city black neighbourhoods' (1987: 36). In light of the data, and in spite of the extraordinary economic success of many refugees, it should perhaps not be so surprising that as gangs have arisen in the ghettos, so have gangs arisen in Little Saigon.

The Role of Education, Family, and Identity

Poverty is one part of the story that helps explain the emergence of gangs, but the role of schools, the family, and self-identity also are significant factors. By examining each of these factors separately, we can understand how they intertwine to push a vulnerable youth into the 'margins', i.e., to comprise a condition of 'multiple marginality', conducive to leading youngsters into gang activities (Vigil 1988).

Schools are probably second only to the family in their importance in the lives of children. For too many refugee youths, however, this important institution came to symbolise frustration, embarrassment, and boredom. The most common problem has been language—while many youths can readily pick up the English language, for some youths, their early experiences in school were particularly frustrating. One gang youth we interviewed explains:

> I know nothing in school. I just go in there and they say sit there, sit there and they point there, point there. I don't say a word. I just listen to where they point. I look at where they want me to go, and I go. I didn't know a single word of English ... I couldn't keep up with the work. It's too hard. I sit in class and the teacher stand up talking and can't get into my head. It's too hard. They pass out work and I just sit there and stare at the work. I couldn't do nothing. I'm tired of that. I got bored.

The language barrier is also a problem in that it often prevents parents from effectively monitoring the performance of their children. One youth we interviewed recounted the time he was called to the principal's office and told to bring in his parents. The school had no translator, so the youth had to act as his own translator for his parents. Thus, while the principal was telling him that he was being expelled for fighting, he told his parents he was being given a special 'vacation'. Given the language barrier, then, Vietnamese youths can manipulate their situation in school so as to avoid detection by their parents. As one social worker told us:

> I've seen a lot of parents who are very ignorant of the American culture or are illiterate even in the Vietnamese language. They cannot control their children because they cannot speak a word of English. The children are the ones calling the shots, not the parents.

While some Vietnamese youths do poorly in school, there are many Vietnamese students who do exceptionally well. Each year, for example, Vietnamese youths are among top valedictorians in Orange County high schools, a fact that is highly publicised and touted in Vietnamese newspapers and in the community. These 'whiz kids', however, may have a paradoxically detrimental effect on other students, particularly those who are not able to cope as well in the school environment. For example, community leaders argue that the stereotype of the Asian 'whiz kid' results in the cutback of programs to help those Asian students that need remedial help. In addition, the inability to match the accomplishments of the 'whiz kids' is a significant source of resentment and loss of self-esteem for youths who struggle in school. One gang member we interviewed said emphatically:

> I just don't look at them or nothing ... I don't like those people. Man, they're too smart. They get A's, and you can't get no A's like that.

> I get mad, I get jealous. You're in your world, I'm in my world.

While English is a major learning barrier, it apparently does not prevent Vietnamese youths from understanding the concept of racism. As a physically distinct minority in a predominantly Anglo or Hispanic environment, Vietnamese students were often easy targets. A 20-year-old gang member told us about his first experiences in grade school:

> The Mexican gang over there [at school] pretty big ... A lot of Vietnamese there got pushed around and I can't understand it. I like to stand up for what we are. Feel I'm big, too.

Another youth told us about his experiences:

> When I was going to school, white people always be calling me nip and gooks and shit. And it hurts. I didn't go to school. I didn't want to get into fights and stuff, so I stopped going to school.

Consequently, given the pressure of racism and the threat of violence, Vietnamese youths banded together to defend themselves. One youth proudly recalls: 'When one white person jumped us, they had to fight the whole school because the Vietnamese stick together ... We just take care of ourselves at school. We like a family'. Indeed, this is probably how the earliest Vietnamese gangs started, as a defensive, protective reaction to racism. As a law enforcement officer we interviewed explains:

> That's what it started out as, and what happened was that the Asian kids were banding together for protection much like the Hispanic kids banded together, and that's basically how they [the gangs] started.

Traditionally, problems at school would be mediated by the family. However, many families were disrupted by the effects of the Vietnam War and the escape to America. In America, the Vietnamese family has faced additional stresses, such as poverty, culture conflict, and acculturation problems. The generational differences within the family can become particularly intense. On the one hand, the children are becoming acculturated at a relatively rapid rate, whereas the parents tend to remain fixed in the culture of their homeland. The clash of the American and Vietnamese cultures, which are sometimes diametrically opposed, can create a great deal of strain. As one Vietnamese social worker explains:

> In Vietnam, your children appreciate you. You could be gone year-round, but your children still behave because they know that their parents are working for them. They are taught that by the Vietnamese culture. Here, it is not a cultural value in the United States. In fact, what the schools do here is to interfere with the family by encouraging the children to question their parents.

The family situation is exacerbated by the fact that most Vietnamese families struggle economically. To survive both parents sometimes need to work twelve to fourteen hours a day, seven days a week. Many of the gang youths we interviewed identified with this situation, and they resented their parents' absence. For example, one youth said:

> When I live with my family, it's no fun ... Because when they opened up their shop, we never had time for each other. The only time we see each other is when we eat. My parents were never there for me.

With the breakdown of the family, which is the most important form of social control in the Vietnamese culture, and the combination of academic failure, racism, and culture conflict, many youths have turned to gangs to establish their sense of identity in America.

CHARACTERISTICS OF VIETNAMESE YOUTH GANGS

In previous work we have described three basic characteristics of Vietnamese youth gangs: a fixation on acquiring money, pragmatism, and fluidity (Vigil and Yun 1990). For the purposes of this case study, we will again explore these characteristics in detail. Unlike Chicano gangs in America, whose focus is on defending their neighbourhood, the focus of Vietnamese gangs is on money. Vietnamese gang youths are materialistic: they want new cars and the latest fashion in clothes, and they spend their nights in motels, pool halls, night clubs, and restaurants. Therefore, most youths start learning criminal strategies to acquire money. One youth's story is typical:

> At first we just play pool and kick back. But I go out and fuck around and I need money ... So I see other Vietnamese, they make money a lot of ways. They rob or they steal car. So some of them told me how to get money to fuck around. So I try to steal a car 'cause I got a man and you give him [a car], he give you eight hundred [dollars] ... and

he don't ask question.

In one city (Westminster) in Orange County, police arrest statistics we examined indicate that Vietnamese males account for approximately 20% of all automobile thefts. Eventually, however, most of these youths turn away from automobile theft in favor of opportunities promising greater rewards. Thus, many youths progress to the next step, home invasion robberies. The victims of these crimes are without exception other Vietnamese, due in part to the Vietnamese tendency to keep large amounts of cash and gold within their homes. The Vietnamese have a customary distrust of banks and, like many other Asian groups, prefer the tangibility of having their cash and gold in their home. Knowing this, the youth gangs will survey a victim's home and at the most opportune time they will invade the home. Victims are then beaten and coerced into revealing the location of their valuables. These home invasion robberies are often efficiently planned and executed. For example, one tactic gangs use is to have one of their girlfriends approach the house, because the victims will be more apt to answer the door if they see a female outside. Once the door is open, however, three to five male youths will raid the house. Meanwhile, other members of the gang will be roaming the neighbourhood in 'look-out' cars. With their cellular phones and pagers, they can warn their 'homeboys' (i.e., fellow gang members) of approaching police. Such robberies can also be very profitable. Youths told us stories of how they could commonly steal $20,000 from a single home robbery, and even losses of up to $100,000 have been reported to the authorities.

Most of the time, however, losses are not reported to the police, and this demonstrates a second characteristic of the Vietnamese youth gang—their sophisticated pragmatism. Given their intense ethnic pride, it is perhaps odd that these youths would victimise their own people. Yet a closer analysis reveals the thinking behind their crimes. One youth simply told us: 'We scared of whites, [of] any other race, 'cause they know a lot of law and they don't keep cash [within their homes)'. Vietnamese, on the other hand, do keep cash at home and also tend to be leery of the police and courts. Most importantly, victims are intimidated by the gang's threat of retribution if they do report the crime to the police. One Vietnamese businessman we interviewed was frank in his assessment of the victim's dilemma:

> You are not going to report the crime. You have to think about your family. I know the police are good guys, but they are not going to

> protect me. Within 72 hours, the criminal can be out on bail. So I'm not going to tell ... The robber will not only go after me, but my children. So am I going to tell the police? No way!

As a result of such sentiment, and to the great frustration of Orange County law enforcement officials, it is estimated that anywhere from 60% to 90% of home invasion robberies are not reported.

Given this sophistication, Vietnamese youth gangs calculate their behaviour logically, in terms of a risk-benefit paradigm. For example, Vietnamese youth gangs will rarely fight each other simply over 'turf', or territory. This is in marked contrast to other ethnic gangs in Southern California—such as the African American and Chicano gangs—whose conflicts often stem from perceived violations of turf. Vietnamese youths simply think such fighting is 'stupid'. As one youth said: 'Black and Ese [jail slang for Chicano] gang, they ... fight for neighbourhood. They shoot each other for nothing. For us, [the] most [important thing is] we try to make money. We don't fight for a little neighbourhood 'cause that's stupid'.

Drug dealing tends to be shunned as well, based on the youth's calculation of the risk-benefit ratio. With the wealth obtained from residential robberies, the youths simply have no need for other sources of 'income'. Moreover, drug dealing is a costly enterprise, with much 'overhead', and the youths feel that there is too much 'competition' already to justify its risk.

Conspicuous gang symbols, such as tattoos and gang colours, also tend to be avoided since they draw attention. Unlike their African American and Chicano counterparts, Vietnamese youths will also emphatically deny they are in gangs when confronted by police. Gang tattoos, if visible, tend to be inconspicuous. For example, one common tattoo is that of a small 'V', composed of five dots, that is placed on relatively inconspicuous parts of the body such as the webbing between the thumb and first finger. Other markers, while conspicuous, are easily altered. One youth we interviewed used to sport a 6-inch Mohawk hairstyle, but he proudly pointed out that his hair was held vertical by a mix of hair gel and egg white. His experimentation found that this formula was the easiest to wash out in case of an 'emergency', where he would need to change his hairstyle to avoid the police. Likewise, Vietnamese youths tend to avoid a single style of dress, as is common for the African American or Chicano gangs. Rather, Vietnamese gang youths tend to dress stylishly, in a 'GQ' fashion (after the name of a popular men's fashion magazine), which in southern California makes their dress relatively non-distinctive.

Indeed, Vietnamese youth gangs seem to be 'fluid'; they move easily and escape detection. They are also 'fluid' in terms of crossing spatial boundaries. As noted, Vietnamese youth gangs do not claim a 'turf', and they tend to travel from city to city, sometimes even from country to country. We have interviewed youths who have been to places as distant as Massachusetts, Canada, and Mexico. As they travel from city to city, they commit home invasion robberies to fund their journey. Their nights are spent in motels and, commonly, fifteen to twenty persons of both sexes will inhabit a single room (because renting multiple rooms attracts suspicion). This geographical fluidity is not the result of an organised national network of Vietnamese gangs. Rather, the youths establish contacts by mere word of mouth and they travel too quickly from city to city to establish any permanence.

Their relatively high level of criminal sophistication notwithstanding, we have found little evidence that the youth gangs are intimately related to the more organised criminal groups in the Vietnamese community (Vigil and Yun 1990). The youths we interviewed claimed to have little knowledge of the activities of organised crime groups (that tend to be more involved in extortion, prostitution, and drug smuggling), but they do look up to these groups as role models. Several informants voiced aspirations of joining such groups, but were unable (or unwilling) to articulate how they would be able to do so.

Although youth gangs may be a stepping stone to higher levels of organised crime, the Vietnamese youth gang structure is actually quite different from most organised crime groups. For instance, there is little or no role differentiation and the membership ranks are in constant flux. Unlike the African American and Chicano gangs which have structured initiation rites (commonly referred to as 'jumping in'), membership within a Vietnamese youth gang (provided that the initiate is Vietnamese, or, in some cases, Cambodian) is established via personal relationships. One youth told us simply that if: '... Somebody like your good friend, they look like they cool, they not stab you behind your back and you know them well, so just kick it together'. Another youth merely stated: 'It's really open'.

Despite the mobility and 'openness' of the youth gangs, intense interpersonal relationships are still formed. One youth said: 'We have a lot of respect and love for each other. We really with together [sic]. We live with each other. We're real close to each other'. Another emphatically declared: 'They were family to me ... I love 'em. Something come down, I'll be there for them ... I'd die for my homeboys'.

Indeed, with the social breakdown of their own biological families, the youths tend to adopt the gang as their family. Most of the youths we interviewed deny that their gang is a gang, asserting instead that they are a family. One youth explained:

> It's just like people trying to live, trying to survive. People my age, I try to help them survive because they help me survive. We're family, we're not a gang. White people say we are gang, but we not a gang—we family.

CONCLUSION

In examining the Vietnamese youth gangs of today, we must account for historical experiences which have played a crucial role in the creation and establishment of these gangs. From their tragic experiences in Vietnam to their alienation and isolation in America, Vietnamese youths in southern California have gravitated to a home that we label as a 'gang'. (It is interesting to note, however, that we have found little evidence from our life history interviews of any organised youth gangs in Vietnam.)

From their perspective, they have had to create their own gang subculture to survive the uprooted, dislocated nature of their lives. Like the dust that is scattered by the wind, their lives seem to be a reflection of the turbulent winds that are still generated by the aftermath of the Vietnam War and America's reluctance to accept those who are different and poor. As a community leader poignantly observed:

> We will still have a lot of the problem with the kids and their lack of being accepted here. They are still retaliating ... It's still the racial and ethnic slurs and the deep, deep feeling that they are not welcomed here and never will be. So the kids that don't have the strength of the family; gangs are the only way they are going to make it (former mayor Kathy Buchoz, Westminster, July 1990).

Although each of the ethnic groups discussed here has had a different history and have a different socioeconomic dynamic, they share a common set of stresses and strains that fit into the multiple marginality framework. In this framework there are numerous ecological, economic, sociocultural and psychological components of marginality. Caught in the margins and under intense socioeconomic strain, families broke down as parents lost firm parenting skills and as the family unit shifted to mother-centered households (McLanahan and Sandefur 1994). As families became less important in the youth's life, street socialisation took over and bought the youth into contact with the negative aspects of street life.

Combining and integrating these factors into the multiple marginality concept helps explain how disaffiliated, disenfranchised, and detached youths formed peer alliances in gangs. Because each ethnic group has different histories and different degrees of intensity of multiple marginality, different qualities in the ethnic gangs emerged. What these gangs have in common, however, is the reality of the streets. On the streets, gangs have access to excitement, danger, and comraderie. As their 'street sense' matures, they learn and adopt attitudes and behaviour that bolster the gang identity and weaken ties to traditional social control institutions. A youth becomes socialised to gang rituals, manner of speech, and dress, which serve to cultivate a loyalty to the peer group that takes precedence over all other relationships and values.

The importance of the street subculture is deepened when the youth realises that there are few other positive developmental experiences in his life. Meaningful employment is hard to find for alienated, poorly trained youths, and school is viewed as drudgery. In contrast, the 'streets' provide a youth a means to achieve self-esteem, a means to prove his manhood by demonstrating his toughness, courage, and daring. Given the predominance of female-centered households, the idea of 'manhood' is especially important as the physical drama of the streets 'beats out' any vestiges of femininity and identity confusion. In offering friendship, emotional support, and a sense of security and protection, the gang offers the vulnerable youth a way to navigate through the crazy, unpredictable pressures of the street. This relationship becomes intensified as youths learn to 'back each other up', so much so that youths from each of the different ethnic groups repeatedly stated that their homeboys were like 'brothers'.

In all these groups, multiple marginality provides a baseline model in understanding how these ethnic youths become attracted to the gang life. In large part, the gang represents a mechanism by which these youth can negotiate their multiple marginality complex and navigate through the realities of the street. Future research needs to be focused upon the means of directing these young people towards ways of meeting these complex needs through more socially acceptable forms of behaviour and institutions.

REFERENCES

Bach, R.L. and Bach, J.B. (1980) 'Employment Patterns of Southeast Asian Refugees', *Monthly Labor Review* 103: 31-8.

Bogardus, E.S. (1934) *The Mexican in the United States*, USC Social Science Series, No. 8, Los Angeles: University of Southern California Press.

Camarillo, A. (1979) *Chicanos in a Changing Society: From Mexican Pueblo to American Barrios in Santa Barbara and Southern California, 1848-1930*, Cambridge: Harvard University Press.

Cooper, J. (1990) 'Refugees have made it a remarkable fifteen years', *Los Angeles Times,* April 13.

Desberats, J. and Holland, L. (1983) 'Indochinese Settlement Patterns in Orange County', *Amerasia* 10: (1) 23-46.

Efron, S. (1990) 'Officials hit same sewing shops again', *Los Angeles Times*, March 21.

Evans, M.C. (1995) 'Older refugees sing the job-market blues', *The Orange County Register*, August 22.

Fainstain, N. (1986) 'The Underclass/Mismatch Hypothesis as an Explanation for Black Economic Deprivation', *Politics and Society* 15: 403-52.

Geertz, C. (1973) *The Interpretation of Culture*, New York: Basic Books.

Gold, S.J. and Kibria, N. (1989) 'Vietnamese refugees and mobility: Model minority or new underclass?', paper presented at the American Sociological Association Annual Meeting, August 10, San Francisco.

Gonzales, A. (1981) 'Mexican and Chicano Gangs in Los Angeles: A Socio-historical Case Study', DSW dissertation, University of California, Berkeley: School of Social Welfare.

Grant, B. (1979) *The Boat People*, Ringwood, Victoria: Penguin Books.

Green, M. (1981) 'The Refugees of Orange County', *Christian Science Monitor,* September 22.

Griswold del Castillo, R. (1980) *The Los Angeles Barrio, 1850-1890*, Los Angeles: University of California Press.

Hill, M. (1928) 'An Americanised Program for the Ontario Schools', in L. Pitt (ed.), *California Controversies*, Glenview, IL: Scott, Foresman, and Co., 1968.

Hudson, H.R. et al. (1995) 'The Epidemic of Gang-related Homicides in Los Angeles County from 1979 through 1994', *JAMA* 274 (13): 1031-6.

Johnson, J.H. and Oliver, M.L. (1991) 'Economic Restructuring and Black Male Joblessness in U.S. Metropolitan Areas', *Urban Geography* 12: 542-62.

Kalfus, M. (1995) 'Poll: Most Vietnamese report Discrimination', *The Orange County Register,* August 21.

Kelly, G. (1977) *From Vietnam to America: A Chronicle of the Vietnamese Immigration to the United States,* Boulder, Colorado: Westview Press.

Klein, M.W. (1995) *The American Street Gang*, New York: Oxford University

Press.
Klein, M., Maxson, C. and Cunningham, L. (1988) *Gang Involvement in Cocaine Rock Trafficking*, Los Angeles: University of Southern California Press.
Liebow, E. (1967) *Talley's Corner*, Boston: Little, Brown and Co.
Levy, F. (1987) *Dollars and Dreams: The Changing American Income Distribution*, New York: Russell Sage.
Liu, W.T. (1979) *Transition to Nowhere: Vietnamese Refugees in America,* Nashville, Tennessee: Charter House Publishers.
Mandel, J. (1982) *Police Use of Deadly Force in Hispanic Communities*, Washington, D.C.: National Council of La Raza.
Marsh, R.E. (1980) 'Socioeconomic Status of Indochinese Refugees in the United States: Progress and Problems', *Social Security Bulletin* 43: 11-12.
Masciola, C. and Zielbauer, P.G. (1995) 'A Vietnamese Island in O.C's Mainstream', *The Orange County Register,* August 20.
McLanahan, S. and Sandefur, G. (1994) *Growing Up with a Single Parent: What hurts, what helps,* Cambridge, MA: Harvard University Press.
Morales, A. (1972) *Ando Sangrando (I Am Bleeding)*, La Puente, CA: Perspectiva Publishing.
Nguyen, L.T. and Henkin, A.B. (1982) 'Vietnamese Refugees in the United States: Adaptation and Transitional Status', *The Journal of Ethnic Studies* 9(4): 101-16.
Office of Refugee Resettlement (1987) *Report to Congress*, Washington, DC.
Oliver, M.L., Johnson, J.H. and Farrell, W.C. (1993) 'Anatomy of a Rebellion: A Political-economic Analysis', in *Reading Rodney King, Reading Urban Uprising*, R. Gooding-Williams (ed.), New York: Routledge Press.
Skinner, K. (1980) 'Vietnamese in America: Diversity in Adaptation', *California Sociologist* 3(2): 103-24.
Soja, E., Morales, R. and Wolff, G. (1983) 'Urban Restructuring: An Analysis of Social and Spatial Change in Los Angeles', *Economic Geography* 58: 221-35.
Stein, B.N. (1979) 'Occupational Adjustment of Refugees: The Vietnamese in the United States', *International Migration Review* 13: 25-45.
Taylor, C. (1990) *Dangerous Society*, East Lansing, MI: Michigan State University Press.
Time (1975) 'A Cool and Wary Reception', May 12.
United States Commission on Civil Rights (1970) *Mexican Americans and the Administration of Justice in the Southwest*, Washington DC: US Government Printing Office.
United States Commission on Civil Rights (1971) *Report I: Ethnic Isolation of Mexican Americans in the Public Schools of the Southwest*, Washington D.C.: US Government Printing Office.
Vigil, J.D. (1993) 'Gangs, Social Control, and Ethnicity: Ways to redirect', in S.B. Heath and M.W. McLaughlin (eds), *Identity and Inner-City Youth:*

Beyond Ethnicity and Gender, McLaughlin, New York: Teachers' College Press.

Vigil, J.D. (1988) *Barrio Gangs: Street Life and Identity in Southern California,* Austin: University of Texas Press.

Vigil, J.D. and Yun, S.C. (1990) 'Vietnamese Youth Gangs in Southern California', in C.R. Huff (ed.), *Gangs in America,* Newbury Park, CA: Sage Publications.

Weikel, D. (1990) 'Crime and the Sound of Silence', *Los Angeles Times,* October 21.

Wilson, W.J. (1987) *The Truly Disadvantaged: The inner city, the underclass, and public policy,* Chicago: University of Chicago Press.

6 Navajo Nation Gang Formation and Intervention Initiatives

Marianne O. Nielsen, James W. Zion and
Julie A. Hailer

INTRODUCTION

The topic of Native American gangs is remarkable for its absence in the emerging gang literature[1] although it has recently caught the imagination of the mass media (e.g. Linthicum 1996; Mydans 1995; Dial 1995). This is not surprising, however, in light of the general neglect in the United States of Native American involvement in the criminal justice system. Because of the greater numbers of African-Americans and Hispanics in the criminal justice system, these latter have received more scholarly attention. Among the notable exceptions to this trend are recent works by Grobsmith (1994), Bachman (1992), Flowers (1988), Pommersheim (1995), French (1982, 1994), Beauvais (1992), LeResche (1993), Deloria and Lytle (1983), and Nielsen and Silverman (1996). A related issue is that most gang-related research and intervention initiatives focus on urban areas (Spergel, Curry and associates 1994), whereas Native American gangs are primarily rural, with some urban ties.

An understanding of the formation of gangs in the Navajo Nation must be placed within the historical and social context of the Navajo Nation itself and, given the limited research in this area, must draw heavily upon impressions and estimates arising from the criminal justice system. Both adult and juvenile Native Americans are greatly over-represented in the criminal justice system. The growing number of Native American young people adopting gang lifestyles has led to community and criminal justice system concerns that arrest and incarceration rates will be even higher for

Native Americans in the future.

The Navajo Nation is a domestic dependent nation[2] that is situated primarily in Arizona but overlaps with the states of Utah and New Mexico. It covers 25,000 square miles and has a population of over 146,000 (Arizona Republic 1993).[3] Over 51% of the Navajo population is aged nineteen or under (Navajo Nation Department of Law Enforcement 1995), a population profile common in many Native American communities. Approximately 32% of the general Native American population is under the age of 15 (Kramer 1995) and about 47% of Native Americans living in non-metropolitan areas are under the age of 20 (Snipp 1991). In the state of Arizona, where the largest part of the Navajo Nation is located, about 9% of the juvenile population (age 0 -17) is Native American, and in New Mexico, which includes a small section of the Navajo Nation as well as several other Indian reservations, 12% of the juvenile population is Native American (Snyder and Sickmund 1995: 3). New Mexico has the second largest Native American juvenile population in the U.S.; Arizona has the fifth. While there are significant numbers of Navajo Nation members living in predominantly non-Native urban communities surrounding the Navajo Nation, we will focus on the population living in the Navajo Nation, which is, in comparison, 'rural'.[4]

Like Indian Nations throughout the U.S.,[5] the people of the Navajo Nation are disadvantaged in terms of education, health, and other social factors. In general, more Native Americans aged sixteen to nineteen withdraw from high school without graduating (18%) compared to the general U.S. population (10%) (Snyder and Sickmund 1995:16); the life expectancy rate for Native Americans (71.1 years) is lower than for Whites (74.4 years) (Snipp 1991); and the unemployment rate for Native Americans (13.3%) is higher compared to the US population (6.5%) (Kramer 1995). About 28% of American Indians live below the poverty line compared to 12.5% of the total US population (Kramer 1995).

Keeping these figures in mind, it is not surprising that Native Americans are over-represented as offenders in the criminal justice system. Native Americans are 0.8% of the American population, but they comprise 2.2% of all arrests (Reddy 1993).[6] Native American incarceration rates are at or above the rates for both African-Americans and Hispanics in some states and for some offences. For example, in Alaska, Native Americans comprise 31% of the incarcerated population but only 15.6% of the state population; in South Dakota, they comprise 25% of the incarcerated population but 7.3% of the state population; and in Montana, they comprise 18% of the incarcerated population but only 6% of the general population (U.S. Department of Justice 1993: 613; Utter 1993: 18-19). According to Flowers (1988: 109), Native Americans have the highest rate for alcohol-associated offences (3209.3 per 100,000 as compared to 1307.2 for African-Americans, 2474.3 for Hispanics, and 1261.1 for Whites). These include offences such as driving under the influence and drunkenness. They are also arrested most often per capita for vagrancy (Flowers 1988: 109). Flowers (1988: 105) states that, over all, Native Americans have the second highest arrest rate after African-Americans. Silverman (1996) using more recent data, suggests that Flowers' rates may be too high. He indicates that Native American arrest rates are higher than those for Whites (but not much higher) and a great deal lower than those for African-Americans.

Native American juveniles follow a similar pattern of criminal justice involvement. As a rough indicator, American Indians or Alaskan Natives under the age of eighteen comprised 2.7% of arrests in rural counties across the U.S. As with their adult counterparts, they were arrested more often than any other group (except Whites) for alcohol-associated offences; in this case driving under the influence, liquor laws, and drunkenness. They were also arrested more often than any other group (except Whites) for 'suspicion', being 12.1% of all arrests compared to 5.6% for Blacks and 82.3% for Whites[7] (U.S. Department of Justice 1993: 447).[8] Native American juveniles comprised 1% of all residents in custody in juvenile institutional facilities, and 3% of those in juvenile open facilities (Snyder and Sickmund 1995: 166).[9]

Native American over-involvement in the criminal justice system, like that of indigenous peoples world-wide, is rooted in the marginalisation that results from colonialism.[10] Native Americans have endured a century and more of government policies that ranged from genocidal to assimilative to supportive of limited sovereignty. The assimilative policies in general were, and still are (to the extent that they can still be found in American Indian law), important contributors to the development of social and economic conditions conducive to the development of Native American gangs.

Assimilative polices were aimed at resocialising, that is, 'civilising' Indians to adopt European-based values and lifestyles. Strategies used included removing Native American children from their families at a young age and either giving them in adoption to White families or sending them to boarding schools where they were forbidden to speak their language, wear Native clothes and hair-styles, or engage in Native American spiritual practices. In these schools, they were taught to devalue their cultural heritage as 'primitive' and, in the process, gained few parenting skills. Other assimilative actions included the efforts of Christian and other religious missionaries; the exclusion of Native curricula from reservation schools; the prohibition and usurpation of Native leadership structures; the enforcement of a variety of laws forbidding Native social, ceremonial and economic activities on and off reservations; forced relocation to predominantly non-Native urban centres; and the suppression of social control practices such as mediation and peacemaking. These strategies, though actively resisted by Native American groups, made it difficult for Native communities to socialise and guide their young people. Factors such as disease epidemics, destruction of community economies, genocide, racism, and the past and present socioeconomic conditions mentioned earlier, only served to exacerbate the problem. In a similar vein, the thrust of federal efforts to create justice institutions for Indian Nations has been to impose European-based police and social work models (a form of institutional assimilation). These efforts have largely failed (Barsh and Henderson 1976). As a result of these processes social disorganisation occurred, as did increasing crime, suicide, and other forms of violence (Bachman 1992). Native American gangs are simply the most recent manifestation.

NAVAJO NATION YOUTH GANGS

Hailer (1996) found that while a few Native American gangs were known to tribal police forces as early as 1985, the number of gangs known grew rapidly between 1992 and 1993. Thirteen of 29 tribal police departments reported gangs on their reservations, including reservations in the states of Washington, Nevada, Arizona, Wyoming, Nebraska, Minnesota, Michigan, Oregon, Idaho, New Mexico, Montana, Oklahoma, and Wisconsin. The number of gangs on these reservations ranged from a low of one per reservation, to a high of 33, with the average number per reservation being three to four. While the vast majority of gang members are male, female gangs and female members of male gangs are now seen as an increasing police problem (Hailer 1996).

According to law enforcement personnel and others working with Native American gangs, these gangs have a number of characteristics.[11] The gangs can be considered 'transitional', that is, the groups are attempting to build gang traditions but have not been around long enough to have set them. They are not ethnocentric gangs in that many have aligned themselves with Hispanic gangs. When examining factors of Native American gang membership, the greatest concentration of gangs can be found within larger communities, pueblos, villages, or administrative and economic clusters of populations within Indian country.[12] Many of the gang members attend common schools, attend schools off the reservation which are experiencing gang problems, or are raised in gang neighbourhoods. Recruitment of Native American gang members begins as early as seven or eight years of age. Conditions in Native communities are not dissimilar to the conditions in inner-cities. There is a high level of substance abuse; a high poverty/low employment rate which forces residents to seek alternative means of getting money; and low self-esteem and loss of identity among residents. Native American youths feel that they are 'between cultures' due to their exposure to the 'traditionalists' on the reservations, and to the non-Native American youths at their off-reservation schools. Some Indian youths see the gang lifestyles as a solution to this identity crisis.

Native American youths in both urban and rural areas join gangs for many reasons. A number of explanations have been put forth by law enforcement agencies, including:

- to acquire a sense of belonging and a sense of attachment
- to escape intolerable conditions at home
- to attempt to escape poverty
- to obtain a perception of being rich and powerful (usually power through intimidation)
- to seek identity and recognition; 'to be somebody' which is something they cannot get at home, in school or through the community
- to experience adventure and excitement
- to get the protection of the gang and against other gangs.
- Other reasons: to ease boredom, get access to drugs and other substances, and/or as a test of bravery.[13]

According to those working with Native American gangs, some gangs are divided by age, and are named after streets, housing projects, geographic locations, etc. Initiates undergo 'rites of passage' such as 'jumping in' (where the initiate sees how much of a beating he/she can take from other gang members), and participating in a criminal act to prove their loyalty to the gang and to earn their 'placa' (moniker).

Native American gangs are also comprised of 'hardcores' who play the role of tutor/teacher to the new or younger gang members. They teach the novices how to talk, walk, act, not show fear, and commit criminal acts. They also teach them the unwritten codes of the gang: never cooperate with the police or persons in authority, take care of business yourself (that is, via the gang), never 'pull a rat' (snitch), and most important of all, let no insult (no matter how small) go unanswered. The adult gang members use the juvenile gang members to commit their crimes as they know that punishments for juveniles (if any) are not severe and 'nothing much is going to happen to them anyway'. Tribal police officers are seeing younger and younger gang members. They feel this is because the juveniles know of the general ineffectiveness of the juvenile system in handling them.

Native American gang members also tend to dress in a particular manner, resembling the clothing styles of Hispanic gangs. The clothing of choice currently on the reservations is some variation of khaki pants (Dickies), Pendleton shirts (brand-name woollen, plaid shirts), over-sized T-shirts and coloured tennis shoes. This clothing is intentionally worn too large as a means of intimidation, or to give the impression that the gang member is bigger than he/she really is, and/or to conceal weapons, and as a statement of style. The use of differing colours is a reflection of the difference in the individual gang's affiliations. Native American gangs will deliberately use certain colours to distinguish themselves from their rival gangs (e.g. blue, red, black, or green).

Native American gang members also use graffiti to mark their territory (law enforcement personnel view gang graffiti as the 'newspaper of the streets'). They also put graffiti, sometimes quite extensive, in their own bedrooms and on their school books. Hand signs are also used by gang members. Flashing a hand sign is a form of solidarity or of insult, or a way of displaying a cryptic message, usually the initials of the gang. Some gang members now have business cards which they distribute.

Native American gangs have come to carry guns, and have become involved in firebombings and drive-by shootings (sometimes of the wrong house). One of the reasons that gang members are coming to the reservations is because they know that they can hide there, due to the abundance of space and low numbers of law enforcement officers available to detect their activities. Drugs are becoming more prevalent on the reservations partly because Native American families are being paid to house these drugs. Again, the expansiveness/isolation of the reservation and low numbers of police contribute to the problem. The drug runners have discovered that many larger cities have greater suppression capabilities by law enforcement agencies while the reservations lack the resources for such efforts.

Native American juveniles are very open about their gang activities and membership. Law enforcement officials feel that this is the case because gang activity is still too new to them and they have yet to be involved with the juvenile system long enough to become hardened and uncommunicative with tribal police. The officers feel that this openness will cease as more Native American youth have increased contact with the system and with other hardcore gang members.

Gangs on the reservations appear to be following the same evolutionary course of well-established gangs, which have grown into forces to be dealt with by the community and the criminal justice system. An example of these progressive steps comes from a reservation in the Southwest United States.

In the mid-late 1980s, tribal police officers began to see graffiti on the walls of the buildings in the community, with a resulting crossing out of the graffiti (which equates to challenges by members of budding rival gangs). Officers then began to see the reservation youths wearing red and black gang colours and established styles of non-Native American gang clothing. There was a progression to fist fights between two groups with an increase in calls to the police of 'shots fired' (at this time the shots were generally fired into the air as a show of force). The next step in this progression was drive-by shootings. This reservation also experienced an influx of narcotics trafficking, and drug houses were established. Neighbourhood parks were taken over and were established as 'outdoors drugstores'. On this particular reservation, the Tribal Council, as a result of educational efforts by the tribal police officers, allowed the officers to seek to suppress gang activities, and even allowed the surrounding municipal police agency *carte blanche* to come onto the reservation. This helped to strengthen law enforcement efforts to fight the growing gang and drug problems. As a result (and while fortunate for this reservation, but not for the neighbouring reservation), the incidents of gang activities were displaced to the neighbouring reservation where law enforcement resources were even more limited. In addition, the Tribal Council at the neighbouring reservation continued to prohibit the surrounding municipal police agency from entering their reservation to assist.

A second example of escalation in gang activities is provided by a different Southwest reservation, the Salt River Pima of Arizona (see Table 1).

Table 6.1: Police Count of Number of Gangs and Frequency of Specific Offences, by Year, Salt River Pima of Arizona

Year	Number of Gangs	Offences	
		Drive-bys	Homicides
1991	1	1	0
1992	3	3	0
1993	5	8	0
1994	14	55	1
1995	22	69	2

Source: Presentation by Sgt Juan Arvizu, Salt River Pima Tribal Police, Scottsdale, Arizona at the Gangs on Indian Country seminar, 1996.[14]

Native American juvenile gangs are still in their infancy. If they follow the evolutionary pattern of other ethnic and racial gangs as they become more sophisticated, numerous changes are likely to occur. Law enforcement personnel believe that many Native American communities are still beset by denial, and are unwilling to acknowledge that their children are involved in gangs. Law enforcement officials predict that Native American communities will continue to see the growth of gangs and numbers of gang members. They also predict that: gangs will become more violent and more mobile; gang members will learn the benefits of being more structured; gang members will outnumber law enforcement resources; the number of gang members on probation and parole will increase; females will play a larger role within the gangs and more female gangs will form; gang members will become more confrontational; and, lastly, more sophisticated weapons will be used.

Many Native American communities control their own criminal justice system, including the juvenile justice system. Section 16 of the *Indian Reorganisation Act* of 1934[15] recognised the 'existing powers' of Indian nations, including the authority to establish criminal justice and juvenile systems. Earlier forms of justice, including informal methods of social control continue to exist in one form or another (sometimes underground) despite the operation of courts and police steeped in Bureau of Indian

Affairs (BIA) ideology and practices. These BIA-influenced structures were and still are limited in jurisdiction so that, for example, all serious felony offences (e.g. homicide, sexual assault) have to be dealt with by the Federal Bureau of Investigation (FBI) and tried in federal courts. Tribal Courts are also limited in jurisdiction so that they can impose sanctions limited to six months in custody or a fine of $500. (This was the original limitation imposed on Indian Nations in the *Indian Civil Rights Act* of 1968. More recently, the Act was amended to provide for a maximum one year term of incarceration and/or a $1000 fine.) The Navajo Nation's jurisdiction over Navajo young people is similarly limited so that young people committing serious offences must be charged by the United States and prosecuted in federal court. Many Navajo gang-related offences, because of their relatively less serious nature, however, fall within Navajo jurisdiction, as do all crime prevention activities.

INSTITUTIONAL EVIDENCE OF GANGS

The Navajo Nation courts and police have both statistical and anecdotal evidence of the existence of gang activity. For example, some judges report the appearance of youths in court dressed in gang colours, accompanied by similarly-dressed supporters. Navajo Nation police say that the 'Vicious Cobras' of Fort Defiance (an administrative community near the capital of Window Rock) were introduced by two brothers, half Navajo and half Puerto Rican, from Chicago. Another example is provided by the 'tagging' with gang graffiti of the partially completed new chapter house in Fort Defiance. Workers reported that youths jumped the high chain link fence topped with razor wire, to paint graffiti (perhaps to mark their disapproval of the building?). Also recently, youths broke into the old chapter house and trashed it. The Chief Justice of the Navajo Nation and the court solicitor recognise this kind of activity and describe it as a *nayee* or 'monster' (Yazzie and Zion 1995). The term relates to Navajo creation narratives and means 'that which gets in the way of a successful life'.

The Navajo Nation Department of Law Enforcement (1995) reported the existence of 28 gangs in thirteen Navajo Nation communities (figures based on detachment estimates). The largest and most recently formed gang is the 'Vicious Cobras' with an estimated 200 members.[16] The second largest is the Westside City in Canoncito with an estimated 50 to 75 members, and the third is the Dragons of Window Rock-Fort Defiance, with about 50 members. The rest range in size from five to 40, with the average number being eighteen. Since recruitment is on-going, these numbers are probably already out of date.

Several Navajo Nation communities with cluster housing sites are notorious for gang activities: a U.S. Department of Housing and Urban Development project in Fort Defiance, Rio Puerco estates, which is sometimes called 'Beirut' for its violence; the small community of Navajo (New Mexico), where youths burned down one Navajo Housing Authority rental house and attempted to burn another; and the Ojo Amarillo project of the Navajo Housing Authority, which was built to house workers of the Navajo Agricultural Products Industry (near Farmington, New Mexico).

The Navajo Nation police use the following (common tautological) definition to describe gangs: 'Criminal street gang means an ongoing formal or informal association of persons whose members or associates individually or collectively engage in the commission, attempted commission, facilitation or solicitation of any felony act or who has at least one individual who is a criminal street gang member'. The gangs are mainly comprised of young males between the ages of fifteen and 21. There are a few female members (no numbers exist on this). The groups have committed acts of vandalism against community business establishments and public property. Problems the schools are having with fights, vandalism, discipline and drugs have been related to gangs. Gang membership has also been associated with increased problems in the home as reported to the police.

A total of 621 offences or 58% of the total delinquency cases committed by youths under the age of eighteen, and handled by the Navajo Nation Family court from 1 April 1992 to 31 March 1993 (the latest figures available), are believed to be gang-related[17] (see Table 2).

The gangs' hangouts include the housing projects, business establishments that cater to youths, and abandoned buildings. The abandoned buildings are occasionally used for 'booze parties', as well. The Navajo Nation is a semi-arid area and one of the prominent geological features near most communities is a 'wash'. It is an eroded gully caused by the runoff from heavy thunderstorms. Youths gather in washes near schools and housing projects to drink and party. Many homes are crowded and there are few recreational areas, so youths will gather in washes or local convenience stores with video games to play and socialise.

Table 6.2: Gang-Related Offences Handled by the Navajo Family Court, 1 April 1992-31 March 1993

Type of Offence	Frequency	Percentage
Assault and battery	140	22.5
Property damage	104	16.7
Disorderly Conduct	98	15.8
Theft	88	14.2
Burglary	44	7.1
Resisting Arrest	36	5.8
Trespassing	33	5.3
Weapon charges	32	5.2
Threatening	30	4.8
Criminal Nuisance	16	2.6
Total	**621**	**100.0**

Source: Navajo Department of Law Enforcement (1995).

The Navajo Department of Law Enforcement (1995) believes the origins of gang activities can be found in poor parenting skills, the ineffectiveness of arrest and detention as social control strategies, the publicity given by the media to gangs, and the lack of regulations that deter young people from, for example, staying out late (curfew laws were only recently passed) and being exposed to undesirable influences (such as video stores renting and selling violent and sexually explicit materials to young people under eighteen). The lack of parenting is characterised as a lack of communication between parents and children, alcoholism in the home, and single parent families. These, the Law Enforcement Department suggest, lead to lack of self-identity and belonging in the children, which in turn lead to low self-esteem, attention-getting behaviour, running away, and violent and destructive behaviour. Arrest and detention are termed ineffective deterrents because they are seen by the young people as a means of getting free food and lodging, and respect. Detention also assists to establish contacts with other gangs and in the establishment of a gang network. The media, such as films and music videos, encourage gang behaviour by projecting an image that it is 'cool to be in a gang'.

Members of the Judicial Branch of the Navajo Nation have a slightly different perspective on the origins of gang activity, focusing more on traditional approaches and the possibilities they offer. They view the problem to be one of Navajo youths who have lost their cultural bearings and as a result feel that the traditional approach of *k'e* (which is difficult to translate but has respect as a major component) may be used to reach out to gang members. One theory being advanced is that youths are using 'war way thinking', *hashkeeji naat'aah*, as befits their age and status, but without being fully aware of the traditional conceptualisation. War way thinking is using certain forms of aggression for the benefit of the community. It utilises secret planning, action which is aggressive, prompt and vigorous, and strong individual leadership. Historical examples would be recapturing Navajos from slavery, or raiding other groups to obtain horses. The essential problem, then, is to divert the activities which are the product of war way thinking to more positive ends. In Navajo thought, words produce actions, so it is important to inculcate positive thinking; *hashkeeji naat'aah* is not evil of itself. Gangs are much like warrior groupings of Navajo history, and if they can be integrated into their communities for positive group activities, that may provide an approach which is distinct from other gang control or 'suppression' efforts in the United States.

Applying these perceptions of the origins of gang delinquency development and operation, a number of remedial approaches have been initiated by the Navajo Nation.

REMEDIAL APPROACHES

Following a series of sensational events, including the vandalism of an office in Fort Defiance and drive-by shootings in Shiprock, the Navajo Nation Council summoned Navajo Nation police leaders, the chief prosecutor and the Chief Justice of the Navajo Nation to a special Council meeting on gangs in October 1993. The representatives of all three organisations reported a lack of funding for suppression activities and a lack of federal support in addressing violent activity. The Navajo Nation Council gave a directive to justice officials to respond more efficiently. Their only option was, and still is, to develop strategic plans to deal with gangs, since there is little hope of increased federal support in a climate where the United States Government is withdrawing financial support from Indian Nations and still fails to commit effective federal law enforcement support to the problem.

Attempts to deal with, and prevent, gang activity have been launched by the Navajo Nation Council and by the two branches of the Navajo Nation criminal justice system. Informal meetings have involved the most visible 'players' in the justice system who deal with gangs: police officers in gang units, Navajo Nation behavioural health workers who meet with both gang members and community organisations, Navajo Housing Authority officials, judges and court staffers. In the absence of financial support, their strategy is to make more efficient use of limited resources and personnel. These groups have also initiated research efforts to discover more about the gangs.

In 1995, the Navajo Nation Council adopted a new curfew law, which includes parental criminal liability for curfew violations and civil liability for personal injury or property damage. The Judicial Branch and Navajo Housing Authority applied for and received federal grants aimed at reducing gang activity, closely coordinating activities with the Navajo Nation Police. The Navajo Housing Authority recognises the link between cluster housing and violent activity, and it has hired security guards for patrols, encouraged project organisations and entered into special agreements with the Navajo Nation Police to patrol projects with identified gang activity.

The Navajo Nation Police have officers in each district command area who devote their efforts to gang activity, and these officers recently met with federal officials to discuss better coordination of federal and Navajo Nation policing and prosecution activities.

Police efforts have been modelled upon gang approaches in non-Native cities, although with a strong emphasis on community involvement and commitment. One detachment, the Fort Defiance District (of the Fort Defiance Agency), formed a gang unit which covers Window Rock, Fort Defiance, Navajo (New Mexico) and other communities with identified gang problems. The district commander lives in a police command post in Navajo, New Mexico. He has assumed responsibility for the overall gang-related activities of the Navajo Nation Police. The Unit consists of three uniformed officers and has as its objectives the identification of high activity areas, the conduct of investigations, and the instilling of community awareness and support for deterrence initiatives. The Gang Unit is also involved with other law enforcement agencies such as the Arizona Department of Public Safety and the FBI in developing a gang task force, intelligence networking, and information sharing. They have also provided training to other tribal law enforcement agencies in dealing with gang activities. In addition to the activities of the Gang Unit, uniformed officers conduct gang awareness seminars and lectures in schools and to the public, and the department has increased patrols in high risk areas (Navajo Department of Law Enforcement 1995).

The police support a number of strategies for future implementation. These include incorporating existing programs or bringing in new programs to the gang initiative such as: summer programs and camps, youth boot camps, Scouts, Mountain Search and Rescue, and Big Brothers/Big Sisters; involving community groups such as schools, community leaders, churches and other interest groups in the initiative; committing juveniles to federal correctional facilities off the reservation for counselling and supervision; and implementing a 24 hour juvenile surveillance program, and a 24 hour hot-line to keep track of gang members and to handle complaints about gang activities. Serious obstacles to implementing some of these strategies are the lack of funding and personnel (Navajo Department of Law Enforcement 1995).

The Judicial Branch has also pledged to do what it can to deal with gangs in accordance with Navajo legal thinking. It has held meetings of the Navajo Nation Judicial Conference (i.e. an assembly of all judges) to discuss judicial options and has made gang initiatives a priority for grant applications. While recognising that serious criminal behaviour with resulting injury to persons and property should not be tolerated, the Judicial Branch points to the success of peacemaking for intervention in driving while intoxicated cases involving both adult and juvenile offenders. Based on the same principles, the Judicial Branch has developed a pilot program which addresses delinquency cases uses peacemaking. This pilot project, initiated in 1992, is called the Yaa da' ya ('upward moving way') and is based on the peacemaking principles used by the Navajo Nation Peacemaker Courts. The Peacemaker Courts, which were first established in 1982, are based on early Navajo dispute resolution practices. Navajo peacemaking follows a traditional Navajo concept of 'talking things out'. The term 'court' has been abandoned in favor of Navajo justice terms. They are *hozhooji naat'aah* or 'planning for good relations-peace-harmony', and *hozhooji naat'aanii*, which refers to the process of talking things out for a restoration of good relations, and to the traditional Navajo civil leader, a *naat'aanii*. The Yaa da' ya project is funded by the U.S. Justice Department's Office of Juvenile Justice and Delinquency Programs (OJJDP) on the premise that traditional methods of dealing with youthful offending are superior to mainstream juvenile delinquency efforts. Thus far the concept has proven to be successful.

The Yaa da' ya project is seen as a prototype for future mediation within and among gangs, and between gangs and the community. The project has shown that it is possible to deal with individual offenders by bringing in their family members, community leaders and support agencies to deal with the problems which underlie offending. The Navajos who conduct the project recognise that in historical times, young people were brought into warrior society in various ways, and that there is war way thinking. In Navajo thought, nothing is 'good' or 'evil' of itself. Navajo thought is empirical, so the focus is upon evil effects rather than evil of itself. The concept to be applied to gangs is to tap the positive aspects of youthful energy (which would otherwise create a classic warrior) to channel it to behaviours which are not evil. The thinking is that if gang leaders are approached with an attitude of respect and negotiation, that will be easier than attempting to use limited law enforcement and judicial resources for suppression. Good thoughts produce good actions, and right relationships are the product of *k'e* or respect. Thus, reaching out to gang leaders with an open hand and respect is a central component of the Judicial Branch strategy. Recognising that such is a difficult process, the courts are also prepared to use their adjudication authority where necessary to deal with offenders who cannot be reached through these traditional processes.

RESEARCH

Because gang activities are such a recent phenomenon in the Navajo Nation, research is desperately needed to describe the parameters of the situation and to develop effective prevention and intervention strategies. Several research projects are currently underway. The President's Office has asked a member of the Navajo Nation Police to collect data on gangs. As well, the Fort Defiance police commander oversees in-house initiatives in conjunction with other Navajo Nation justice officials, including police, prosecution, courts, probation officers and other interested agencies.

A San Jose State University-sponsored research project is investigating the extent of gang activity on American Indian reservations as well as the composition and characteristics of Native American gangs across the USA. The Navajo Nation is included as a case study. Data sources include surveys sent to law enforcement officials of the various tribal police departments and Bureau of Indian Affairs-Law Enforcement Services agencies across the country, and informal interviews with the Navajo Law

Enforcement officers. The project explores which reservations are experiencing gang activity, the reasons behind the occurrence of gang activity on these reservations, the degree of violence of these activities and finally, an examination of what the law enforcement agencies of jurisdiction are doing in response to gang formation and activities on their particular reservation (Hailer 1996).

A third project is under the directorship of the Navajo Nation Judicial Branch and is funded by the Office of Juvenile Justice and Delinquency Prevention. It is designed to document the youth gang situation including its history, influences on the gangs, and the activities of the gangs; and to document current data bases. Its second goal is to devise promising strategies for prevention and intervention that incorporate Navajo *nayéé* thinking. A *nayéé* is a monster; it is that which gets in the way of a successful life. In the case of the gangs, they are only *nayéé* if they lead their members down a wrong path that harms them and/or the community. The negative effects (such as drug use, violence and community disruption) must be stopped, not the gangs themselves. As a result, the research asks: how do you deal with a monster? The Navajo maxim is: 'Think carefully and proceed cautiously'. The first thing which must be done is to observe the monster from a place of relative safety. Watch it closely and carefully. Note its habits—how it moves and bears itself. Look for its weaknesses. Having observed the monster carefully, select weapons which can be used to kill or weaken it. The weapons selection process is both personal and objective. That is, while you can select weapons, you must also prepare yourself individually to gain strength. In ancient times, the Hero Twins, Monster-Slayer and Born-for-Water, went through intensive preparations and survived many challenges before they were worthy to receive weapons from their father, The Sun. (The Twins' mother, Changing Woman, later pointed out that she, as a single-parent family head, taught the Twins their strength and ability to survive hardship.) Then, when the warrior is prepared and the weapons are in hand, it is time for prompt, aggressive and vigorous action. Navajo thinking combines the values of careful planning in discussions with others and, in the war way, vigorous action against a foe. Once careful preparations are made based on careful observation, it is time to dedicate to all-out action against a monster.

These approaches respond to Navajo culture and current thought on Indian programming, both of which outline the need to incorporate the grassroots from the beginning of the project and to build on Indigenous knowledge. The project will interview gang members, criminal justice system members, school teachers and administrators, and community leaders. The end result of this project will not only be the preparation of material on the development and activities of the Navajo gangs, but will be a plan based in Navajo narratives and law to intervene in the development and operation of the gangs.

The Judicial Branch gang study team met in early June 1996 to finalise approaches to the study and coordination plan. The team identified stakeholders in the process (interested government agencies and community organisations), discussed how to bring more active 'players' into the process, and developed questionnaires for gang members and stakeholders. In addition, the team discussed issues posed by classic research studies of Navajo culture: anomie, loss of culture as a variable, parenting, family composition, population mobility, and the impact of assimilationist Bureau of Indian Affairs programs, including boarding school and relocation to urban areas for employment. Navajo Nation Police have pointed out that Navajo Housing Authority cluster projects, which select occupants based on income level and a 'first-come, first-served' eligibility standard divorced from actual residence arrangements, are high crime areas. Some of these issues are prompts for more detailed research into issues such as spatial relations, urbanisation, housing project composition and other variables.

Such issues may point to the reasons Navajo gangs are unique and why they are emerging in Indian Country across America; and may suggest approaches which address Native American conditions. The preliminary assessment of the team as it began the actual operation of the project is that while urban models of research may be utilised to construct a research model for the Navajo Nation, there are many distinct problems which must be addressed in the context of Navajo society. The literature on Navajos is large, and there is insufficient space to do a preliminary survey here, but it offers supplementary information to help frame strategies for a final report. Another unique aspect of the project is that its head, Philmer Bluehouse, is a former Navajo police officer with six years experience in peacemaking. He says that he has turned from the war way of the police, *hashkeeji naat'aah* to the peace way of Navajo peacemaking, *hozhooji naat'aah*. The Navajo Nation chief justice, Robert Yazzie, has a hands-on approach to the project, insisting that it use Navajo thinking in its approaches. The team is supplemented by a Navajo researcher who is a gang member. The Navajo component of the team will take the lead, assisted by four social scientists and a lawyer who is experienced with Navajo judicial planning. Thus, the effort is Navajo-driven in conjunction with individuals who are experienced with the literature on Navajos and field work.

This research approach attempts to integrate field research techniques, literature accounts of Navajo society, and the practical experience of Navajo actors who guide the process. Aside from the goals of the project to identify the nature and extent of gang activity in the Navajo Nation, it will be interesting to see the product of a joint effort of academics and justice system officials who will attempt to join the elements of Navajo tradition with justice planning processes.

CONCLUSION

Native American gangs are the newest entrants into the world of North American gang life and activities, and very little is as yet known about them. The existence of Native American gangs is not surprising given the impact of colonialism and resulting social conditions in many Native American communities. Native American young people have social and personal needs that are not being met by the existing social institutions in these communities. Instead, they have adopted an institution from outside Native communities—the youth gang—that fulfils some of these needs, though at the price of interpersonal violence and community disruption.

Native American gangs are still in the transitional stages, however, which means that the opportunities for intervention are still exceptionally timely. As well, Native American youth come from very different cultural traditions than those of other ethnic and racial juvenile gangs. Native American youth gangs are a distortion of *hashkeeji naat'aah* or war way thinking.

Navajos are currently reviving modes of thought which are based in Navajo creation narratives, ceremonies, songs and other expressions of their culture. Many such ways of thinking are 'survivals' or unconscious attitudes brought forward from traditional culture. Navajos are looking to their traditions for a more conscious articulation of their base values to address contemporary social problems, including gang activity. In this ideological framework, the gangs should not be eliminated, but rather should be redirected. Youth gangs are a source of status, honour, self-esteem and fellowship. These are positive aspects of group life that are still needed by the youth living on today's reservations. The gangs themselves are not 'evil'; though some of their effects are. The challenge is to turn the gangs into forces that act for the good of the community and are part of the community. This can be done by going into the past for traditional values and practices, and bringing them into the present, for the good of everyone.

This is, however, not the only route that is being followed. Both the Navajo Judicial Branch and the Navajo Nation police are quite aware that the gangs were imported from outside the Navajo Nation, and that some 'outside' strategies are also needed to deal with them. Respect, negotiation and community-level social control mechanisms such as peacemaking, are vital parts of Navajo community life, but not necessarily vital parts (yet) of Navajo gang member life because of the imported values that many gang members have adopted. Law enforcement and adjudication, gang units, and courts, are also needed. Navajo Nation criminal justice personnel are very aware that such a balanced criminal justice approach is necessary. Navajo Nation gangs are unique because of their Native American origins; but they also share characteristics with other ethnic and racial minority gangs. Intervention, therefore, must be equally diverse and innovative in order to be effective.[18]

REFERENCES

Arizona Republic (1993) 'The Two Worlds of the Navajo', 12 September 1993, P. NV-2.

Armstrong, Troy, Melton, Ada Pecos and Guilfoyle, Michael (1996) 'Native American Delinquency: An overview of prevalence, causes and correlates', in Marianne O. Nielsen and Robert A. Silverman (eds), *Native Americans, Crime and Criminal Justice*, Boulder: Westview Press.

Bachman, Ronet (1992) *Death and Violence on the Reservation*, New York: Auburn House.

Barsh, Russel Lawrence and Henderson, J. Youngblood (1976) 'Tribal Courts, the Model Code, and the Police Idea in American Indian Policy', in Lawrence Rosen (ed.), *American Indians and the Law*, New Brunswick: Transaction Books.

Beauvais, Fred (Guest Editor) (1992) *Journal of the National Center of American Indian and Alaska Native Mental Health Research—Indian Adolescent Drug and Alcohol Use: Recent Patterns and Consequences*, 5(1).

Cohen, Albert (1990) 'Introduction' in C. Ronald Huff (ed.) *Gangs in America*, Newbury Park: Sage.

Cohen, Felix S. (1982) *Handbook of Federal Indian Law*, Charlottesville: Michie Bobbs-Merrill.

Covey, Herbert C., Menard, Scott and Franzese, Robert J. (1992) *Juvenile Gangs*, Springfield, Ill.: Charles C. Thomas.

Cummings, Scott and Monti, Daniel J. (1993) *Gangs—The Origins and Impact of Contemporary Youth Gangs in the United States*, Albany, NY: SUNY Press.

Deloria Jr, Vine and Lytle, Clifford M. (1983) *American Indians, American Justice*, Austin: University of Texas Press.

Dial, Marla (1995) 'Gang Activity Reported on Navajo Lands', *San Francisco Chronicle*, April 25.

Flowers, Ronald B. (1988) *Minorities and Criminality*, New York: Praeger.

French, Laurence A. (1994) *The Winds of Injustice: American Indians and the U.S. government*, New York: Garland.

French, Laurence A. (1982) *Indians and Criminal Justice*, Totowa, NJ: Allanheld, Osmun.

Grobsmith, Elizabeth S. (1994) *Indians in Prison: Incarcerated Native Americans in Nebraska*, Lincoln: University of Nebraska Press.

Hagan, William T. (1993) *American Indians,* Chicago: University of Chicago Press, (3rd edition).

Hailer, Julie (1996) 'Taking the Black Road: Gangs in Native America', paper presented at the Academy of Criminal Justice Sciences Annual Meeting, Las Vegas, Nevada, March, 1996.

Hirschfelder, Arlene and de Montano, Martha K. (1993) *The Native American Almanac: A Portrait of Native America Today*, New York: Prentice-Hall.

Huff, C. Ronald (1993) 'Gangs in the United States', in Arnold P. Goldstein and C. Ronald Huff (eds), *The Gang Intervention Handbook,* Champaign, Ill.: Research Press.

Jaimes, M. Annette (ed.) (1992) *The State of Native America: Genocide, colonisation, and resistance*, Boston: South End Press.

Jennings, Francis (1993) *The Founders of America: From the earliest migration to the present*, New York: W.W. Norton and Co.

Knox, George W. (1993) *An Introduction to Gangs*, Buchanan, ML: Vande Vere Publishing.

Kramer, Joyce M. (1995) 'Social Welfare of the Indigenous Peoples within the United States of America', in John Dixon and Robert P. Scheurell (eds), *Social Welfare with Indigenous Peoples*, London: Routledge.

LeResche, Diane (Guest Editor) (1993) *Mediation Quarterly—Special Issue: Native American Perspectives on Peacemaking*, 10(4).

Linthicum, Leslie (1996) 'Surge of Violence on the Reservation', *Albuquerque Journal*, Sunday, February 4: A1, A10.

Miller, J.R. (1989) *Skyscrapers Hide the Heavens,* Toronto: University of Toronto Press (revised edn.).

Mydans, Seth (1995) 'Gangs Reach a New Frontier: Reservations', *The New York Times*, Saturday, March 18: 2, 9.

Navajo Nation Department of Law Enforcement (1995) 'Gang activities on the Navajo Nation', March 27, Internal document.

Nielsen, Marianne O. and Silverman, Robert A. (1996) *Native Americans, Crime and Justice*, Boulder: Westview Press.

Pommersheim, Frank (1995) *Braid of Feathers: American Indian law and contemporary tribal life*, Berkeley: University of California Press.

Reddy, Marlita A. (ed.) (1993) *Statistical Record of Native North Americans,* Detroit: Gale Research.

Silverman, Robert A. (1996) 'Patterns of Native American Crime', in Marianne O. Nielsen and Robert A. Silverman (eds), *Native Americans, Crime and Justice*, Boulder: Westview Press.

Snipp, C. Matthew (1991) *American Indians: The First of This Land*, New York: Russell Sage.

Snyder, Howard N. and Sickmund, Melissa (1995) *Juvenile Offenders and Victims: A National Report*, Washington: Office of Juvenile Justice and Delinquency Prevention (OJJDP).

Spergel, Irving A. (1995) *The Youth Gang Problem: A community approach*, New York: Oxford University Press.

Spergel, Irving A., Curry, David and associates (1994) *Gang Suppression and Intervention: Problem and response*, Research Summary, Washington: Office of Juvenile Justice and Delinquency Prevention (OJJDP).

Trigger, Bruce G. (1985) *Natives and Newcomers: Canada's 'Heroic Age' reconsidered*, Montreal: McGill-Queen's University Press.

U.S. Department of Justice (1993) *Sourcebook of Criminal Justice Statistics, 1992*, Washington: U.S. Government Printing Office.

Utter, J. (1993) *American Indians: Answers to today's questions*, Lake Ann: National Woodlands Publishing.

Yazzie, Robert and Zion, James W. (1995) '"Slay the Monsters"': Peacemaker Court and violence control plans for the Navajo Nation', in Kayleen M. Hazlehurst (ed.), *Popular Justice and Community Regeneration*, Westport: Praeger.

NOTES

1. A search of the literature found no research on Native American gangs, although their existence was mentioned in a few places. Spergel (1995: 59-60) for example, reports: 'American Indian gangs have been active in Minneapolis and in several southwestern states'.

2. 'Domestic dependent nation' is a legal term that means Indian nations have the right, within specific limits set by American federal law, to control their own internal affairs including the administration of justice. The Navajo Nation is a 'nation' by virtue of such recognition in its 1868 Treaty with the United States. The right of Indian Nations to establish justice institutions is part of retained Indian Nation sovereignty (Cohen 1982:334).

3. According to the 1990 Census, about 1,960,000 people or 0.8% of the total U.S. population identified themselves as 'American Indian, Eskimo or Aleut' (Kramer 1995).

4. Snipp (1989: 315) estimates that slightly more than 50% of Native Americans live outside metropolitan areas, which makes them one of the least-urbanised groups in the United States.

5. Native Americans are not 'a people', although pan-Indian movements exist. Native Americans vary widely in terms of their cultures, languages, economies, histories, and community needs and priorities. There are 515 tribal groups in the United States, including 197 Alaskan Native villages (Hirschfelder and de Montano 1993). The term 'Native American' is an inclusive term that includes American Indians, Native Hawaiians, Alaskan Natives (a term which also embraces Alaskan Inuit, Aleuts, and Indians) and individuals of mixed descent who identify with their Native American heritage. Native American communities and individuals also differ widely in terms of their acculturation to dominant U.S. values and lifestyles.

6. See Silverman (1996) for a discussion of the reasons that arrest is not a good indicator of Native American involvement with the criminal justice system. Serious problems in census reporting of Native Americans is the main issue. Incarceration rates are more accurate, but are also farther removed from the criminal event.

7. Figures for Asians and Pacific Islanders were not given in this category by the Department of Justice.

8. Comprehensive incarceration statistics for Native American juveniles are not reported by the U.S. Department of Justice. While separate statistics are available for African-American, Hispanic and White juveniles, Native Americans juveniles are usually lumped into the 'other' category.

9. For a recent and comprehensive overview of Native American juvenile involvement in the criminal justice system see Armstong et al. (1996). This is an edited version of a report prepared for the federal Office of Juvenile Justice and Delinquency Prevention in 1992.

10. The following overview of the processes and impacts of colonialism is, of necessity, short and generalised. For more comprehensive descriptions of the historical relations between Native Americans and colonial forces, see Hagan (1993), Jennings (1993), Jaimes (1992), Miller (1989), and Trigger (1985).

11. The following section is based primarily on information gathered from handouts and presentations at a training seminar on 'Gangs On Indian Country' held in Las Vegas, 23-25 January 1996 which was attended by one of the authors (Hailer).

12. 'Indian country' is both a legal and popular term to denote Indian areas, including 'reservations' of homelands by treaty, statute or presidential executive order; individual Indian land allotments; and 'dependent Indian communities', or areas which are predominantly Indian in population.

13. These explanations are very similar to the explanations given in scholarly studies as to why members of other minority groups become involved in gang activities (Cummings and Monti 1993; Knox 1993; Covey et al. 1992; Cohen 1990).

14. It is important to note that Scottsdale is part of the metropolitan area of Phoenix, Arizona, a very large urban community with many gangs and gang problems.

15. This act was introduced as a response to the 1928 Merriam Report. This report was one of the first 'modern' government documents describing the social conditions of Indian peoples. It identified Indian self-government as a means of dealing with their political powerlessness.

16. Window Rock, the Navajo Nation capital, is a small community with small 'bedroom suburbs' of Tse Bonito, St Michaels, and Fort Defiance nearby. Most of the 'Vicious Cobras' appear to live in Fort Defiance, which is seven miles north of Window Rock.

17. It should be noted that there is a great deal of debate in the literature about the identification of so-called 'gang-related' offences and 'personal' offences committed by a gang member, as well as about what in general comprises a 'gang' (see, for example, Spergel 1995:21; Huff 1993:4-7).

18. The authors wish to express their gratitude to Jeff Ferrell, Dan Wall and Harmon Mason for their valuable comments on earlier drafts of this chapter.

7 Street Gangs and Criminal Business Organisations: A Canadian Perspective

Robert M. Gordon

INTRODUCTION

It is only in the past few years that Canadian social scientists have taken a significant interest in the issue of criminal gangs, groups, and organisations. As students of the field continually discover, there is very little research addressing the topic of gangs from a Canadian perspective, despite emerging evidence that street gangs,[1] criminal business organisations,[2] and other similar groupings have been active in Canadian cities since well before the Second World War (Rogers 1945; Dubro 1992; Young 1993).

The apparent lack of interest on the part of Canadian social scientists is, to some extent, a product of Canada's proximity to the American criminological machine. Until a few years ago, American research tended to dominate Canadian academic and public discussions of gangs as well as both federal and provincial policy-making and the development of programs in the area. There was little incentive to move beyond the importation of explanations, policies and programs, in part because the most visible and potentially troublesome form of gang—the street gang—tended to be an episodic, and therefore less critical, social phenomenon. As Young (1993) has pointed out, for example, street gang activity in Vancouver since 1945 has tended to follow a wave-like pattern and it is only the most recent wave (covering the period from 1985 to approximately 1994) that has stimulated a serious interest in the development of indigenous solutions.

A kindling of interest in the gang phenomenon may also be a function of the appearance of a more confident and better equipped Canadian criminology. Some of the responsibility for the lack of indigenous research rests at the door of past Canadian social scientists (especially criminologists) who, understandably, tended to focus on more easily researched topics. Unless a researcher has contacts within bona fide gangs or criminal groups, gang research requires special access privileges, for example, to government file data, incarcerated gang members, or gang members who are on probation and known, primarily, to corrections systems. Such privileges are usually only granted when a social phenomenon becomes a significant social problem requiring a rapid solution. The emergence of street gangs as a social problem in Canadian cities (or, at least, their *definition* as a social problem), accounts for both the research that has been conducted in the last three years (Fasilio and Leckie 1993; Mathews 1993; Gordon 1993, 1995; Gordon and Nelson 1996), and the research projects that are in progress in, for example, Manitoba and British Columbia.[3] Some of this recent work will be examined in the discussion that follows.

RECENT CANADIAN GANG RESEARCH

The choice of the year 1993 for the release of several pieces of Canadian gang research was purely coincidental. Three reports, each written for either the federal or the provincial levels of government (Fasilio and Leckie 1993; Gordon 1993; Mathews 1993), and an unpublished M.A. thesis (Young 1993) examined different aspects of the gang phenomenon and provided not only the answers to some pressing policy-related questions (e.g., to what extent are Canadian gangs dominated by the members of visible ethnic minorities?) but also the building blocks for more comprehensive research that is currently in progress.

A study by Fasilio and Leckie (1993) of the Canadian media's coverage of gangs and gang activity undertaken for the federal Solicitor-General made an extremely valuable contribution to what was then an emerging debate over the role of the news media in amplifying the street gang 'problem' and in creating a moral panic. The authors analysed the media's focus on, and characterisation of, gangs and attempted to determine if variations existed within and between the different regions of Canada (e.g., whether the coverage in Atlantic Canada was different from that in British Columbia). To this end, they undertook a content analysis of major national news magazines (e.g., *MacLean's*) and the major daily newspapers published in selected urban centres over a four month period (July -

October 1992). These centres included Winnipeg, Edmonton, Vancouver, Ottawa, Toronto, and Montreal—the cities generating the largest number of stories. The sample was, therefore, not representative of the full range of media (television and radio were excluded) and did not capture every Canadian urban centre. The selection process yielded a total of 120 gang-related news stories for analysis, out of a universe of approximated 6,000 stories (two percent of all stories).

Perhaps predictably, Fasilio and Leckie found that the media characterised gangs and gang activity as widespread, a significant threat to society, and a relatively new phenomenon. Subsequent research (discussed below) and more recent events demonstrate that this characterisation was wrong in most respects. Gangs were depicted as a subject of 'growing social concern' and the product of an ailing society, themes that, according to Young (1993), have been trumpeted by Canadian newspapers during every wave of urban street gang activity since at least 1945. The analysts noted the absence of any historical reference or perspective in the stories, and a focus that accentuated polarisation along ethnic lines: 'asian gangs' were a particular menace. One consequence, the authors argued, was an unjustified increase in the fear of gangs and gang activity and a similarly unwarranted concern over the extent to which immigrants (especially those who were members of visible ethnic minorities) were responsible for gang-related crimes. Journalists depended heavily on law enforcement officials for commentaries on gang violence, the locations of gang crime, and the extent to which gangs constituted a threat to society. The reasons why gangs emerged were largely ignored apart from some vague references to the consequences of immigration policies and practices. Generally, in the authors' view, the media were unintentionally contributing to the creation of a moral panic.

Some regional variations in coverage were noted. The volume of gang-related news in western Canada, and particularly the prairie provinces, was probably over-represented (22.5 percent of stories), while Atlantic Canada was under-represented. Nevertheless, the way in which gangs were characterised was fairly consistent across all regions with one exception. In Quebec, news stories tended to be less concerned with 'asian gangs' in favour of a more diverse coverage, one that focused on the problem of 'youth gangs', the Mafia, and Jamaican gangs. This, the authors argued, probably reflected the ethnic composition of Quebec's population and, therefore, both the membership of gangs and the perceptions of such membership. For example, according to the 1991 census, only 1.2 percent of Montreal's population was of Chinese ethnic origin compared with nearly eight percent in Toronto and over 16 percent in Vancouver.

To some extent, Gordon's research on gang members in British Columbia correctional centres provided a counterfoil to the news media's pre-occupation with 'asian gangs' and 'youth gangs' (Gordon 1993). Interestingly, the research—which was conducted for the provincial Attorney-General as part of a census of all prisoners in correctional centres in the province (see Gordon and Nelson 1993)—attracted absolutely no media interest, despite the public release of the report and the currency of the topic.

The research was only intended to be a preliminary study. The correctional centre files of 41 male inmates (adult and youth) who were identified as active gang members by the police and by corrections personnel (e.g., probation officers) were examined, in depth, by a team of researchers. No female gang members were identified. The inmates were also asked to participate in an interview and, somewhat surprisingly, 34 agreed to take part in this component of the research (10 adults and 24 young offenders). The goal was to obtain information about the organisation, activities and membership of gangs in the province (especially in the Greater Vancouver area), and the reasons why young people in particular became involved with gangs. A secondary objective was to design and test some research definitions and instruments for use in a later study.

The mean age of the gang members in the research sample was 19 years and over 92 percent of the subjects were 25 years of age or younger. The majority of incarcerated gang members were young adult males, rather than young offenders (i.e., young people between the ages of 12 and 17 who commit crimes), and this finding was of importance in combating both the false perceptions created by the news media's use of the term 'young gangs' and the acrimonious criticism of the federal *Young Offenders Act*, which, at the time, was emanating from both victims' rights groups and their conservative political allies who were clamouring for harsher punishments for young offenders. Also of importance was the finding that, with respect to issues of ethnicity and immigration, the largest single group of incarcerated gang members were those of Caucasian ethnic origin who were born in Canada (40 percent). The next largest group were of Asian ethnic origin (34 percent), the majority having been born in Canada. There were very few gang members of East Indian, Aboriginal, and Hispanic origin, and only one black gang member in the sample. Overall, 32 percent of incarcerated gang members were not born in Canada, a proportion considerably higher than the immigrant inmate population as a whole—11 percent on the day of the corrections census. The proportion was also higher than the proportion of immigrants in the provincial population and, therefore, the expected percentage (22 percent). This finding lent support to an hypothesised relationship between immigration and gang membership although, as Gordon and Nelson (1996) have pointed out, any apparent relationship must be viewed with extreme caution because the actual numbers of gang members in the study who were not born in Canada (14) is extremely small especially when compared with the size of the immigrant population in the province as a whole (approximately 750,000 people).

The gang members who were interviewed were surprisingly forthcoming with confirmed information about their lives and the reasons why they became involved in gangs. The subjects felt that they were not coerced or otherwise pressured into joining gangs and the process of becoming involved happened gradually, rather than abruptly. There was a slow drift towards involvement which was often initiated by a close relative or a friend who was already a member of a gang or who knew a gang member. A prospective member would spend time on the periphery of the group but might eventually be drawn in, undergo an initiation ceremony, and then become a full member. As Gordon (1993, 1995) points out, the process was neither strange nor surprising and was akin to the process that is followed when a young person joins a legitimate 'gang' such as the boy scouts, a hockey or baseball team, or a marching band.

A key to understanding involvement in gangs, especially a young person's involvement, is the availability of choices: if an individual has no access to a 'legitimate' gang, or is not encouraged to join such a mainstream group, an 'illegitimate' gang may be selected instead (Cloward and Ohlin 1960). With this hypothesis in mind, the researchers analysed, in particular, the file data of all 41 subjects. Nearly one half of the subjects had backgrounds of both family and school problems including, drug, alcohol and physical abuse in the family coupled with school records characterised by truancy, fighting, suspensions and expulsions. The picture was one of troubled individuals from troubled backgrounds in trouble, and when these problems were related to the professed reasons why the subjects became involved with gangs (as gleaned from the interview data) it became clear that the choice of an illegitimate, rather than legitimate, group was a function of the lack of alternatives. The subjects reported a desire to find a secure and nurturing surrogate family. For over one third of the subjects the gang was a haven in an otherwise heartless world.

The reasons why the rest of the sample (just under two thirds of the subjects) became involved with gangs were more difficult to explain. Approximately one third appeared to have joined a gang, not because of severe problems at home (although the files of some subjects indicated family and school problems), but primarily in order to continue associations with friends, to make money, and for the relief of boredom: considerations that were not likely to be satisfied through membership of a legitimate 'gang'. The reasons why the remaining gang members (eight subjects) became involved with gangs could not be determined from the information available to the researchers. Contrary to the researchers' expectations, over 75 percent of subjects stated that there were no barriers to leaving a gang. Gang members remained with their gangs, not out of fear of reprisal, but because they found membership to be rewarding. They were with their friends—their 'family'—and leaving the gang would involve a major life adjustment.

Research conducted in Toronto by Mathews (1993), for the federal Solicitor-General, also involved interviews with gang members: specifically, youth gang members. The study—which was intended to be a preliminary examination of the youth gang issue—was undertaken to provide young people with an opportunity to add their voices to the emerging discourse on gangs and groups, to broaden the discussion of the issues, and to have an impact on both problem definition and the development of an effective, comprehensive response.

Youths who were known to be involved in gang activity were approached by experienced social services and law enforcement personnel and asked to participate in the study. Twelve youths ranging in age from 14 to 21 years agreed and were interviewed. Additional interviews were conducted with police officers, school officials and social workers, as well as the parents of gang members and some victims of gang activity. The number of research subjects was extremely small, especially given the size of the population of the Toronto Metropolitan Area, and this weakness undermines the study's usefulness.

Some of the results were, nevertheless, helpful. As Mathews points out, the term 'gang' can be a misleading way of describing different kinds of gatherings of young people. The term 'gang/group' is preferred as a better way of capturing the phenomenon; and analysts and policy-makers should be thinking in terms of a continuum ranging from groups of friends who spend time together and occasionally get into trouble to more serious, organised criminal groups or gangs. This problem of definition was also recognised by Gordon (1993) who used the results of the British Columbia study to develop a typology and a set of definitions that have been used subsequently in major studies of gangs in Winnipeg and Vancouver. These definitions are set out elsewhere in this chapter.

Mathews also found that a reliance on official discourse and documented rates of violence did not capture the nature of the fear experienced by victims, or the climate of unrest and violence in schools. Research participants stated that youth gang and youth group violence was significantly under-reported and that physically smaller, weaker, younger, isolated and friendless youth were most often the victims of gang/group violence and extortion. The research suggested that the institutional practices of schools contributed to the perpetuation of such violence. Some teachers and administrators vying for promotion were unwilling to admit to the presence of gangs in their schools. Large class sizes, a lack of teaching resources, and poor facility management and design each contributed to the increasing violence of gangs/groups in Toronto's schools.

The fourth study to be released in 1993 was conducted by a graduate student in the School of Criminology at Simon Fraser University; namely, Young's (1993) work on the history of (youth) gangs in Vancouver. The study filled a significant gap in Canadian gang research by providing the first socio-historical analysis of youth gang activity in a large Canadian city, in this case, Vancouver from 1900 to 1985.

The primary sources of data were the main provincial newspapers and this constituted both a strength and a weakness of the research. On the one hand, the research had to proceed with the assumption that the patterns of reporting reflected more than just the patterns of news media interest: that they accurately reflected the gang phenomenon. Since there is evidence of media amplification (see, Fasilio and Leckie 1993), this assumption may be wrong. On the other hand, there were no other accessible sources (e.g., government archival materials) with the same amount of rich information stretching back to the turn of the century.

Young manually and electronically scrutinised each daily edition of a major newspaper—*The Province*—to locate, read and analyse any and all gang-related articles during the 85 year period and, when articles were found, these were cross-checked against stories in other newspapers. These data indicated that Vancouver had experienced waves of youth gang activity that clustered into three distinct periods: the period of the 'corner lounger gangs', which apparently lasted from 1924 to 1931; the zoot suit and hoodlum gang period from 1944 to 1959; and the period of the 'park gangs' from 1969 to 1975—a time when youth gangs were named after the city parks where they gathered. The most recent wave of street gang activity began in 1985; and although the wave appears, at the time of writing, to be virtually spent it was in full swing at the time Young conducted his research.

Having identified the periods of gang activity, Young then attempted to explain the wave-like pattern during the post 1945 period by focusing on two independent variables: inward migration and unemployment rates. A preliminary analysis of these variables indicated a slight positive relationship between inward migration rates and reported fluctuations in gang activity. Unemployment rates and fluctuations in gang activity were inversely related but Young cautions against the use of these results for purposes other than the construction of hypotheses for future research.

'LOS DIABLOS': A CANADIAN STREET GANG

A reasonable understanding of gangs and gang activity in Canada can be gleaned from an account of the rise and fall of the quintessential Vancouver street gang of the 1980s and 1990s: 'Los Diablos'.[4] Although there may be some variation in gang activity and gang membership in the cities currently most affected by the gang phenomenon—Vancouver, Winnipeg, and Toronto—an example drawn from Vancouver research is instructive.

'Los Diablos' and other Vancouver street gangs associated with the most recent period of gang activity are in some ways similar to both the 'hoodlum gangs' of the 1950s (e.g., the 'Alma Dukes' and the 'Vic Gang') and the 'park gangs' of the early 1970s (e.g., the 'Riley Park Gang' and the 'Clark Park Gang') (Young, 1993). 'Los Diablos' came from and generally concentrated its activities within a particular area, eventually adopted 'colours' and rituals, and seemed to be as interested in conflict with rival gangs as it was in profitable criminal activity. Like both its predecessors and other, more recently active, gangs 'Los Diablos' was comprised primarily of older adolescent and young adult males. Although young women have been occasionally involved with Vancouver street gangs—usually as associates or 'employees'—the so-called 'girl-gangs' that purportedly exist in other Canadian cities have not appeared in Vancouver.[5]

'Los Diablos' was formed in the mid-1980s (probably in 1986) in the Killarney area of south east Vancouver. The exact origins of the gang are unclear but it seems to have started with a small group of youths who called themselves 'Towa'. The reasons for the creation of 'Towa' are unknown but 1985/86 was a year when other street gangs and 'wannabe' groups[6] began to appear in larger numbers in the Greater Vancouver area (Girrard 1993; Gordon 1995). It was a year that marked the beginning of the most recent wave of street gang activity in the city (Young 1993).

The Killarney area is (and was) a quiet, middle class, residential neighbourhood consisting of modest single family homes. It is a far cry from the kind of disintegrating and socially disorganised inner city neighbourhoods commonly associated with street gang activity in North America. It is, however, an area in transition as immigrants, particularly from non-European countries, begin to make their homes there. Both 'Towa' and, later, 'Los Diablos' reflected the emerging ethnic composition of the neighbourhood and both gangs were comprised of young people of East Indian, European, Fijian, African, Chinese and Iranian descent.

'Towa' members concentrated primarily on property crime (thefts and break and enters), assaults, and some extortion but their activities took a more serious turn in 1986 when the gang became allied with a criminal business organisation known as 'Lotus'. This alliance coincided with a change in the demographic composition of 'Towa'; principally, an infusion of individuals of Hispanic ethnic origin following the arrival in Vancouver of refugees from the political turmoil in Central America. Many of these new members had lived previously in Los Angeles and had been connected with street gangs in that city. It was these new members, with their recently acquired skills and knowledge of American street gangs, who began to alter the face of 'Towa'. The name of the gang was changed, to 'Los Diablos' ('The Devils'). The gang's activities became more organised and sophisticated and expanded beyond the immediate confines of the Killarney neighbourhood to the rest of south-east Vancouver.

By 1987, the gang enjoyed considerable recognition and notoriety, and a high status amongst many adolescents. The gang was probably at its peak at this time, with an active membership of between 60 and 75 young adult and adolescent males. It was also around this time that the gang came into conflict with a rival street gang known as 'Gum Wah', which was closely associated with a criminal business organisation, the 'Red Eagles'. There then ensued a period of violent exchange between 'Los Diablos' and the 'Red Eagles'/'Gum Wah' which included the occasional execution-style murder, fire-bombings, stabbings and, in the summer of 1988, a gun battle that became known as the Woodland Bridge shooting and which apparently established the gang as a force to be reckoned with.

Although 'Los Diablos' was a group that had to be taken seriously there was an amateurish element to its activities. This is reflected in a police account of the Woodland Bridge shooting in which the demise of one gang member was reported, with barely concealed mirth. Despite a significant exchange of gunfire only three individuals were injured, two with minor wounds. The third casualty, and the source of much amusement, was a gang member who accidentally shot himself in the testicles while drawing a handgun from the waistband of his pants.

It was in the wake of the Woodland Bridge incident that 'Los Diablos' began to copy the more obvious mannerisms of American street gangs, especially those in the Los Angeles area. Members began to wear colours (red, white and black clothing), to use hand signals and street (territory) markings, and to initiate new members by requiring one of two possibilities: a short beating at the hands of other gang members (taking five, or the beats); or the commission of specific crimes to prove their worth. Similar practices were used by other Vancouver street gangs at the time (Gordon 1993). The reasons for these developments are unclear but the changes came in the wake of the release of the movie 'Colours'. Gang members were heard copying the dialogue and the terms used in the film (especially the term 'homes' or 'homeboy') and territorial graffiti (notably wall markings) began to proliferate throughout the Vancouver area.

The 'gang war' between 'Los Diablos' and 'Gum Wah' continued throughout 1987 and 1988, with running street fights, battles in shopping malls, and the occasional mobile gun battle. Some 'Los Diablos' members also began to take a serious interest in cocaine trafficking and operated as 'cells' led by particular individuals and known by that person's last name (e.g., 'Doe's cell'). Indeed, by this time, 'Los Diablos' was best described as an amalgam of groups or cells that operated in alliance with each other and that could be mustered quickly by using pagers or cellular telephones. Some cells also formed into allied street gangs, concentrated in particular suburban areas: e.g., 'Los Panchos' (in the suburb of Burnaby); the 'Sparrows' (in the suburb of Coquitlam); and 'Bario Latinos' (in the Kingsway-Joyce area of Vancouver).

A further complication emerged in the fall of 1988 when a dormant street gang more commonly associated with Vancouver gang activity in the 1970s, re-emerged. The 'East Vancouver Saints' began to engage 'Los Diablos', which promptly responded, and by the Spring of 1989 'Los Diablos' and its allies (including a gang known as 'Mara Latinos') were involved in conflicts with both 'Gum Wah' and the 'East Vancouver Saints' and its allies (two additional street gangs—'Patook' and 'Viet Ching'). These conflicts involved drive-by shootings, molotov cocktail bombings of the homes of rival gang members, and both gang fights and beatings of individual gang members.

By the end of June 1990, the demographic profile of 'Los Diablos' changed again, from a predominantly Hispanic group, to a predominantly Indo-Canadian (East Indian) group. It was estimated that 80% of the gang's members were of Fijian East Indian origin and the gang was led by a high profile Fijian individual. There was evidence of the friendly movement of gang members from one gang to another, one goal being to form several ethnically homogeneous gangs—an enterprise that ultimately failed. By the August of that year several senior members of 'Los Diablos' had been released from prison and attempted to wrest control of the gang away from the newer Fijian membership. What followed—a major, internal fight involving the competing factions—was a defining moment for the gang. It signalled the beginning of the gang's disintegration as a significant and cohesive force. There is evidence that attempts were made by some gang members to mitigate the effects of the internal conflicts and rivalry but, by the summer of 1992, the gang was in steep decline. The *coup de grace* came with the arrest of the gang's high profile leader and his conviction for murder, followed by the murder of some remaining key members of the gang who were involved in drug trafficking.

THE LESSONS OF 'LOS DIABLOS'

What can be learned about Canadian street gangs from the account of 'Los Diablos'? First, several key characteristics are evident, each of which point to the reasons such gangs form and are maintained but then eventually fade away. The periodic appearance, disappearance, and reappearance of street gangs in cities such as Vancouver is an interesting feature of Canadian street gang activity but the reasons for these cycles remain unclear. Second, the account casts light on the relationships among street gangs and other groups, notably criminal business organisations. It also helps to explain the formation and maintenance of gangs, and reinforces the distinctions between gangs, groups and organisations which are critical for effective anti-gang policy making and program development.

One of the most obvious characteristics of street gangs such as 'Los Diablos' is their transient quality and relative instability, especially when compared with criminal business organisations. A brief case study of such an organisation—'Lotus'—is provided below. The history of 'Los Diablos', for example, indicates continuous change and instability across a number of key areas. There were changes in the ethnic composition of the gang, in the leadership and core membership, in the alliances the gang formed and ended with other gangs and organisations, and in the kinds of criminal activities that were preferred by the gang, the gang's different 'cells', and by individual members. The gang was riven with dissent and rivalry, and seemed to flourish more as a result of fear and myth than consistent concrete accomplishments. 'Los Diablos' was certainly a constant presence in the Vancouver area during the late 1980s and early 1990s but, contrary to public (i.e., media created) impressions, it was not a finely tuned and highly organised criminal machine.

Instability and transience were the hallmarks of other Vancouver street gangs and 'wannabe' groups during this period. Gangs and groups appeared and disappeared with breathtaking speed, some disbanding almost as quickly as they were formed. Those that did not disband completely often amalgamated with other gangs or groups, frequently creating new gangs with new names (Gordon 1995). Indeed, attempting any analysis of the field during the peak activity period (the late 1980s/early 1990s) was virtually impossible and comparable to trying to herd cats.

In the spring of 1991, for example, there were about nine street gangs in the Greater Vancouver area, in addition to 'Los Diablos', including the 'Bacada Boys', 'Patook', and 'Persian Pride'. By the fall of 1993, most of these gangs had disappeared or were in rapid decline but new street gangs had appeared, often formed by the members of disbanded or disintegrating gangs. The short-lived suburban gang known as 'Los Cholos', for example, was purportedly created by disenchanted members of 'Los Diablos'. At the time of writing, only a handful of active street gangs can be identified in the Greater Vancouver area (e.g., 'CTB' or the 'Chinatown Boys', and the 'New Dragons'). Some members of now defunct street gangs have continued as criminal groups[7] but the numbers of street gangs and street gang members, and the amount of street gang activity, have fallen dramatically when compared with the situation in 1991.

The example of 'Los Diablos' helps to illuminate the relationships among street gangs and criminal business organisations. Where links existed, as they often did, organisations used gangs for such things as extra legal dispute resolution ('enforcement') and the distribution of goods and services (e.g., retailing drugs). The example is also particularly useful in identifying where some gangs came from and why they were created. Clearly, large street gangs can be the seedbed of new gangs, not only when the 'parent' gang dies and the remaining members disperse (as in the case of 'Los Diablos') but also when the members of a flourishing gang decide to expand into other parts of a metropolitan area. 'Los Diablos' was the parent of at least three allied street gangs ('Los Panchos', the 'Sparrows', and 'Bario Latinos') and probably influenced the creation of numerous, although happily short-lived, 'wannabe' groups throughout the Greater Vancouver area. New street gangs may also appear in response to threats posed by existing gangs, and a new wave of gang activity may be a product of a vicious circle of threat or perceived threat, reaction, reinforced threat, further reaction, and so on. The emergence of the 'East Vancouver Saints' in the fall of 1988 provides a good example of this phenomenon because the gang appears to have been resurrected as a mutual protection society solely in response to a localised fear of 'Los Diablos' and its allies. This claim is supported by the fact that the 'Saints' disbanded shortly after 'Los Diablos' began to disintegrate. Additionally, groups of allied gangs and organisations appear as the fear of another gang or group of gangs and organisations spreads and as the warring factions step up the conflict. As the 'Los Diablos' example indicates, at least two groups of gangs and organisations were active in the Greater Vancouver area during the late 1980s and early 1990s. 'Los Diablos', 'Lotus' and their allies were in conflict with 'Gum Wah', the 'Red Eagles', the 'East Vancouver Saints' and their allies, and were probably collectively responsible for a great deal of the gang-related criminal activity in the city at that time as well as the formation of other gangs and groups.

Germane to the issues of instability and transience amongst street gangs is the age of the members of gangs. Preliminary results from the Greater Vancouver Gang Study, for example, indicate that just under one half of the members of gangs, groups, and organisations involved in the study were youth (those 12 to 17 years of age inclusively) and that those identified as members of *street gangs* were, on average, 19 years of age. Perhaps more importantly, 84% of the subjects were males between the ages of 14 and 26: the group at greatest risk of involvement in all kinds of predatory street crime but a group comprised of individuals who usually discontinue such activity as they grow older. The evidence is not yet fully confirmed, but there is some support for the conventional 'maturation hypothesis' as a partial explanation for the periodic disappearance of Canadian street gangs. Gang members may simply grow older and lose interest in street gang life as more sedate and rewarding options present themselves. This sentiment was expressed by some gang members in British Columbia correctional centres who were interviewed in a study conducted in 1993 (Gordon 1993). The reasons why gangs reappear after a 10 year hiatus—a pattern that has characterised street gang activity in

Vancouver since 1945—remain unclear.

Another key characteristic reflected in the account of 'Los Diablos' is the ethnic composition of such gangs. Preliminary results from the Greater Vancouver Gang Study indicate considerable ethnic diversity amongst gangs and gang members, very few gangs being comprised predominantly of a particular ethnic group, and despite the frequent use of ethnically specific gang names (see also Gordon 1993; 1995). For example, the North Vancouver street gang known as 'Persian Pride', which was extremely active in the late 1980s and early 1990s, consisted of young adult males from several ethnic groups even though the name suggested a street gang dominated by individuals of Iranian ethnic origin. 'Los Diablos' passed through a period when young males of Hispanic ethnic origin dominated the gang (and gave it its name) but these individuals were later displaced by East Indian gang members of Fijian ethnic origin. Even gangs and criminal business organisations with Chinese or Vietnamese sounding names such as 'Gum Wah' and 'Lotus' had (and continue to have) an ethnically diverse membership and include individuals of European ethnic origin (caucasians) who were born in Canada.

The clear evidence of ethnic diversity found amongst the membership of Vancouver's street gangs is important for a number of reasons. It is of value with respect to the politics of gangs insofar as evidence of diversity helps to combat inaccurate, and sometimes vindictive, commentary about particular ethnic minorities. The evidence is especially useful when responding to the cavalier and extremely misleading use of terms such as 'Asian gangs' so popular in the Canadian news media. Evidence of diversity helps to normalise the membership of street gangs: if a metropolitan area is ethnically heterogeneous one would expect to find that diversity mirrored, qualitatively and quantitatively, in a wide variety of organisations, institutions, and groupings including street gangs and criminal business organisations.

There is, however, some evidence that street gangs in Vancouver and other Canadian cities may have memberships that are comprised disproportionately of individuals from particular ethnic minorities, albeit in relatively small numbers. In the Greater Vancouver Gang Study, for example, more than three quarters of the research subjects were members of visible ethnic minorities.[8] Eighty-three of these subjects (65.6%) were members of non-aboriginal visible ethnic minorities compared with an estimated 13.5% in the general population of the province (Gordon and Nelson, 1996). The largest single ethnic group was comprised of those of Asian ethnic origin (45%)[9] and, of these, nearly one half were Vietnamese.

In each case, the ethnic groups were disproportionately represented although the actual numbers were small, relative to the size of the groups in the general provincial population (Gordon and Nelson 1993; 1996).

Similar disproportionate representations along ethnic lines have been noted in the case of street gangs in both Winnipeg and Toronto. In Winnipeg, the two principal street gangs—the 'Indian Posse' and the 'Manitoba Warriors'—members of which were involved in a recent riot in the provincial correctional centre at Headingly, Manitoba[10]—are comprised predominantly of young aboriginal males.[11] Other street gangs in the city reflect other visible ethnic minorities—Filipino and Chinese/Vietnamese in particular—but it is the aboriginal gangs which appear to pose the greatest problem for criminal justice agencies. Recent reports of street gang activity in the Toronto metropolitan area suggest a disproportionate number of gang members of Caribbean, Hispanic, and Portugese ethnic origins.[12]

Ethnicity is clearly a relevant factor in understanding the Canadian street gang phenomenon but not, alone, sufficient to explain the creation and maintenance of gangs, or their eventual demise. It is only when ethnicity is combined with variables such as immigrant status and socioeconomic status that a more useful picture emerges. Preliminary results from the Greater Vancouver Gang Study indicate that just over one half of the subjects in the study were immigrants to Canada: a significant over-representation given that about 22% of people in the general provincial population were not born in the country (Gordon and Nelson 1993; 1996). Sixty-five of the subjects in the study (50.7%) were immigrants who were members of visible ethnic minorities and the largest single group of immigrants was from Vietnam (19.5% of the research population). In both cases, there is a significant over-representation when compared with the general population of the province although it is important to note that the actual numbers of people involved is extremely small.

As many analysts of the street gang phenomenon have pointed out, ethnicity, immigrant status and socioeconomic status are of relevance where these variables combine with limited language competency and a lack of marketable skills to produce a variety of social and economic vulnerabilities: poverty, family disintegration, a lack of supportive community networks, and the lack of rewarding employment, to name the main concerns (Huff 1990; Mathews 1993; Spergel 1995; Gordon and Nelson 1996). In Vancouver, for example, while the socioeconomic status of the subjects in the gang study ranged from 'upper middle class' to 'economically disadvantaged', the largest single group (36 percent) were economically disadvantaged and the majority of these individuals were from visible ethnic minorities. A similar picture—one of cultural disenfranchisement, economic impoverishment and a lack of legitimate opportunities—has been recognised as significant for an understanding of gangs and groups in other Canadian cities (Mathews 1993).

Ethnicity, immigrant status, economic disadvantage, and the lack of legitimate and rewarding opportunities are possibly *more* important in understanding involvement in, and the maintenance of, criminal business organisations than street gangs. In the Vancouver gang study, for example, 22 of the 24 subjects who were identified as members of organisations were not born in Canada and were almost invariably of Chinese or Vietnamese ethnic origin. Unlike street gangs, criminal business organisations are more stable, more constant, and as the following brief case study illustrates, involved in more serious and organised forms of criminal activity.

'Lotus': A Canadian Criminal Business Organisation

Unlike 'Los Diablos', 'Lotus' is an *active* Vancouver-based criminal business organisation. It is generally thought that the organisation first appeared in the late 1960s but its origins are murky.[13] Likewise, little is known about the organisation's early activities although it may have started as a street gang with a predominantly Chinese-Canadian membership. It is clear that the organisation was in conflict with the members of other Chinese gangs and groups in the late 1970s and it is believed to have been actively involved in armed robberies in British Columbia and Alberta at that time. It was also involved in extortion and targeted mainly Chinese businesses.[14]

In the mid-1980s, the organisation amalgamated with another criminal business organisation—Jung Ching—to form an organisation comprised primarily of individuals of Chinese ethnic origin, including Chinese members who were from Vietnam and who spoke only Vietnamese. In the main, the organisation's more visible activities—occasional shootings and assaults—were extensions of its general business activities: operating social clubs; gambling; drug distribution; prostitution; restaurant extortion; and credit card frauds. Occasionally, however, the business activity entered the public domain; the best, but most tragic, example of such activity being the organisation's involvement in the high profile kidnapping and eventual murder of a Vancouver restaurant owner and his wife (the 'Ming slayings'). The organisation's members were also vulnerable to attack by rival gangs and organisations and these exchanges spilled over into the public domain, often in spectacular ways. For example, in January 1987 a member of 'Lotus' was shot and killed while watching a film in a Chinese movie theatre in Vancouver by an individual working for a rival organisation. This incident—the so-called 'Golden Princess Theatre shooting'—proved irresistible to the media and led to considerable public alarm about 'gang' activity in the city.

By December 1989, there was considerable evidence that 'Lotus' was operating a major, commercial, break and enter scheme in the Vancouver area, using young people to hit predetermined and directed targets. In addition, the organisation was engaged, with an allied street gang ('Los Diablos'), in an increasingly violent war with the street gang known as 'Gum Wah', a rival criminal business organisation (the 'Red Eagles'), and their allies. This took the form of frequent drive-by shootings, as well as beatings and stabbings in restaurants, bars and, in the case of the younger members of the organisation, in high schools.

The following summer, 'Lotus' began to diversify by organising a variety of criminal activities in addition to its regular itinerary. Different groups, or cells, within 'Lotus' were assigned to commit robberies aimed at different types of targets: one group were assigned to fast food restaurants; another to high profile jewellery stores; and yet another to hotels. Some groups were slow in starting but this hallmark activity was to continue for more than a year. One cell within 'Lotus' also kidnapped the daughter of a local millionaire but were quickly identified and arrested. By the early 1990s, 'Lotus' were deeply involved in the distribution of drugs, for resale, the primary 'retail' outlet being members of the allied street gang, 'Los Diablos'. Drug distribution through a set of interconnected cells continues to be the primary business activity for 'Lotus'.

Although allied to 'Los Diablos' over a long period of time, 'Lotus' stands out as a significantly different entity. It has proved to be a more permanent and more stable form of organisation having successfully survived numerous conflicts with rival organisations and gangs, primarily over market share in the field of drug distribution. This is not to suggest that all Canadian criminal business organisations, unlike street gangs, are permanent. Some merge with each other (e.g., 'Lotus' and 'Jung Ching' amalgamated in the mid-1980s), and some go out of business. One of 'Lotus'' rival organisations—the 'Red Eagles'—have disbanded.

Criminal business organisations exhibit greater ethnic homogeneity than street gangs but their membership is not solely Chinese or Vietnamese; 'Lotus', for example, had (and has) several Euro-Canadian members. The members also tend to be older—in the Vancouver gang study the average age was 28 years—although the membership can include adolescents. Also, a criminal business organisation's activities can be city-wide and even national in scope—they tend not to be tied to particular neighbourhoods or operate in set areas of cities, as was the case with 'Los Diablos' and other Vancouver street gangs.

Although organisations like 'Lotus' tend to be dominated by individuals from visible ethnic minorities, many of whom were not born in Canada, a preliminary analysis of the data gathered for the Greater Vancouver Gang Study indicates that organisation members are less likely to be economically disadvantaged than the members of street gangs. The reasons for this are perhaps self evident: the members of criminal business organisations are usually employed in extremely rewarding, although illegitimate, fields of work that exhibit growth rather than decline (e.g., drug trafficking). Generally speaking, given language and cultural difficulties as well as a lack of marketable skills, the members of criminal business organisations would not be able to compete successfully in the legitimate labour market for employment that was equally rewarding. Given a choice between menial work for minimum wages in the kitchen of a restaurant and an exciting and highly lucrative position working within a criminal business organisation, it is doubtful whether many young adult males would forgo the latter occupation in favour of the former.

CONCLUSION

The extent to which the situation in the Greater Vancouver area, as reflected in the findings of the Greater Vancouver Gang Study, are mirrored in other Canadian cities remains unclear at this time. It is expected that the work in progress, for example in Winnipeg,[15] will provide some interesting comparative data and important new information particularly with respect to aboriginal street gangs. Work, scheduled to begin in Vancouver in the spring of 1997 as an extension of the Greater Vancouver Gang Study should also provide further insight into the relationships among ethnicity, immigrant status, and membership of street gangs, criminal groups, and criminal business organisations. The results of this forthcoming research, which is being conducted as part of the national 'Metropolis Project',[16] should help the federal and provincial governments to identify the resources, services and strategies that are necessary to address key issues and problems associated with immigration.

In the meantime, the results of the limited number of research projects that have been recently completed in Canada, and that have been identified and briefly canvassed in this discussion, provide partial answers to some of the questions posed by Canadian gang analysts, researchers, and policy-makers. There is, for example, a better understanding of why street gangs in Canadian cities appear and then disappear in a wave-like fashion, although a comprehensive, comparative historical analysis has yet to be attempted. There is a better understanding of the relationships among gangs, groups and organisations and of the key demographic and other differences among their memberships which point to some of the reasons individuals become involved in this area of criminal activity.

The distinctions which must be made between gangs, groups and organisations are also better understood and this bodes well for the development of effective, indigenous, anti-gang policy and programs. Clearly, the best strategy for combating entrenched and highly effective criminal business organisations (notably, vigorous and targeted enforcement and prosecution by specialist units) is unlikely to be of tremendous value when dealing with occasional suburban irritations. Noisy but transient groups of adolescent 'wannabe' gang members require a different approach.

Although there is a great deal about Canadian street gangs and criminal business organisations that remains murky, it is clear that Canadian policy-makers and program developers occupy a happier position than their counterparts in the United States. Street gang and 'wannabe' group activity is not yet an entrenched feature of the Canadian urban landscape and there is still enough time, energy, and commitment to develop sound ways of addressing gangs and gang-related issues. It is highly unlikely that any form of government policy or programming will *prevent* a resurgence of street gang and related activity. In Vancouver, and on the basis of the pattern of gang activity since 1945, this renewed activity is predicted to begin around the year 2005. It may, however, be possible to develop ways of responding more confidently and cost-effectively when the next wave arrives.

At a minimum, some important features of the Canadian social welfare and criminal justice systems should be preserved, if not strengthened. One explanation for the impermanence of street gangs and 'wannabe' groups in Canadian cities (despite the nation's proximity to the United States) is the array of social safety nets that keep these cities reasonably healthy. Although inner city areas have their share of problems they are not home to large populations of disenfranchised, dissolute, and desperate youths and young adults living with no hope of positive change. Canadian cities have a reasonably effective educational, health and social service apparatus staffed by generally optimistic personnel who are interested in building communities and community services and who are concerned to address the various issues and problems that seem to be related to the entrenchment of street gangs: urban decay, family disintegration, cultural and language barriers, impoverishment, and unemployment.

On the criminal justice side, Canada has relatively strict firearms control and, at present, the federal government seems to be prepared to make such control even stricter, with considerable popular support. Some provincial governments also seem willing to regulate the supply and use of firearms to the extent they are able within their constitutional mandate. Criminal business organisations may not be touched by the effectiveness or otherwise of the social safety net but they will be affected by initiatives such as restricted access to firearms and ammunition and by fully staffed and supported enforcement and prosecution units working in collaboration with the communities most affected by organised criminal activity (e.g., restaurateurs who are subjected to extortion). Utilitarian theories of deterrence may not be popular explanatory or policy tools at this time but they should not be dismissed in situations where criminal activity is organised along business lines and undertaken primarily for profit.[17]

REFERENCES

Cloward, Richard A. and Ohlin, Lloyd E. (1960) *Delinquency and Opportunity: A Theory of Delinquent Gangs*, New York: Free Press.

Dubro, J. (1992) *The Dragons of Crime: Inside the Asian Underworld*, Toronto: Octopus Publishing.

Fasilio, R. and Leckie, S. (1993) *Canadian Media Coverage of Gangs: A Content Analysis,* Ottawa: Solicitor-General Canada.

Girrard, M. (1992) *The Print Media's Portrayal of the Youth Gang Phenomenon in British Columbia*, unpublished B.A. (Hons.) thesis, Vancouver: School of Criminology, Simon Fraser University.

Gordon, R.M. (1993) *Incarcerated Gang Members in British Columbia: A Preliminary Study,* Victoria: Ministry of Attorney-General.

Gordon, R.M. (1995) 'Street Gangs in Vancouver', in J. Creechan, and R. Silverman (eds) *Canadian Delinquency*, Scarborough: Prentice Hall.

Gordon, R.M. and Nelson, J. (1993) *Census '93: The Report of the 1993 Census of Provincial Correctional Centres in British Columbia*, Victoria:

Ministry of Attorney-General.

Gordon, R.M. and Nelson, J. (1996) 'Crime, Ethnicity and Immigration', in R. Silverman, J. Teevan and V. Sacco (eds) *Crime in Canadian Society* (5th edn) Toronto: Harcourt Brace.

Huff, C. Ronald (ed.) (1990) *Gangs in America*, Newbury Park: Sage Publications.

Joe, D. and Robinson, N. (1980) 'Chinatown's Immigrant Gangs', *Criminology* 18: 337-45.

Mathews, F. (1993) *Youth Gangs on Youth Gangs*, Ottawa: Solicitor-General Canada.

Rogers, K. (1945) *Street Gangs in Toronto: A Study of the Forgotten*, Toronto: Ryerson Press.

Spergel, Irving A. (1995) *The Youth Gang Problem: A Community Approach*, New York: Oxford University Press.

Young, M. (1993) *The History of Vancouver Youth Gangs: 1900-1985*, unpublished M.A. thesis, Vancouver: School of Criminology, Simon Fraser University.

NOTES

1. Defined in the Greater Vancouver Gang Study as 'groups of young people and young adults who have banded together to form a semi-structured organisation the primary purpose of which is to engage in planned and profitable criminal behaviour or organised violence against rival street gangs. Street gangs can be distinguished from other groupings by (i) a self perception of the group as a gang, (ii) a name that was selected by and is used by gang members, (iii) some kind of distinctive identifying marks such as clothing or colours. The members will openly acknowledge gang membership because they want to be recognised as gang members by other people, but street gangs will tend to be less visible than "wannabe" groups'.

2. Defined in the Greater Vancouver Gang Study as 'organised groups that exhibit a formal structure and a high degree of sophistication. These groups are comprised primarily of adults, including older adults. They engage in criminal activity primarily for economic reasons and almost invariably maintain a low profile, which is a key characteristic that distinguishes such organisations from street gangs. They may have a name, but the tendency is to avoid such identifying features'.

3. The principal project is the Greater Vancouver Gang Study. The research was conducted under the auspices of the provincial Interministerial Committee on Criminal Gangs and Youth Violence with funding provided by the Ministry of the Attorney-General (British Columbia) and the Department of Justice (Canada). The research began in 1993 with a preliminary study of known gang members in

British Columbia correctional centres and culminated in a detailed analysis of all gang members known to the provincial correctional system in the Greater Vancouver area in 1995 (128 subjects). The results of the study are expected to be made public late in 1996. The methods and instruments used in the Vancouver study are being used in a tandem study in Winnipeg, Manitoba.

4. The following account of the history of 'Los Diablos' is drawn from a variety of British Columbia law enforcement and corrections sources including archival materials and interviews with personnel.

5. There is some evidence that some Vancouver street gangs have been involved in organised prostitution, employing young women for this purpose. Gangs comprised primarily of young women are reported to exist in Toronto and Winnipeg but the evidence is primarily anecdotal. See, 'Girl-gang violence alarms experts', *Globe and Mail*, 12 September, 1995.

6. Defined in the Greater Vancouver Gang Study as 'young people who band together in a loosely structured group primarily to engage in spontaneous social activity and exciting, impulsive criminal activity, including collective violence against other groups of youth. A "wannabe" group will be highly visible and its members will openly acknowledge their "gang" involvement because they want to be seen by others as gang members. The group will have a local gathering area and a name, selected and used by its members, which may be a modified version of the name of either a local or an American street gang. The group may use clothing, colours, or some other kind of identifying marks. The group's name, meeting ground, and colours may fluctuate'.

7. Criminal groups are defined in the Greater Vancouver Gang Study as 'small clusters of friends who band together, usually for a short period of time, to commit crime primarily for financial gain. They can be composed of adolescents and adults (young and not so young) and may be mistakenly, or carelessly, referred to as a gang'. Some criminal groups are created without any connection to street gangs or other organisations. Other criminal groups may be formed by the more tenacious members of defunct street gangs or criminal business organisations, one Vancouver example being the creation of a criminal group with a predominantly Iranian membership from the residue of a North Vancouver street gang known as 'Persian Pride'.

8. The main groups were those of Canadian aboriginal (Native Indian), East Indian, Asian, Hispanic, African, and Middle Eastern ethnic origin.

9. Being individuals of Chinese, Japanese, Korean, or South East Asian ethnic origin.

10. *Vancouver Sun*, 9 May 1996: A 3.

11. *Globe and Mail*, 18 May 1996: D 5.

12. *Globe and Mail*, 5 August 1995: A 1 and A 5.

13. The following account of the history of 'Lotus' is drawn from a variety of British Columbia law enforcement and corrections sources including archival materials and interviews with personnel.

14. For an account of gangs and gang activity in the Chinatown area of Vancouver during the late 1970s see, Joe and Robinson (1980).

15. See note 1 above.

16. The Metropolis Project is a set of research projects funded by the federal government through four 'Centres of Excellence'. The Project will analyse different facets of immigration and ethnicity in Canada.

17. The author wishes to acknowledge the assistance of the Greater Vancouver Gang Study project management team and the project researchers, especially Sheri Foley, Lynda Fletcher-Gordon, Lee Van Chu, and Kim Nickel, in the development of this chapter. The Greater Vancouver Gang Study is funded by the Ministry of the Attorney-General (British Columbia) and Justice Canada. The views expressed in this chapter do not necessarily reflect those of the funding agencies.

8 Masculinity and Violence: An Ethnographic Exploration of the Bodgies, 1948-1958

Judith Bessant and Rob Watts

INTRODUCTION

If currently there is concern about the incidence of the adolescent 'gang problem',[1] and historians have begun to reveal its long history internationally,[2] then in Australia there has been relatively little historical interest in the phenomenon. Jon Stratton's study of the 'bodgies and widgies' of the 1950s is therefore a landmark event in recent Australian social history.[3] Stratton has made an important contribution to that history and to social theory (Stratton 1992).[4] Stratton's is an ambitious survey of the formation of a 'youth culture', which had its origins in gatherings of young people at the Woollomooloo Railway Station Cafe in Sydney in the late 1940s. By the mid-1950s the bodgies' distinctively styled clothing, haircuts, threatening manners, and unattractive morals were attracting widespread attention—and criticism (Stratton 1984: 14-16).[5] The 'bodgie style', increasingly affected after 1954 by American film and rock'n roll music, had already spread to New Zealand. Stratton's work reminds us that 'bodgies and widgies' were a prominent feature of Australian urban life in the 1950s, yet for all of its strengths it seems to us problematic.

Stratton's work clearly situates the 'bodgie and widgie' culture in a widely admired tradition of research about 'youth cultures' (Cohen 1980; Hall 1980; Brake 1980). We take exception to this tradition on two grounds. First there are reasons, adduced in the post-structuralist critique of neo-Marxist cultural studies, to reject much of the fundamental framework of that theory (Bessant and Watts 1992). Secondly there are good grounds for pressing for a more ethnographically sensitive reading of the activities of bodgies and widgies which bypass the more functionalist and essentialist 'cultural studies' analysis Stratton offers. This may help us better to enter into the life-world of the bodgies and widgies and to make sense of what they did in terms that avoid either condemnation or romanticism, the two besetting sins of traditional interpretative approaches strongly shaped by a variety of 'functionalist' dispositions.

A CRITIQUE OF YOUTH CULTURE THEORY

While this is not the place for a full theoretical confrontation with Stratton and the tradition he exemplifies, we do need to spell out some of the principal concerns we have. Stratton explicitly distances himself from the older styles of theorising adolescent gangs. The long dominant view in a host of twentieth century social science monographs on delinquency, found in adolescent gangs (and bodgies and widgies) the authentic 'anti-social delinquent'. On this account the 'anti-social' is correlative with immorality. This is the representation of 'delinquents-as-outsiders' fabricated by a 'therapeutic-functionalist' model of deviancy. This discursive tradition, prompted by Cyril Burt's early work, welded together a quasi-Freudian psychological and a structural-functionalist sociology of adolescence and its vicissitudes (Burt 1926; Kett 1977). This model was widely adhered to in Australia (1920 to 1970) and was doubtless widely admired in other countries. It sought to define a 'normal process' of socially necessary and psychologically inevitable adolescent maturation, adjustment, and development into appropriate social roles and adult psychological capacities. On this basis, 'deviant' exceptions were thus identifiable, given, as Manning's classic study of Sydney 'bodgies' suggested, the prevalence of 'social dysfunctions' such as unhappiness in early childhood, broken homes, strained and tense homes, lack of parental supervision and appropriate moral and spiritual training. The bodgies' 'delinquency' was thus born of the complete frustration of (normal) urges and the resultant feelings of anxiety. Inferiority, deprivation, and inadequacy force the child to seek substitute satisfactions in conduct that we call 'delinquent' (Manning 1958: 85-6).

Delinquency became a marker of failure in the all-important task of adjustment to socially functional roles and institutions. To this underlying 'scientific-moral' vision of the 'good society' was allied a recurrent 'social scientific' interest in discerning the invariant factors which *determined* that some people would become deviant (Orcutt 1983: 2-37). This tradition has been exemplified in the 'juvenile delinquency' paradigm and its stress on the precariousness of socialisation in the great task of social adjustment to socially functional roles (Cohen 1955; Downes 1966; Matza and Sykes 1961). For Stratton the Birmingham 'school' and its 'breakthrough' text, *Resistance through Rituals* (1976), holds the key to a more adequate theorisation of the emergence of adolescent gangs as expressions of 'youth culture'[6].

It should be noted that Stratton (and others like White), do not rely on a simple or narrow class-based analysis. As White indicates there is an apparent openness to diversity in the response of young people to the structural inequalities of race, class and gender (White 1990: 195-99). This stance is in effect a 'new structuralism' which builds in considerably more space for contradiction, even as it 'reads off' choice from a limited range of structurally given options. White argues for example, that there are a range of given structural positions:

> being young in each case is conditioned by the position of individuals as members of a class, a gender, and an ethnic group. The diversity of cultural influences 'available' to young people is in turn influenced by the limits of and pressure on their daily lives (White 1990: 196).

This is glossed by White (following Hall and Jefferson, and Hebdige) as follows:

> given the structural and cultural restrictions placed upon the 'choices' available to young working class men, both in terms of job opportunities and spare time activities, attempts are often made at a subcultural level 'magically' to resolve the dilemmas facing them (ibid).

This 'new structuralism' allows a plurality of structures (class, gender, and ethnicity) and stresses that choice and diversity, albeit within limits, is open to the actor in a given situation. A 'youth subculture' becomes a space inscribed by a set of structures, in which young people seek to resolve the contradictory pressures on them. Stratton for example suggests:

> that many young people identify themselves as members of a particular subculture. This membership depends on mobilising the

> appropriate 'dress, music, argot, and ritual' ... and represents attempts at producing magical solutions to contradictory ideological pressures. These contradictory pressures are themselves a product of middle class attempts to incorporate hegemonically working class behaviour (Stratton 1984: 10).

What is important here is the ongoing effort to read off the culture of young people, that is the patterns of meaning, ritual, and behaviour, from the given or prior system of power relations (class, patriarchy, and racism), and the functioning of social control agents. The two choices that are left available to young people are *co-option* or *resistance*. Thus Stratton modifies the thesis of Cohen, Willis, and Hall et al., that working class subcultural groups actively resist hegemonic middle class interventions. Stratton suggests that a major part of the bodgie and widgie youth culture was constituted as a consumer category (Stratton 1984: 11).

Stratton argues there were two phases in the 'bodgie and widgie' phenomenon. The first was constituted before a youth market had been established by various industries in the middle to late 1940s. A second bodgie and widgie 'youth culture' began around 1954 and had much more to do with commodifying music, clothing, and style with young people as the targets of popular culture and advertising campaigns.

What Stratton offers is a more sophisticated, modified version of a Birmingham 'youth culture' model. Stratton remains convinced, along with Cohen (1980); and Hall et al. (1976), that as a 'class actor' the meaning of 'youth cultures' is found only in its capacity or inability to resist co-option (Stratton 1992: 17-31). Accepting that Stratton has modified the youth culture model,[7] he nonetheless draws on it to sustain much of his assessment of the 'bodgie and widgie' culture (Stratton 1992: 10).

> The second generation of bodgies and widgies constituted a working class youth culture whose members, whilst celebrating their access to a range of new consumer goods nonetheless had to resolve their recognition that other goods were beyond their purchasing capacities. In turn they fell back on an articulation of their class position often found in the assertion of a variety of oppositional values (Stratton 1992: 21).

Here Stratton deploys the familiar notion of youth culture-as-class argument which exists to manage contradictions through symbolic or 'magical' oppositional activities. As Stratton puts it, working class youth cultures 'inevitably fail in the long term to win space precisely because they are fighting on a symbolic rather than a material level' (Stratton 1992: 30). Stratton further uses this model to distinguish between first and second generation bodgies; the latter being described as insufficiently oppositional to warrant being called a 'youth culture', unlike the first generation of Melbourne bodgies who satisfy his requirements of oppositionality: 'Here the culture was much more clearly working class and much more obviously oppositional to the dominant conservative middle class culture' (Stratton 1992: 24).

There are a number of important criticisms to be made of the University of Birmington's Centre for Contemporary Cultural Studies (CCCS) style of 'youth culture' analysis—criticisms which Stratton has not addressed (McRobbie 1980; Tait 1992). Firstly we remain unconvinced of attempts, by Giddens and others, to connect structural position and lived experience, including beliefs and actions. Coward has suggested there is a determinism in the CCCS framework, which constrains the members of the 'youth culture' to choose only from a limited repertoire of options about how to behave (that is, to 'resist' or 'be co-opted') (Coward 1977). Given that the social formation is said to be simply an expression of the division between capital and labour (or of black versus white, or male versus female), it follows that the cultural expression is 'read off' from the dominant-subordinate relationship be it defined economically, sexually, or racially.

On this reading 'youth culture' becomes a cultural manifestation of a pre-given structure (of class, gender, or race) which sits outside the fields of culture. This renders insoluble the question of how 'structure' and 'meaning' or 'experience' can 'get it together'. In this way we preserve an active suspicion about a relationship which so many others assume exists. Totalising notions that imply a relation for example between 'the working class' and 'working class culture' we would rather treat as an invitation to join a research project than as a theoretically established given.

McRobbie has trenchantly criticised the neo-Marxist emphasis on class and age as the primary elements in the constitution of youth cultures, to the neglect of gender and race/ethnicity (McRobbie 1980). Admittedly the more sophisticated proponents of the 'youth culture' model like White have taken this criticism on board by expanding the range of structures (again the articulation of the relations between structures and lived experience tend to be assumed rather than demonstrated). Another problem is the frequent urge to romanticise the 'resistance' of the working class kids and their culture, a tendency with a long history in the relationship between the 'working class' and left intellectuals (Clarke 1982; Walker 1986).

Then there is the problem with the youth culture tradition's reliance on the idea of 'social control'. A considerable literature on the idea of social control suggests it should no longer be given the kind of tacit use-value it retains in contemporary social theory and research. Van Krieken has raised a number of issues about the continuing reliance on social control themes including: (i) the failure to demonstrate the role of the state and/or welfare agencies in securing social order and (ii) the possibility that the 'victims' of social control actively desired state intervention or that there was a compatibility of interest between state and working class rather than the more usual assumption of contradictory interests which most social control theorists assume (van Krieken 1992: 269-70).

Van Krieken's call for a recognition of power as asymmetrical negotiations, alliances, and compromises, construing power as a social relationship, is a position we endorse. Finally as Tait (1992) suggests the 'post-structuralist' project associated with Foucault and his treatment of the power/knowledge nexus undercuts the emphasis on resistance to hegemony or to 'social control' in 'youth culture' theory.

The neo-Marxist understanding of 'power', developed by the Birmingham school after Gramsci and its local exponents, sees it as a totalised generality, possessed by the 'ruling classes' (or dominant gender or race) and used in a hegemonic fashion to coerce or socialise the 'lower classes', who don't have 'it'. Further, there is the tendency already referred to, to see everywhere a range of state agencies and professional agents committed to 'social control' activities in ways which fail to acknowledge the problems involved in much of the social control model.[8]

Foucault's reworking of the idea of power has major implications for the continued use of notions of 'hegemony' or 'social control', so vital to the 'youth culture' model. Rather than understanding 'hegemony' or 'social control' as the unitary exercise of coercive mechanisms (or as the use of consensual techniques) to realise the intentions of a unitary source or agent of power, Foucault (1980) sees a multiplicity of techniques and practices which flow into and around a range of cultural institutions and social sites. If hegemony is therefore to have any theoretical use-value it can only be by pointing to the profusion of techniques for constituting reality and knowledges. Any notion that a 'youth culture' is simply and only counter-hegemonic or a site of resistance to social control, or merely a site where symbolic means are deployed to handle contradictions, needs to be very carefully rethought.

Australian theorists, including Hunter, have pushed this argument so far as to broach the idea of 'culture' itself (Hunter 1988). Again the effect of these telling arguments is to embarrass the 'youth culture' model. Hunter rejects the notion that culture is a generalised entity. Functionalists and structuralists of various persuasions have long argued that culture and even consciousness itself refers to a 'total' way of seeing, thinking, and valuing. Culture is a total way of life. (For the 'youth culture' model this premise is essential to their argument that youth culture is a total way of life, in imitation of the alleged 'culture of the whole society' and from which its differences can then be determined even as it remains tied to the 'total way of life'. For Stratton the social and moral order is referred to as a 'middle class moral order' (Stratton 1992: 197). For Hunter 'culture' is best understood as 'a signpost pointing in the general direction of a patchwork of institutions in which human attributes are formed and which, having no necessary features in common, must be described and assessed from case to case'. 'Culture' then is a more fragmentary practice of 'limited and specific cultural programs'. By implication there is no totalised entity which can be called 'working class culture' or 'working class consciousness'.

What do Stratton's theoretical dispositions mean for the kind of study he produces? On the face of it there are a consiberable number of fine and interesting descriptions of the life experience of young people in the fifties around their sexuality, leisure activities, and clothing and music preferences. However, the ethnographic material has been shaped in ways which may not have been recognisable to the young people themselves. In this way it remains an outsider's account, its interpretations driven by a pre-existing agenda. As a study of a 'culture' or a 'subculture' Stratton's work shows a limited interest in the experiences and meanings of the young people he writes about. (When his subjects' experience demonstrates the resistance/co-option themes which his youth culture model calls for, Stratton seems to pay more attention).

On the rule of thumb suggested by Geertz, who asks if the interpretation offered by the anthropologist would be acceptable in principle to the group s/he is anthropologising, Stratton's account would not pass that test. He agonises about problems which for his, and our respondents, was never at issue (like were there really 'bodgies and widgies'? and concludes that they were essentially 'mythical') (Stratton 1992: 191).[9] This is a very serious problem for any interpretative project claiming to speak meaningfully about other people situated across a historical and hermeneutic gap. That gap we now turn to, and illustrate with a single episode in the life of one 'bodgie'.

THE BODGIE CULTURE OF THE FIFTIES

It is 1956. The place, a network of narrow laneways in Footscray, a western suburb of Melbourne, Australia, and home to thousands of immigrants from Italy and Greece and to an even greater number of Australian-born working class women, men, and young people. The houses are aging, many built in the late nineteenth or early twentieth century. Most days there is a ubiquitous stench from the local meatworks, and a haze of smoke from the numerous local foundries belching out sulphurous oxides and the ash which coats the washing hung out on backyard clothes lines.

The action, a 'blue' (fight) near a lane between a local 'gang' of Australian adolescents and several 'dagos' (Italians):

> After beating the dago's mates to a pulp and leaving them lying there unconscious, our gang went up the lane to where the dago was holding two of the boys at bay with his knife. ... Knuckles became enraged and lost all reasoning ... he threw away all caution and charged at the dago. It was a courageous but foolish move. The dago swung his knife in three fast successive blows and stabbed Knuckles three times low in the stomach. Knuckles' first two punches smashed into the dago's face as he was stabbing him and the dago reeled back. ... With all this happening so fast, the boys rushed in and commenced smashing and punching [the dago] until he was lying on the ground in a pile of blood. Even as he lay there, they continued to kick him about the head and body until he was scarcely recognisable as a man at all. I wondered if he was dead. I hoped so. To see my mate Knuckles in such pain nearly brought tears to my eyes (Dick 1968: 164).[10]

This was violence in its most immediate and direct expression. In a century of repeated, and highly organised violence, often by states against their own citizens it may be thought small beer. Yet it raises a problem; how do we understand such violence?

What we have in this memory is not only a slice of that almost completely unrecorded and unwritten about history-from-below which historians are now trying to reconstruct, but an interpretative puzzle. Acknowledging the difficulty of encountering such an 'otherness' as the lives we report on, we begin with the problem of how we can make sense of the kind of masculine violence and solidarity. Do we treat it, as the respectable professionals, the 'child savers', the police, the journalists or the politicians of the day would have done, as reprehensible, as savagery, and as a sign of that delinquency which comes of failed parenting (Manning 1958:1-13)? Or do we see it, after the 'new criminology', as 'resistance' by the working class to changed conditions imposed on them by a careless state or a rampant capitalist economy hungry for new raw labour (Taylor, Walton and Young 1975)? Or do we see in it as the first stirrings of an embryonic 'youth culture' anticipating if only in hypothetical steps, some larger pattern of symbolic or magical management of contradictions as they confront adult authority, and middle class-culture (Brake 1980)? How much was this 'fight' a choreographed moment of repeated social interaction which might fit Geertz's notion of a hermeneutic anthropology (Geertz 1973)?

At the time the dominant model available would have brought together a functionalist sociology obsessed with social order and social conformity with an ersatz Freudian model of 'normal psychic development', based on empirico-positivist methodologies. Thus E.A. Manning a psychologist of the 1950s saw the bodgies as victims of failed socialisation and as symptoms of inadequate adjustment to the social roles which reality was demanding of them. 'Terry Cooke' had a view of such social science research identifying the gap between the outsider's and the insider's perspectives:

> Some psychologists had been studying us bodgies and widgies, and boy, were they way out! We often read the articles they printed about us and we didn't think that any of those psychologist blokes had ever met a bodgie let alone studied us. One bloke reckoned he dressed up as a bodgie and lived, ate, slept, and ran with a pack of us for twelve months while he made notes. We reckoned it was a lot of bulldust (Dick 1968: 169).

Our sense of why the functionalist-positivist paradigm is problematic has recently been stated in Katz's revision of traditional deviance theory. Katz begins with a devastating critique of that dominant tradition of deviance theory characterised by its search for 'causal invariance' usually detected in the offenders' psychological backgrounds or social environments (Katz 1988: 1). Katz notes:

> 1) whatever the validity of the hereditary, psychological, and social-ecological conditions of crime, many of those in the supposed causal categories do not commit the crime at issue, 2) many who do commit the crime do not fit the causal categories, and 3) what is most provocative, many who do fit the background categories and later committed the predicted crime, go for long stretches without committing the crimes to which theory directs them (Katz 1988: 2).

Katz suggests that very little of the mainstream tradition of criminological research has significant explanatory power, capable of saying why it is that people kill, thieve, or vandalise—or at least enact the 'socially' disapproved forms of these activities. (If this is the case, and we think it is, Katz's own insensitivity to feminist insights is also a concern in his work).

A different framework needs to be developed. It seems that we should be able to understand *both how and why* it is people do things of which others have habitually disapproved or disallowed. Furthermore, this exercise should begin with the lived experience of those 'doing evil'. Such an interpretation should not begin by assuming some fundamental division of the population into 'good' and 'bad', or 'successful' and 'failed' members, and then look to isolate the allegedly differential factors that force 'the bad' to do evil. It may be more illuminating to assume that there are a number of common ethical dispositions shared by groups of people normally more disposed to accentuate their apparent differences within a given social setting than to accept that perhaps they share a great deal with the Other.

Much of what follows is an initial attempt to explore the implications of an alternative framing assumption which may be closer to an 'insider's view'. We will suggest that in the life-world of the 'bodgies and widgies', and for many teenage groups of young Australian males in the 1950s, we are re-encountering sets of distinctively moral emotions, some of them to do with experiences and issues preoccupying many young men—such as honour, potency, filling up space in impressive ways and possessing territorial integrity and control, all of which enhance their status and their dignity.[11]

We take our cue both from Katz's attention to 'moral emotions' and from Charles Taylor's philosophical anthropology which suggests that human beings *constitute themselves* in their inner life and in their relations with each other *as moral beings* (Taylor 1985).[12]

The moral nature of much human behaviour seems also to be at the heart of Katz's revision of deviance theory. Katz's resolution is to ascertain the 'positive attractions within the lived experience of criminality' by focusing on the 'seductive' qualities of crime which make it 'sensible' and even 'sensually compelling'. Katz's is a phenomenological project which attempts to focus on passions, the expressive creativity, and the bodily sensations involved in doing things others define as criminal, and to do this in a way which respects the cultural and social constraints of class, gender, and ethnic rules, and structures for relationships and actions. For each kind of crime, Katz proposes a distinctive path of action, a unique way of defining the meanings of this action and an emotional process involving 'seductions' and 'compulsions' to act in a certain way. As Katz indicates much of the behaviour he examines (for example murder, theft, and vandalism) revolves around fundamental moral emotions—'humiliation, righteousness, arrogance, ridicule, cynicism, defilement and vengeance' (Katz 1988: 7). (Here Katz relies on a strategy like Taylor's to broaden the ambit of the 'moral'). Katz suggests that the doing of evil is not the consequence of material deprivations so much as it is a morally driven experience.

As Katz sees it, doing evil is often about 'overcoming a personal challenge to moral—not material—existence', suggesting that for young people shoplifting or vandalism is impelled by a 'shifting melodrama about the self', in which 'getting away with it' as a demonstration of personal competence, especially if it is accomplished before adults' eyes, becomes a powerful attraction (Katz 1988: 8).

We turn now to some aspects of life in the teenage gangs in southern Australia who adopted a 'bodgie style' in the 1950s.

The Coming of the Bodgies

Young males saw in the 'bodgie' style of the late forties or early fifties a seductive, diverse means of self expression. For some of them, the coming of the bodgie style flowed easily and smoothly into their experience in local teenage 'gangs'. As Irene reported:

> See all the bodgies used to be in one group. They all sort of came together in one great sponge and they all stuck together. There were gangs within different suburbs too that couldn't stand what they used to call the greasy longhairs which they used to call us ...

('Irene', interview, June 1992).

There were 'working class gangs' who did not attract bodgies just as there were bodgies and widgies who just 'hung about', but equally it is clear that there were 'gangs of bodgies and widgies' for whom territory and territorial status mattered just as deeply as the bodgie style. Lorraine recalls as a widgie that:

> I actually lived in Hampton so we did have territories...[we] went to the Sunday dances at the life saving club and things like that. That was our home territory. A lot of us did travel to the City because that was where it was all happening and most people went to Melbourne Friday or Saturday night because very little happened in the suburbs so that was where you did collect anyway for entertainment. But then during the weeknights or Sundays [it] was your local territory and you hung out there. You sort of had beach areas, park areas that was yours or surf life saving clubs that you dominated in. ... People knew their territory and they kept to it ('Lorraine', interview, October 1992).

It seems that membership of a gang or a local group had little to do with being a bodgie or widgie, which in many cases anyway, often came years after involvement with 'gangs', and more to do with traditional forms of collective life being reaffirmed including a strong sense of territorial patriotism.

If it was complex for outsiders to work out, it seems that the relationships between 'being a bodgie', being 'tough' and being a member of a local group or 'gang' in which a certain pride could be invested, were clearer to those involved. For some bodgies, entrance into a gang was a matter of normal life and an almost 'natural' choice that came as part of existing friendships. As Brian remembered, being a member of a gang came with the suburb and the school.

> Growing up in Sunshine meant that you had to join the local gang. There was no other way, you just had to do it. Everybody had their gangs and different areas ... well there would always be a place, you would meet at someone's place whose parents weren't too strict on things. The kids hung around milkbars. Basically people at school [was one of the ways gangs were created] ('Brian', interview, May 1991).

For Des becoming a bodgie entailed transcending the exile to Preston—imposed on him by his parents for his extra-legal activities as a thirteen year old—and involved returning on weekends to the suburb (Richmond) where he had grown up. As an eight year-old in Richmond in the 1950s Des had been challenged and provoked by the mystery of the space in which he lived and especially that which the great factory complexes posed:

> I remember being surrounded by factories. As kids we used to do a fair bit of breaking in of factories and ransacking them for things that we needed. It was mainly to get into the place and take some of the mystery away from them. They just used to overpower our lives. There was about five of us. There was a place called Rola—they used to make things for radios. It was only about when we got to about fourteen or fifteen that we started to take things of any value. One of the biggest things we used to go and get was things to make billy carts with, particularly at Heinz. Basically it was getting into areas that we felt were overpowering all the time and finding out our territory ('Des', interview, October 1992).

Making sense of one's territory, affirmation of the locale, its traditions and its boundaries mattered because it was a source of pride in terms of other locales, and because to be in the gang was to proclaim one's elite status *in one's own territory*.

Becoming a Bodgie

At some point in the lives of our story tellers came a moment when they plunged into the identity which bodgie clothes, language, hairstyle and what a later generation would call 'attitude' conferred on them. In the initial decision or moment of encounter with new modes of being, many could identify clearly what it was that the new identity offered.

Those first encounters were often uncomplicated responses to the appeals of new clothes styles and the expressive opportunities they appeared to open up to young men to be smooth, sexy, and sophisticated. Fred offers insights into that first encounter; his description and its meticulous detail about the clothes nearly 40 years on provides its own comment about the experience.

> I remember the release of [the film] *The Blackboard Jungle*, in

Melbourne in 1954 which is what started the rock 'n roll craze here, because of course it contained the music 'Rock Around the Clock'. I remember a team which was at the old Astor tearing out the first six rows of seats to give us room to dance ... we simply ripped them out of the floor 'cos they were in the way ... We'd have put them back if we'd been asked.

We were pretty fussy about our appearance. Shoes, except for suede shoes had to look like a mirror ... I would bone them with the handle of a tooth brush and spit 'n polish them. One had to be immaculate or girls wouldn't look at you ... Cutaway tailored shirts ... I used to have mine hand-made at a cost of five guineas each ... I was paying about fifteen times the cost of a normal shirt. Ties were compulsory. Nobody ever wore a shirt without a tie.

Coat lapels were narrow, single buttons, single breasted jacket with single buttons. Buttons had to be at exactly belt buckle height. The bottom of the coat had to be a precise length. Measurement was derived from standing upright, bending your fingers at the first knuckle and the lip of the coat should exactly rest in the rim of the knuckle, the first and second knuckle. If it didn't the coat wasn't the correct length. Clean lines were very important. It was absolutely out to wear braces, they were banned. Key chains were very popular. A genuine bodgie key chain, and bodgie was the term, had to be precisely four feet long. Now if it was three feet six, it was a fraud, if it was five feet long it was pretentious, so you wore a four foot long chain which attached to the belt at the front, hung down to your knee, then came up and went in your right hand side pocket.

Normally you would carry fifteen or sixteen keys of any description at the end of the chain. If you got into a fight you had the perfect weapon. You could swing this thing around, keep you foes four feet away, and inflict considerable damage, and you couldn't be had up with carrying an offensive weapon by the police. It was very in.

I had one hairdresser ... who was the only man in Melbourne I'd allow to put a pair of scissors to my head, and my hair was cut regularly every two weeks. The duck tail had to meet precisely in the back; if the hair overlapped I was very unhappy.[13]

Gordon recollects as a barber's apprentice in 1954 encountering the combination of bodgie clothes and rock 'n roll:

> My word I was proud to be a bodgie! ... We were rebels, there are no two ways about it. I used to have the big blow out the front, with ... aaah ... hair like Tony Curtis, wear a red jumper and black tight trousers ('Gordon', interview, May 1992).

For some the clothes were all that being a bodgie meant. Allan recollects that:

> If you can picture three foot wide shoulders tapering to about a six inch waist (laughs), then very narrow pants ... the coat jacket would come down half way between your thighs and your knees. Gaberdine was the thing, pink, beige, those cut away collars, with gaudy hand painted ties, that was an era! ('Allan', interview, May 1992).

For some its appeal seemed to lie in its breach of local Australian working class stylistic markers. For Barry in the late 1940s as a sixteen year old in Port Melbourne it was friendship with Donny and Donny's bebop music which marked their identity as bodgies. The two boys spent hours listening to Donny's record collection featuring the music of Cab Calloway. As an apprentice with a part-time job as a concreter and living at home, Barry was almost able to afford the 25 pounds for his first bodgie jacket (three weeks' wages). Within months he had become a regular dancer at the Palm Grove near St Kilda where the legacy of the American invasion of the war years was still in evidence in the Saturday night swing bands, the jazz bands, and the jitterbug.

For some the new clothes and music were like a rush of colour into a hitherto grey existence. For Clem Gorman living in Perth thousands of miles from Melbourne and Sydney, the bodgies came in 1955 offering him colour and life in a suburban city:

> They arrived in the Golden West in 1955 and immediately set about reshaping parts of it in their own image ... They took over a corner beside the bandstand at the Canterbury Court Ballroom on Friday nights,and they lived in shared houses around Northbridge. I met them during this period of their travels, and although being middle class, I could not actually join their gang, called 'The Saints', I

> became what was known as a 'hub cap' a middle class boy who aped bodgie style and mannerisms ... It was a brief flash of defiance, a short burst of artillery across society's bows which turned out to be popcorn mixed with jaffas ... In a dull suburban Australia recovering from war it was a tonic (Gorman 1990: 54).

Defiant—or simply colourful—music, clothing, and dancing were not always the crucial factor. For Lorraine it was the dramatic novelty of access to motor bikes. Lorraine linked up with a group by buying her own motor bike, and with her need for independence and for identifying herself as a rebel:

> It could have been the appeal of the dress or motor bikes, or just the sense of freedom, of being a rebel ... A motor bike was so cheap ... and it gave you a freedom when you could get around on one. ... I had my own motor bike because I was a real rebel and not many girls had a motor bike ('Lorraine', interview, October 1992).

Rebellion came after years of what she calls:

> ... a very strict Catholic school and living in convents and I thought there was more to life than this. Being a rebel was just letting it all hang out after years of oppression and it was great ('Lorraine', ibid).

For Des the memory is of the music associated with bodgies and the rift which rock 'n roll inserted into the apparently serene and smooth certainties of his family's musical taste in 1954:

> We used to have a radio that we used to sit and listen to in my ... house and [we'd] hear all this music like 'How Much is that Doggie in the Window', and Perry Como's 'Catch a Falling Star and Put it in Your Pocket'. And then there was this change when Bill Haley's 'Rock Around the Clock' came out. That made a difference ... the beat to it was so challengingly different and fun ('Des', interview, October 1992).

Pressed to say a little more Des added that becoming a bodgie:

> started mainly with all the familiar faces and people that I had grown up with around there and they had all transformed into bodgies and I had joined them but I didn't have my own clear decision ('Des', ibid).

For adolescents like Des the decision to become a bodgie may have had a lot to do with the media and the developing youth music industry. But perhaps it was just to do with the exuberance involved in wearing stylish clothes.

> Roycie had a younger brother about thirteen years old who ... had a black sports coat with pink crosses on it which we all admired and Roycie had lent me a black sports coat and I wore that out that night and I was absolutely star turned when we went up to the cinema ... and then [we] wander[ed] around the streets and would feel pretty excited about ourselves being dressed up ('Des', ibid).

Sometimes it seemed as if the bodgie clothes were a heaven sent opportunity to escape the inevitable fate of becoming like their fathers.

This was established unequivocally by rejecting a 'drab' Australian style in favor of a sophisticated and/or tough American style. For Eric, aged eighteen, the opportunity to wear very expensive hand tailored clothes offered the chance to be in a crowd of 'smooth' bodgies.

> I went out and bought five hundred pounds worth of clothes—Peter Jackson's, Cosgroves ... I got hand made shirts, hand made shoes, the whole bloody lot. It was an awful lot of money. I paid one hundred and fifty pounds for a pair of shoes ... As far as going to dances went, you had to look spot on, be on your toes ('Eric', interview, December 1992).

For Lorraine, apart from the motor bike as a sign of rebellion, the clothes lifted her up and out of the drabness around her:

> I think I was firstly attracted because I loved motor bikes and the group I was with all rode motor bikes. The guys wore leathers and skin tight jeans and everything. Virtually what attracted me was ... the way the girls looked. At the time we used to wear mostly a skin tight black skirt with a slit up the back, and very high heel shoes

> and dark stockings, sometimes fishnet which were always very sexy to me ('Lorraine', interview, October 1992).

The bodgie style had multiple appeal. It conferred status; it incited the fury of the police; it marked out a rejection of Australian drabness. And as Terry recollects, Bootlace also indicated that, 'You'll kill the sheilas, they really go for us, they're sick of the squares' (Dick 1968: 59). For many young men it seemed the style offered a new self-definition which collated sexiness, toughness and differentness. For others, the bodgie dress offered functional attractions. Brian recollected the virtues of suede shoes with thick crêpe soles, often referred to as 'brothel creepers':

> I always wore rubber soled shoes ... nobody could hear you coming, never leathers. If you went dancing you wore suede shoes. You always wore something so people would never hear you. You could walk up on people—you could be two feet behind them and they wouldn't know you were there ('Brian', interview, May 1991).

MORAL EMOTIONS AND BODGIES

While 'bodgie culture' had distinctive and novel features, it was also superimposed on ongoing sets of localised masculine attitudes, practices, and preferences which had their own history and appeal. In this sense, the observer-moralists of the 1950s probably got it wrong when they attributed to the visible aspects of 'bodgie culture', culpability for patterns of rape, violence, and vandalism, which had their origins in more durable patterns of pre- and post-war gangs. It is to some of the important moral emotions that we turn now.

Numerous factors connected the older pre-war gangs and the emergence of bodgie culture in the fifties. It is the complex dialogue between continuities, such as the xenophobia, the reliance on violence to affirm status, the petty thieving and vandalism, the drinking and sexual activity *and* the novelty and discontinuity which bodgie clothing, music, jargon, and collective life embodied, that matters. Gang life represented a proud continuity with the past.

> Nearly everybody in Footscray belonged to a gang of some sort in their life-time. My old man used to belong to one of the razor-slashing gangs that were around [Footscray] years ago and he

> and his mates often talked of 'the good old days when we were in the mob' (Dick 1968: 155).

Bodgie culture also entailed a major rupture with the older solidarity of their parents, culture which, in its search for security organised itself into an almost tribal-like community which admitted few points of internal difference for the first 40 years of the twentieth century. Bodgie culture enacted the first rupture in the older tribalism by segmenting the older culture along generational lines, using markers such as clothing, musical taste, and hairstyle to insist that young people could be and were 'different'. At the same time continuities in terms of local patriotism around the football club, the organisation of large gangs, mateship patterns, sex and drinking, and the semi-ritualised warfare with the forces of 'law 'n order 'n decency', was continued almost without change under the new cover of bodgie lifestyle. For some young people in Preston, Richmond, or Footscray, joining a gang was an almost 'natural' choice. For others, the gang wasn't a gang, just an informal group. Lloyd remembers his group as if it were a social club:

> It wasn't a gang ... but there was a group of guys who hung around together all the time ... four or five car loads of us. So there was about eighteen or 20 guys who used to hang around ... if you weren't doing anything during the weeknight you'd go around to one of their places ... Or you might just go for a walk and do some perving on the birds, the guys would always go cruising on the Saturday afternoon and Saturday night and we'd ride up and down the main streets ('Lloyd', interview, January 1991).

At the same time it is also clear to some of our informants that being 'mates', and being in a gang, had only a contingent relationship with being a 'bodgie'. There was often more choice about becoming a 'bodgie' than the mates you had—or the gang you joined. As Terry remembered it:

> Quite a lot of our boys had become bodgies now, but about half of our mob were squares. Mainly all the tough ones and good fighters were squares, they didn't have to be bodgies to be tough because they were already tough (Dick 1968: 171).

Being a bodgie was not as important as being a member of the Footscray mob, 'the greatest street gang there was in Melbourne' (ibid:154). This sense of local patriotism was embodied in a number of ways. It was often sufficient that the suburb itself identified the gang. Brian recollects the pride of being part of the Oaks (from Oakleigh), the Carnegie Boys, or the Footscray Boys ('Brian', interview, May 1991). Territoriality was also established by the practice of sending a car load of 'scouts' from one gang into another gang's territory.

> Someone would cruise through in a car. There might be one car with six blokes in it or something, and you would see them and say: 'They're down there', and the next thing you are on a train and down comes the gang ('Brian', ibid).

As in the matter of joining any 'elite' club, whether it be the Melbourne Club or the Masons or the Footscray Boys, access came slowly though getting to know the 'right people' and being accepted and known by them. Terry's membership claims were especially enhanced after he became an apprentice cabinet-maker and two of his work mates (Ape and Knuckles) proved to be leader members of the gang. Terry, as a bodgie, joined the gang as did Barney and Argles who were not. Membership was clinched by Terry being protected by Knuckles and Ape. In turn Terry's mates, Barney, Argles and Joey, won membership. As Terry Cooke remembers it, his best mates who were members of key gangs, weren't bodgies.

> Barney and Argles weren't bodgies yet and I didn't think they ever would be either for that matter. They were just not the type. Not that they weren't good blokes by any means; they were the best mates I had, but they were just not interested in becoming bodgies (Dick 1968: 153).

The lived experiences of our informants begins to reveal, in their own terms, some of the appeals and moral imperatives which gang membership both offered to them and required of them as young males.[14] This happened just as surely as membership of any other social institution can do, in which collective *and* personal identity are both integrated and oriented to powerful moral imperatives. Being a nurse, a soldier, or an academic, has its own ethical identity just as much as being a member of the Footscray mob had for its members.

Far from characterising the appeal of gang membership in terms of a gender-neutral 'youth culture', the gang provided diverse masculine activities. The 'discovery' that gangs are intensely masculine expressions is hardly novel, but what that means is not always as clear.

Connell has illuminated some of the distinctive aspects of masculine expressivity in his discussion of how men fill up space and move around in it. (Connell 1983; 1987). He deploys Berger's notion that men — conventionally — have a spatial presence dependent on the promise of power (Berger 1972). Connell insists that much of this power is literally embodied, that is, it is realised in men's bodies. Men's experience of sport for example, apart from the sensuousness of the experience of speed, or the aerobic effect, is also about how men come to feel powerful and skilful in the use of their bodies. (By 'force' Connell means the 'irresistible occupation of space'; by 'skill' he means 'the ability to operate on space or the objects in it, including other bodies' [Connell 1983: 18]). The acting out of the desire to be forceful and skilful, Connell suggests, is basic to masculine sociability *and* to self-definition, offering both sensuous rewards and political advantage. And it has to do with occupying space:

> To be an adult male is distinctly to occupy space, to have a physical presence in the world. Walking down the street, I square my shoulders and covertly measure myself against other men (Connell 1984: 18).

Masculine preoccupations with sport, with fighting, with the quantity of assets, sporting victories, with penis size and the quantity/quality of erections, or with winning (drinking contests, market advantage or games), appear to play a fundamental role in constituting maleness. Central to 'masculinity' is the equation between maleness and dominating or filling up space. (This is a volumetric preoccupation which feminist theory has long noted in much male knowledge). This formulation also points to the underlying fragility and precariousness of masculinity, in that many men fall prey to fears that they are not 'big enough' or 'strong enough' indices of 'maleness'; anxiety and a fear of inadequacy drives many men into repeated affirmations of their capacity to be forceful, large, and skilful.

These preoccupations are part of what Connell has more tendentiously called a hegemonic discourse about masculinity which begins with the notions that most men are essentially heterosexual, are 'naturally' more powerful than women, and enjoy and have a distinctive primacy in the 'public sphere' just as women have a primacy in the domestic or 'private sphere'. These elements of the 'masculine discourse' are sustained by the 'hydraulic model' of male sexuality (in which sexuality for the male is a 'natural and overwhelming almost uncontrollable force' [Weeks 1985:

80-1]). Within that overarching discourse, adolescence for the male is construed as a time of restlessness, of defining new powers, of testing capacities to control explosive urges and learning to adjust urges to enact 'anti-social' violence and sexuality (Hudson 1984: 35). And there are significant legitimations for adolescent boys to explore their adult male identities through affirmative and ritualised violence whether on the streets or on the sports field. We cannot hope to offer a fully developed discussion of masculinity—and its discontents here—nor our dissatisfaction with parts of Connell's formulation. Enough however has been said to suggest how we might begin to see in bodgie culture one expression of Australian masculinity in the post-war period.[15]

Our approach to understanding the experiences of being a bodgie stresses a localised, highly particular combination of behaviours, rules, and moral emotions which seems to have been integral to the collective experience of being a bodgie for many of those who laid claim to this status. Being a bodgie was a masculine expression of the drive to perfect claims to being a 'hard man' and of occupying space in particular ways. It worked through an often precarious search for forms of self and collective governance.[16] Membership of the collectivity conferred some of the strength of the group on to even the weakest members, members like Ritchie who 'was a weak sort of bloke who was always trying to create the impression that he was tough'.

Leadership in such fluid groupings was both impermanent and subject to many vagaries. For some bodgies there were clearly identified leaders, although the degree of informality was at odds with what the press identified as incumbents of such titles as the 'King of the Bodgies' and the 'Queen of the Widgies'.[17] Some storytellers recollected that there were local 'Kings of the Bodgies' who were young men who stood out for some reason or other.

> Well nobody really called them that. They just seemed to be. I mean I suppose that they were acknowledged by the town [Lismore] as amongst the leading elements of that particular group and therefore seen as someone deviant in their behaviour ('Jim', cited in Stratton 1992: 50).

For the most part, they had never heard the phrase nor observed the phenomena. But for a member of a bikie gang the issue of who got to be leader was necessarily a complex matter:

> It was a dictatorial structure really. Whoever was [leader] was not necessarily the strongest, but whoever could gather the most support. You weren't elected to lead a bikie group, you were there by associations ... Whoever can muster the numbers. The leader personally is usually a reasonably smooth talker but not necessarily a strong fighter or a physical fighter. If he had the support of a few musclemen, well then he could take the lead ('Jim', cited in Stratton 1992: 50).

Collective expression of strength and fearsomeness was much more a preoccupation than issues of leadership. It was a proof of their elite status that their activities were seen as so threatening, or that the media would set the alarm bells ringing and that special policing responses were mounted. As Brian recollects:

> Some of the gangs were that big that people were frightened to go out on to the streets and public transport. They had a special [police] squad from Russell Street called the 'bodgie squad'. And they used to crunch heads. They crunched heads and they were there to clean the place up. They were given a free rein. They'd never take you to court (though) I presume some of them must have ended up in court. They handed out some decent wallopings ('Brian', interview, May 1991).

Being part of a bodgie gang or any feared gang brought access to some morally uplifting activities such as protecting the weaker and more vulnerable gang members, even as it offered up more traditional masculine trophies, in the bloodied faces, the wounds won in the heat of battle, and the sexual favours of women.

Access to gang life offered entry into a masculine world of rules and behaviours to do with notions of honour, of dealing with challenges to one's dignity, and the making of claims to elite status, all of it within the security of collective solidarity. At the same time however, membership of gangs, which for many teenagers stretched between the ages of twelve and eighteen, was precarious. That precariousness had to do with the likelihood that, if being in a gang at twelve was acceptable, being in a gang at eighteen lay one open to accusations of still being involved in 'kid's play'.

Dealing with the culturally constructed indeterminacy of adolescence and its relations of enforced and imputed dependency was not easy. For young working class bodgies the allure of adult pursuits was apparently irresistible. As Brian recalled it:

> We were too young for pubs when you got to pub age it was a different group and different things and you grew out of that stage. You just move on to the next rung ... like kids would to play pinball machines and they'd get a bit old for that and they'd move onto the next sphere of life ('Brian', ibid).

Yet snooker, pinball machines, and the rest were not always sufficient to lay clear claim to adult status. Hence the constant invitation to allay such fears by demonstrations of aggression, violence, intimidation or more symbolic forms of terror, such as staking a claim over territory like a milk-bar. Such behaviour demonstrated they 'really meant it' and should be taken seriously. There was also the precariousness involved in moving from the terrifying violence of beating up other gang members or knifing 'dagos' in the streets at night, to the relative ordinariness of a Sunday family lunch. And for some it had to do with dealing with fear. As William Dick put it in 1965: 'The tough guy isn't happy. He's dead scared underneath. He's scared all the time' (cited in Craig 1965: 4).

Dealing with this precariousness led to an emphasis on collectively mobilising constant sources of challenge, in the form of choreographed challenges to 'out-groups' like the 'dagos' or to the police, or the parading in menacing postures, or the endless discussion in military fashion of 'attacks' and 'defences' against the enemy 'out there'. For many bodgies, these fights were collective experiences. As Craig remembered it:

> They weren't individual fights, they were all-in fights. They'd start over nothing ... you'd just walk past and you'd knock someone and then it would be on ... People would go out at night time and they'd get done over—so square-up night might be Friday night. You'd go hunting these people down ... you'd know where to find them (Craig 1965: 4).

Fighting seems from the reports of our respondents to have been about honour. For gang members there were many ways in which insults to honour might be resolved. Picking a fight typically involved either a deliberate attempt to move in on a gang member's female companion (variously called 'sheila', 'brush' or occasionally 'girl friend'), or it might require a mounting crescendo of personal insults. Brian remembers for example the way fights were started at dances:

> We were at Collingwood Town Hall ... one bloke got up and started dancing with this sheila and of course that was another bloke's girl. And someone got up and said to the bloke: 'You're dancing with my woman, sport', and he said, 'I only asked her for a dance mate, not a bloody root'. All of a sudden there was a chair in the air and that was the end of the night. The coppers had to come in and close the place down. That was a decent brawl ('Brian', interview, May 1991).

Chris remembers on one occasion an ambush which began with a widgie member of another gang 'leading' him on, arranging a date and then leaving him to confront a dozen or so ice-blade wielding gang members. He escaped narrowly from a very severe attack. On other occasions it would be a more casual affair:

> We didn't have a tough leader, some gangs did have them but we didn't. There was no-one up front telling us what to do. Things would just happen ... I'd say 'let's get outside and let's give it to them'. The word would just go around, 'There's going to be a blue on outside after' ('Chris', interview, December 1992).

The gangs of the fifties were a doubly collective phenomena, as groups of self-aware symbolically formal entities with names ('The Preston Boys' 'The Saints', 'The Phantoms') and leaders, *and* as groups whose very rationale depended on the existence of other similar and antagonistic groups. Violence was as essential to the gang members as the secrecy and silly handshakes are still to the Masons. It imbued a mundane reality with a glorious, even transcendent significance as other men, caught up in the violence of boxing, business conflict, ice hockey or war-making have long experienced and understood.

Membership of gangs was essentially about the construction of situations in which awesome struggle and heroic loyalty were conjoined in violence. Adopting the postures of an elite who wield, to the full, the powers of terror entails the absolute necessity that on occasion real violence be done, to avoid the humiliation of the posture being seen as just that.

There was certainly a code of rules for appropriate behaviour in which 'squaring up' or restoring a certain harmony to the relations between bodgies and the forces of order, took a high priority. 'Squaring up' seems to have been focused primarily at the non-legal end of the forces of order, especially at the bouncers who kept order at the dances and at the concerts. Brian recalls the general gist of the code of 'squaring up':

> You'd see bouncer pick people up by their arms and legs and run them deliberately into brick piers and drop them. I have seen some bad things like that. It doesn't matter if there were ten or twenty of them you would square up. There are easy ways to square up. You would sit in a park and watch when these people would leave, find out what they drive. There were many ways to square up. You'd get a bouncer and you'd break his leg ... and he'd remember what it was for. You'd never go hunting him again it was squared up and that was that. It was over and done with, providing you squared up and that was the end of the story ('Brian', interview, May 1991).

Squaring up involved a recognition that in a head to head confrontation with an adult bouncer the young bodgie stood little chance. Squaring up entailed waiting and then intervening to secure retribution on the bodgie's terms. In regard to police responses to such brawling, it appears that, in the bodgie's view at least, most police preferred to exercise discretion as the better part of valour. As Brian remembers it:

> The police would not normally turn up [at the big brawls at the Town Hall] ... Oh they might turn up two hours later after the action. They weren't stupid. If you were a policeman would you come, when there was anything from 30 to 100 blokes fighting ... It was the police that would get the hiding ('Brian', ibid).

Yet it is also clear that the 'bodgie squad', one response of police to the bodgie menace, was seen as a refracted cause for pride if only because it was so tough. The bodgie squad appears to have made its appearance in 1954-55. As Brian recollects the men who were in the bodgie squad were tough and able, the toughness and the ability in its own way reflecting its own commendation of the bodgie groups:

> They were hand picked these people, they were tough people. Sure, they ended up with broken arms and things like that, but not too often. And sure, they might have got a hiding from time to

> time. They were hand-picked blokes and they were tough blokes ('Brian', ibid).

In this contest with indubitably masculine authority figures the young men in ways not always clear to themselves felt themselves vindicated and affirmed.

There are many other elements of the lived experiences of Australia's bodgies we have not reported here. It was an aggressively masculine culture and yet the experiences of the widgies, the women, of the subculture, had their own integrity and significance. The relations between the sexes present researchers in the 1990s with major problems of capturing and representing these relations which appear to have little connection with contemporary moral frameworks about how relations between the sexes ought to be. Likewise the complex interpenetration of the media and bodgie culture, in which the media played a dual role as creators of a 'moral panic' and as creative sources of icons and as mirrors of bodgie culture is worthy of examination.

What we have focused on here is the way some young men constructed patterns of meaning and value around recurrent issues to do with power, honour, and territoriality. In one sense our attempt to recapture the lived experience of bodgie life is a small gesture towards the restoration of what Philip Rieff has luminously called the 'feeling intellect'—that attempt to 'recognise what it cannot see directly, the authority that directs each self in its own will to be someone' (Rieff 1990: xi). In that person and in their context we see a recurrent human impulse to experience the self as a distinctively moral agent, albeit here in ways which reflect distinctively masculine preoccupations. These ways may in turn invite moral emotions on the part of the reader like admiration or disgust. Undoubtedly we see here attempts at inspiring respect, earning integrity, exercising authority or compelling righteous fear. It matters considerably that so much of what Terry and his mates did might then—or now—be seen as 'mindless', as 'anti-social behaviour', as delinquency requiring correction, or more recently as acceptable forms of 'working class resistance'.

As Rieff reminds us, we all need to cultivate that 'humane and perceptive inner distance' from the immediately given social context—an inner distance which may help save this society from 'its intoxication with one damnable simplification after another' (Rieff 1973: 5). We would like to think that we have helped to restore some of that inner distance. If we have also restored to memory part of what has been repressed, we may sustain the possibility of a more intelligent discussion of how and what it means to be human.

REFERENCES

Berger, J. (1972) *Ways of Seeing*, Harmondsworth: Penguin.

Bessant, J. and Watts, R. (1992) '"Idols of the Mind" Beyond Culture and Towards an Ethnography of Youth Culture', *Australian Law and Society Conference*, La Trobe University, December 1992.

Braithwaite, J. and Barker, M. (1979) 'Bodgies and Widgies as Folk Devils of the 1950s', in P. Wilson and J. Braithwaite (eds), *Two Faces of Deviance*, St Lucia: University of Queensland.

Brake, M. (1980) *The Sociology of Youth: Culture and Youth Subcultures,* London: Routledge and Kegan Paul.

Burt, Cyril (1926) *The Young Delinquent*, London: London University Press.

Clarke, G. (1982) 'Defending Ski Jumpers: A Critique of Theories of Youth Subcultures', *CCCS Occasional Papers.*

Cohen, A.K. (1955) *Delinquent Boys: The Culture of the Gang*, New York: Free Press.

Cohen, P. (1980) 'Sub Cultural Conflict and Working Class Community', in S. Hall et al., (eds) *Culture, Media, Language*, London: Hutchinson.

Connell, R.W. (1983) 'Men's Bodies', in R.W. Connell (ed.), *Which Way is Up?*, Sydney: Allen and Unwin.

Connell, R.W. (1987) *Gender and Power: Society, the Person and Sexual Politics*, Sydney: Allen and Unwin.

Coward, R. (1977) 'Class, Culture and the Social Formation', *Screen* 17.

Craig, B. (1965) 'Writing his Way to the Top', *Australian Women's Weekly,* 8 December: 4.

Dick, William (1968) *A Bunch of Ratbags*, London: Collins.

Downes, D. (1966) *The Delinquent Solution,* London: Routledge and Kegan Paul.

Foucault, Michel (1980) 'Truth and Power', in C. Gordon (ed.), *Power/Knowledge: Selected Interviews and Other Writings*, New York: Pantheon.

Geertz, C. (1973) *The Interpretation of Cultures*, New York: Basil Books.

Gorman, C. (1990) 'The Bodgies - Acne with Padded Shoulders', in C. Gorman (ed.), *The Larrikin Streak*, Sydney: Sun Books.

Hall, S., Clarke, J., Jefferson, T. and Roberts, R. (eds) (1976) *Resistance Through Rituals: Youth Subcultures in Post-War Britain*, London: Hutchinson.

Hudson, B. (1984) 'Femininity and Adolescence', in A. McRobbie and Nava, M. (eds), *Gender and Generation*, London: Macmillan.

Hunter, I. (1988) *Culture and Government: The Emergence of Literary Education,* London: Macmillan.

Katz, J. (1988) *Seductions of Crime,* New York: Basic Books.

Kelt, J. (1977) *Rites of Passage: Adolescence in America, 1790 to the Present,* New York: Basil Books.

Manning, A.E. (1958) *The Bodgie: A Study in Psychological Abnormality,* Sydney: Angus and Roberston.

Matza, D. and Sykes, G. (1961) 'Juvenile Delinquency and Subterranean Values', *American Sociological Review:* 26 (5): 664-70.

McDonald, J. (1951) *The Bodgie,* (B.A.Thesis), Department of Anthropology, University of Sydney.

McRobbie, A. (1980) 'Settling Accounts with Sub Cultures: A Feminist Critique', *Screen Education,* Spring, 34: 37-49.

Orcutt, Robert (1983) *Analysing Deviance*, Englewood Cliffs: Prentice Hall.

Rieff, Phillip (1974) *Fellow Teachers,* New York: Harper and Row.

Rieff, Phillip (1990) *The Feeling Intellect,* Chicago: University of Chicago Press.

Sercombe, H. (1992) 'Youth Theory: Marx or Foucault?' *Youth Studies Australia*, 11: 3.

Stratton, Jon (1984) 'Bodgies and Widgies: Youth Cultures in the 1950s', *Journal of Australian Studies*, 15: 10-24.

Stratton, Jon (1992) *The Young Ones*, Perth: Black Swan Press.

Tait, Gordon (1992) 'Reassessing Street Kids: A Critique of Sub-Culture Theory', *Youth Studies Australia*, 11 (2): 12-17.

Taylor, C. (1985), *Philosophical Papers*, (2 vols), Cambridge: Cambridge University Press.

Taylor, I. Walton, P. and Young, J. (1975) *The New Criminology: For a Social Theory of Deviance*, London: Routledge Kegan and Paul.

van Krieken, Robert (1991) *Children and the State*, Sydney: Allen and Unwin.

van Krieken, Robert (1992) 'The Poverty of Social Control: Explaining Power in the Historical Sociology of the Welfare State', in M. Muetzelfeldt (ed.), *Society, State and Politics in Australia,* Sydney: Pluto Press.

Walker, J. (1986a) 'Romanticising Resistance, Romanticising Culture: A Critique of Willis' Theory of Cultural Production', *British Journal of Sociology,* 1.

Walker, J. (1986b) 'Romanticising Resistance, Romanticising Culture: Problems in Willis' Theory of Cultural Production', *British Journal of Sociology of Education*, 7 (2): 259-80.

Weeks, J. (1985), *Sexuality and its Discontents: Meanings, Myths and Modern Sexualities,* London: Routledge.

White, Rob (1990) *No Space of their Own*, Sydney: Cambridge University Press.

Willis, P. (1977) *Learning to Labour: How Working Class Kids get Working Class Jobs*, Farnborough: Saxon House.

NOTES

1. On current international concerns see, Youth Affairs Administration, *The World Youth Survey 1989*, Prime Minister's Office, Tokyo, 1989; J. Walker et al., *A Comparison of Crime in Australia and Other Countries, Trends and Issues, 23,* Canberra: Australian Institute of Criminology, 1990; National Committee on Violence, *Violence: Directions for Australia*, Canberra: Australian Institute of Criminology, 1990; M. Brusten, J. Graham, N. Herriger and P. Malinowski, (eds), *Youth Crime, Social Control and Prevention*, Pfaffenweiler: Centarus Verlagsgeselleschaft, 1986; P. Wilson and J. Arnold, *Street Kids, Australia's Alienated Young,* Melbourne: Collins Dove, 1986, and C. Alder and D. Sandor, *Homeless Young People as Victims of Violence*, Report, Criminology Department, University of Melbourne, 1990.

2. For an overview of American history of gangs see P. Kratcoski and L. Kratcoski, *Juvenile Delinquency,* Englewood Cliffs: Prentice-Hall, 1979: 70-103. See also, J. Gillis, *Youth and History*, New York: Norton, 1974; I. Warner,'Masculinity, Crime and Juvenile Gangs: A Cross Cultural Comparison between Australia and Japan', (unpublished), Melbourne, October 1991.

3. Stratton builds on a body of work including J. Braithwaite and M. Barker, 'Bodgies and Widgies as Folk Devils of the Fifties', in P. Wilson and J. Braithwaite, (eds), *Two Faces of Deviance*, St Lucia: University of Queensland Press, 1979.

4. See his first intervention J. Stratton 'Bodgies and Widgies—Youth Cultures in the 1950s', *Journal of Australian Studies*, 15, November 1984: 10-24.

5. There is no definitive account of the meaning or origin of either 'bodgie' or 'widgie'. Most now accept that it had its origins in Sydney c.1942-45 and probably had something to do with the activities of Australian and American 'black market' dealers in clothing which was not always in perfect order; the English expression 'bodger' was used to describe such imperfection.

6. At the same time Stratton is interested to go beyond the interactionist approach of Braithwaite and Barker who, following Cohen, in effect dispose of any focus on young people in their pursuit of the way the media and other social agencies constructed a 'moral panic' (Braithwaite and Barker 1979).

7. Stratton is careful to indicate some weaknesses in the youth culture model; he is for example critical of Cohen's failure to adequately specify the boundaries around youth culture. Even so Stratton himself ends up with a certain confusion about how much his 'youth culture' is genuinely autonomous and counter-hegemonic, and how much it has been compromised by 'middle class media'.

8. See variously S. Cohen, *Visions of Social Control*, Polity Press, Cambridge, 1985; D. Chunn and S. Gavigan, 'Social Control: Analytic Tool or Analytic Quagmire?, *Contemporary Crises*, 12(2)1 : 107-24; J. Higgins, 'Social Control Theories of Social Policy', *Journal of Social Policy*, 9(1) 1980: 1-23, and

R. van Krieken, 'Social Theory and Child Welfare; Beyond Social Control', *Theory & Society*, 15(3) 1986: 410-29.

9. To be fair, Stratton's analysis is working at the discursive level as he wishes to suggest that there was a categorical conflation between 'teenagers' and 'bodgies and widgies' built into a 'moral panic'. At the substantive level however for some young people there was no doubt about their experience as bodgies or widgies. On other occasions Stratton's analysis clearly leaves the world of the bodgie; 'As the bodgie and widgie were constructs, images that one could voluntarily and literally buy into because so much of their construction was based on the newly available mass-produced goods, there was another possibility to be considered. The image provided a possible vehicle for assimilation for immigrant youths into Australian society'. (Stratton, *The Young Ones*, 1992: 42). Apart from not being clear what possible experience 'assimilation into Australian society' could possibly refer to, this latter claim would come as a considerable surprise to the Australian-born bodgies we have interviewed.

10. Dick's 'novel' about bodgies and widgies in the 1940s and 1950s was defined by Dick as '95% autobiography'. It has come to occupy a privileged position as an ethnographic source. The Department of Criminology at the University of Melbourne prescribed his text in 1965, and we have relied on it heavily (Craig 1965).

11. We are not saying that all bodgies did or experienced the things we discuss here. There was a vast range of experiences and dispositions in which being a bodgie could involve everything from just liking to dress up occasionally through to hard core 'criminal activity', while we stress the moral nature of much of the behaviours and expression of 'bodgies' and 'widgies' and gang culture in the 1950s it is not necessarily our kind of morality.

12. What Taylor seems not to do as well is to deal with the ways in which gender helps to constitute the distinctively moral character of so much *different* interaction and behaviour.

13. The voice belongs to Fred Mackenzie. Fred was interviewed for a 3RN radio documentary called 'The Johnny O'Keefe Story', broadcast in April 1992 (quoted by courtesy of the ABC).

14. We hope to avoid any conflation between notions of 'human' and 'masculine' by suggesting that people may have common intentions, for example in regard to honour and respect, but that these intentions are fragmented or mediated by many factors including gender, in terms of how these qualities are represented, realised or sought out.

15. Needless to say this formulations avoids many questions about the extent to which 'masculinity' is a cross-cultural phenomenon, and/or a trans-historical phenomenon.

16. This idea of 'governance' is used in Foucault's sense of a project oriented to securing 'self-control' and 'control over others'. Without subscribing either to his theoretical ambitions or to his deployment of this idea, we have drawn some

insights from G. Wickham, 'A Sociology of Governance', *Australian Law and Society Conference*, LaTrobe University, December 1992.

17. The *Sydney Morning Herald* in December 1956 carried a story about a girl in a Melbourne Court whose lawyer, Frank Galbally, insisted was the 'Queen of the Widgies' (*Sydney Morning Herald,* 18 December 1956). A search of the Melbourne press revealed nothing to substantiate the Sydney story.

9 Media Depictions and Public Discourses on Juvenile 'Gangs' in Melbourne, 1989-1991

Ian Warren and Megan Aumair

INTRODUCTION

> Gang wars, brawls, and feuding may sound like a recipe for an action movie, but such behaviour is becoming a way of life for some Melbourne secondary students (*Sunday Herald-Sun* 25 April 1994).

In the last decade there has been an increased public focus on the emergence of a 'gang problem' in larger Australian cities. Fostered largely by press reports of collective criminality and representations of gang activity in North American popular culture, the tenor of this issue concentrates on the negative aspects of male collective identification and the threat such groups pose for the broader community. Public discourse suggests that there is a rising threat to public safety caused by groups of young adolescent males involved in destructive criminality and random violence. Yet little is known of the actual characteristics of the gang phenomenon, or the reasons why groups of young males frequent areas of public space. Indeed, the media tends to show only one side of a multi-faceted problem of social acceptance and collective youth culture in the public realm.

This essay presents the results of research conducted on 'gangs' in an inner suburban area of Melbourne in 1991. The aim of the study was to provide a detailed ethnographic account of youth gang activity (Hammersley and Atkinson 1989), and the relationship between gangs and the general community in light of the popular media imagery of the 'gang problem'. The study was designed to elaborate some of the common perceptions of juvenile gangs which emerged in press reports, through extensive consultation in one locality. The research provides a detailed critique of the conceptions of 'gangs' in urban Australia which supplements the extensive data on gangs in the United States (Huff 1990; Sanchez-Jankowski 1991).

The research involved a multi-method approach to exploring the phenomenon of youth gangs. Given the fact that there are a number of disparate conceptions of the gang phenomenon and youth crime, the research attempted to gain an understanding of the different problems posed by those groups for different members of the community. A large number of young people and professionals who have regular contact with young people were approached. This facilitated community consultation on matters involving social research in our society (VCCAV 1990). Organisations such as schools, the public transport authority, youth services, ethnic and migrant services, and members of the Victoria Police were interviewed using an open-ended question schedule designed to elicit the opinions and degrees of interaction each organisation had with young people in the community. These were supplemented by interviews with young people themselves, and their experiences in light of the gang debate. Further, a general public opinion survey of local shopkeepers provided a broader guide for assessing public perceptions. Media accounts over the three years preceding the study were also analysed to illustrate the range of public discourses focusing on the gang phenomenon.

Research of this nature does not provide a full account of the trends of youth gangs Australia-wide, nevertheless the results do provide a general picture of the encounter between groups of young males and the community in the public domain.

Definitions and Discourses

Central to the issue of gangs in modern society is the image which the term 'gang' evokes in the broader community. Public discourses on the subject of gangs are directly influenced by media portrayals of gang criminality and by the messages of other cultural agents regarding socially acceptable behaviour (Walton 1993). While it is difficult to attribute blame for the moral panic on gangs solely to the media, the media do have a dominant role to play in the way issues relating to crime, criminality, and social control are perceived by the rest of society. Underlying the issue of media and cultural depiction of gangs is the power vested in media organisations to shape community perceptions of social issues. Coverage of other areas which tend to incite moral panic has often been found to be imbalanced, with content written in a form which is easy to accept without questioning the intention of journalists and the images they create (Kelsey and Young 1982: 5; Coleman et al. 1990).

Historically there have been a number of anomalies associated with the use of the term 'gang' to describe the behaviour of males in the public domain. Common parlance in Australia suggests a highly negative connotation which is reflective of the 'bushranger' violence of Ned Kelly's gang, or the organised criminal activities of Squizzy Taylor and John Wren in inter-war Sydney and Melbourne. Yet this imagery is juxtaposed against the positive team ethos encouraged by a gang of sportsmen or boy scouts. While linguistically the term has both positive and negative connotations, the most vivid in terms of historical discourse has been the negative, where gang activity is seen to represent a threat to the security of the state.

The term 'gang' has become a convenient catch phrase used by the print media in particular to convey a negative perception of the activities of groups of young males in the public domain in contemporary society. Very often this has criminal connotations, associated with the subcultural activities of gangs in the United States derived from visual imagery in popular culture. Graphic representations of gang violence, drugs, and criminality in movies such as *Colors*, *New Jack City*, and *Boyz 'n the Hood* and the racist violence exhibited by gangs of neo-Nazi Skinheads in the film *Romper Stomper,* paint a picture of a growing problem in modern cities. While many of these movies have a fictitious basis, the imagery and meanings such depictions evoke have the ability to feed into the gang debate by moulding the perceptions of the public, and by creating a mentality of fear associated with groups of young males, particularly in public areas.

During the period from 1989 to 1995 the media utilised this imagery, often with comparisons with the experience in the international setting. This works to create a modern day discourse on male collective behaviour and gang deviance based specifically upon experience which is different from the Australian experience. The difficulty with such analyses is that they make rash and often unfounded comparisons with the characteristics of very different societies:

> Victoria was becoming like Los Angeles which last year reported 60 warring gangs within a radius of 5 km in one section of the city ... Victorian youth were resorting to crime as a means of survival and a way of expressing their anger at the recession which had widened the gap between the 'haves and the have-nots' (*Herald-Sun* 8 August 1991).

Several studies have indicated that gangs in the United States serve a variety of organising purposes in the communities they comprise, some of which have criminal consequences, others which are more communitarian in nature (Huff 1990; Sanchez-Jankowski 1991). These range from the provision of recreational options for young members of the community, protection from outsiders in insular communities, to political lobbying for public works in certain areas. Moreover, the more detailed the information on gangs becomes, the more difficult it has been for scholars in the United States to come to a definition of gang behaviour which reflects community perceptions of an organised entity surviving purely upon criminal activity (Spergel and Chance 1991: 23; Aumair and Warren 1994). These findings challenge the commonly portrayed characteristics of gangs, engaged in orgies of drive-by shootings, large scale drug distribution, prostitution rackets, and random violence directed at innocent and vulnerable members of the community.

Popular imagery, in film and the press, does not reflect the different social and organisational realities of youth culture in contemporary Australian society. Yet the conclusion to be derived from such discourses is obvious: gangs of young males are undermining the fabric of law-abiding society through systematic and random violence. The point of this study was to explore whether this is the case, and whether these perceptions are shared by the community at large.

Environmental Characteristics of the Region

Some studies, particularly in the United Kingdom, have emphasised the importance of environmental characteristics in dictating the course of social phenomena, and in influencing the broader public and control responses to such issues. Keith (1993) for instance places great emphasis on the environmental features which surrounded the race riots in Brixton, Hackney, and Notting Hill in the early 1980s. His findings indicated that there were certain areas of importance to the black communities which became the source of increased police and media attention. The creation of 'no-go' zones, battle zones, and the use of police raids in certain recreational areas frequented by black youths was a central feature of the riots which generated not only a control response, but black retaliation to persistent police harassment. In historical terms, the work of Cohen (1979) illustrates the process of law enforcement in 'cleaning up the streets' in a working class suburb of 19th century urban England. This study illustrated how specific areas were important, not only in providing an open and public forum for members of working class communities to fraternise and engage in minor forms of recreation, but in the eventual determination of the elite classes to remove these people from the public areas through the legal authority of the police. White (1990) provides a working paradigm for assessment of the relationship between young people and the community in areas of public space in Australia.

Our study focused on the urban business district of an inner suburban region of Melbourne. The immediate vicinity had several characteristics which attracted groups of young people to the area for a variety of recreational and social reasons. The city centre was a hub for a number of public transport facilities (trains, trams, and buses) which enabled young people to get to and from school and to attend recreational areas after hours. This made the inner city a regional centre catering for a wide range of young people from outlying suburbs. The inner city comprised a shopping centre attracting people of all ages. The construction of a mall theoretically catered for collective relaxation in the public setting, although it is arguable that such facilities cater mainly for shoppers rather than for the general public. Several secondary and tertiary education facilities encircled the main shopping region, giving additional justification for the presence of large numbers of young people. Further, there were a number of youth amusement venues, including video game outlets, pool halls, and a ten-pin bowling alley.

As a result, the regular presence of young people was not only expected in the inner city, it was encouraged by the facilities provided in the area. The mall acted as the consumption and recreation centre of the region. The lay-out was conducive to social gathering, with an abundance of seating facilities in an environment enhanced by trees, freshly painted buildings and artistic work carried out by local youth. Essential community services, shopping, entertainment, and public transport were within walking distance of the mall. Young people therefore were frequently seen in and around the area.

A profile of the local population also helps to highlight the ethnic diversity and the working-class traditions of the area. Census statistics from 1991 indicate that 44.3% of the population were born overseas: 13.1% in South-East Asia (10.6% in Vietnam) and 15.4% in southern Europe (3.5% in Italy and 3.5% in Greece). Many of the Asian immigrants came to the country as refugees with little or no family support and few had any form of support structures at all. This necessitated collective association within cultural groups which could in some way provide support and a sense of belonging.

Fifteen percent of the population in this region was aged between fifteen and 24 years at the time of the 1991 census. Official unemployment in the area was 12.7% (Australian Bureau of Statistics 1991). A continued decline in the level of employment has been one of the most striking trends in the youth labour market over the past two decades (Sweet 1990). A report by the Department of Employment, Education and Training in early 1995 found that the area under investigation suffered the worst official unemployment rates in the country. The survey of regional labour markets during the first three months of 1995 showed that official unemployment in this area was 14.3%, and that the official teenage jobless rate was 55.7%. Despite the so-called 'recovery' and the Federal Government's Working Nation Program, this region had 6,000 fewer jobs in 1995 than at the same time in 1993 (Department of Employment, Education and Training 1995).

High youth unemployment, exacerbated by a fall in the number of manufacturing jobs, has become a characteristic of the region. In addition, the 1991 census found that 18.1% of households in the region earned less than $12,000 per annum compared to the Melbourne Statistical Division average of 11.1% (Australian Bureau of Statistics 1991). This indicates that a far greater number of households in this area were in deprived circumstances compared to the Melbourne average.

There are conflicting interpretations of employment and unemployment statistics in relation to the social demographics of particular geographical regions, and the characteristics of those who inhabit these areas. Gregory and Hunter (1995) argue that the economic gap is widening in Australian society which has implications for the ways people in various communities spend their time on a day to day basis. The argument runs that the poor are increasingly living together in one set of neighbourhoods, and the rich in another. Unemployed people in depressed neighbourhoods may be associating with other unemployed people, which leads to a continual exclusion from available job opportunities. Further, individuals living in depressed neighbourhoods may develop behaviour patterns that make it difficult for them to find work. The result is that in geographical regions where there is a depressed working economy, unemployment statistics may reveal high concentrations of youth or migrant unemployment which has implications for the prospects of these people breaking the cycle of joblessness.

This argument is of great importance to the present discussion. It continues to be an observable fact in this region that large numbers of young people congregate in public space at all hours of the day. When this feature is combined with the relative absence of few, low, or no cost recreational options for young people, the streets, or other areas of public space, take on greater significance as a place for young people or newly arrived migrants to gather and spend their time (White 1990).

Young people are one of the most vulnerable groups in society. They are confronted constantly with decisions, attitudes, and processes which are beyond their control. Choice in the direction of their lives is influenced by the conditions of the society in which they live (Moysey 1993). Given the profile of the community under review this is clearly evident. In response to contemporary socioeconomic realities a variety of youth cultures develop. Some elements of these cultures advocate anti-adult and anti-social behaviours. They convey this through personal appearance, musical preferences, and sexuality. Other aspects of other youth cultures conform to adult and societal expectations, particularly those emphasising success. Some conflict does exist within certain youth cultures in Australia. However, as the evidence will suggest, the seriousness of these conflicts is not comparable to the kind of gangland violence in the United States which is associated with territory, masculinity, and ethnicity (Polk 1993).

Characteristics of Melbourne Inner-City 'Gangs'

There was general unanimity expressed by those working in the area of youth relations, and by young people themselves, about the characteristics of inner city Melbourne youth 'gangs.' The responses indicate that, in spite of extensive media publicity to the contrary, gangs are not of great concern in this region. Indeed, when viewing the issue over time, there was little difference between the activities of groups of young people today, and those of similar groups in the 1950s.

Central to the conception of the gang phenomenon was the way in which the term 'gang' was used. The results indicate a considerable variation between the characteristics of a 'gang' in popular discourse, and the activities of groups of young people in this particular region. While the activities of young people were reflective of amorphous structures and types of collective behaviour, the term 'gang' implies a more cohesive, unified structure, with a deliberate and ongoing criminal purpose. As one respondent with several years of teaching experience in this area indicated:

> In order to belong to a gang there is certain behaviour and attitudes and values which you have to hold and maintain, and also display, in order to be part of it.

The characteristics of groups in this region did in some cases reflect certain identifiable subcultural characteristics which suggest a common identity. This was particularly so in the case of migrant groups who have shared experiences of lifestyle and socialisation in the community, and other subcultural groups such as 'headbangers', 'jocks' or 'rappers' who exhibit particular styles indicative of contemporary heavy metal music culture (long hair, torn jeans, and t-shirts with graphic representations of death, human bodies in varying degrees of decomposition, and occasional satanic references), contemporary sports fashion (such as tracksuits, soccer or football jerseys, and elaborate athletic footwear), or bastardised versions of Afro-American rap culture (reversed baseball caps, overly baggy denim jeans of various colours, and elaborate athletic footwear). However central to the term 'gang' was an ongoing and identifiably criminal purpose which implied an illegitimacy of formation. This resulted in the term having negative, and criminal connotations reflective of portrayals in popular discourse. As such gangs were by definition an organised and criminal threat to the community.

In contrast youth collectives in Melbourne inner-city were by and large social groups, comprised mainly of young males with common traits of sociocultural identity. The collective was more a peer group, where there were no formal requirements of entry and few informal codes of organisation. Subcultural traits were common, enabling individuals to distinguish between different 'styles' of youth behaviour. However these factions were similar to other forms of peer interaction among both adults and youths in organised settings. Therefore, those who were fanatical about heavy metal music and culture would congregate together because the music and the culture gave them something in common. The characteristic of formation for a criminal purpose was not central, despite the fact that criminal activity did at times occur among and between groups. The normativity and premeditated criminal behaviour, characteristic of popular conceptions of gang behaviour, were generally absent.

While youth crime was seen to be specifically attributable to the gang phenomenon, the incidence of crime among the Melbourne youth under study was sporadic, and seldom involved random interpersonal violence. The majority of criminal behaviour was related to the status of young people, and reflected the social surroundings of the area, and the recreational options available for these groups. Thus graffiti and damage to public property was a prominent feature, particularly in and around public transport facilities. Shop windows were sometimes broken, however incidents involving organised robberies were rare. Minor pilfering from larger shopping centres was common, yet seldom attributable to organised and identifiable groups of young people. By and large, the crimes which occurred were reflective of general crime patterns experienced by young people in most urban communities; rates for violent crime were low compared to levels for adult offences, while minor property offences were relatively more common (Mukherjee and Dagger 1990: 67-69).

There were some instances where interpersonal violence did occur between rival groups. Examples of this behaviour provided some evidence of ethnic-related conflict between groups who, on occasion, engaged in an organised 'punch-up' often stemming from long standing community rivalries, or misunderstandings, which sometimes involved interference with the 'women' of a particular group. While these issues were of some concern, particularly given the ethnic composition of the participants, their frequency was low, and posed little threat to the broader community. Indeed, it was pointed out by one person, who had been a gang member in the 1950s, that there was little difference between this behaviour today and that which had occurred throughout urban Australian history:

> They are no different to the bunches of young louts who used to knock around here 30 or 40 years ago except that they were all Aussies [then] rather than being ethnically based ... In terms of their purpose and role, why they were formed, and what they got

out of it there are no obvious differences.

Moreover, the youth-focused nature of such confrontations means that it is difficult for such violence to spill over into other areas which affect the general community. As with young people involved in organised sports, these activities involved participants who voluntarily assumed the risks (Young 1993).[1]

When questioned about the reasons for committing crime, young people indicated that boredom was a primary feature. This was particularly relevant in the case of minor vandalism and victimless crimes, such as under-age drinking or minor drug use. Breaking the rules provided a more engaging opportunity for immediate gratification. This again was not a regular occurrence, and was often attributed to a few bad apples in the group. The issue of individual status was important. Youths often felt compelled to join their peers in a common activity which might lead to a deviant act. However crime on the whole was not a primary objective of these groups, and its systematic and organised occurrence was denounced by the groups themselves, police, teachers, and youth workers.

The lack of understanding about the purpose of congregation was the central theme expressed by youth workers and migrant workers about the demarcation between public perceptions and youth culture in the gang debate. In most cases the purpose was social in nature: the group provided a means by which young people, and young males in particular, could identify collectively. Yet few members of the community were seen as adopting this perspective. There was a common misconception about the use of community space, especially in relation to groups of young people from migrant communities. Its effects were also seen to impinge on the broader issue of male youth culture in the public domain. The issue for migrant youth was however very different, because not only did they congregate together for social reasons, but collective socialisation also provided an avenue for peer support where problems and experiences of assimilation in a new culture could be shared and resolved as a group.

The main case in point in the present study related to Indo-Chinese youth in the region. This population faced difficulties which necessitated strong networks of peer support both in private and public space. As most respondents working with these groups explained, it is impossible to divorce the cultural backgrounds and experience of many Indo-Chinese youth from the current trends in collective socialisation in contemporary Australia. Yet the general consensus was that the broader public have little idea of the difficulties such youths face in negotiating cultural difference.

Respondents said that many young people have settled in Australia from an environment which has stifled their adolescent development. There were vast cultural differences between the upbringing and environment of their homeland communities and the norms and values which prevailed in contemporary Australian society. Several intersecting factors made the assimilation process difficult, particularly for young people. This included long years spent in concentration camps where death was an every day occurrence, the absence or loss of parents and other supportive family structures, rejection by sponsors when arriving in Australia, language and other cultural barriers, limited educational development by western standards, and difficulty in negotiating social and community support and income services, particularly as a result of a general unawareness of the mechanics of Australian bureaucracy.

In a number of cases, teenagers from these backgrounds are by necessity forced to be fully independent in a culturally alien and alienating environment. These problems are exacerbated in the realm of public space, where there is increased competition with other young people for the use of community recreational resources. Thus, tauntings from groups from other backgrounds, often based on visible racial differences, compounded by low socio-economic status, combined with the above factors to make the transition process from the homeland to the new country a daunting experience for many from this population. While respondents were cautious to point out that many of these problems did not apply to all Indo-Chinese youth, they were prevalent in this region in light of the trends of mass settlement encouraged by cheap housing and business rental.

This evidence suggests that these groups have a particular need for collective peer identification not only for recreational purposes, but to facilitate an ongoing support network which attempts to negotiate and offset some of these difficulties. This aids in the overall integration process for these groups. In some ways this informal network replaces more formal mechanisms of social welfare due to the specific nature of the problems faced by these groups. As one worker in the migrant community indicated, a self-help network is required as the problems are generally 'too complex for the competence of the agencies which are designed to provide the assistance required'.

While it was acknowledged that some minorities participated in criminal activity on a more sustained level, their presence was largely hidden from the mainstream community. The semi-organised criminal activities of such groups—such as drug use, illegal gambling, and prostitution, however, tended to be masterminded by older members of these communities and were viewed as the exception rather than the rule. Moreover their victims were likely to be the less powerful members of these communities, such as the women, or those with substance addiction. Thus there was little scope for the broader public to be affected by, or made aware of, these problems. Many respondents however indicated that the presence of these groups was of no greater frequency than those from other ethnic backgrounds, including Anglo-Australians.

The final point to emerge from interview evidence was the variable of masculinity. Most gangs regardless of class, ethnic background, or indeed age involved groups of males. Females were peripheral to the activities of such groups and seldom used the public realm as an area for recreation. In most cases, young females were also seen as a primary source of conflict between different groups, particularly where sexual and emotional relationships were involved. Indeed, one of the main sources of conflict between groups occurred when outsiders tried to threaten or make a pass at the girlfriend of a gang member. This would lead to the rest of the group supporting the affected individual and often led to aggressive and recurrent confrontation.

The most important finding of the study was that criminal activity was in most cases a transient and sporadic phenomenon for most groups. The perception that there were organised youth gangs persistently engaging in criminal activity, was seen by most youth service workers and the police as distanced from the fundamental purposes of collective social interaction and peer support. While there was some criminal activity which caused concern, the phenomenon of a sustained gang problem for criminal justice purposes was clearly the exception rather than the norm. The youth posed little actual threat to the broader community.

Public Perceptions

As the data indicated that the gang phenomenon was of little concern to major organisations involved in youth policy and criminal justice, it was decided to assess the factors which influenced public opinion and perceptions. The aim was to assess the general public's belief that there was a 'gang problem', and the sources of information available in the public realm which contributed to that belief. Following is a summary of the results of a survey carried out amongst local shopkeepers in the region to assess their concerns over groups of young people congregating in community space. Shopkeepers were targeted, given their permanence in the region and the nature of the services they provided to the public. Moreover, shopkeepers have a vested interest in the safety of shoppers and clients both during and after opening hours. A total of 47 shopkeepers were approached in the main shopping area, and 32 completed questionnaires. Most respondents were female (65.5%) and the ages of respondents ranged from fifteen to 40.

A small percentage of shopkeepers (56.3%) were aware of gangs operating in the area. However of primary interest was the way these were characterised by the individual respondents. The main indicator of a person being a gang member was the way in which the individual or group of young people dressed. Gangs were seen as a threat to shoppers and shop owners on the basis of the image which young people, and particularly young males, portrayed to the general public. Other visible features such as a common ethnic identity, and an identifiable ring leader were also recognised as indicating a gang presence.

The majority of respondents believed that the types of offences gangs were likely to engage in were vandalism (47%) and theft (42%). Other offences attributable to gangs included assault (21%), substance abuse (21%), and loitering (10.5%). However, there was generally a high perception of fear of collective gang violence. The fear of groups of young people was particularly widespread, and predictably, was more of an issue for females than males. Over half of the respondents (57.2%) demonstrated a general fear of collective criminality, with the majority (42.9%) being female. The age of negative responses was evenly distributed—although, interestingly, the younger the respondent the less concern there was over the behaviour of youth gangs.

Most people feared victimisation from young people in the mall area or at the local railway station and, as expected, the majority of respondents (62%) said they felt more vulnerable in the evening than during business hours. Again, females were more likely to express concerns about their safety in these areas. Perhaps the most pervasive finding related to the sources from which people derived their information on the incidence of gang criminality. Table 1 shows that the majority of people interviewed received their information on gangs and gang behaviour from secondary sources, comprising mainly hearsay (42.1%) or the media (32.2%).

Table 9.1: Sources of Information about Gang Crime, Melbourne

Source of Information	Males (n. and %)	Females (n. and %)	Total (n. and %) *
Experience/Observation	4 (12.9%)	3 (9.8%)	7 (22.7%)
Hearsay	2 (6.6%)	11 (35.5%)	13 (42.1%)
Media	6 (19.4%)	4 (12.9%)	10 (32.3%)
Police	-	1 (3.2%)	1 (3.2%)

* As there were multiple responses to this question percentages total over 100%.

The results of the shopkeeper survey suggest several things. First, the actual incidence of gang activity in the region was relatively infrequent. Only a small percentage of respondents (22.7%) had actually observed or been victims of gangs. Indeed, when queried about this point, 16.1% of respondents said that they had been victims of collective youth violence in the last twelve months. Of these, two respondents said this had been in the mall after normal working hours. Yet this level of victimisation is low, compared to the 70.9% of respondents who felt there was a 'gang problem'. This is indicative of a perception amongst the majority of respondents of a youth presence which is threatening to the safety and well-being of local shopkeepers. Interestingly, of the 29.1% of individuals who did not perceive a 'gang problem', 16.1% were female, 9.8% were male, and 3.2% were so unfamiliar with the nature of the community that they were unable to comment on the issue.

The implications of these results are that the perceptions of a 'gang problem' are more often than not based upon secondary evidence rather than direct victimisation or first hand interaction with local groups of young people. The negative connotations therefore associated with gangs are seldom based on actual experience. Those who express no fear either do not see collective youth behaviour to be a threat to personal safety, or are oblivious to the existence of gangs in the region.

However, over 53% of respondents perceive a negative gang presence which is primarily based on second hand accounts or hearsay related to the behaviour of young people in public space. The implications of this level of fear in terms of public representations of youth behaviour in the popular print media are outlined below.

In addition, only one individual stated that the police were her major source of information on issues related to gang criminality. Clearly this issue requires further exploration, but it does illustrate two points. First it supports interview evidence that police do not view gangs as a major issue of concern in the overall crime debate. As one police officer explained, domestic assault was a greater problem for police than the behaviour of young people in public places. Secondly, and as a result of the greater concern of police about criminal behaviour in the private sphere, this point may indicate an absence of police consultation with the community on a broader scale. When this is compared with the high level of public reliance on the media and hearsay for information, the evidence suggests that the lack of liaison between the police and members of this community may be a contributing factor to exaggerated local perceptions of a gang problem. Finally, over 70% of respondents said that they relied upon secondary sources for information regarding gang activity or its possible threat. This suggests that there is little personal contact with, and few instances of personal victimisation by, groups of young males.

The Media and Gangs

One of the central themes relating to the media involvement in the gang debate was a sustained level of media attention given to the assumed rising gang problem in the Melbourne metropolitan area during the two years preceding this project. In particular, both the local and greater Melbourne press contained a number of articles claiming an overall rise in levels of collective youth criminality which threatened the safety of the general public. Underlying the issue of media reportage is the power vested in media organisations to shape community perceptions over social issues through selective discursive interpretation and presentation of such information as 'News'.

Content analysis of print media reportage on the gang issue during the period 1989-1991 revealed that the media consistently used the term 'gang' when referring to any group-related behaviour involving young males in the public spaces of Melbourne. In doing this they projected an image of young people in groups as threatening and potentially violent even when they might be congregating legitimately in public space. This helped to mould the public's perception of an increasing and threatening 'gang problem'.

There were a number of recurring images of gangs which appeared in the press during the period of study. These allowed the public to construct a profile of the typical gang member, the gang victim, and gang-related offences. Of particular interest in media reporting of gang crime incidents was the use of words and phrases, specific events which sparked an increase in reports of gang crimes, the changing definitions of gangs in the media, the influence of the 'expert' arguing the case, and the American influence. On the other hand, a clear definition of what a gang was, the socialisation aspects of congregation, the cultural impetus for social gathering, and the need to maintain and express masculinity in the face of unemployment and disadvantage, were usually omitted from these media reports.

Both newspaper headlines and the content of articles relating to gang activity indicated that there was a particular construction of truth as much designed to sell newspapers as it was to provide the public with information. Nevertheless, these portraits have a strong impact upon public tolerance of youth culture in general, as seen in the article below:

> **Youths Attack Shoppers: Teen Gang Violence**
>
> Teenagers and women have become targets of violent youth gangs ... there was a perpetual problem in a Footscray car park ... where ten to 20 youths habitually gathered around the so-called 'beer garden near the bus stop ... the youths consumed alcohol in the area on Friday nights and then headed down ... to the 7-Eleven store, leaving a trail of violence and graffiti behind them'. Police have also had reports of 'gangs hanging around the Food Court in the shopping centre where thefts have occurred', Detective Senior Sergeant ... said (*The Western Times* 24 April 1991).

This report communicates strong condemnation of the behaviour of this particular group of young males. However, while sensationalising and suggesting a persistent and violent problem, the report fails to provide any additional illumination on the problem. For example, the use of public space by the youths for recreation is self evident, yet there is no voice for the young people to justify or explain why they are using this space, and what alternatives for socialisation there may be. Moreover, there may be environmental characteristics of the venues noted in the extract (car parks, shopping centres) which may also contribute to the perception of a public threat if youths are congregating in these areas. For instance the lack of lighting in the car park may be a feature which heightens public fear. In this report the young people are at fault and are the primary cause of a broader threat to general public safety.

This trend is particularly evident in reports dealing with the behaviour of gangs of young males from non-Anglo Saxon backgrounds. There were a number of articles which produced negative images of Indo-Chinese youth and their collective behaviour in public. The following extract illustrates this point:

> **Viet Gang Fear**
>
> Gangs of Vietnamese youths are running protection rackets and threatening Asian shopkeepers ... Police say gang members—ranging in age from sixteen to 22 are demanding money from Asian shops and businesses. They threaten violence and property damage if their demands are refused ... Gang members, often sporting 'mod haircuts' and 'trendy clothing', will enter an Asian shop and demand money (*The Western Times* 30 May 1990).

Similar discourses on the behaviour of this group generate images which could be generalised to apply to all Vietnamese youth. The visual description of the youths' hair and clothing creates in readers' minds an association between these images, and the criminal activities they fear will be committed. When such young people are encountered, labelled by the media as 'gang members', readers are left no doubt as to who are the potential perpetrators and of their potential victimisation.

The stereotypical power of such reportage to those outside the Indo-Chinese community is indeed powerful. The media have a certain construction of an 'ideal community' reality which is challenged not only by the presence of youth from migrant backgrounds, but by the congregation of young people in general. Thus, the public activities of both are adversely represented within the deviant and criminal discourse, but they impact in different ways. In the case of ethnic gangs, while the lack of a motivation for good behaviour in the public domain is also prevalent, the difficulties of assimilation into the broader community experienced by so many young people of this group, are seldom addressed. Greater incomprehension, and therefore fear, is likely to be generated regarding them.

Later observations indicate little has changed in terms of media portrayal of the behaviour of young people in public since our study. Evidence from 1994 indicates similar portrayals which work to further marginalise young people from the mainstream of the community. The result is that the press uses the term 'gang' as a convenient 'put-down' of the activities of young people generally. 'Rampaging youth' are spotlighted (*The Knox News* 27 April 1994). Calls, however, for greater parental control are rarely accompanied by a recognition that young people may be 'hanging out' in order to escape abusive home environments.

It is clear that public opinion is shaped by the negative reporting of gangs in the popular press. While it is difficult to discover a direct causal nexus between public attitudes and press reportage, articles in the press have generated fear relating to the gang issue. This leads to a misunderstanding by the broader community of the motives young people have in congregating in public places. When combined with frequent comparisons with the United States, and in particular Los Angeles, where similar moral panics have emerged over gangland confrontations and criminality which threaten the public welfare, the result is a public discourse relating to groups of young people which is not only negative, but factually incomplete.

CONCLUSION

The results indicate little new in terms of the role of moral panics over the behaviour of young people in public space. Research on youth subculture in the United Kingdom—whether on 'Mods and Rockers' (Clarke et al. 1976), football hooligans (Coleman et al. 1990), or muggers (Hall et al. 1978)—illustrates the effects of popular discourse upon the crime debate. The existence of a phenomenon, which is promoted by the media, and then generates negative concern in the public domain, works to marginalise and criminalise those who fit the description of the phenomenon, without understanding the deeper implications of this process.

As interview data from young people and community workers show, there was little actual concern over the extent of a gang problem in the region under study. What was evident, however, was a general public and media misconception of the nature of youth behaviour in public space. While potentially applicable to all young people as a class of citizens, negative stereotyping has a specific impact upon youths from non-English speaking backgrounds. Given their need for support these groups are far more likely to have justified reasons for collective congregation in the public domain. However they are also more likely to attract media attention and community disapproval for the deviant activities of a few. They are also more likely to be categorised as 'ethnic gangs' within the public discourse.

The relationship between race and deviance needs further exploration and clarification at the theoretical level. The variable of race is not uniform but contextual. Not all issues relating to race apply equally to all members of a particular ethnic group. As Yinger (1986) suggests, the variable of race has a number of intersecting strands which differentially affect different members of a group. This ultimately makes generalisation about the impact of issues which affect people from such groups a hazardous task:

> What helps men may hurt women; what helps the young may hurt the old; what helps the skilled may hurt the unskilled. We cannot be content with analysis at the racial or ethnic group level alone. On the whole, the least advantaged in the various groups involved are also the least aided by emphasis on ethnicity (Yinger 1986: 30).

When race and social disadvantage intersect with age we can have a situation of severe deprivation. Young people in the present study fit into this framework. Not only are young people in general disadvantaged in terms of recreational options which necessitates utilisation of public space more frequently than adult populations, but migrant youth are particularly susceptible to adverse stereotyping in matters involving youth relations and youth culture. The negative description of groups of Indo-Chinese youth has the potential to affect all young people of this background, because of their visible and cultural similarities. While generalisations such as this are largely dependent on individual interpretation of negative reportage, the discourse leaves an impression that all groups of ethnic youth are a potential threat to the safety and well-being of the general community. This is a microcosm of the broader picture. The behaviour of one group of young males has the potential to affect all such groups in the public domain.

While people from non-English speaking backgrounds are at special risk of being viewed as comprising a significant proportion of an emerging crime problem (Francis and Cassell 1977), official statistics indicate that people from migrant backgrounds are under-represented in recorded crime rates (Hazlehurst 1986). Yet a significant proportion of media attention, particularly in relation to law and order issues, is devoted to the negative stereotyping of members of these communities (Bell 1993). The effect is to create a public image of many migrant groups whose behaviour appears contrary to the constructed ideal of social appropriateness. Therefore, while there are numerous cultural contradictions of the 'Australian norm', the popular conception of that norm is almost inevitably used as the reference point in media discussions of social and criminal justice issues regarding migrants. Different norms seldom appear in the picture unless they are related to the artistic or culinary delights of 'multicultural Australia'.

These features intersect at two points in the debate on youth criminality. The tenor of press reportage during the period under study suggests that young people in general are likely to receive adverse publicity. Press reports often ignore the reasons underlying the need for young people to utilise public space on a regular basis (reliance on public transport, lack of alternative facilities for recreation, unemployment, and the promotion of these locations as areas for public congregation). However these issues have more serious social implications for young people from different cultural backgrounds.

Absent from the media discourse on the issue of gangs is any discussion of the reasons for the congregation of young people, particularly those of Indo-Chinese origin. Press reports exploit fears which groups of youth create for the community, yet there is little information suggesting that there might be a legitimate purpose for this congregation. While there are obvious social reasons which explain why all groups of young people congregate in public space, the need for additional peer support in the case of Indo-Chinese youth is seldom discussed. The result is a media portrayal which confines explanation of the behaviour of these groups to terms of criminal intent through the use of the term 'gang', while the real needs of ethnic youth are left largely untouched. Members of the public interviewed clearly relied upon this information as their main source of information on the issue of gangs.

The fact that the public are influenced by media reportage and hearsay relating to the debate on juvenile gangs is not surprising, given the history of media involvement in other forms of criminal debates internationally (Coleman et al. 1990: 41-108; Hall et al. 1978). What is of concern in the present debate is that much of the media concern over the gang problem uses the experience of the United States as its reference point. A number of articles describe Melbourne as 'the new Los Angeles'. They have alluded to gangland brawls in describing the behaviour of young people on Melbourne's streets and have fuelled the public's anxiety on this issue. While data does suggest that there is some underground gang activity in Melbourne, there is little to suggest that the general public are in constant danger of victimisation. Indeed, the most likely victims of sustained criminality are those who are most disempowered in these migrant communities themselves, particularly young women. It is these populations who have the fewest opportunities in terms of financial independence or access to resources which would give them support if they did become victims of crime.

Most media organisations will claim that there is a public interest in disseminating material on crime issues. The concerns which are highlighted in the present study do not suggest that criminal reportage by the press should be abandoned. It is however important to consider the way in which the discourse on gangs is permeated through press reports. Similar information can be portrayed to the public in very different ways. Through less sensationalist headlines, and the presentation of a broader range of facts, some of these concerns could be resolved. Improved guidelines by media organisations, and greater powers of watchdog bodies such as the Press Council could help to promote community understanding rather than trepidation regarding migrant communities, and young people in general.

While many of the issues raised in this research require further examination, one feature which transcends most of these concerns is the question of masculinity. The socialisation of young males is clearly central to an understanding of gang-like behaviour. Future research should be directed to analyse the characteristics of masculinity, the way in which young males feel the need to take up public space, and their perceived necessity to congregate in public. While the implications of this have only been briefly elucidated in this study, further exploration of this phenomenon is warranted given the demands placed on males to dominate the public realm in contemporary culture. By focusing on these issues, a greater understanding of the behaviour and cultures of masculinity in relation to the behaviour of young people may emerge.[2]

REFERENCES

Aumair, M. and Warren, I. (1989) 'Characteristics of Juvenile Gangs in Melbourne', *Youth Studies*, 13: 40-44.

Australian Bureau of Statistics (1991) *Census of Population and Housing Basic Community Profile, 1991*.

Bell, P. (1993) *Multicultural Australia in the Media: A Report to the Office of Multicultural Affairs*, Canberra: Australian Government Publishing Service.

Clarke, J., Hall, S., Jefferson, T., and Roberts, B. (1976) 'Subcultures, Cultures and Class' in S. Hall and T. Jefferson, *Resistance Through Rituals: Youth Subcultures in Post-War Britain*, London/Birmingham: Hutchinson in Association with the Centre for Comparative Cultural Studies, University of Birmingham.

Cohen, P. (1979) 'Policing the Working Class City' in B. Fine, R. Kinsey, J. Lea, S. Picciotto, and J. Young, *Capitalism and the Rule of Law: From Deviancy Theory to Marxism*, London: Hutchinson.

Coleman, S., Jemphrey, A., Scraton, P. and Skidmore, P. (1990) *Hillsborough and After: The Liverpool Experience*, First Report, Centre for Studies in Crime and Social Justice, Ormskirk, Lancs: Edge Hill College of Higher Education.

Department of Employment, Education and Training (1995) *Unemployment Statistics*.

Francis, R. D. and Cassell, A.J. (1977) 'Culture Conflict Amongst First-and Second-Generation Migrants', *Australian and New Zealand Journal of Criminology* 10: 85-94.

Gilmore, D.D. (1990) *Manhood in the Making: Cultural Concepts of Masculinity*, London: Yale University Press.

Gregory, R.G. and Hunter, B. (1995) 'The Macro Economy and the Growth of Ghettos and Urban Poverty in Australia', Discussion paper No 325, Canberra: Australian National University.

Hall, S., Crichter, C., Jefferson, T., Clarke, J., Roberts, B. (1978) *Policing the Crisis*, London: Macmillan.

Hammersley, M. and Atkinson, P. (1989) *Ethnography: Principles in Practice*, London: Tavistock Publications Ltd.

Hazlehurst, K.M. (1987) *Migration, Ethnicity and Crime in Australian Society*, Canberra: Australian Institute of Criminology.

Huff, C.R. (1990) *Gangs in America*, Newbury Park: Sage Publications.

Keith, M. (1993) *Race, Riots and Policing: Lore and Disorder in a Multi-racial Society*, London: University College London Press.

Kelsey, J. and Young, W. (1982) *The Gangs: Moral Panic as Social Control*,

Wellington: Institute of Criminology, Victoria University of Wellington.

Moysey, S. (1993) 'Marxism and Subculture', in R. White (ed.), *Youth Subcultures: Theory, History and the Australian Experience*, Hobart: National Clearing-House for Youth Studies.

Mukherjee, S.K. and Dagger, D. (1990) *The Size of the Crime Problem in Australia* (second edition), Canberra: Australian Institute of Criminology.

Polk, K. (1993) 'Reflections on Youth Subcultures', in R. White (ed.), *Youth Subcultures: Theory, History and the Australian Experience*, Hobart: National Clearing-House for Youth Studies.

Sanchez-Jankowski, M. (1991) *Islands in the Street: Gangs and American Urban Society*, Berkeley: University of California Press.

Spergel, I. and Chance, T. (1991) 'National Youth Gang Suppression and Intervention Program', *National Institute of Justice: Reports*, No. 224.

Sweet, R. (1990) 'The Youth Labour Market: A Twenty Year Perspective', Discussion paper No 243. Canberra: Australian National University.

VCCAV (1990) *Violence in and Around Licensed Premises*, Melbourne: Victorian Community Council Against Violence.

Walton, P. (1993) 'Media and Murder: Some Problems of Culture, Representation, and Difference', paper presented at the Second National Conference on Violence, Canberra: Australian Institute of Criminology, June 1993.

White, R. (1990) *No Space of Their Own*, Cambridge: Cambridge University Press.

Yinger, J. Milton (1986) 'Intersecting Strands in the Theorisation of Race and Ethnic Relations', in J. Rex and D. Mason, (eds), *Theories of Race and Ethnic Relations*, Cambridge: Cambridge University Press.

Young, K. (1993) 'On Sports Crimes: Risk, Masculinity, and Consent', *Socio-Legal Bulletin* No. 10: 8-13.

NOTES

1. As Young indicates, the traditional legal conceptions which have exempted sports participants from criminal liability for serious and premeditated injury on the field have worked under the premise that athletes assume the risks of their voluntary participation in the sporting pastime. Young goes on to point out however that the 'voluntary participation' defence ignores the fact that many sports participants at the professional level are not fully instructed when they are first contracted on the nature of the risks they face.

2. This research was funded by the Australian Research Council and supervised by Dr Joachim Kersten from the University of Melbourne. We would like to thank Dr Kersten for his input and inspiration for the ideas expressed in this essay.

10 'Pulling the Teams Out of the Dark Room': The Politicisation of the Mongrel Mob

Pahmi Winter

> It's not a case of us not wanting to be involved in society ... but if you don't have the skills and you don't have the opportunities, you don't participate (Harry Tam, Mongrel Mob Advisory Panel National Coordinator).

INTRODUCTION

Gangs have been a feature of New Zealand society since the 1950s. There are bikie gangs, skinhead and white power gangs and, more recently, Asian triads. However, it is the ethnic gangs of predominantly Maori membership that most New Zealanders associate with the term 'gang' and its connotations of violence and lawlessness. Police figures estimate New Zealand has around 6,000 gang members, 64% of which belong to ethnic gangs (Meek 1992).

Ethnic gangs first came to public attention through a television documentary about the South Auckland Stormtroopers in 1971. During the 1970s, public discourse regarding the growing phenomenon of ethnic gangs identified them as a 'juvenile crime problem'. A decade later, public discourse on ethnic gangs framed them as a serious social crisis and a threat to public order and safety. By the mid 1980s, after a decade of rapidly increasing rates of unemployment and violent crime, the 'gang problem' had become politicised as a law and order issue.[1] The police, members of the judiciary, politicians, and the media exacerbated public anxieties about the gang 'threat'. They pushed for a 'get tough' response through hard-line policing and legislative policies as the most effective solution to the problem of increasing gang membership, visibility, and involvement in crime and violence (Kelsey and Young 1982). In New Zealand in the mid 1990s 'law and order' remains high on the political agenda. However, the institutional response has now broadened from a reactive stance to include a new discourse, that of 'crime prevention'.

In April 1992, the Prime Minister's Department set up a Crime Prevention Action Group (CPAG). In its preliminary report, the CPAG committee recognised that recidivist offenders are responsible for a significant proportion of crime. They also noted that repeat offenders tend to:

> rate poorly on a number of socio-economic indicators and are characterised by unemployment, poor health, low educational achievements, low income, and substance abuse in some form. In some circumstances, lack of skills especially in relation to parenting along with the presence of family violence creates a cycle of deprivation from generation to generation (CPAG 1992:41).

The Crime Prevention Action Group commented in their report:

> The small group of people who fall into this category can be described as 'multi-problem families' ... One of the most distinctive characteristics of multi-problem families is that they are socially isolated from the community and often cut off from family and other potentially supportive networks ... Multi-problem families often have different values, expectations of behaviour, skills and abilities to access services than members of the surrounding community ... (ibid: 41-2).

The members of 'multi-problem' families characterise the habitual clients of social welfare and health systems and are over-represented in courts and prisons. The model accurately represents the context of many gang members lives: that is, a history of economic and cultural deprivation, low self-esteem, and destructive behaviour. The problems of poverty, low education, poor parenting, a lack of life and job skills, substance abuse, and an overwhelming sense of alienation and social isolation dominate their lives and those of their families.

THE SOCIAL HISTORY OF THE MONGREL MOB

The emergence of the Mongrel Mob and other gangs within New Zealand society can be linked to the structural and economic upheavals of industrialisation and urbanisation following World War Two (Comber 1981; CPAG 1992; Newbold 1992). The post-war emergence of a 'youth culture' rebelling against the ethos of austerity and conservatism cultivated by the war years elicited a moral panic about 'teenage' gangs and lawlessness which has occupied a permanent place in public consciousness ever since (Newbold 1992:100).

During the fifties, youth gangs were predominantly Pakeha (European New Zealanders). Ethnic gangs like the Mongrel Mob did not appear until the 1960s. These gangs, which are mainly Maori, take their origins from the rapid migration of rural Maori who moved to the larger New Zealand cities in the 1950s in response to the growing need by manufacturing industries for an urban labour force. The shift from close-knit, self-sufficient communities to the isolation of the suburbs undermined extended kin networks and destroyed, for many, their links with their land, their people, and their culture. The pain of cultural dislocation and social isolation was numbed with alcohol and expressed in violence.

For many Maori youth whose families have disintegrated or been unable to provide material and emotional support, a gang provides identity and a sense of belonging. Their common experience of feeling abandoned and isolated, of frustration, anger, and a shared history of trouble with authorities, draws new young recruits (prospects) to the gang. The culture of the gang celebrates the ethos of 'rape, pillage, and plunder', signifying their rejection of the values and standards of a society they feel has failed them.

In New Zealand, after 1975, gang numbers increased as economic conditions worsened and rising unemployment exacerbated socio-economic pressures on Maori. Previously, most gang members tended to grow out of their interest in gang membership by their late 20s (Comber 1981). Many, by this age, had established their own families and no longer needed or desired the gang lifestyle. Unemployment interrupted this settling down process through diminishing gang members' opportunities to provide the economic base on which a secure and stable family life depends (Tam 1994b).

In the capital city of Wellington in the mid 1970s, Maori youth workers working with swelling numbers of street kids established the Work Trust Movement. The movement's proponents encouraged gangs to set up charitable trusts to cater for gang members' education, work, accommodation and recreational needs. This concept was applied nationally and was successful in providing training through employment for many gang members. However, the increasing severity of the economic recession, and the consequent rise in unemployment, affected the ability of gang work trusts to provide jobs for their members (Tam 1994a). The limited opportunities available to gang members to generate an income legally diminished even further, and criminal offending by gang members increased, as did police targeting of gangs and their associates. During the 1980s, the number of gang members and their associates in New Zealand prisons rose to 25% of the total inmate muster (Braybrook and O'Neill 1988), and prison culture became dominated by gang affiliation and gang-related rivalry (Meek 1992).

The efforts of the police to turn the ethnic gangs into a law and order problem in the late 1970s (Pratt 1988) were successful in mobilising public support, largely due to the simplistic and conflict-oriented reporting of gang-related incidents and issues by the New Zealand media. Their representation of groups like the Mongrel Mob as anarchic and evil resulted in public anxieties and antipathy being inflamed into a moral panic about incipient 'urban terrorism' (Kelsey and Young 1982). The media's moral crusade against the ethnic gangs justified increased targeting of these groups by the police and the judiciary. In response to a perceived demand by 'the public' to 'do something' about the ethnic gangs, the government set up a Committee on Gangs. The Comber Report, released in 1981, identified as a solution to 'the gang problem', setting up:

> points of contact within the bureaucracy for gangs (and other work trusts and community employment groups) to help them to negotiate the system of employment and related policies, and to liaise between departments ... (Comber 1981: 29-33).

As a consequence, the government established a Group Employment Liaison Service (GELS) under the auspices of the Labour Department, which was specifically to provide assistance to gangs to help them secure work for their members and remove the economic impetus to commit crime.

The Mongrel Mob had not had a long-term involvement in the work schemes set up by the Work Trust movement. That initiative had been picked up by the rival Black Power gang and therefore many Mongrel Mob members perceived work trusts to be a 'Black Power thing'. Since rivalry between the two gangs was intense, they did not see it as an attractive option. This perception changed, however, after Harry Tam of the Mob's Dunedin chapter successfully applied for a position as GELS fieldworker for Otago. Through his work with Mob chapters in the South Island and as facilitator for GELS fieldworkers dealing with the Mob in other areas of the country, the gang began to see the opportunities of involvement in such activities provided for them. In a lecture given at Waikato University Tam explained:

> When our fellas went to work they were able to accumulate money and assets, and when other chapters came to visit we were able to host functions and they were probably quite impressive by Mob standards. So I suppose that provided an incentive for some of these other chapters to look at these things we were doing (Tam 1994c).

However, a change of government in 1984 introduced a non-interventionist political climate and the subsidised work schemes established by the National government were phased out.

The incoming Labour Government then began a series of economic reforms which resulted in the number of unemployed rising from around 109,000 in 1986 to 220,000 in 1990 (Easton 1990). Maori and other Polynesians bore the brunt of economic and structural reform in New Zealand at this time as traditionally, on leaving school, they moved into unskilled and semi-skilled labouring jobs in primary production like forestry and the meatworks, and the manufacturing industries.

The community workers who started the Work Trust movement associated predominantly with Black Power and had encouraged them to organise and adopt a positive development strategy. As a consequence, leaders within Black Power had developed close links with the National government's prime minister, Robert Muldoon, and had acquired some respectability. The Mongrel Mob, by contrast, became even more threatening and anarchic in the public imagination.

THE POLITICISATION OF THE MONGREL MOB

The Mongrel Mob are currently, and have been for some time, the folk-devils of New Zealand society. Reviled as the embodiment of evil, they are perceived by most to be a malevolent threat—violent, destructive, and irredeemable. For many, the Mob and crime are synonymous. Indeed there is a strong connection between the Mob and criminal activity although the New Zealand police say it is less in the mid-1990s than at its peak ten years ago.[2] Most Mob members are more than familiar with the criminal justice system. They appear regularly before the courts, many are in prison or serving community-based sentences, and are harassed by police when out in public. Yet crime is not the central focus or *raison d'etre* of the gang, and they cannot be compared to the organised crime syndicates typified by the Mafia or Asian Triads. To the contrary, ethnic gangs like the Mongrel Mob are loosely structured and 'leadership beyond local groups is far less significant than is portrayed by the police.' (Meek 1992: 257) Criminal activity by gang members tends to be the result of individual decisions rather than planned and coordinated by gang leaders.

Nevertheless, the rates of criminal offending by Mongrel Mob members, and their detection, are high. Marea Brown, a career education consultant who has been working with the gang for several years, estimates that 50% of the Mob nationally are currently serving time. In 1993, Brown conducted a survey of 40 Mob members in the Northern Region (the top half of the North Island). This sample constituted half of the known Mobsters living in the region. Her survey showed that all of the members in the surveyed area had been in prison: 30% of them were before the courts or in prison at the time of the research; 75% of them had appeared in court in the last two years and 33% of their partners had also been before the courts in that time; 24% of the women surveyed have been in prison. Three families had children who were currently before the Youth Court (Brown 1993).

While Brown's survey might be taken as confirmation that the public is right to reject the Mob as a criminal subculture beyond redemption, the survey in fact reflects a more complex state of affairs within what is indisputably a criminally inclined subculture. An interest in 'positive development' within the Mongrel Mob occurred in reaction to hardening official and public attitudes towards them and deteriorating social and economic conditions. It emerged as an initiative from within the gang and is concerned with helping Mob members to be active in improving the quality of their lives and the lives of their families.[3]

The Labour Government's commitment to an ideology of market liberalism led to the reduction of benefits and the phasing out of subsidised employment schemes.

> As they were wound down and out, the Mob found itself in a situation where, for a long time in a long history of what you could consider

> 'negative development', they were now focusing on positive development. But now the resources weren't there for them to use. Of course, everyone else in disadvantaged positions also found themselves in that situation. I guess that's where MAP (Mongrel Mob Advisory Panel) came from. A lot of our members at that time were becoming more aware of what was happening (Tam 1994c).

In 1991, the Mongrel Mob's Wellington chapter laid a complaint with the Secretary of Labour regarding what they perceived to be inequities in the Department's dealings with them. The chapter was aware of how the local chapter of the Black Power gang was benefiting from the close relationship it had established with the Labour Department agency GELS through its long-term involvement in the work trusts. The Wellington chapter of the Mongrel Mob felt that its long-standing feud with Black Power was preventing them getting the same kind of service.

> They [the Mob] were quite critical of those sorts of groups. At that same time, the CEO of GELS was Denis O'Reilly. He had a background of close involvement with Black Power and our guys, to a certain extent, when the goods weren't there, they attributed it to Denis. It was very convenient to say: 'Denis is Black Power, he stopped the goods coming to us'. Denis also employed a number of other fieldworkers who had gang affiliations and Black Power affiliations—and some of our guys sat down and weighed it up and said: 'Two Black Power, 1 Mob—things aren't right here!' They saw it strictly through the patches rather than through what the causes were.
>
> At that time, I saw a need for training for our people, particularly with the times of change. I saw that our skill base was going to need to be up-graded if we were going to participate in the new environment (ibid).

The matter was discussed further at a meeting convened by GELS fieldworker Harry Tam in Dunedin. Mob leaders decided they needed to take a more constructive approach on the matter and it was agreed that the Mob present a set of recommendations to GELS which would enable them to improve the way the government dealt with them.

> The wananga (teaching session) was to train our people in basic communication skills, negotiation skills, and media skills. At the end

> of the wananga, we had a good chance to talk and assess the situation. It was at that point that we brought up the idea that the Mob had to have its own people in place — and we need to train them and access resources to get our people up into the positions where they are capable of doing it for their own people rather than relying on government departments and what have you. And that, basically, was the birth of MAP (ibid).

The Auckland chapters of Mongrel Mob then convened a hui (meeting) which was attended by a number of former Mob presidents. A discussion paper was circulated which included an analysis of the factors and events leading up to the lodging of the 1991 complaint to the Secretary of Labour. The paper identified the emergence of 'positive development' initiatives within the gang and discussed the reluctance of GELS field workers to work with the Mob, and their lack of understanding of the gang. At a subsequent national meeting in September 1992, it was decided that an Incorporated Trust be established to serve as a national organisation for coordinating positive development initiatives for Mongrel Mob gang members and associates. This group was called the Mongrel Mob Advisory Panel, now known as MAP.

> Basically, the purpose of MAP was to serve two roles—to get people into leadership positions who could facilitate resources and to try to get a foot in the door with different government departments and community agencies that could deliver to us. So MAP had a political purpose. We really needed to get alongside government departments and let them know what the needs of our people were.
>
> At the same time, after a lot of talk, we were able to clarify exactly what the situation was—why the assistance wasn't coming down. And the reality of it was that it had dried up for everybody, not just the Mob. We therefore needed to refocus on utilising our own resources, be a bit more imaginative rather than just waiting to pick up what was offered (ibid).

In April 1993, at a full presidents meeting held in Porirua, a presentation was made outlining what the aims and objectives of MAP were. The presidents then voted unanimously to support the MAP initiative. Their acceptance of it was crucial to MAP acquiring credibility with the 'troops' as a gang initiative.

> Having the presidential support has done a lot. When you talk about change, change is very threatening to a lot of people who are settled in their ways, and we don't actually talk about change within the Mob. What we talk about is creating a better way of doing things. I mean, if we can work and generate the income to serve our needs and our family's needs, its a better way of getting income than robbing banks, than doing time. It's a better way (Tam 1994c).

The organisation of MAP consists of a national coordinator and six regional representatives covering six regional areas of Northern, King Country, Bay of Plenty, Hawkes Bay, Lower North Island, and the South Island. The national coordinator is responsible for the provision of training, advice, and support to the regional representatives, gathering and disseminating information to the regional representatives, coordinating national MAP meetings, and facilitating connections with government and community agencies. The responsibilities of the regional representatives include gathering and disseminating information to all chapters in their areas as well as keeping MAP's national coordinator informed of local developments, coordinating regular meetings of chapters in their area, providing assistance and advice to their chapters regarding applications to and negotiations with government and community agencies, and helping their chapters undertake education, work, accommodation, and recreation initiatives (Tam 1994b).

GELs fieldworker and patched Mob member, Harry Tam, became the National Coordinator of MAP. He defines MAP's focus as providing Mob members with the means of pursuing 'legitimate channels to success' through providing better access to social services, employment, recreation, education, and vocational training. By extending the range of choices and options available to their members, MAP seeks to help them to improve the quality of their and their families' lives by enabling them to break out of the cycle of socio-economic deprivation and destructive behaviours. MAP's Northern regional representative, Edge Te Whaiti, uses the metaphor of 'pulling the teams out of the dark room' to explain how he sees their objectives. 'The dark room' is a metaphor for the gang members' common experience of being physically isolated in jail, and the experience of social isolation, deprivation, and poverty. It is this which binds them together as patch brothers—the gang provides a sense of belonging, support, and meaning that they have been unable to find elsewhere.

Tam identifies education and home ownership as two factors which are crucial to breaking the cycle of deprivation. Providing the foundation for a stable and supportive family environment elicits a sense of pride and achievement in the owners, strengthens the family's asset base and is crucial to ensuring that their children's education is not disrupted by frequent shifts of home and school.

> Getting our people into home ownership is very important. I feel that if our kids are going to get into education, they need a good home base and home ownership is a good way to contribute to providing those things (ibid) .

Harry Tam's Dunedin chapter has played a key role in developing practical strategies for achieving MAP objectives which other Mob chapters can adopt. It became a registered trust which enabled them to become a registered provider under the Training Opportunities Programme (TOPS) administered by the Labour Department's Education and Training Support Agency, as well as contracting out their labour and work skills. They have also established what they refer to as their '$100 housing scheme' for members. This started with a loan from Mana Enterprises,[4] Housing Corporation, and the Labour Department's agency for assisting the long-term marginalised unemployed, the Community Employment Group or CEG. The funding was used to buy and restore an old house which was then sold to finance the purchase of land the crown had bought for motorway extensions which were no longer required. The trust negotiated a deal with a private house building company, Colonial Homes, for kitset houses which trust members could erect. The home-owner pays the trust $100 a week which covers mortgage repayments, rates, and insurance.

> First we got funding to do a business plan because we set it up as a private sweat equity business. To get capital we went to Mana Enterprises. To get that loan, we had to deal with the local tribal authority. We enlisted the support from local kaumatua [male tribal elders] from the tangata whenua [local indigenous 'people of the land'] from local areas. When you enlist their support, it is not a one way relationship. We've got to participate in the things that they do too. So through that community development process, or positive development as we call it, things get happening (Tam 1994c).

The initiative shown by the Dunedin Mob's Ngati Mahi Kuri Trust is evident in several other chapters. For example, in Tauranga, on the east coast of the North Island, the Mob chapter has a fishing quota and boat which provides work and income for their members.[5] The Wellington chapter's trust provided work for 55 members in 1994 through work contracts and Labour Department schemes such as Taskforce Green.[6]

Extending the chapter organisation, through each becoming its own registered trust, creates a structure that enables the chapter to operate as a business, to provide training programs and be eligible for state funding to resource these. One important and valuable aspect of the Mob providing collective employment and vocational training for their own people is that it opens these options up to people who feel too alienated from the rest of society to consider enrolling in courses at polytechnics or other training centres.

The desire for training, and the attractiveness of being able to train with people one is comfortable with, was identified in a survey of Northern Region Mob members, affiliates, and partners commissioned by Edge Te Whaiti. The survey was funded by CEG and undertaken by Marea Brown for MAP's Northern Regional representative to support a funding application to CEG. This was sought to provide a salary and funding to enable him to establish education and training programs for Mob members, their partners, and affiliates of chapters from Waikato north. Evidence of the demand and need for these programs was provided by Brown's survey findings.

The survey showed 95% of the group were unemployed, with 93% classified as long-term unemployed (out of work for six months or longer); 87.5% had been unemployed for six years or less and 10% had been unemployed for over ten years.

The survey indicated low levels of education and vocational skills: 82% of the men surveyed and 66% of the women left school at age fifteen or under; 88% of the group have no educational qualifications and/or vocational skills; 10% of those that did have qualifications gained these in prison. The other 2% acquired theirs in training institutions after they left school.

Brown found that while 88% of the survey group were not involved in education or training, most indicated they would be willing to participate in further education and training if this could be made available to them in their area, and that the programs could be delivered to them as a group.

Urban-based respondents were interested in gaining motor trade skills (motor mechanics, auto-electrical work, welding and panel beating), spray painting and sign-writing. Women respondents expressed an interest in child-care, secretarial, and computing skills. Rurally-based respondents expressed an interest in training for primary industries such as fishing, oyster farming, mussel farming, horticulture and forestry. Driving education programs (car licence, heavy traffic licence, and defensive driving courses) were requested by most. Half of the group did not have licences although most of them drove. Interest was also expressed in training for setting up a small business, and a number were interested in learning Te Reo Maori (the Maori language), and doing courses in Maori Health and Maori arts and crafts.

All of the survey group self-identified as Maori. Although the Mob is not an exclusively Maori gang, most members are Maori. The extent to which a Maori kaupapa (philosophy or principles) informs the life of gang members depends upon the chapter, and the nature of the community within which it is located. For example Pat Aramoana, the president of the Opotiki chapter in the Bay of Plenty, is strongly committed to using tribal values and customs as the basis for improving the well-being of his people. This commitment to a Maori perspective is evident in rurally-based chapters located in areas where a large number of the local population are Maori and tribal traditions still figure strongly in daily and ceremonial life.

Ironically, the president of the Waikato Chapter, Sonny Fatupaito, is a New Zealander of Samoan and African-American parentage but has a strong commitment to encouraging his people to honour and practice tikanga Maori (Maori custom) in all aspects of their lives. He speaks Te Reo Maori and is committed to seeing the Mob establish a marae where Mob members can meet together with their whanau [family] and provide their members with 'a stronger sense of themselves, more purposeful lives and yet still satisfy their sense of belonging that the gang provides for them' (Brown 1993).

However, most urban chapters do not draw on a Maori kaupapa. While they may practise aspects of tikanga Maori in their daily lives, and participate in cultural programs in prison, many city-based Mob members do not make a special point of celebrating their Maori heritage. This is largely due to their not having the knowledge or connection with their people and, for many, being Maori has not been a positive experience, given their history as a colonised people. Edge Te Whaiti, MAP's Northern Regional Representative, typifies the senior gang member who is of Maori descent and familiar with a Maori perspective but does not express this overtly or deliberately in his way of living. In this he is not only typical of the gang member, but also typical of many young males from the urban indigenous underclass.

Te Whaiti was released from prison two years ago after serving a six-year sentence. On his release, he immediately began to prepare an application to CEG to set up personal development, life-skills and vocational training programs for Mob members in the Northern Region. He wanted to set up a work contract scheme similar to that which the Mob's Wellington and Dunedin chapters had already got underway through CEG funding. However, what was unique about Te Whaiti's plan was that he also wanted to set up educational programs that would help his people learn a wide variety of skills that could enhance their lives. This was indeed a significant advancement in the realisation of MAP's positive development vision.

His motivation to work for the betterment of his people was stimulated by his involvement as a key player in the Gang Mediator Scheme which successfully reduced tension and conflict between the Black Power and Mongrel Mob gangs in Auckland Medium Security Prison (Paremoremo) and Mt Eden Prison.

By the late 1980s intergang rivalry, particularly between the Mongrel Mob and Black Power, had become a feature of New Zealand prison culture and a serious problem for prison managers. In the Auckland prisons, Black Power dominated Mount Eden and the Mongrel Mob controlled Paremoremo (Meek 1992). Despite the prevailing managerial policy of prisons formally being 'neutral ground' and therefore not recognising and legitimating the existence of the gangs, the Auckland Maximum Security Prison Custody Manager allowed Te Whaiti to negotiate with Black Power leaders. The outcome was the appointment of mediators from each gang. Their role was to maintain communication between the two groups, liaise with prison management, sort out disputes with the gangs, and to visit the remand wing at Mt Eden Prison to inform new prisoners belonging to the gangs of the behaviour expected of them (Meek 1992: 272).

> The success of the initiative at the two Auckland institutions led to two GELS officials [one of whom was Harry Tam] visiting a number of institutions to promote the scheme. An evaluation in December 1989 found that the appointment of mediators had resulted in improved relationships between gang members and staff and an increased level of involvement of gang members in constructive activities within prisons such as culture groups and hobby work (ibid).

Te Whaiti's positive experience of working with institutional authorities, and the achieving of an outcome which benefited all, gave him a sense of new possibilities and directions: 'After we got that cleaned up', Te Whaiti explains, 'I asked myself, "what now?"' In his words, he decided to use his long sentence to work on improving his quality of life after release, and he was interested in setting up something for the Mob which would enable them to do the same.

Te Whaiti was shifted from maximum to medium security in 1990 and it was here that he set up, with two other Mob members and Marea Brown's assistance, the Heirs of Tane Trust.[7] The Trust is guided by a Maori kaupapa and seeks to help members develop personal qualities and social skills which will enable them to stay out of prison after release. The foundation program is based on a model called Moral Ethics and Values. Its objective is to assist and encourage participants to become aware of, and to examine critically, their values and beliefs. In learning to adopt positive and pro-social values, the individual acquires the ability to value himself and others and to choose not to act destructively. The Trust's sessions are guided by a strong emphasis on kawa (protocol) and connection to wairua (spirituality), strengthening of wairua, whakapapa (genealogy) and self-identity, carving and whaikorero (oratory), communication and relationship skills and learning how to 'live safely within the world' (Brown 1993).

The program developed by Edge Te Whaiti and Sonny Fatupaito in Paremoremo was subsequently made available at Wellington Prison and MAP went on to negotiate with the Justice Department regarding the program being implemented in other prisons. However, there is considerable resistance to this initiative, and the developing relationship between MAP and the Justice Department, from the prison officers' subgroup of the PSA (Public Service Association).

MAP's National Coordinator Harry Tam interprets this resistance as an indication of the desire prison officers have to preserve the status quo in prisons. The 1990 reorganisation of prison structures and the introduction of a case-management approach has been perceived by prison officers as threatening their interests. Tam believes that PSA subgroups use the threat of gang violence in prisons to strengthen their industrial negotiating position. This is because gang-related tensions in prisons translate into higher manning numbers required when moving those prisoners around. Programs and policies which reduce violence and conflict between gang members mean fewer prison officers are needed. Another contributing factor is the introduction of social work concepts into the custodial management of inmates as a result of the 1990 restructuring. This shift in custodial arrangements requires skills not traditionally held by custodial staff in New Zealand prisons (Currie 1989). Continuing inter-gang rivalry and gang-related violence within prisons justifies employing the 'hard man' type of custodial staff. It also means high numbers of custodial staff must be maintained to meet maximum security regulations which require three prison officers to move a gang-affiliated inmate within or between prisons.

Ironically, although imprisonment is a disempowering and negative experience, MAP views prison as fertile ground for their people to make positive personal changes and acquire useful skills that will enable them to help their fellow Mob members once released. MAP appreciates that for the Mob member doing time, the pressures which fuel destructive behaviour are reduced. There is an opportunity to reconsider values and attitudes, and to get a fresh sense of hope and direction. This is due to the Justice Department restructuring of Penal Division which prioritised 'providing inmates with the opportunity to change' (Corrections Mission Statement—Penal). Before then, inmates had access to programs of varying quality on an intermittent and haphazard basis, with many of the custodial staff acting as obstructively as possible when it came to inmates getting to their classes (Currie 1989). After the 1990 restructuring, a system of individual case management was introduced. On entry, inmates were assessed and placed in the programs which most suited their particular needs.

THE OBSTACLES TO POSITIVE CHANGE

The MAP representatives are motivated by a desire to help their people to create more satisfying and safer lives for themselves and their families. They know this depends on desisting from crime, making their peace with 'the system', and learning to work with that system to get the resources and support they need to help themselves. Yet despite the real progress that has been made towards this goal, the realisation of the MAP vision remains a long way off, if indeed it is possible at all. There are many serious obstacles preventing 'the teams' being released from their 'dark room' of deprivation and criminality.

One of the most significant obstacles is the culture of the gang itself, which has traditionally identified with the slogan 'rape, pillage, and plunder'. The gang culture has been shaped by a value system formed in reaction against conventional society and its norms. This set of beliefs is internalised during the socialisation process each individual undergoes in becoming a member of the gang. The gang mind-set accepts destructive behaviour and criminality as part of the everyday world. Its taken-for-grantedness undermines the ability of gang members to act constructively and to make positive changes in their lives.

For any adult, personal change is difficult and challenging. For those within the Mob seeking to realise the MAP vision, they are doubly handicapped by low self-esteem and low self-awareness, no skills, limited money or assets, and a profound sense of alienation from 'normal' society. The condition of their lives, and their frustration with its seeming inevitability, make it difficult for them to move beyond the habitual self-destructive behaviours of their youth. For those that do dare to hope, when they cast about for a better way of living, the experience of societal rejection and indifference drives them back to the group that offers solidarity, support, security, and respect.

The MAP representatives are those who have committed themselves to 'pulling the teams from the dark room'. Yet they are in a catch-22 situation where, to be in a position to assist gang-members make positive life-changes, they have to be patched. This is essential to their credibility in the eyes of the gang members they seek to help. Being a member of the gang, however, means to inhabit the gang life-world and to participate in a gang culture that is shaped by an anti-social ethos and is very resistant to change. The intractable nature of this double-bind was illustrated in December 1994 when, after twenty months of negotiations with CEG, MAP's Northern Regional Representative Edge Te Whaiti finally secured an agreement from them to fund a salary for him. This would enable him to establish his project for personal development and vocational skills programs for Mob members in the region. A few days later, however, Te Whaiti and other members of his chapter (Notorious) were arrested and charged with conspiring to distribute Class A drugs (LSD). On learning of this development, CEG immediately withdrew their funding.

This turn of events has consequently halted the MAP initiative in the Northern Region and seriously undermined the positive development strategy for Mob chapters. It removes the glimmer of hope for Mob families and those members in prison who saw, in the MAP initiative, the possibility of their being involved in something that promised a better quality of life. It is also a profound blow to those who were supporting the Northern Regional initiative in a professional capacity (e.g. police gang liaison officers, prison education staff and independent consultants like Marea Brown). They have lost credibility in the eyes of their colleagues, and particularly those who did not support them in their association with the Mob and who believed that helping people like the Mob was a waste of time, money and energy.

Thus, opposition to supporting positive development within the Mob has become further entrenched. For future Mob members who seek to bring their people 'out of the dark room', the odds against them succeeding are even greater than before. The scant support from outside the gang has diminished even further, and state and community agencies will be even more suspicious and intractable in their attitudes to the group, despite their statutory obligation to encourage and assist the 'severely-disadvantaged' and 'at-risk' unemployed into work and training.

While the anti-social and criminal culture of the gang is a factor in the collapse of the current MAP initiative in the Northern Region, the reticence of CEG to deal with the Mob must also be taken into account. CEG's target group are the long-term unemployed, particularly those impeded by substance abuse problems, criminal records and gang affiliations. Despite its formal brief, the agency was very slow to respond to the proposal put forward by Te Whaiti, taking twenty months before it agreed to support his plan. This was partially due to the close links between the CEG Regional Manager in their area and the Black Power gang, and also CEG's previous experience of the collapse of a King Country Mongrel Mob initiative which they had resourced, owing to a misappropriation of funds.

CEG resistance to the Mob is compounded by the recent introduction of performance contracts for managers within government departments and agencies, and the emphasis on managerial accountability in the public service. The implications of these changes for MAP are considerable. As MAP's National Coordinator points out:

> Greater responsibility on the regional managers to be accountable for projects which they support and recommend for approval often has an adverse effect for the gang target group (Tam 1994a:10).

In a recent discussion paper he prepared, Tam criticises the considerable delays the Mob experience when dealing with government and community agencies:

> Delays in processing and delivery is rampant although there have been changes in the processing mechanisms (through regional offices etc.) and there has been some improvement. However, for groups that are gang based then processing and delivery is as slow as ever. (In the [Wellington] Trust situation, this took three years). It appears that often an application is processed through the regional offices in a

> reasonable time frame but there are substantial delays in the final approval at head office level. The reason for this is often because of the over-sensitiveness of the final approving authority in head office. It appears these decisions are often made on the basis of how sensitive gangs are with the media and politicians at that given time, i.e. if there is negative media coverage of a particular gang, then the approval will best be declined or at the best delayed (Tam 1994a: 10).

The media's maintenance of the stereotype of the Mob as evil and irredeemable also contributes to Mongrel Mob members remaining trapped in a cycle of deprivation and criminal offending. When a crime is committed by someone whom police claim is a Mob *associate,* headlines and news items invariably implicate the Mob as the driving force. When journalists and editors misrepresent a situation with alleged Mob involvement through sensationalist and/or incorrect reports, public and official attitudes towards the Mob harden.

This was evident in the case of Edge Te Whaiti. His approach to CEGS coincided with the trial of a young man for a murder in South Auckland. The accused claimed that he had merely accompanied several Mongrel Mob members who were responsible for planning and carrying out the attack. However, the two gang members he identified from a police photo-file voluntarily gave DNA samples which tested negative, supporting their denial of any knowledge of, or involvement with, the woman's rape and murder. This, however, was ignored by the media and newspapers consistently headlined their coverage of the trial with statements such as 'LIFE AND DEATH IN MOB RULE' (*Sunday Star-Times* 19 July 1994), 'MONGREL MOB MATE GETS LIFE FOR RAPE AND MURDER' (*Sunday News* 19 July 1994), 'MOB MEMBERS PLANNED RAPE ATTACK' (*New Zealand Herald* 11 June 1994), 'MOB RULE' (*New Zealand Herald* 30 July 1994).

The consequences for MAP of media sensationalism and misrepresentation for the Mob should not be underestimated. For example, CEG officers were reading headlines such as these before they went to work and made decisions regarding MAP applications. Not surprisingly, the representatives of the Mob and their plans are perceived through a mediated lens which constructs the Mob within a discourse of fear and threat; of 'decent people' powerless against diabolic forces. The fact that Mob members persist in maintaining their gang allegiance and wear the gang patch on official business is experienced by most New Zealanders as intimidating, and thus an indication that members have no remorse or genuine desire to be 'decent' people. Therefore, they are not seen to be suitable recipients of taxpayers' funds.

What this attitude fails to appreciate is that the patch is a most effective solution to the invisibility of the dispossessed and ignored. It symbolises the precious fact of belonging and bequeaths an identity that gives the wearer courage and meaning. It is also unrealistic to expect a gang member to go without their patch while on gang business. To the Mob member, the patch is them and they are the patch. As some members mature and establish their own families, the need for the patch and kinship with the gang lessens, and they move on with their lives. But for others, their relationship with the gang persists because their need to belong, for connection, is not met elsewhere.

CONCLUSION

This case-study of the Mongrel Mob and the emergence of a positive development ethos within the gang raises important issues for all concerned about crime, and its costs, both human and economic. The Crime Prevention Action Committee noted in its preliminary report that:

> Interventions targeted at multi-problem families can only be effective if they succeed in addressing the associated issues of social isolation and the need for re-integration with the local community. The characteristics of this group are such that there will be difficulties with both the delivery and effectiveness of programs if these issues are not considered and planned for carefully (CPAG 1990: 42).

Despite the negative prognosis made regarding the likely success of the MAP 'positive development' initiative, it is self-evident that the success of crime-prevention strategies by state and community agencies is ultimately contingent on the commitment of client-groups to the same outcomes. The MAP initiative provides an effective intervention that parallels those of official crime prevention strategies for it is a self-help model which provides gang members with the means of integrating into society, of taking control of their lives, and of making positive and healthy changes without having to abandon the support of the only encouraging social environment they have encountered. The success of the Dunedin Ngati Kuri Mahi Trust chapter in reducing offending and improving the quality of life for its members suggests that positive development within the Mob is not impossible. Their success shows Mob members elsewhere the possibility that things can be different and better, and provides encouragement to other chapters to persist until they are able to achieve the same for their members.

However, to do this, they need the support of the community. Also, official agencies have to come to terms with the fact that while dealing with the Mob is risky financially, and managers may feel vulnerable given the new accountability regime, to not do so is even more costly, in both economic and human terms. As Harry Tam sees it:

> It may be considered a valid reason that because the target group is a gang, greater levels of scrutiny may be required in order to avoid accountability and administrative problems. However through previous experiences of other schemes and in particular, through the GDA Pilot Projects (Group Development Assistance Pilots), it is clear that the delays in themselves is a collision course for failure of the actual project (Tam 1994a: 10).

In a 1993 lecture to mark the Year of the Family, Judge Mick Brown, New Zealand's principal Youth Court Judge called on communities to accept ownership of the problems of crime and violence. This has considerable relevance for those working within state and community agencies. Criminal recidivism cannot be explained solely by reference to the personal inadequacies and belief systems of the recidivist. The failure of the community to respond to, and to support their 'multi-problem families', including those of gangs, when they seek the means of reintegration into society has also to be taken into account. The continued support of the Mob by agencies like CEG and the Safer Communities Councils has been jeopardised by the collapse of the initiatives in the Northern region. Yet it is crucial that the rich potential of the MAP initiative is not ignored.

Policy makers and public servants, indeed society in general, cannot afford to forget that crime and violence occur when backs are turned, when an individual's worth, dignity, and needs are continually denied. As Greg Newbold put it: 'in the world of the poor, violence is a consequence of an empty present, buttressed by a hopeless future' (Newbold 1992:102).

I believe we as a society have to ask ourselves, at what cost do we want our pound of flesh? To reject gang members from the list of those eligible for state assistance on the grounds that they are still involved in crime is not consistent with the reality of the world that we live in. So-called 'respectable' people are committing crimes every day, some of them of such magnitude and by people with so much power that they cease to be considered 'crimes'. Those being committed in corporate and governmental suites, in homes and in the workplace, seem to be forgotten in the moral calculus used to weigh up the future of the Mongrel Mob. If crime prevention initiatives are to be effective, that calculus has to take into account the role the 'respectable classes' play in keeping the Mob and others like them in their place.

The Mob is ageing. Marea Brown's survey showed that 90% of its members are 26 or older, with 63% over 30 years of age. Mob leaders are maturing, and as they get older, their interests and concerns reflect a different life-stage. They are more concerned about their future, their health, and that of their families. For many, the code of being staunch is being reinterpreted according to the concerns of a human approaching their middle years—they want security, a better life, for their kids not to have the wasted years of life inside prison as they have done.

Desistance from crime by gang members is dependent upon their being allowed the opportunity to find a place within society. Reconciliation and healing require a commitment on both sides. It is not sufficient to expect these people to change their values and attitudes. Members of the 'respectable' classes also need to change theirs. This is an opportunity we can ill-afford as a society to ignore. For, as Edge Te Whaiti put it: 'at the end of the day, it's about the common good, what's good for all of us. It will be the community as a whole that will benefit'.[8]

REFERENCES

Berger, B. (1987) 'Multi-problem Families and the Community' in J.Q. Wilson and G.C. Lowry (eds), *From Children to Citizens*, New York: Springer-Verlag.

Braybrook, Beverley and O'Neill, Rose (1988) *A Census of Prison Inmates*, Wellington: Department of Justice.

Brown, Marea (1993) 'Background to the Mongrel Mob Survey in the Northern Region', unpublished paper, Auckland.

Comber Report (1981) *Report of the New Zealand Committee on Gangs*, Wellington: Government Printer.

Crime Prevention Action Group (1992) *Strategy Paper on Crime Prevention*,Wellington: Prime Minister's Department, October.

Currie, C. (1989) *Art in Prison: An Evaluation of a New Zealand Prison Programme*, Wellington: Institute of Criminology, Victoria University of Wellington.

Easton, Brian (1990) 'Queue Up and Be Counted', *New Zealand Listener*, August 13: 20.

Kelsey, Jane, and Young, Warren (1982) *The Gangs: Moral Panic as Social Control*, Wellington: Institute of Criminology, Victoria University of Wellington.

Meek, John (1992) 'Gangs in New Zealand Prisons', *Australian and New Zealand Journal of Criminology*, December 25: 255-77.

Newbold, Greg (1992) *Crime and Deviance*, Auckland: Oxford University Press.

Tam, Harry 1994(a) 'Group Development Assistance Fund Review Discussion Paper', unpublished paper.

Tam, Harry 1994(b) 'A Brief Look at the Development of the Mongrel Mob', unpublished paper, Dunedin.

Tam, Harry 1994(c) Lecture given at Waikato University, Hamilton, August.

NOTES

1. See John Pratt's 'Law and Order Politics in New Zealand 1986' in the *International Journal of the Sociology of Law* 1988, 16: 103-26 for a review of the factors contributing to the politicisation of the crime problem in New Zealand.

2. New Zealand Police, Det. Murray Bardsley, Hamilton Office NZ Police, personal communication, 1994.

3. Harry Tam, Mongrel Mob Advisory Panel National Coordinator, personal communication, 1994.

4. Mana Enterprises (now defunct) was an organisation administered by the Ministry of Maori Affairs (later Ministry of Maori Development) which made loans to Maori business enterprises.

5. Commercial fishing in New Zealand is managed through the quota system. Fishing enterprises purchase a quota which entitles them to take a specified quantity of certain specified species of fish.

6. Taskforce Green is a subsidised work program run by the Labour Department for those who have been unemployed for more than 26 weeks. It provides full-time waged work on community or environmental projects for a maximum of 26 weeks.

7. Tane is the Maori god of the trees and forests. Tane also signifies the male principle.

8. This paper is dedicated to the MAP members Harry Tam, Edge Te Whaiti and Sonny Fatupaito in recognition of their struggle, and with thanks for sharing their story.

11 Urban Raskolism and Criminal Groups in Papua New Guinea

Sinclair Dinnen

INTRODUCTION

The growth of violent gang crime provides a major focus of law and order debate in Papua New Guinea (PNG). In Melanesian Pidgin, the words 'raskol' and 'raskolism' are popularly used to refer to gang members and juvenile gang crime. As well as being the source of acute levels of personal insecurity within the country, raskolism has become a defining feature in overseas depictions of modern PNG. A recent article in an Australian magazine claimed that:

> hundreds of rascal gangs around the country are seemingly out of control, responsible for the vast majority of crimes that have turned modern PNG into a law and order nightmare. In the space of two decades, the capital Port Moresby has gone from a sleepy Australian colonial town to a violent Melanesian city. These days it isn't just expatriates who live in barbed wire compounds but anyone who can afford to. This underlies the sense of siege that pervades the city which, with its graffiti-splashed compounds, is in parts beginning to resemble a South Pacific version of South Central Los Angeles (Bohane 1995: 14).

This essay focuses specifically on urban criminal groups and, in particular, on those operating in the capital Port Moresby where my fieldwork was conducted. The purpose is to identify and discuss the social dynamics underlying this complex phenomenon. The first section deals with the rise of raskolism in Port Moresby from the mid-1960s onwards and, in doing so, examines state responses to lawlessness, as well as the social organisation of the Melanesian gang. The second section presents a detailed ethnographic account of a recent criminal group surrender in Port Moresby. This story provides important insights into the political aspect of raskol behaviour and, in particular, processes of voluntary exit from crime. The essay concludes with a broad analysis of the social and economic dimensions of urban raskolism.

The Rise of Raskolism

Raskolism has had a relatively short history. Until the early 1960s, little concern was expressed by colonial authorities about crime rates in PNG. In 1959, for example, it was claimed that 'the incidence of crime continues to be low' (Territory of Papua 1959-60: 80), while in 1960 there was 'no evidence that urbanisation is producing delinquency'.[1] According to Po'o—himself a former gang member—criminal gangs were unknown in Port Moresby before the mid-1960s (1975: 33). Harris has claimed that the term 'raskol' was first used in the mid-1960s (Harris 1988: 3-4). By the mid-1970s, however, the term was being applied to most forms of juvenile crime and fear of the raskol had become pandemic.

Most accounts locate the rise of raskolism within the context of rapid urbanisation that began in the decade preceding Independence in 1975, in parallel with the dismantling of colonial controls over the movement of the indigenous population.[2] Emphasis has been placed on the role of the early gang as a support mechanism for young male migrants from rural villages confronted with an alien and disorienting urban environment. During this initial phase gang activities appeared to be confined to petty crime and a variety of 'relatively harmless pursuits' (Parry 1972: 44). The deprohibition of alcohol in the early 1960s has also been identified as an important contributing factor, with Harris claiming that it was 'the spark which ignited the flame' of urban gang growth (Harris 1988: 8).

In 1971, the President of the Police Association suggested that there were 50 gangs in Port Moresby.[3] A similar estimate was made by Po'o in 1975 (1975: 34). In 1976, Young claimed there were twenty gangs operating in the city (1976: 5). According to Harris there were six active gangs in 1963, rising to twenty by the late 1970s, and then falling to about twelve by the mid-1980s (1988: 43). Another former gang member, Utulurea claimed that there were 30 operating in 1981 (1981: 111).

Urban arrest figures from the mid-1970s suggested an increase in the overall volume of acquisitive crime, as well as a rise in non-acquisitive offences. These increases in recorded crime have been attributed to the gradual spread of raskol activities from low visibility settlements[4] to more established middle class suburbs in Port Moresby during the period 1968 to 1975 (Harris 1988: 11). Rising crime rates also reflected a growing sophistication in criminal organisation, as well as the influence of better educated criminals who were familiar with the residential areas chosen for breaking and entering operations.[5] The wider social contacts of these individuals also facilitated the dispersal and sale of stolen property, thereby beginning a 'process of vertical integration of gangs into larger criminal networks' (ibid: 13). These changes marked the transition of urban raskolism from being principally a means of psychological support to becoming an efficient vehicle for material advancement (ibid: 13-14). These developments have, in turn, been linked to the deteriorating institutional capacity of law enforcement agencies.

The late 1970s and early 1980s witnessed a process of consolidation, as the larger groups struggled to assert their dominance in particular neighbourhoods. This often involved violent inter-gang conflict. A series of take-overs and amalgamations eventuated, with the larger entities extending their influence through sub-branches in other areas. At the same time, new gangs continued to emerge in the settlements springing up in the outlying parts of town. As the size of criminal associations grew during this period, their membership became more ethnically heterogeneous (ibid: 27). 'Payback' rapes and other assaults occurring in the context of inter-gang conflict marked the beginning of a substantially more violent phase in the evolution of urban raskolism (Dorney 1990: 304-5). These developments have been accompanied, in turn, by rising levels of personal insecurity on the part of the wider urban population. This is reflected in the ever more elaborate security measures guarding official and commercial premises, and the more prosperous private residences.

The recent history of Port Moresby gangs has seen the continuation of the processes of organisational rationalisation and specialisation. The widespread availability of firearms—factory and home-made—has contributed significantly to an increasingly violent urban environment. A growing trade in marijuana has opened a new and lucrative market for criminal entrepreneurs. Criminal groups are now well-established in most urban centres (Hart Nibbrig 1992; Goddard 1992, 1996), as well as in many rural areas (Reay 1982, 1987; Borrey 1994). Evidence also suggests a developing nexus between raskol groups and certain political and business leaders who use criminal 'muscle' for electoral, commercial or personal reasons. While deficiencies in available criminal justice data make it difficult to quantify crime patterns, the general impression is one of gradual deterioration with state controls increasingly overwhelmed by escalating levels of criminal violence.

The evolution of raskolism in PNG has occurred within the broader context of decolonisation and significant related processes of social and political change. In particular, it has evolved in parallel with rapid population expansion unmatched by economic growth. Between 1966 and 1977, Port Moresby experienced a dramatic 12.2% growth rate (King 1992: 22) and doubled in size during the first decade after Independence in 1975 (Dorney 1990: 299). Whereas most early growth was the result of migration, recent growth reflects a natural increase in fertility among urban residents. Despite persistent calls to repatriate 'troublemakers', many of today's urban youth have only tenuous links with rural villages. In practice, a growing proportion of the urban population constitute 'permanent urban dwellers' (Morauta: 1980). Available indicators suggest a marked decline in the quality and delivery of government services in recent years. The 1994 UNDP Human Development Report placed PNG at the bottom of the Pacific region for life expectancy, adult literacy, and the status of women (UNDP 1994). Striking contrasts in wealth and lifestyle in the urban milieu are exemplified by the modern high-rise apartments that house the national and expatriate elite and the sprawling and neglected settlements that have proliferated in most urban centres.

Of the current national population approximately 43% are under the age of fifteen (Dalglish and Connolly 1992). According to the 1990 national census figures relating to Port Moresby and its environs, approximately 50% of the total National Capital District (NCD) population of 195,570 were aged under twenty years and approximately 62% under 25 years (National Statistical Office 1993). In 1992 the then Deputy Prime Minister, Sir Julius Chan, claimed that 52,000 young people left school annually seeking employment in the labour market (*Post-Courier* 13 August 1992). The formal economy has the capacity to absorb only 10,000 of these, leaving 42,000 to seek alternative avenues in the informal sector. In this context, the growth of raskol crime has been regularly linked to the lack of economic opportunities available to the growing body of annual school leavers.

STATE RESPONSES TO RASKOLISM

The institutional weakness of the formal criminal justice system—itself a symptom of the overall weakness of state processes in PNG—has had an important influence upon the evolution of raskolism in both urban and rural contexts. This relates to insufficient resources, which seriously limit the coverage afforded by state controls, as well as increasing the relative ease with which criminals evade detection. It also relates to the counter-productive impact of militarised policing which has become the standard response to crime and social disorder. This, in turn, may be seen as an attempt to compensate for the weakness of the state by drawing on the strength of its ostensibly strongest part.

Dorney (1990: 296) has described the police force handed over to PNG on the eve of Independence as 'the most crippled of any government agency' and one whose responsibility in 1975 'covered only 10% of the land area and 40% of the population'. Rapid localisation, lack of technical skills, a persistent shortage of resources, serious disciplinary problems, and burgeoning levels of crime and disorder, have all contributed to the deficiencies of policing in the post-Independence period. Related—if less visible—difficulties have been experienced in other law and order institutions. Reviewing criminal justice performance in 1984, almost ten years after Independence, the Clifford Report concluded that:

> Simple observation convinces us that the situation is critical—that the criminal justice system is in serious danger of losing the battle to manage and process, let alone constrain, the existing rates of crime (Clifford et al. 1984: 136).

The report recognised that the development of a more effective criminal justice system depended on achieving a much closer articulation between state institutions and informal processes of social control operating at local levels in PNG. While its insights have received rhetorical support from policy makers and criminal justice professionals, there have been few reforms along the lines suggested. In practice, reliance upon reactive and militarised responses to escalating lawlessness has increased despite their obvious expense and often counter-productive effects.

A favoured policing strategy has been to raid settlements—usually in the early hours of the morning—in search of suspects and stolen goods. Raids are typically conducted in a heavy-handed fashion, resulting in the confiscation of items of value that cannot be accounted for with a written receipt. Complaints of harassment, criminal damage, and assault are common. Several provincial governments have also directed coercive administrative measures against 'problem' communities believed to be implicated in urban crime.[6] These have included the repatriation of migrants[7] and demolition of illegal settlements.[8]

Serious outbreaks of localised violence tend to be responded to through the imposition of blanket restrictions on movement and special policing operations. These responses, in turn, reflect the failure of routine criminal justice processes. Announcing the declaration of a state of emergency in the NCD in 1985, in response to raskol violence, the then Prime Minister Michael Somare explained that:

> the law and order situation in the National Capital District has reached a point where the life and safety of a large number of our citizens is now under threat ... In the last few weeks, crimes of despicable violence and cruelty have been committed. The Police have advised that, while house breaking and other non-violent crimes are declining, crimes of violence are escalating rapidly ... The threat that these criminals represent has spread rapidly. The Police can no longer—using their normal powers—control it.[9]

Emergency measures have had little lasting impact in suppressing urban crime. Criminal groups lie low during such operations and 'wanted' criminals escape to rural villages or other towns. While temporarily restoring order in the immediate area, these strategies disperse criminals to places where state controls are weaker. Suppressive measures may well have contributed to overall law and order problems by accelerating the geographic spread of raskolism.

The crisis management approach to crime control has produced a familiar pattern in recent years. An increase in raskol activities, or perception of such, increases pressure for government action. Responses typically include the announcement of a draconian, and largely symbolic, law and order package,[10] special policing operations and, in the most serious cases, the imposition of a curfew.[11] Relative tranquillity returns until the next build up when similar responses are forthcoming, and so on. This happened again in 1991 when the Namaliu government announced a formidable set of legislative proposals.[12] Curfews were imposed in the NCD, Western Highlands, Oro, Morobe, Madang and Sepik Provinces. Addressing the nation on the eve of the NCD curfew, the Prime Minister claimed that:

> Criminal gangs today threaten your personal safety, they make life miserable for all. You and your fellow citizens live and sleep in real

> fear. Our businesses are being hit hard by robberies and our transport, banking, commercial and rural sectors are all being undermined by crime (INA 1991: 31).

A similar situation occurred in 1993, leading the Wingti government to announce the anticipated law and order package, including the controversial Internal Security Act (Dinnen 1993c). Although unsuccessful, a senior government minister called for the declaration of a nationwide state of emergency (*Post-Courier* 20 April 1993: 5) and women's groups demanded a curfew in the NCD (*Post-Courier* 22 April 1993: 1-2). This pattern continues. Calls were made for the imposition of curfews towards the end of 1994 following a number of violent raskol crimes in Lae and Port Moresby (Dinnen 1995). In this case, PNG's financial crisis was cited as the main reason for not implementing such measures (*Post-Courier* 24 November 1994).

THE MELANESIAN 'GANG'

The close association drawn between raskolism and relatively recent processes of urbanisation has encouraged a view of the raskol gang as an integral part of the pathology of modernisation. As such, PNG's raskols have often been viewed as analogous to criminal groups that emerged during periods of rapid change in other national and historical contexts. Many overseas criminologists have assumed that Port Moresby gangs differ little from their counterparts elsewhere.[13] For anthropologists, raskols have been conceived as essentially urban and 'modern' and, hence, of significantly less interest than rural and more 'traditional' phenomena.[14] Such views have, in turn, been reinforced by media coverage depicting PNG's raskols in terms of familiar western gang imagery.

Recent research takes issue with the view of the PNG gang as an essentially 'modern' entity and instead draws our attention to important continuities linking their organisation to more enduring Melanesian social traditions (Schiltz 1985; Harris 1988; Goddard 1992, 1996; Borrey 1994). My own fieldwork in Port Moresby between 1991 and 1994 suggests that the contemporary urban gang exhibits a rich mixture of social traditions. Amongst other things, the social organisation of the Melanesian gang demonstrates the resilience of pre-capitalist traditions and the manner in which these have successfully adapted to socioeconomic change.

In practice, criminal group organisation appears to be much more fluid than that depicted by earlier observers and the media. My informants were generally agreed that there were four broad criminal groupings operating in Port Moresby in the early 1990s. These were: 'Bomai', 'Koboni', 'Mafia', and '585'. Although territorially divided, there was little evidence of territorial or other patterns of inter-group conflict.[15] Raskol group structure, like that of the Melanesian clan-tribe, is essentially segmentary. Each of the four encompassing groups consist of an indeterminate number of loosely associated subgroups operating from the home territory or other parts of the city. These subgroups have their own names and leaders and exercise a significant degree of operational autonomy. The continuous flux in size and configuration of criminal groups—generally following the fortunes of individual leaders— suggests close parallels with traditional political organisation. This is also reflected in the constantly shifting alliances between different entities. While the history of the current major groupings can be traced back to smaller and more ethnically homogeneous groups, their size and segmentary configuration ensures that they reflect the ethnic heterogeneity of the overall urban environment. In practice, smaller subgroups are likely to retain a more homogeneous ethnic composition.

Entry into criminal groups in Port Moresby appears to be a casual affair with no indication of the formal initiation rites previously described by Harris and others (Harris 1988: 26; Young 1972: 7; Utulurea 1981: 112). A prospective 'member' might be invited to participate in a criminal operation and his performance informally assessed by colleagues.[16] More typically, an individual will drift into group crime at a relatively early age and his association with a particular group is developed over years of escalating involvement. Exit from crime appears to be equally informal. Acquiring family responsibilities, criminal group surrender, deciding to concentrate upon legitimate economic activity or employment, tiring of crime, religious conversion, or simply growing older are among a list of factors that might induce an individual to discontinue criminal activities. Some of these individuals might, in turn, return to crime at a later stage for an equally diverse range of reasons. In this respect, Matza's notion of drifting in and out of delinquency is particularly apt in the PNG context (Matza 1964; Clifford et al. 1984: 175).

Loyalty to the group appears to be the only discernible 'rule' of membership. Betrayal of group secrets, and in particular betrayal to the police, is the most serious breach and one likely to attract violent reprisals. It is difficult to identify any clear criterion of membership and, by extension, to distinguish between members and non-members. Goddard (1992: 25) has noted how self-professed gang leaders are unable to state with any precision how many members there are in the groups they lead. My own informants were unclear about the number of subgroups associated with their own. The indeterminate character of the criminal group, in turn, challenges the usefulness of the 'gang' concept with its implicit delineation between members and non-members.

In the urban environment, Schiltz (1985: 158) observed that 'gang leadership shows many striking similarities with traditional bigman-ship'. Kulick (1993: 10) identifies a number of features linking raskol leaders to traditional 'great-men', notably their reputations as 'belligerent and audacious warriors'. Harris (1988: 26) has also indicated parallels between gang leaders and the Melanesian big-man. Among my informants, leadership was clearly of central importance. While the number of leaders, like that of members, remained uncertain, there was a definite leadership hierarchy. At the apex of this was the 'father', who was the senior leader of the constellation of criminal groups comprising each major entity. The term 'father' in this context denotes the 'highly personalised bond of loyalty and dependence' linking criminal leaders and their followers (Schiltz 1985: 145). Below the overall leader were a number of subgroup leaders. Leaders had typically acquired their status through long years of criminal notoriety, usually involving lengthy bouts of incarceration. They were generally much older (often in their late 20s or 30s) than their teenage or mid-20s followers.

Criminal leaders are often well known within their residential communities and may adopt an active role as community leaders. In contrast to the stereotype of raskol groups terrorising local neighbourhoods, urban groups are often extremely well integrated into their immediate surroundings. The interests of raskols and their neighbours frequently overlap. The survival of the former depends on the cooperation of the latter. While raskols have the capacity to intimidate other residents, and such incidents are not uncommon, excessive intimidation and disruption are likely to prove counter-productive. Raskol groups ultimately depend on the community as a safe haven to operate from and to hide in.

Community members are unlikely to inform on their resident raskols except under extreme provocation. Longstanding antipathy between such communities and the police constitutes a major disincentive. As well as inviting criminal retaliation, requesting police intervention might result in heavy-handed raids that inflict extensive collateral damage.[17] Strong bonds of kinship and association will generally transcend externally imposed criminal labels. While older residents express disapproval of raskolism in general terms, there is a noticeable reluctance to condemn the activities of local criminals. Community support is also likely to be more directly manipulated through the selective redistribution of the proceeds of crime..

An important source of ideological integration between criminal and other residents of the more socially disadvantaged urban communities lies in the powerful sense of grievance they share. Frustration and anger is expressed about local socioeconomic conditions, government neglect and corruption, and the widening and highly visible inequalities in the urban context. Such views are prevalent and appear well founded in light of available social and economic indicators, as well as reported cases of official corruption and malpractice.[18] Youth leaders have become particularly adept at articulating a powerful rhetoric of disadvantage that connects with these broader currents of popular discontent and specifically legitimates raskolism in terms of deepening socioeconomic inequalities, corruption, and state violence. Raskol invective is directed at government, politicians, public servants and members of the economic elite for their conspicuous privileges and unwillingness to share these with others.

EXITING CRIME THROUGH GROUP SURRENDER

The mass surrender of self-proclaimed criminal youth groups dates back, at least, to the early 1980s (Giddings 1986) and has since become a regular occurrence throughout PNG. The mass surrender phenomenon raises a number of interesting questions. In the first place, what motivates groups to choose this course of action? The stereotype of the 'raskol gang', conveyed in the media and elsewhere, is of a group of ruthless and well organised criminals capable of operating with minimal chances of apprehension or detection. Why, then, should a number of these groups voluntarily give themselves up to authorities and risk the legal and other recriminations that might follow?

The larger surrenders tend to be elaborate and ceremonial affairs and are usually the outcome of intensive preliminary negotiations. These negotiations, in turn, often involve a brokering party, typically a church group or community organisation and, occasionally, the police as in the following case study. As we shall see, some church groups have adopted a high profile and entrepreneurial role in contacting criminal groups and persuading them to surrender. Such groups can play an important role in assisting the surrendering youths in their subsequent reform plans. Mass surrenders are also likely to include the handing over of large quantities of firearms, ammunition and other implements of crime. A review of local newspaper reports over the past few years indicates the prevalence of this practice and the variations in size of the groups and quantities of commodities surrendered:

- 4 youths with ammunition at Rabaul, East New Britain Province (*Post-Courier* 4 September 1991: 4);
- 6 youths with half a kilogram of marijuana at Kagua, Southern Highlands Province (*Post-Courier* 21 June 1993: 4);
- 17 youths with weapons and marijuana from the Sinasina district of Simbu Province (*Times of PNG* 16 September 1993: 5);
- 17 youths with firearms and ammunition in Popondetta, Oro Province (*Post-Courier* 20 September 1993: 4);
- 20 youths from Lae, Morobe Province, with weapons including a Japanese-made automatic pistol and assorted homemade guns and ammunition (*Post-Courier* 15 February 1993: 4);
- 34 youths in South Lavongai, New Ireland Province (*Post-Courier* 10 December 1993: 4);
- 35 youths in Kimbe, West New Britain Province (*Post-Courier* 8 March 1993: 17);
- 45 youths in Mendi, Southern Highlands Province (*Post-Courier* 3 October 1994: 3);
- 65 youths with firearms in Vunadidir, East New Britain Province (*Post-Courier* 28 October 1993: 15);
- 70 youths with homemade weapons at Badili, National Capital District (*Post-Courier* 19 October 1992: 3);
- 100 youths with homemade weapons in the Toma area of East New Britain Province (*Post-Courier* 24 September 1993: 3);
- 100 youths with weapons in Mendi, Southern Highlands Province (*Post-Courier* 14 December 1992: 3);

- 400 youths from the Kokoda district of Oro Province, with homemade guns (*Times of PNG* 3 September 1992: 5).

The cases reported during this period covered thirteen separate surrenders, involving a total of 913 youths, in eight out of PNG's nineteen provinces. Many more surrenders are likely to have taken place without attracting the attention of the urban-based media.

The ceremonial character of the mass surrender, including the handing over of criminal implements, resembles aspects of customary exchange ceremonies and raises issues of continuities in long-standing social traditions and the manner in which these have interacted with introduced institutions and processes. The surrender also constitutes a significant political forum for dialogue and negotiation between socially marginalised groups and the state and provides us with important insights into how raskol groups understand and relate to the world around them. It is clear from such cases that the state is perceived primarily as a controller and distributor of desirable resources. Other questions concern the role and motivations of the brokering parties and, of course, the longer-term outcome for the surrendering group.

The following case study tells the story of a surrender that occurred in Port Moresby in 1992. The narrative covers the period from the time of the surrender in October 1992 to the end of 1994. I have changed the names of all the informants involved in the actual surrender.

FROM GGB-MAFIA TO METROPOLITAN YOUTH LEAGUE

In October 1992, the PNG *Post-Courier* newspaper announced the surrender of 70 members of the GGB-Mafia gang at a ceremony held at Badili Police Station in Port Moresby. Gang members were reported to be tired of being hunted by the police and to have decided to abandon their criminal activities for 'normal' lives. They claimed that many of their associates had been shot dead by police over the previous two decades. A spokesperson announced the formation of a new youth group, to be called the Metropolitan Youth League (MYL), that would seek government recognition and funding assistance (*Post-Courier* 19 October 1992: 3).

The young men involved in this surrender were mainly of Goilala descent and lived in the Rabia Gini settlement, popularly known as 2-Mile Hill. This is a densely packed urban settlement clinging precariously to the slopes of the 2-Mile Hill, under the shadow of one of Port Moresby's tallest landmarks and most luxurious residential blocks, the Pacific View Building. 2-Mile has long been notorious as a 'haven for black market beer sales and criminals' (*Post-Courier* 5 October 1990: 11). The visual contrast between Pacific View and the settlement it towers above is striking. Originally settled in the late 1950s by small groups of migrants, the settlement started growing at a significant rate in the 1960s (Norwood 1984: 49). It remains one of the most neglected of the city's inner settlements in terms of infrastructure and services. Although there are several water taps, raw sewage flows down the streams cutting across the residential area and, as yet, there is no established electricity supply. The settlement comprises groups of clustered dwellings inhabited by people from the same original district. Just over 30% of the estimated 3,000 inhabitants are from the mountainous and undeveloped Goilala region of the Central Province. Other residents come from Kerema (Gulf Province), Daru (Western Province), Finschafen (Morobe Province), Simbu Province, and the Eastern and Southern Highlands Provinces (Department of Village Services and Provincial Affairs 1993). The ethnic composition of the larger community is reflected in the resident youth groups which comprise a mixture of mainly Goilala, Kerema, and Simbu youth.

The name GGB stands for the Gaire Goilala Boys, or GoiGai Boys as it is sometimes known. Whereas Goilala youth appear to have been the main ethnic constituency during its formative period, the current array of subgroups exhibits the multi-ethnic composition shared by most contemporary urban criminal groups in PNG (Harris 1988: vi). According to my informants, Goilala involvement can be dated back to the Goipex gang in the late 1960s, with a change of name to G105 in the mid-1970s, before becoming the GGB-Mafia in the 1980s. Both Goipex and G105 were Goilala groups.

Operational alliances subsequently forged with criminal groups in the Gaire area, to the south of Port Moresby, are reflected in the current name. The Mafia is one of the four major Port Moresby criminal associations that evolved from an earlier process of consolidation involving a number of groups centred around the Hohola suburb in Port Moresby (Harris 1988). By the late 1980s the Mafia had affiliated subgroups in many parts of the city, including the Badili area at the foot of the 2-Mile Hill, as well as in other towns. After the October surrender, GGB leaders publicly claimed that the GGB-Mafia had up to 800 members in Port Moresby alone, with more in other urban centres (*Post-Courier* 11 November 1992: 6). In practice, it is not possible to accurately estimate numbers. Lack of a clear definition of membership, shifting alliances, and the tendency to claim simultaneous 'membership' with different groups render precise quantification impossible. Indeed, as we have noted above, the loose and fluid linkages which are characteristic of 'raskol' groups suggest that the gang label now widely used in the context of juvenile crime in PNG may not be appropriate (Goddard 1992).

Those involved in the particular surrender discussed here were mainly young men in their mid-teens to early twenties who had been born in the city or spent most of their formative years there. In many cases, parents had moved to Port Moresby from their relatively undeveloped rural villages in search of work and a better quality of life. Few of the youths interviewed mentioned any desire to return to the village and most expressed a strong empathy with their immediate neighbourhood and the urban environment in general. While ethnic identities remained strong,[19] the shared experience of growing up in the same urban community helped forge strong social relations with those from different ethnic backgrounds.[20]

Individual profiles suggested a typical background of interrupted formal education, a drift into minor crime at a comparatively early age, occasional stints of unskilled employment, and an incremental involvement in group crime. Peter, a 22 year old involved in the surrender and subsequent formation of the MYL, is representative. Born in Goilala, he was brought to Port Moresby by his parents at the age of four. His father got a job as a labourer with the Lands Department and the family lived at 4-Mile. Upon retrenchment, the father invested his savings in a small plot at 2-Mile in the proximity of relatives and wantoks from home.[21] Peter had been back to his father's village on several occasions for feasts and other ceremonial events but expressed no interest in returning permanently. He attended community school at Badili and dropped out in grade eight. By that time he was stealing from stores, snatching bags, and engaging in other acts of petty theft. His drift into crime occurred in the company of older boys and his involvement escalated by his late teens to more organised and serious activities, including housebreaking and car theft. While he had never been convicted by a court, he spent several short periods on remand in Bomana Gaol. Like many of his peers, Peter had held a number of unskilled positions, working in stores and as a security guard. These bouts of employment were invariably short-lived, with Peter being dismissed for poor time-keeping or simply leaving because of the monotonous and low-paid character of the work. When he was working, his small pay packet had been rapidly 'eaten-up' by family and wantoks at 2-Mile, leaving him with little for himself.

Several other youths claimed more serious criminal involvement and regularly boasted high criminal status. There was little, however, to suggest that they had the experience or commitment associated with hard core criminals. Jimmy, the group's spokesperson, was a 22 year old Goilala youth. He was born in Port Moresby after his parents left their home in the Upper Kunaimaipa area of Goilala in search of work. His father worked with the Housing Commission and he initially lived at a Housing Commission compound in Badili. The family went back to Goilala when Jimmy was about eight years old and he attended a local mission school before going on to High School to complete grades seven to ten. He returned to town aged about sixteen and stayed with wantoks at the Administrative College. After a couple of years he moved back to 2-Mile where his mother, four brothers, and two sisters had returned from Goilala. His father remained in the village.

Jimmy claimed to have spent a great deal of time looking for employment. He did get a temporary job as a security guard but had to leave when the expatriate company owner left the country. Like many of his ethnic group, he claimed that discrimination against Goilalas was pervasive and that this was a major obstacle to securing employment. Jimmy became involved in a range of acquisitive crimes, including housebreaking and robbery, and built up his own personal following among Goilala youth living at 2-Mile. These activities were explained as the only way of supporting his dependent mother and younger siblings.

Jimmy's following was made up of younger Kunaimaipa boys, as well as some non-Goilala associates from 2-Mile. While his group operated fairly independently, he acknowledged the standing of more experienced criminal leaders from the same area. At the time of his surrender, most of these older youth were in prison serving sentences for past crimes. They included the alleged principal leader or 'father'[22] of the GGB, and several other senior and experienced leaders.[23] The previous 'father' had been shot dead by police at Badili in July 1991,[24] a fate apparently shared by his immediate predecessor in the mid 1980s. At the surrender ceremony in October, group representatives claimed that approximately 32 of their members had been killed by the police in the twenty years or so since the formation of the original group. Indeed, this was one of the reasons given officially for their decision to surrender. (A number of the youth involved informed me of their belief, repeated to me by many other urban youth, that the police had a 'hit-list' of 'hard-core' criminals and were deliberately eliminating them whenever the opportunity arose.)

Jimmy had been trying to secure funds to start a group project for some time prior to the surrender. In the course of these attempts he had met

Arthur, a senior expatriate police officer. Arthur led the Police Community Relations Directorate and was actively involved in expanding the scope of its operations. This principally involved the development of community auxiliary policing which had commenced in selected parts of the National Capital District in 1991. Auxiliary policing entailed the appointment of settlement and village residents as special constables to work in their own communities under the supervision of the regular community police. By the middle of 1992, considerable success was being claimed for the pilot projects in the National Capital District (NCD) with an apparently dramatic drop in local crime rates (Dinnen 1993b). Arthur was engaged in disseminating this successful approach and in seeking government and other funds for further development.

From the police point of view, the surrender of a major urban gang presented an ideal and, in Arthur's case, timely public relations opportunity. Arthur encouraged Jimmy to get the group to give itself up and register as a youth group with the city authority, the National Capital District Interim Commission (NCDIC). He also proposed calling the new group the Metropolitan Youth League. The registered group would be able to compete with other community organisations for NCDIC cleaning contracts and could also apply to government agencies and international donors for project assistance. In the following weeks Arthur and his officers spent a great deal of time encouraging and assisting Jimmy and it is clear that they played a key role in the brokering of this particular surrender. Jimmy's original plan had been to register his boys as a youth group. He had never seriously contemplated surrender. The change in plan was, nonetheless, welcomed as a practical way of securing funds. Jimmy believed this strategy was likely to benefit from the active support of a senior and respected expatriate police officer.

Rumours of the impending surrender circulated rapidly and Jimmy soon received threatening notes from imprisoned GGB leaders declaring their opposition to the proposal and anger at his lack of consultation. These individuals were mostly Goilalas, aged in their late twenties with a long history of criminal involvement. Their opposition was later explained in terms of their deeply ingrained suspicion towards the police. Relations between police and urban youth in PNG, criminal and otherwise, has historically been characterised by mutual suspicion and conflict. Likewise, previous experience of politicians and government agencies has generated little faith in the value of official pledges of assistance. Anger was also directed at Jimmy's perceived attempt to represent himself as a leader of the GGB-Mafia. One of these older leaders, Stephen, later described

Jimmy as 'just a schoolkid' intent on building his name. Whereas Jimmy had only intended to mobilise his own immediate followers, it was widely believed at the time that he was trying to speak on behalf of the larger entity. Subsequent newspaper reports reinforced this misperception by identifying the surrendering group as the GGB-Mafia and naming Jimmy as one of its leaders.

Arthur and Jimmy visited the leaders in prison to clarify some of the misunderstanding and argue their case for proceeding with the surrender. Although later denied by Arthur, Stephen claimed that a number of specific 'promises' were made. These allegedly included the prospect of establishing a workshop for unemployed youth to be funded by Australian aid. This proposal appealed to Stephen and Joe, another Goilala leader, who were shortly due for release and who hoped to utilise the skills they had acquired in the prison joinery. Arthur was also alleged to have promised the purchase of a dump-truck with private sector donations and reportedly said he would help secure cleaning contracts with the city authorities. Stephen and his colleagues were also impressed with Arthur's status as a senior and well connected expatriate officer. Their decision, conveyed to Jimmy, was to approve the surrender. They now accepted that those involved would consist of Jimmy's followers, leaving others to do as they wished.

ARRANGEMENTS FOR SURRENDER

Detailed arrangements for the surrender were subsequently worked out between Arthur and Jimmy. Arthur drew up a formal *Memorandum of Understanding between the Department of Police and the Metropolitan Youth League*. Under its terms, the police undertook to:

(a) accept the surrender of the members of the gang, their weapons and ammunition, in a recognised form of ceremony;

(b) inform gang members as to the nature and type of any outstanding criminal charges, warrants and offences for which they might be classified as wanted persons;

(c) arrange for outstanding charges to be heard before a magistrate and for the charge to be lawfully determined, with the fact of the individual's voluntary surrender being taken into account by the court;

(d) in cases of a minor charge, the Police Department would recommend to the court that the accused, on conviction, should be sentenced to a fine, suspended sentence or community work order;

(e) in serious cases, the police would advise the court of the voluntary surrender of the accused, in order that the court could take this into account when passing sentence;

(f) the Police Department would guarantee the safe conduct of all persons who voluntarily surrendered under the provisions of the Memorandum of Understanding for a further period of 14 days; and

(g) the Police Department, through officers of its Community Relations Directorate, would maintain a close liaison with the group and provide guidance and support, in cooperation with other agencies, to assist with their rehabilitation, training and the acquisition of skills necessary to effect their rehabilitation.

In return, the Metropolitan Youth League agreed to:

(a) deliver all arms, ammunition and offensive weapons under their control to the Police Department, where they would be handed in at a recognised form of ceremony;

(b) advise police of those members of their organisation who might be classified as 'wanted' persons, in order that their cases might be dealt with;

(c) register with the National Capital District youth office under the name of 'Metropolitan Youth League' and to make their members available for work parties, etc., as allocated by the NCDIC Youth Office;

(d) maintain liaison and contact with the Community Relations Directorate of the Department of Police, who would make an officer available for Youth Liaison purposes; and

(e) work in liaison with the Community Relations Directorate of the Police Department to effect the surrender, rehabilitation and fostering of understanding between youth gangs, police and community, and

> make a positive contribution to the maintenance of peace, law and order in Papua New Guinea. *(Memorandum of Understanding between the Department of Police and the Metropolitan Youth League,* 16 October 1992*)*.

Despite the formal and legalistic tone of the Memorandum, it had little practical effect. Arthur subsequently checked the 70 names of MYL members against police records. Only two were wanted for outstanding charges and as these were of a minor nature Arthur had them struck out. No charges were ever laid against any member of the surrendering group. While available criminal justice data in PNG, including police records, are notoriously unreliable (Clifford et al. 1984: 15-42; Walker 1985), this is further confirmation of the low criminal status of those who surrendered. Other evidence suggests that many of those who surrendered had little, if any, criminal experience. Interviews with Jimmy and released leaders indicated that the more criminally active youth were awaiting the eventual outcome of the surrender.

The formal surrender took place on 16 October 1992 in the precinct of the Badili Police station. Weapons handed in included home-made rifles, ammunition, knives, and bows and arrows. Arthur, who acted as master of ceremonies, had arranged for the attendance of the media and a number of official guests. Three government ministers were present, including the Minister for Police. Short speeches were delivered by Arthur, Jimmy, an Acting Deputy Commissioner of Police, and a well-known local evangelist. The Memorandum of Understanding was formally signed by the Acting Deputy Commissioner on behalf of the Commissioner of Police and by Jimmy as Executive Officer of the newly formed Metropolitan Youth League.

Others who attended the ceremony included most of Jimmy's followers, other local youth on the lookout for any immediate opportunities, and an assortment of onlookers from the Goilala community at 2-Mile. Jimmy formally asked for forgiveness on the part of the former gang and made a plea to government representatives for financial support for the newly formed Metropolitan Youth League:

> We need your assistance and we would like government bodies that are directly responsible for youth development to help us get a sub-contract with NCDIC so that we can keep our members busy with useful activities and not turn back to crime (*Post-Courier* 19 October 1992: 3).

The media subsequently ran a number of stories on the surrender. In one, titled 'Bad Boys Come Good', the story differed markedly from that subsequently given by Jimmy and other participants but conformed to the standard depiction of the dynamics of group surrender:

> with continuous police community relations in the settlement and tireless efforts by church leaders, some members of the GGB Mafia Gang came to realise that crime will eventually destroy them and that there was no purpose in the lives they were leading (*Post-Courier* Weekend Magazine 23 October 1992: 1).

PROBLEMS ESTABLISHING THE MYL

Arthur issued special identity cards to each member of the newly formed Metropolitan Youth League (MYL). These certified that the holder was a member of the Police and Citizen's Youth Employment and Assistance Program and were designed to appeal to potential employers and donors. In the following weeks Arthur and Jimmy explored various avenues for acquiring job placements and financial assistance. Initial signs were promising with a number of businesses expressing interest. Within a short time, 28 MYL members were working as security guards, shop assistants, and carpenters for a local company. A handful of others got similar work in other enterprises and there appeared to be good prospects of securing a cleaning contract with the NCDIC. Arthur helped prepare a lengthy proposal for submission to the Australian International Development Assistance Bureau (AIDAB) for K8,000 funding for a proposed poultry project. One company agreed to donate chicken wire, while another promised K1,500.

In November 1992, Arthur arranged for three imprisoned GGB-Mafia leaders to hold a press conference at the Corrective Institutions Service Headquarters in Port Moresby on 10 November 1992. The immediate purpose was to appeal to prison escapees to give themselves up. Ten alleged hard core prisoners had escaped from Bomana on the morning of Sunday, 25 October 1992, in what was reported to have been a well-planned operation (*Post-Courier* 27 October 1992: 1). Of the ten, eight were from Goilala. Earlier in the same week, two other convicted murderers from the same area had also escaped from Bomana. Jimmy told Arthur of his suspicion that the escapees were looking for him because of his role in the surrender and was duly given some police protection. One of the escapees did, in fact, contact him at 2-Mile but the purpose was to solicit money rather than wreak revenge.

In the course of the press conference, the three prisoners stated that only a small number of the GGB-Mafia had actually surrendered in October and that most remained sceptical of the venture. They circulated a letter recently received from one of the escapees. In it, the escapee spoke of the treachery of those who had surrendered and threatened to take revenge on them. While the leaders dutifully called on the escapees to give themselves up, they also urged authorities to devote more attention to the country's unemployed youth and proposed a massive injection of funds into youth projects. In the words of one:

> We want to take part in the development of this country. If the government can give us the opportunity, we will prove that we do have something to offer this country (*Post-Courier* 11 November 1992: 6)

Arthur also took the opportunity to appeal to business houses for support and to publicise the fact that 28 members of the Metropolitan Youth League had already found employment and that 30 others were likely to be offered jobs in the near future.

The surrender and accompanying publicity raised high expectations on the part of all involved. Despite what was said in the media reports, Jimmy's decision to surrender was principally based on its appeal as a strategy for securing project funds and opening up employment opportunities. The emphasis in media stories upon the fear of the police and the impact of religious conversions was at variance with available evidence. As already stated, Jimmy's group was not composed of hardened criminals and few were, in fact, known to the police. While many of those who surrendered were likely to have had first-hand experience of police brutality, it is unlikely that any believed themselves to be objects of special police interest. Likewise, the churches played little role in the events leading up to the surrender. Jimmy informed me that few of his followers, himself included, had any real interest in religion and were, if anything, hostile towards church groups who rarely helped the community. The surrender, in their view, was primarily a strategy for pursuing altogether more secular ends.

The police also had their institutional interests in mind by facilitating the surrender. News of their involvement in preventative, as opposed to reactive, police work provided a welcome contrast to their popular image as a reactive and repressive force. In addition, the community relations branch, with its recently launched community auxiliary initiative, was likely to receive timely publicity that might help secure the financial support needed for further expansion. Jimmy and Arthur also stood to gain in terms of the kudos attaching to their respective individual contributions. In the immediate aftermath of the surrender Jimmy was constantly pursued by journalists and received warm receptions at the various business and government offices he visited. On a visit home to Goilala he was delighted to see that students at his old mission school had stuck his newspaper clippings to the noticeboard. In effect, he had become something of an overnight celebrity. At the same time, whereas the police could claim considerable success upon the surrender taking place, the longer-term success of Jimmy's strategy depended upon him achieving tangible results in the months to come.

During the early part of 1993, Jimmy—by now President of the League—continued to express cautious optimism about the prospects of the enterprise. Real problems were, nevertheless, beginning to appear. Principal amongst these was the lack of administrative skills necessary for completing lengthy and technical funding documents. Related to this, the bureaucratic procedures governing the administration of project funds in PNG are complex and cumbersome. For many of the youngsters, the long delays constituted a continuous source of confusion and frustration. The proposal for Australian aid for the poultry project had been passed on to the PNG Office for International Development Assistance (OIDA) who are required to approve all international project assistance.[25] They subsequently sent the League a request for the following documentation:

- A project file or feasibility study;
- A letter of proof from the Lands Department (this letter was required to ensure that the proposed land was not subject, or likely to be subject, to a lands dispute);
- Projected cash flow;
- Quotations from three suppliers on materials and equipment to be purchased;
- A sketch of the project site or any other designs for the intended project;
- Confirmation from market outlets intending to take in some of the future produce.

Without the basic skills and experience required, the group remained largely dependent on the assistance of individuals such as Arthur. At the same time, Arthur was under mounting pressure from the expansion of the community auxiliary scheme and other projects and was spending increasing periods away from Port Moresby. The necessary documentation was never completed and the application proceeded no further.

The Department of Home Affairs and Youth, the government department charged with promoting the interests and welfare of the nation's youth, proved particularly unhelpful and assistance was sought from the voluntary sector. An initial approach was made to the American Peace Corps organisation. While sympathetic, the Peace Corps, like many other overseas voluntary organisations, required that volunteers be provided with secure accommodation by the project participants. Given the MYL's lack of resources, this requirement was difficult to meet. The newly formed National Volunteer Service was also approached and provided some temporary assistance.

Meanwhile Jimmy was coming under mounting pressure from followers and detractors alike. He was receiving daily visits from those expecting jobs and cash. The initial interest expressed by business houses receded as time passed. In the absence of immediate results, a number of those involved in the surrender were questioning the wisdom of the surrender strategy. Accusations were resurfacing that Jimmy and his followers had been 'tricked' by the police. Jimmy also faced the continuing hostility of some of the imprisoned leaders who had subsequently been released. Stephen, for example, was claiming that Jimmy had reneged on a promise to deliver him the leadership of the MYL upon his release. In addition, the relationship between Arthur and Jimmy was becoming progressively strained with Arthur complaining of Jimmy's endless demands, and Jimmy countering with complaints about Arthur's increasing lack of interest.

Problems were also appearing in respect of those who had secured jobs immediately after the surrender. Accusations were made that contracts promised by employers had not materialised and that pay rates were lower than originally agreed. On the other side, there were complaints of petty pilfering and poor time-keeping. Of the 28 youths employed by one company, only five remained in employment by May 1993. While the funding application for the proposed poultry project continued to languish at OIDA, it also became clear that the original site chosen at Badili, near the 2-Mile settlement, would have to be changed. Local health regulations prohibited the raising of livestock within the city limits. The new plan was to use some customary land at Laloki, on the outskirts of the city. Even if the funding application proceeded—which it did not—the next problem would have been how to transport the produce to city markets.

Several meetings were held in the middle of the year in an attempt to generate wider public interest in the issue of funding and supervision of youth projects. Jimmy, as well as other youth leaders, appeared on talkback radio shows appealing for assistance and a meeting was arranged with the Deputy Prime Minister and Minister for Finance, Sir Julius Chan (*Post-Courier* 21 April 1993: 1). Once again, sympathy and support were expressed but no tangible assistance was forthcoming. By August, the League appeared to be falling apart. Several of Jimmy's original followers had abandoned him and switched their allegiances to other leaders, or were simply hanging out in the settlement and drifting back into petty crime. In September, Jimmy returned to Kunamaipa in Goilala with about twenty of his closest followers. Gold deposits had recently been discovered there and a new and potentially lucrative opportunity presented itself. Attempts were simultaneously being made to secure funding to start a vegetable project in the village and then sell the produce in Port Moresby.

Jimmy came back to town in January 1994 and resumed his strenuous rounds of visiting government offices, business contacts, and sympathetic individuals. Initially he was seeking funds to purchase a large freezer for storing the vegetables prior to their transportation to town. Despite the failure to secure funding assistance, Jimmy's entrepreneurial drive showed no sign of faltering. By mid-1994 he had embarked on his most ambitious project to date. This entailed incorporating MYL as a company and then submitting a tender to carry out cleaning for government offices in Port Moresby. He had met a senior official in the Department of Trade and Industry who informed him that the cleaning contract was up for renewal. This official helped Jimmy draft the *Memorandum and Articles of Association for the Metropolitan Youth Corporation Pty Ltd* and encouraged him to apply for a Small Business Scheme Loan from the Rural Development Bank.

CASH, PRESTIGE, AND DEVELOPMENT

Contrition for previous crimes and the desire to become law-abiding citizens had little to do with the decision to surrender by Jimmy and his group. They were never very heavily involved in criminal activity in the first place and had a lot less to be forgiven for than implied by the media reports. In practice, Jimmy and his followers had to work quite hard at projecting the kind of 'criminal' image appropriate to the surrender strategy. Their individual and collective pasts differed little to those of thousands of other socially marginalised urban youth and certainly did not amount to the extraordinary 'life of violence, stealing and hurting others' subsequently depicted in the media (*Post-Courier* Weekend Magazine 23 October 1992: 1). While such an image may have suited Jimmy's purposes, it was vigorously contested by the older youth interviewed, who ridiculed Jimmy's claims to high criminal status. Evidence from this and similar cases suggest that mass surrenders tend to attract groups of youth whose criminal commitment is of a qualitatively less serious kind than that of the numerically small 'hard core' criminal for whom crime has become an established way of life. Such a strategy has less appeal to the latter, who would be more likely to face a lengthy period in prison.[26]

The decision to surrender in this case was perceived by all the main parties as a strategy for acquiring funds, either through project assistance or employment opportunities. This was the prospect that Arthur held out when persuading the group to surrender. Throughout the period immediately preceding and after the October ceremony, he was actively engaged in trying to secure contracts, jobs, and funding assistance for group members. It is also one of the main reasons the imprisoned leaders withdrew their initial opposition to the surrender strategy. Jimmy's tireless quest for funds and jobs attests to the same purpose.

Having established the importance of securing funds, we can proceed to ask why this was considered so important. On the face of it, the answer appears to be relatively straightforward. Money is necessary to procure the essentials of survival in any cash economy—that is, food, clothing, shelter, transport etc. Lack of legitimate opportunities for acquiring the necessary cash (i.e. employment) encourages those excluded to explore illegal means to the same ends. This view has particular force in the contemporary urban context where the option of falling back upon the subsistence sector is limited. It is also the view propounded in the post-surrender media reports. Commenting on the criminal history of Jimmy's group, one report stated that:

> For them, there was nothing wrong with stealing. Stealing was the only means of surviving in a big town like Port Moresby (*Post-Courier* Weekend Magazine 23 October 1992: 1).

At the same time, while the forces driving the activities of Jimmy's group obviously included considerations of material survival, there is little doubt that they also went well beyond these.

At this point, it is necessary to broaden the discussion and consider some aspects of the wider socioeconomic position of contemporary Papua New Guinean youth, as well as some of the specific social dynamics that have informed their collective responses, criminal and otherwise. This will also provide an opportunity for demonstrating that the switch from crime to reform strategies, exemplified in the mass surrender, entails a much less significant transformation in underlying social commitment than the initial contrast suggests.

Most accounts of the current crime situation in PNG focus selectively upon the highly visible area of gang crime, and usually seek to explain it in terms of the criminogenic effects of rapid socio-economic change and its particular impact on youth (Department of Provincial Affairs 1983; Clifford et al. 1984; UNDP/ILO, 1993). Population growth, the adequacy and appropriateness of the formal education system, and lack of employment opportunities are regularly cited as the principal underlying causes of discontent and disorder amongst the young. Such views are also reflected in the rhetoric of disadvantage articulated by the young themselves. Unemployment, in particular, has achieved a prominent explanatory status in discussions of the rise of raskolism. As we have seen, PNG's raskol problem has often been portrayed as little different to that evident in other countries sharing similar developmental profiles. At the same time, available empirical evidence suggests that the social responses of youth groups in PNG, whether these be criminal associations or otherwise, have their own distinctive aetiology.

There are a number of difficulties associated with attempts to connect unemployment causally to youth crime, some of which apply in other national contexts and some which are distinct to the Papua New Guinean environment. Addressing the issue of employment/unemployment in PNG is notoriously difficult. In addition to the lack of reliable statistical data, there is the fact that the vast majority of the population remain outside the formal wage sector. The 1980 national census, for example, estimated that only 9.7% of the total population were counted in the formal wage sector (Mannur 1987: 29) and this figure is likely to have decreased further since 1980 because population growth has exceeded growth in wage employment (McGavin 1991: 53). Even when we leave the problems of definition and quantification to one side, the relation between unemployment and crime is by no means as straightforward as its proponents suggest. For a start, it is clear that most unemployed people, however defined, do not resort to the criminal lifestyles usually associated with raskol groups.

Evidence also indicates that many of those involved in raskol activities have at one time or another occupied waged positions. While some like

Jimmy might lose their jobs for reasons beyond their control, others like Peter relinquish employment opportunities either through direct choice or indirectly by failing to fulfil basic requirements (e.g. maintaining regular hours). For those who have had jobs, the experience has often been one of unrelenting monotony and low material rewards. This is related to the kind of menial work available to those with limited or no formal educational qualifications. The progress of the MYL members who secured employment in the immediate aftermath of the surrender is a case in point. Amongst other things, their rate of attrition reflected a low level of commitment to the discipline of wage labour. This observation is at variance with the popular and reductive equation drawn between unemployment and raskolism—either as cause or solution. It also indirectly draws attention to the positive attractions of the raskol option in terms of non-material factors such as excitement and prestige. In this sense it is clear that 'the popular stereotyping of raskols as unemployed school drop-outs is too simplistic and therefore a misleading generalisation' (Schiltz 1985: 155).

The benefits of waged employment in PNG have also to be viewed within the context of extended Melanesian kinship networks and the social obligations these engender. Having a job brings with it the demands and expectations of relatives and wantoks which can effectively undermine the incentive to work. One observer has described how the employed person in such a situation becomes 'a channel for the flow of cash and commodities' (Goddard 1992: 22). Another remarks that in the urban context 'too many demands being made on the income of young people in their first jobs becomes an intolerable burden' (Monsell-Davis 1993: 11). Peter's experience falls into this category. The decision to relinquish employment for crime may in certain cases be as much about escaping the demands of kin, as being a response to a small and restricted labour market. Whereas the waged worker can expect regular visitations from cash-hungry wantoks on fortnightly pay days, the raskol has significantly more control over his resources owing to the irregular and surreptitious nature of criminal work. Moreover, crime promises a level of material rewards that far surpasses the wages for unskilled labour.

This is not, of course, to deny the criminogenic impact of deepening structural inequalities, including those relating to access to education and formal employment. The broader background of socio-economic change and emergent structural inequalities constitute the primary context of many aspects of contemporary criminality in Papua New Guinea, amongst both the relatively deprived and the relatively advantaged (Dinnen 1993a). It is clear, for example, that the absence of legal means for individual and collective advancement, such as employment opportunities, is an important factor in influencing criminal choices. At the same time, however, these macro processes do not in themselves explain the specific form or range of responses adopted by particular groups. While structural processes of recent origin provide us with the background to many contemporary areas of disorder, an explanation of the foreground requires analysis of the social and situational dynamics underlying criminal behaviour.

Success in both capitalist and pre-capitalist Melanesian worlds depends, in varying degrees, upon the accumulation of wealth. Whereas, the capitalist ethic promotes individual accumulation as an end in itself, Melanesian societies tend to view wealth for its instrumental value in the pursuit of more fundamental social objectives, notably the pursuit of prestige. Access to resources, and the manner of their distribution, constitutes a fundamental social dynamic linking the conduct of social relations in both modern and traditional settings. In this context, Monsell-Davis has stated that:

> Reputation, including moral and ethical superiority, is commonly based on access to, and command over, resources and their distribution. The expectation of reciprocity, and the idea of prestige associated with giving (along with the concomitant fear of being perceived as repudiating proper social relationships if one rejects a request for help), are important elements of continuity in modern Melanesia (Monsell-Davis 1993: 6).

In this sense, access to material wealth provides an important means for achieving other social ends. Insofar as employment provides opportunities for acquiring necessary wealth, its absence, low returns or restricted access, may encourage crime as an alternative strategy to essentially the same ends. The inherent versatility of cash as a form of transactable wealth has made it the most attractive medium for both criminals and non-criminals engaged in prestige building strategies. On the one hand, it is difficult for law enforcement agencies to link cash directly with specific crimes and, on the other, it is capable of being used in a wide variety of social contexts. In her study of Highland migrants to Port Moresby, Strathern noted how 'money has become the sole operator, the only medium through which status and relationships can be expressed' (Strathern 1975a: 315). In her view, money in PNG has become the 'coin of social commerce' (ibid: 300). Borrey's research on rural crime also emphasises the centrality of cash in the building of prestige and power across a number of different social settings in contemporary PNG (Borrey 1994).

From this perspective, the emphasis shifts from viewing raskolism exclusively as a means of material survival, to an appreciation of its role as a strategy for pursuing more familiar Melanesian social objectives. Low levels of popular allegiance to the normative and institutional order embodied in state law,[27] as well as minimal risk of apprehension, enhance the appeal of group crime as a strategy for this purpose. This view of crime as an essentially goal-oriented activity is supported by the practice among youth of referring to their criminal activities as 'wok' (work) and, in this sense, indistinguishable from other goal-oriented activities, such as wage labour, aimed at the same ends.

KINSHIP, LEADERSHIP, AND PRESTIGE

Many observers have noted the resilience of long-standing Melanesian forms of kinship obligation and prestige building and the manner in which these have interacted with a range of contemporary institutions and processes. The role of leader/follower reciprocal obligations is central to understanding the social organisation of raskolism and provides another illustration of significant continuities connecting modern and traditional institutions in PNG. Like Schiltz (1985) and Harris (1988), Goddard (1992) has argued that today's criminal leader shares many of the characteristics of the traditional 'big-man' and, in particular, his pursuit of prestige and power through manipulating social relations with others. His success, like that of the big-man, depends on his entrepreneurial skills in the building and manipulating of relations of patronage with a range of individuals and groups. Whereas the big-man builds his power through the accumulation of traditional items of wealth and their redistribution and ceremonial exchange, the criminal leader constructs his power-base upon acquisitive crime and the strategic redistribution of the proceeds among criminal associates and kin. The object of redistribution in both cases is to create and sustain highly personalised relationships based on obligation and dependency and, in the process, to build up the prestige and influence of the donor. It is in this context that criminal leaders—and aspiring leaders—boast of their influence and status among peers and view themselves as big men of crime.

Concern with prestige and reputation is as evident among those opting for the surrender strategy as among those actively engaged in raskol activities. Surrender constitutes another avenue for pursuing essentially the same social objectives. In this sense, raskolism and surrender are different means to the same ends. It is clear, for example, that Jimmy's endeavour to secure jobs and resources for MYL members was as much about building up his own name and standing as it was about procuring the necessities for material survival in the city. This was the basis for the hostility expressed by Stephen and others who constantly sought to 'rubbish' his claims to leadership status. Jimmy relished the attention he was getting from the media, officials, business houses and, of course, from among his peers, in the aftermath of the surrender. Whereas his status as a criminal leader may have been negligible, his role in the surrender gave him the 'name' he so clearly desired. In this respect, his subsequent endeavours for funds, jobs, and contracts was about consolidating and developing this newly acquired status.

The pervasive desire by youth for cash in hand and the patterns of conspicuous consumption, noted by Borrey (1994), relate to expectations that items will be redistributed within given social relations and that all will share, in varying degrees, in the material rewards and prestige of the successful individual or leader. Contemporary leaders, whether their 'wok' is in politics, the public service, business, or crime, are all expected to engage in this social process, in much the same way as the traditional Melanesian leader. Individual accumulation without redistribution is not only unlikely to enhance the status of the individual concerned but may well attract the retributive attention of those who thereby feel excluded.

Expectations of reciprocity on the part of those involved in redistribution have a direct bearing on the practice of handing over firearms and ammunition at mass surrenders. Amongst other things, such acts engender expectations on the part of the surrendering group that the recipients will reciprocate by delivering the funds, clemency or other resources sought. The surrender of weapons also signifies the group's intent to abandon criminal strategies while simultaneously providing a reminder of their power to disrupt and engage in violence should their expectations be disappointed. Raskol groups are acutely aware of their disruptive potential and their ability to thwart official efforts to provide a stable law and order environment. In this vein, Schiltz quotes a Port Moresby gang leader telling political leaders that: 'We determine Papua New Guinea's image abroad; we control the country's economy; we are the carpet you walk on; and we are your time bombs' (Schiltz 1985: 142).

For Jimmy and his boys, the surrender provided an important opportunity for initiating potentially rewarding social relations with those in positions of authority and influence. Like other youth groups throughout the country, they held extremely high expectations of the 'government' or the 'state', as lying in its control of vast and desirable resources. Expectations of it are, in turn, premissed on it conducting relations with its subjects in much the same way as any other powerful group or leader. The state's control of resources, thus, provides it with a unique status and potential in the context of Melanesian patterns of wealth distribution and the manipulation of social relations. Borrey has recently used the analogy of the state as big-man to describe these popular perceptions:

> for lots of people the State is a surrogate big man or leader who in the process of wealth accumulation (like mineral and logging projects) is expected to redistribute some of this wealth back to the people (Borrey 1994: 7).

The inevitable failure of government authorities to live up to such high expectations leads to acute disappointment and anger. This anger is further fuelled by the regular flow of extravagant promises by political leaders, which are rarely fulfilled in practice. This is part of the reason for the markedly anti-government, anti-politician invective articulated by youth leaders. From the same perspective, violent crime may be viewed as a way of punishing those seen as having reneged on their promises and, at the same time, a way of forcing them back into more familiar and appropriate exchange relations. Schiltz refers to this as the 'equalising dimension' of 'raskolism' (Schiltz 1985: 149).

The perennial quest for cash and prestige has led to a number of innovative strategies on the part of youth and other groups.[28] These invariably involve some attempt to tap into government or private sector resources. Youth group 'walkathons' have become a favoured tactic in this respect and have occurred in parts of country. Such groups travel considerable distances, often by foot, to get to Port Moresby, the seat of the National Parliament and the central repository of public and private sector resources. The object is to attract maximum media coverage and meet with politicians and other prominent figures, with a view to acquiring funds for a variety of 'development projects'. In the past, youth groups often succeeded in procuring funds in this way and were able to return home in triumph. As more and more groups resorted to this strategy, however, public opinion grew increasingly sceptical and the potential returns from the walkathon diminished accordingly.[29] As an attempt to access resources, gang mass surrender provides a more spectacular version of the same phenomenon.

At first glance, the long-term outcome for surrendering groups appears to be largely dependent on the provision of adequate funding for project development and appropriate levels of technical and administrative assistance. At the same time, the progress of particular projects is inevitably complicated by the social dynamics of prestige and obligation discussed above. Such considerations are rarely anticipated by project planners and, once manifest, are likely to lead to dismay on the part of proponents of economic growth and individual production. For participants, on the other hand, it is these underlying social factors that are likely to be considered more important than considerations of accumulation and growth. The measure of success is, in this sense, largely a question of perception.

CONCLUSION

The immediate significance of the mass surrender is that it is a strategy for securing funds and a process for developing new avenues for prestige building. The pursuit of funds and prestige, in turn, underlies a range of contemporary social behaviour in Papua New Guinea, including raskolism. In this sense, the move from raskolism to reform, via the mass surrender, represents a continuation, rather than change, in underlying social commitment.

The same phenomenon illustrates the innovative way in which social groups that find themselves increasingly marginalised in the emergent capitalist order are able to create negotiating space with those in political and economic power and, in the process, open up new opportunities for individual and collective advancement. An irony shared by both walkathon and mass surrender options, is that they both lead participants to inflate, and occasionally invent, criminal backgrounds for the purpose of accessing the funds sought. The manipulation of raskol identities and reconciliation rituals evident in the mass surrender illustrates the sophisticated way in which certain groups are able to turn their marginal and officially stigmatised status to advantage.

None of this is to deny the broader context of socioeconomic disadvantage faced by Papua New Guinean youth today, including the routine abuse they experience at the hands of the police. As mentioned previously, the broad genesis of current trends in crime consists of structural inequalities of recent origin. This context is critical to explanations of the evolution of raskolism. At the same time, it is important to move beyond the generalities of structural analysis if we wish to appreciate the specificities of criminal organisation in contemporary PNG. In this respect, our analysis illustrated the manner in which raskolism represents a rich mixture of different social traditions.

While lack of reliable criminal justice data makes quantification difficult, most observers are agreed that raskolism continues to increase. This is most apparent in the urban centers but is also the case in most rural areas. Highway hold-ups have become a growing hazard for travellers in many parts of the country. This is particularly so along sections of the Highlands Highway which provides the sole road link between the populous Highlands region and the eastern ports. Raskolism concentrates around the areas of highest development—where criminal opportunities are greatest. Mass surrenders are unlikely to have a significant impact in reducing raskol activities until they are more effectively connected to sustainable alternatives to crime. At present the lack of organised support and guidance for surrendering groups increases the likelihood of re-entry to crime after the initial enthusiasm, goodwill and resources have dissipated. In order to exploit the considerable potential for crime reduction presented by the surrender phenomenon, serious attention has to be paid to ways of formalising its connection to employment, education and social development options.

REFERENCES

Biles, D. (1976) *Crime in Papua New Guinea*, Canberra: Australian Institute of Criminology.

Bohane, B. (1995) 'The New Bushrangers', *The Bulletin*, 27 June 1995: 14-19.

Borrey, A. (1994), 'Youth Unemployment and Crime', paper presented at the National Employment Summit, 11-12 May 1994, Port Moresby.

Clifford W., Morauta, L. and Stuart, B. (1984) *Law and Order in Papua New Guinea*, Vols I and II, Port Moresby: Institute of National Affairs and Institute of Applied Social and Economic Research.

Dalglish, P. and Connolly, M. (1992) 'Too Much Time, Too Little Money—the Challenge of Urban Street Youth in Papua New Guinea', *Street Kids International,* Toronto: 1-47.

Department of Provincial Affairs (1983) *Report of the Committee to Review Policy and Administration on Crime Law and Order*, Port Moresby.

Department of Village Services and Provincial Affairs (1993) *Village Services*

N.C.D. Settlement Survey, Port Moresby.

Dinnen, S. (1993a), 'Big Men, Small Men and Invisible Women—Urban Crime and Inequality in Papua New Guinea', *Australian and New Zealand Journal of Criminology*, 26: 19-34, March.

Dinnen, S. (1993b) 'Community Policing in Papua New Guinea', *Criminology Australia*, 4(3): 2-5, January/February.

Dinnen, S. (1993c) 'Internal Security in Papua New Guinea', *Criminology Australia*, 5(2): 2-7, October/November.

Dinnen, S. (1993d), 'Paradigm Lost—'Third World' Criminology and the Fall of Global Theory', *Asia Pacific Law Review*, 2(2): 1-25, Winter.

Dinnen, S. (1995) 'Papua New Guinea in 1994—the Most Turbulent Year?', *Current Issues in Criminal Justice*, (March) 6(3): 395-407.

Dorney, S. (1990) *Papua New Guinea—people, politics and history since 1975,* Sydney: Random House Australia.

Fitzpatrick, P. (1980) *Law and State in Papua New Guinea*, London: Academic Press.

Giddings, L. (1986) 'Some Alternatives to States of Emergency', in Louise Morauta (ed.), *Law and Order in a Changing Society*, Political and Social Change Monograph 6, Canberra: Australian National University.

Goddard, M. (1992) 'Big-man, Thief: The social organisation of gangs in Port Moresby, *Canberra Anthropology*, 15(1): 20-34, April.

Goddard, M. (1995) 'The Rascal Road: Crime, prestige and development in Papua New Guinea', *The Contemporary Pacific* 7(1): 55-80, Spring.

Hart Nibbrig, N. (1992) 'Rascals in Paradise: Urban Gangs in Papua New Guinea', *Pacific Studies* 15(3): 115-34.

Harris, B.M. (1988) *The Rise of Rascalism: Action and reaction in the evolution of rascal gangs,* Port Moresby: Institute of Applied Social and Economic Research.

INA, (1991) *Developments in Law and Order,* Port Moresby: Institute of National Affairs: 1-66.

King, D. (1992) 'The Demise of the Small Towns and Outstations of Papua New Guinea: Trends in Urban Census Populations and Growth from 1966 to 1990', *Yagl-Ambu, UPNG Journal of the Social Sciences and Humanities,* 16(3): 17-33, September.

Kulick, D. (1993) 'Heroes from Hell—representations of "rascals" in a Papua New Guinean village', *Anthropology Today,* 9(3): 9-14, June.

Life Outreach Ministries (1989) 'Operation Tanimbel Crusade '8', Port Moresby.

Matza, D. (1964) *Delinquency and Drift,* New York: John Wiley and Sons.

Mannur, H.G. (1987) 'Employment and Unemployment in Papua New Guinea', *Yagl-Ambu*, 14(1): 26-55, March.

McGavin, P.A. (1991) 'Wages, Incomes and Productivity in Papua New Guinea', Port Moresby: Institute of National Affairs, discussion paper No. 48.

Monsell-Davis, M. (1993) 'Safety Net or Disincentive? Wantoks and Relatives in the Urban Pacific', Port Moresby: National Research Institute, Discussion Paper No. 72.

Moore, D., Richardson, B. and Wuillemin, D. (1984) 'A Comparison of Rural and Legal Ranking of Crimes in Papua New Guinea', *Melanesian Law Journal*, 12: 149-58.

Morauta, L. (1980) *Permanent Urban Residents in PNG: Problems and prospects*, proceedings of the 1979 Waigani Seminar on Urbanisation, Port Moresby: University of Papua New Guinea: 290-302.

National Statistical Office (1993) *1990 National Population Census—Final Figures Census Division Populations*, Port Moresby.

Norwood, H. (1984) *Port Moresby: Urban Villages and Squatter Areas,* Port Moresby: University of Papua New Guinea Press.

O'Neill, N. (1976) *Crime, the Criminal Justice System and Urbanisation Policy*, Port Moresby: 1-29.

Oram, N. (1976) *Colonial Town to Melanesian City—Port Moresby 1884-1974*, Australian National University: Canberra.

Parry, G.L. (1972) 'Organised Juvenile Crime in Port Moresby', *South Pacific Bulletin*, 22(1): 43-4, 60.

Po'o, T. (175) *Gangs in Port Moresby*, Port Moresby: Administration for Development, 3: 30-37.

Reay, M. (1982) 'Lawlessness in the Papua New Guinea Highlands', in R.J. May and H. Nelson (eds), *Melanesia Beyond Diversity,* 2: 623-37, Canberra: Research School of Pacific Studies, ANU.

Richardson, B., Wuillemin, D. and Moore, D. (1987) 'Ranking of Crime Seriousness by the People, the Law and the Police in Papua New Guinea', *Melanesian Law Journa*l, 15: 49-68.

Schiltz, M. (1985) 'Rascalism, Tradition and the State in Papua New Guinea', in Susan Toft (ed.), *Domestic Violence in Papua New Guinea,* Port Moresby: Law Reform Commission of Papua New Guinea, Monograph No.3.

Strathern, M. (1975a) 'No Money on our Skins: Hagen migrants in Port Moresby', *New Guinea Research Bulletin,* 61, Port Moresby: 1-467.

Strathern, M. (1975b) *Report on Questionnaire Relating to Sexual Offences as Defined in the Criminal Code*, Port Moresby: Law Faculty, University of Papua New Guinea.

Territory of Papua, *Annual Report for 1959-60*, Port Moresby.

United Nations Development Programme (1994) *Pacific Human Development Report—Putting People First,* Suva, Fiji.

United Nations Development Programme/International Labour Organisation (1993) *Papua New Guinea: Challenges for Employment and Human Resource Development*, Suva, Fiji.

Utulurea, G. (1981) *Gangs in Port Moresby,* Point: Youth and Development, 1: 109-17.

Walker, J. (1985) *Crime and Justice Statistics in Papua New Guinea,* Canberra:

Australian Institute of Criminology.
Wolfers, E.P. (1975) *Race Relations and Colonial Rule in Papua New Guinea,* Sydney: Australia and New Zealand Book Company.
Young, F.D. (1976) *Pasin bilong Rascal: Juvenile Crime in Port Moresby*, Port Moresby Research Report 209, Port Moresby: Psychological Services Branch, Public Services Commission.

NOTES

1. *Corporal Punishment of Native Offenders—Papua and New Guinea*, letter from the First Assistant Secretary to the Minister of Territories, dated 8 December 1960, A452/1, 61/3271, Australian Archives, Canberra.

2. During most of the colonial period a series of administrative and legal provisions served to preserve the towns as European enclaves by restricting the mobility of indigenous people. These discriminatory measures were gradually repealed before Independence. See: O'Neill 1976: 7; Wolfers 1975; Fitzpatrick 1980: 169-70.

3. Inspector J. Bonono, *Post-Courier* 26 July 1971 quoted in Oram 1976: 154.

4. The term 'settlement' was originally used to describe the areas where new migrants to town 'settled'. These were on land rented from traditional landowners or the state and, sometimes, land that was occupied without permission (i.e. squatter settlements). For a history of early settlements in Port Moresby, see: Oram 1976. More recently, 'settlements' has become a generic term for socially deprived urban communities—whether populated by migrants or long-term residents or both.

5. Clifford noted that one gang was reputedly led by a university student and made up of high school students (1976: 17).

6. For an illustration of the popular association drawn between settlement communities and crime, see: 'Eviction of illegal squatters, Lae City', *Post-Courier* 30 May 1991: 16.

7. Voluntary repatriation schemes have been tried in Lae (Morobe Province), East New Britain Province, and Western Highlands Province. See, respectively: 'Premier welcomes plea to repatriate squatters', *Post-Courier* 21 November 1991; 'Mixed reaction to repatriation', *Post-Courier* 4 September 1991: 18; 'Premier Roika moves to evict town squatters', *Post-Courier* 4 December 1991: 4. Several unsuccessful attempts have been made to introduce forcible repatriation: 'MP lobbies support for Repatriation Bill' *Post-Courier* 1 November 1991: 4.

8. The Morobe Provincial Government was actively involved in the removal of squatter settlements around Lae under the auspices of the 'Stretim Morobe' campaign, *Post-Courier* 22 May 1991. While voluntary repatriation raises few objections, the legality of involuntary repatriation and destruction of communities

is significantly more contentious. See, for example: 'Court bid to halt Morobe eviction', *Post-Courier* 2 October 1991: 2.

9. Michael Somare, Draft Hansard, Tenth Day, 12 June 1985: 20.

10. In practice, relatively few such measures get implemented owing to resource and capacity problems.

11. Prior to 1987 a curfew could only be imposed under a state of emergency declared by the Head of State under Section 228 of the PNG Constitution. *The Curfew Act* 1987 allows for curfews to be declared independently of states of emergency, by empowering the Head of State to proclaim a curfew over specified areas, between specified hours, for specified durations.

12. In March 1991 the National Security Advisory Council submitted a package of measures for consideration by the National Executive Council that included: the re-introduction of capital punishment for murder, rape, and drug offences; the tattooing of convicted offenders; more maximum security facilities; introduction of ID cards; vagrancy laws; and the forced repatriation of 'unemployed people and troublemakers' (*Post-Courier* 15 March 1991: 1). In practice the only measure enacted was the reintroduction of capital punishment for wilful murder.

13. One early observer in this tradition considered them to be reminiscent of the 'mods and rockers' and 'bikies' of post-war Europe and Australia (Biles 1976: 16).

14. A recent observer, himself an anthropologist, commented that: 'If one read only anthropological works about Papua New Guinea, one could very easily miss the fact that rascalism is one of the most salient and talked about topics in the country' (Kulick 1993: 9).

15. 'Territory' in this context appears to relate more to the neighbourhood in which a criminal group resides, rather than to an area over which they proclaim exclusive operational rights (Schiltz 1985: 145).

16. From the outset PNGs raskol gangs have been predominantly a male preserve. Some reports exist of female members but these are the exception rather than the rule. In so far as women have consensual associations with criminal gangs in PNG, these appear to be supportive rather than active. Otherwise, women figure prominently as victims of violent group crime—notably rape.

17. One such raid in my informants' settlement in early 1991—in response to the destruction of an unmarked police car and an assault of its driver—resulted in numerous complaints about the indiscriminate use of tear gas, police assaults, and sexual harassment of women (Dinnen 1993b: 3).

18. Prime Minister Rabbie Namaliu told the 1991 National Crime Summit that the Ombudsman Commission was currently investigating 90 of the 109 members of the National Parliament for alleged misdemeanours and misappropriation of funds (*The Australian* 12 February 1991). More recently the former Governor of the Bank of Papua New Guinea, Sir Mekere Morauta, described corruption as 'systemic and systematic' (*The Press* [Christchurch], 3 July 1995: 26).

19. This is particularly the case amongst Galilee youth whose villages are mostly accessible by road from Port Moresby. This strong ethnic identity is also reinforced by popular stereotyping of Galilee migrants as being prone to violence and crime.

20. One informant told me that loyalty in the criminal group and residential community generally transcended ethnic differences and that there were few serious ethnic conflicts amongst Port Moresby criminals. This was repeated to me by others on different occasions who emphasised their self identity as 'city people' (author's field notes).

21. The term 'wantok' in Melanesian Pidgin literally means someone who speaks the same language (i.e. 'one talk') but is commonly used to describe the relationships of social obligation binding relatives, tribesmen, clansmen, as well as much looser forms of association (Monsell-Davis 1993).

22. The overall leader of the group was called 'apai' in the Kunaimaipa language of Goilala. This appears to be another kinship title used as a term of respect. Jimmy's group communicated with each other in Kunaimaipa but were also fluent in Melanesian Pidgin and Hiri Motu, and most could speak some English.

23. Such leaders, whom Harris calls 'lieutenants' (Harris 1988: 27), are often referred to as 'kakana' by Port Moresby youth. 'Kakana' is a term of respect used to refer to the elder brother of a man, or a woman's elder sister, in the Hiri Motu language spoken by people from the Central Province.

24. In July 1991, a local newspaper reported the fatal shooting by Port Moresby police of a 32 year old male, from Tapini, Central Province. The victim was known to police 'as a hard core criminal with a history of armed robberies and multiple escapes from prison' and was on the run after escaping from Buimo Jail at the time of the shooting (*Post-Courier* 17 July 1991: 4). Considerable controversy followed an ABC Radio Background Briefing Report, broadcast on Sunday 25 October 1992, which revealed that the deceased had, in fact, been shot by an Australian police adviser attached to the Australian International Development Assistance Bureau (AIDAB) Police Support Project.

25. Considerable confusion was caused when the *Post-Courier* newspaper prematurely reported that the MYL had secured a K8,000 grant from AIDAB (*Post-Courier* 3 November 1992). At this stage the application for assistance was still being processed.

26. A public declaration of reform on the part of 'hard core' criminals is more likely to occur after a period of imprisonment for the same reason (see for example: 'Once feared 'King Eric' is a new man—tears at Nadzab as 'born-again' former gangster returns', *Post-Courier* 13 July 1993).

27. Low levels of popular allegiance to the substance and procedures of the introduced law in PNG are well known (Dinnen 1993d). Available research also confirms the existence of significant differences between many of the values embodied in the criminal law and those adhered to in a selection of contemporary

Papua New Guinean communities and organisations (see for example: Strathern 1975b; Moore, Richardson and Wuilleman 1984; and Richardson, Wuillemin, and Moore 1987).

28. Such strategies are by no means confined to youth groups (which, in practice, often include older adults) but are also evident, in varying degrees, among women's groups and other associations including local government councils, provincial governments etc.

29. This change in fortune is reflected in the case of two reported walkathons involving youth groups from Simbu Province. In the first case, sixteen youths arrived in Port Moresby in September 1993 after walking from Wau in Morobe Province. Weapons and marijuana were surrendered in Port Moresby which the group had carried all the way from Simbu (*Times of PNG* 16 September 1993: 5). They were given a cheque for K5,000 from a government minister and a lift back to Simbu in a chartered government flight. A second group arrived in the capital in October 1993. Unlike their predecessors, they received no official reception or government funds and were reported to be seeking emergency relief and transport home from the National Disaster and Emergency Services *(Post-Courier* 13 October 1993: 20).

12 Rituals, Rites and Tradition: Rethinking Youth Programs in South Africa

Don Pinnock with
Mara Douglas-Hamilton

> *Boys everywhere have a need for rituals marking their passage to manhood. If society does not provide them they will inevitably invent their own* (Campbell 1968).

INTRODUCTION

Just before Christmas a mother of two young children stopped at a traffic light at about 6.30pm in the evening in downtown Johannesburg. Suddenly eight youngsters, aged around fourteen, surrounded her car and began hacking at the rubber around the windows with knives, trying to get at her. The woman drove the car forward and felt a bump as the tyre ran over the foot of one of the attackers. But another one clung to her car's bonnet obscuring her vision and causing her to narrowly miss a mini-taxi. The taxi driver, quickly assessing the situation, pulled out a pistol and began firing at the youths who ran away. Their action was undoubtedly criminal. If the youngsters were brought to court it would be the job of a prosecutor to prove that this was an unprovoked attack. And it would be the task of a magistrate to impose a sentence that would cause the young men to feel society's wrath and to deter them from ever undertaking such action again.

But would these steps, seemingly so central to the necessary course of justice, be of any use to the victim, the youths, or to society? If one is to judge by the escalation of teenage lawbreaking and recidivism despite decades—even centuries—of whipping and imprisonment, the answer is: probably not.[1] To the contrary—and particularly if the young men were gang members—each step of the legal process would serve to reinforce those traits the law officers would most like to eliminate, embedding the youngsters deeper in gang culture and increasing their taste for wild anti-social performances.

There are at least two reasons for this. First, the South African justice system was not designed with young people in mind and it does not act in ways likely to win their allegiance or change their attitudes. The reason for *this*, at least in part, is the inheritance of a legal system designed for control and not for social restoration or personal transformation. Jim Consedyne has noted that:

> the law imposed by the English, wherever they colonised, was the law of a conquering empire. The English did to others what the Roman Empire had attempted with them—impose its own form of imperial law. In essence it was hierarchical and centralised. In criminal matters it was retributive in nature, vengeful and punishing in effect (Consedyne 1993:13).

A second reason is that collective adolescent behaviour—particularly where it relates to gangs—seems to be little understood by law officials trained in Western legal procedures. Indeed few adults can accurately remember the emotional turmoil of adolescence, the pressures to conform, perform, and win respect. Why did the youngsters attack the woman? In their absence it is impossible to answer for them. But in their action can be sensed a certain naive wildness, an unplanned theatricality, which seems to have placed more value on *ritualistic performance* than on the apparent goals of the action (why lie on the bonnet hacking at the windscreen rubber when a brick through the window would have done the job?). This does not condone their behaviour. But to understand such action—and I will argue that we need to do this in order to develop policy concerning young people at risk—we will have to remember something important about our own adolescence: teenagers, above all things, are myth-makers, creating and recreating situations and whole webs of significance little understood by the pragmatic adult world.

The failure of this understanding is presently crystallised in the institutions we have created to correct adolescent rule-breaking. Their aim seems to be to inflict emotional and physical pain and social isolation—despite the absence of proof that this ensures compliance, improves behaviour, or produces well-adjusted adults. Indeed, gang formation is an attempted defence against personal pain and isolation which state-inflicted punishment simply compounds. This pain is considerable and understandable. And it was made worse by the massive social engineering under apartheid which placed terrible strain on families. Earlier work on gangs in South Africa has suggested that the effect of poverty and the policy of apartheid created social stress to which gangs were a teenage response (Pinnock 1983). This view is captured by American sociologist Sarah van Gelder:

> The result of this uprooting and neglect is that the solid core of contributing adult members crumbles, and the institutions that provide the foundations of community fall apart. The community safety net is left in tatters. Parents, exhausted by long hours required to make ends meet or demoralised by their inability to cope with the hardships of poverty, may turn to drugs and alcohol. Kids are left on their own in ... adultless communities (in Consedyne 1993: 18).

The attempt by young people to *solve* these problems is more instructive than their causes and is best understood, not at the level of socio-political explanations, but at the level of *meaning*. To quote David Matza: 'The process of becoming deviant makes little human sense without understanding the philosophical inner life of the subject as he bestows meaning upon the events and materials that beset him' (Matza 1964: 176). What does ganging, lawlessness, and excess mean to adolescents? And what can we learn from it in order to lead them to the calmer waters of adulthood? This is a key question in the design of any new youth justice system.

RITUAL AND ADOLESCENCE

In order to understand what is meaningful for young people—and without this understanding we cannot hope to be involved in what is meaningful to them—we need to understand what adolescence *is*. In his book *Circle of Life: Rituals from the human family album*, David Cohen (1991) has described adolescence as a rope bridge of knotted symbols and magic between childhood and maturity, strung across an abyss of danger. It is clearly the most confusing time in our lives and a time deeply misunderstood by Western culture. It is also a period of intense *feeling*. And of feeling misunderstood. In a recent South African survey of beliefs and attitudes, young people were asked to respond to the proposition:

'Hardly anyone I know is interested in how I really feel inside'. Nearly six in ten African youths strongly agreed with the statement[2] (Kotze et al. 1994: 325).

But adolescence is also hugely creative. It is a time of anticipation for something indescribably other—a longing for magical transformation and a rejection of the mundane. It demands ritual space, a time and a place where young men and women can become introduced to the unknown man and woman inside themselves. They need to discover when childhood ends, when and how adulthood begins, and what their culture expects of them. Robert Bly, in his book *Iron John*, has noted that 'adolescence is a time of risk for boys, and that risk-taking is also a yearning for initiation ... Something in the adolescent male wants risk, courts danger, goes out to the edge—even to the edge of death' (Bly 1990: 29).

But Western cultures have largely lost what most pre-industrial cultures knew: these needs and excesses have to be dealt with by ritual guidance and initiation, not by punishment and imprisonment. Bly sees a crucial link between excess and initiation:

> We need wildness and extravagance. Whatever shuts a human being away from the waterfall and the tiger will kill him ... The boy's body inherits physical abilities developed by long-dead ancestors, and his mind inherits spiritual and soul powers developed centuries ago ... The job of the initiator, whether the initiator is a man or a woman, is to prove to the boy or girl that he or she is more than mere flesh and blood (ibid: 55).

Mircea Eliade, in his reports of initiation experiences in dozens of cultures all over the world, mentions that initiation of boys begins with two events: the first is a clean break with the parents, after which the novice goes to the forest, desert, or wilderness (ibid: 28).

In older, more socially cohesive cultures, these requirements are recognised for what they are. When girls reach menses, they are secluded and taught the art of womanhood by older females in their community. Boys typically face an ordeal or trial where they earn and affirm their passage to manhood. In each case there is a conscious recognition that adolescence involves a process, a becoming, a transformation. It is a time filled both with danger and enormous potential for growth (Cohen 1991: 45). But, wherever adolescents are, their need to test their mettle, to become heroes and to be accepted is paramount.

For this reason elaborate rituals have developed around the heroic deed.

While hunting is no longer a vital skill in most of the world, many people in traditional societies still consider the first hunt to be a necessary milestone on the road to adulthood. Among the !Kung, for example, a boy traditionally cannot marry until he has made a kill. Risking one's life is ever present in these hunts, but the necessary challenge can also be found elsewhere. In Vanuatu, adolescents dive from high towers to prove they are courageous enough to become men. Elastic vines attached to their ankles are just short enough to prevent them from crashing to their deaths.[3] Other rites of passage are more spiritual. After Jewish *bar mitzvah* at 13 a boy becomes a Son of the Commandment and becomes accountable for his actions. He can now be counted in the quorum for public prayer and publicly bless and read the Torah and the prophetic Haftorah (Cohen 1991: 78). Behind all of these actions is the mentor, the father or mother figure, the wise one, the shaman, guiding, approving, channelling the wildness to calmer shores. And for boys this seems particularly important.

But in cultures which have lost their ancient roots—through migration, poverty or dilution—young people continue to have (and act on) the same needs. And where ritual is absent it will be created—and often in bizarre forms. In the suburbs of Cape Town young gang members have to 'break a bottle-neck'—be the person to light a broken bottle-neck filled with a mixture of dagga and mandrax. Among older members, the inner circle of the gang may be gained by hunting and killing an 'enemy' gangster. Here teenage rituals continue to be enacted daily which are far older than the justice system which judges them. Elaborately, often unconsciously, young people engage in rituals of transformation which have a single goal: adult respect. In this painful and dangerous journey can be found echoes of African initiation ceremonies, Jewish *bar mitzvahs*, ancient hunting rituals, Boer kommando lore, images of Hollywood, Christian holy communions, Khoi trance dances, Arthurian legends and many other rituals through which, for millennia, young people have attempted to prove themselves worthy of adulthood.

The short answer to why we do these things is that we do them in order to grow up. But we do not grow up gradually and comfortably, we do it in spurts followed by periods of stability. In the span of a life, the changes which take place over the few teenage years are staggering. And at these times the greatest point of growth for adolescents is not their legs, or their genitals, but their spirit. Heroes, performance and ritual are spirit food.

Human longing for ritual is deep, and in our culture often frustrated. Tom Driver has suggested that ritualising is our first language, not our 'mother' but our 'grandmother' tongue, and as such it is something we do not outgrow. Human beings did not invent rituals, but rather that rituals have invented us (Driver 1991: 13). Sally Falk Moor says they 'provide daily regenerated frames, social constructions of reality, within which the attempt is made to fix social life, to keep it from slipping into the sea of indeterminacy' (in ibid: 137). Ritual is so basic to our creation of society that to lose ritual is to lose the way. It is for this reason that when we feel a prolonged or acute absence of moral guidance, when we do not know in our conscious minds what we ought to do, the ritualising impulse, laid down for us in structures older than consciousness, is brought into play. At times like this—and adolescence is one of these times—we are often without formal life-paths and have to rehearse in the dark, so to speak, without a script.

These crucial actions which we engage in as we pass from one state of being to the next are best understood as a rite of passage, a term developed by French anthropologist Arnold van Gennep. He found that the many cultures he studied created ritual ceremonies around moments of individual life crises such as birth, social puberty, marriage, fatherhood/motherhood and death. These ceremonies differed only in detail from culture to culture. But, essentially they were those crucial moments when we shift the gears of life. And we did this by taking the collective wisdom of an entire culture, or a single village or street, and presenting this knowledge in the form of a comprehensible drama.

According to van Gennep, transitions from group to group, from situation to situation, and from age to age, are implicit in the very fact of existence. Life, he says, is made up of a succession of phases: Rites of Separation, Rites of the Threshold and Rites of Incorporation (in Gluckman 1962: 12; van Gennep 1960: 3). *Separation* involves symbolic behaviour signifying the detachment of the individual from his or her fixed point in the social structure. It is a process whereby the individual differentiates himself or herself from the rest of the community. In the condition of *liminality* the state of the 'traveller' is ambiguous, passing through a realm that is undefined. The initiate is neither where he was, nor where he is headed. At this stage there is a suspension of the rules, and the individual is often impelled to do what is forbidden (Stivers 1982: 105). During *incorporation*, rituals are used to symbolise the individual re-entry into the community and into the new group. They generally involve by sharing and coming together.

Rituals of transformation are useful in understanding adolescence. But they have also been among the guiding principles of all homogeneous societies which place social cohesion and restitution above control and punishment. And they are part of the tradition of Africa. For this reason—and because adolescents can only be influenced by what is meaningful to them—an understanding of the use of ritual is essential to the construction of the goals and sanctions of a new youth justice system in South Africa. To build the new we must learn from the old—be it from a human being, a ritual, or an entire culture.

GANGING AS A RITE OF PASSAGE

Fathers are important. The love unit most damaged by the Industrial Revolution has been the father-son bond. Not receiving any blessing from your father is an injury and, as Robert Moor has said: 'If you're a young man and you're not being admired by an older man, you're being hurt' (in Bly 1990: 31). A gang is a group of young men with no older men around them. This absence has many causes. One is the destruction of the older inner-city suburbs and their 'stoep culture' of older people (in the hard new suburbs without verandas one was either inside or out on the street). But there are deeper reasons. When a father, absent during the day, returns home at six, his children receive only his temperament and not his teachings (Bly 1990: 96). And when mothers spend long hours away from home similar absences may appear in a daughter's psyche. When a son does not see his father as a hero, a fighter, or a knight, it is possible that he is replaced with demons. In Bly's words:

> When a boy grows up in a 'dysfunctional' family ... his interior warriors will be killed off early. ... it's likely that the early death of a man's warriors keeps the boy in him from growing up. It is possible that it also prevents the female in the boy from developing ... The inner boy in a messed-up family may keep on being shamed, invaded, disappointed and paralysed for years and years (ibid: 146-9).

Gangs are contradictory and 'imagined' communities whose members are young men (and less often young women) who have newly reached the age of sexual maturity but do not live in a culture which provides them with any ritual pathways for becoming sexually active. So they become simply active. When their situation is complicated by poverty, racism, broken homes or drugs, it can seem a trackless waste. Rituals take on a life-or-death quality and ritual occasions are fraught with perils because the aggressive impulses of human beings are accompanied by very few restraints—perhaps none at all except those few maintained by a culture deeply divided by apartheid and poverty. There is an ever-present danger that aggressions usually held in check by social pressure may come free. The search for 'respect' in the crossing to adulthood takes on larger-than-life proportions.

In this atmosphere police attention, arrest, lashes or prison become the dangers of the hunt, the dizzying dive to the end of the rope, a rite of passage through the hallways and rooms of the enemy into the bosom of the admiring gang. In the desperation of the streets, peer admiration is the only form around. And in this atmosphere violence is high. In the absence of learned moral codes and social restraints we are a creature which kills.

Separation

Separation for youths on the street corner begins by constructing 'us' and 'them'. Through a dual process of differentiation and alignment, the youths break their ties of childhood which bond them to their adult (and very often female) community by trying to gain acceptance into the adolescent group. They do this by acquiring a gang disposition.

Disposition. Due to the 'delinquent' nature of an adolescent group such as a gang, the child's mere association with the group is enough to spark off the process of separation. It can begin from the moment a youth flashes his first gang sign. According to one gang member, 'the community labelled me a gangster because I always stood at the entrance of the shop with my friends' (Subject F).[4] Being labelled a gang member has severe negative connotations. Another boy commented: 'I felt the community turned against me and I could not understand because I grew up in front of them—some will do anything to get me out of the community' (Subject A). The response of the family to the child's association with a gang is, in a sense, both desired by the youth and startling. Although it is partly informed by the youth's desire for independence, the extreme rejection, due the group's criminal associations, seems unexpected:

> They told me they would leave me and if I am in trouble then I would have to sort it out by myself—when I got into trouble I went to them and they told me I have to bear the consequences (Subject B).

Unlike traditional societies where the breaking of childhood bonds may be exalted in a formal ceremony, in the ghetto streets it is a more gradual process of assimilation of gang disposition: conforming to certain gang criteria, posturing on the street corner, adopting a style of talking, mobilising around certain territories and around certain real and imaginary symbols. This disposition involved a performance of both machismo and belonging that manifested in both language and action[5].

Language. Language is one of the most distinctive features of a gang disposition. It is a particular argot specifically used by gang youths to differentiate between those who are a part of the normal community and the gang community. The gang youths favourite topic of conversation is about gang fights. The stories are about battles, guns or styles of fighting, demonstrating their toughness and daring. Central to this language is the gun:

> The nicest thing about the gang is the sound of the gun. It makes the enemy scared and it makes you feel brave when you see the enemy running from you (Subject C).
>
> It was nice to hear the sound of the gun in the gang fight. Every time I hear a gun shot I imagine that it is me standing with a gun in my hand. That was my only wish before I was a gangster, to stand with a gun in my hand ... I just thought it would be fun to join a gang, to go out in the night and walk with a gun to shoot someone (Subject A).

They describe all their close shaves, shouting 'bang! bang! bang!' with great elation. Or they talk about different guns: 22s, 58s and how one makes the sound 'buff' and another 'boof', or the amount of damage they cause. One boy explained:

> You see there are different styles of how you can handle a gun—for instance if I have two 16-shooters [on the front hips], I don't want to have to cock the gun, I just want to take out the guns and shoot like the cowboys (Subject B).

They also engage in extensive explanations of their different styles of fighting and how one gang can be identified by their particular technique. Patterns of fighting are a way of differentiating themselves from competing gangs. They are a way of exalting 'their' side and glorifying the hunt. According to one youth from the 'Americans' gang:

> Each gang has got his own way of fighting. The Americans don't fight in the daylight. We fight at night and split our team into groups of three or four. We surround our enemy and send two without guns to go and look for the enemy. When they find the enemy they start running and the rest of us come out with the guns, in for the kill. That is why the 'Americans' are so powerful (Subject H).

The gang youths also had a particular style of expression, not only in spoken language, but in their use of certain signs and hand signals to describe events. They had a way of visually expressing events. For example there are hand signs that express 'someone running away in a gang fight', or 'someone shooting a gun', or 'two gang members pairing up together to go and make trouble'—called 'coupling'. There are also hand signs for stabbing someone, having sex, checking out the scene, talking to someone, telling a story, and for a woman.

Together with this stance and style, the gangs also have sayings and mottoes that mark off symbolic difference such as: 'When two killers meet one must die'. Many of the sayings have a fatalistic acknowledgment of their position in life and a cynical view of themselves:

> I want them [his gang] to be losers, But still the winners of my pride.
> I was born free, But not to stay free.
> I broke my mother's heart to please my friends.
> Born to Kill.
> Born to lose
> When days are dark, friends are few.

Language expresses the relationship to both the community and the gang. Their talk about how they love the sound of guns, how they like to make people run, and how all they want to do is go out and shoot someone, are rituals of *entrance*.

Posturing on the Street Corner. Gang disposition also develops on the street corner where ghetto youths spend most of their time 'hanging out' on their turf, prowling around, and displaying themselves to the community. These displays of belonging are affected performances to appear tough, hard, and dangerous. The street corner is a site of public display. The following note was jotted down during observation:

> At home base, as usual, on the corner with the gang. A group of

> school kids came out for their lunch break and walked passed us. Within seconds the whole gang seemed to mobilise into a performance process. Their behaviour became very affected, displaying their identity with the group, acquiring a macho disposition, jeering at the pretty girls, and strutting around. The atmosphere changed, the group was on edge and there was an element of unpredictability. They slightly cold-shouldered me in front of the youths walking by.[6]

This gang, the 'Americans' in Manenberg, Cape Town, seemed quite different inside their leader's house. There the leader's mother was boss, outside they were boss; inside was private, outside was public. Within the house little defined them as a gang. They simply appeared to be a group of friends laughing, joking and spending time together. Outside the performance began the moment they became aware of being in the public eye.

Ritual symbols and identity. Mobilising around visual, or even imaginary symbols, parallels gang identification through territory and serves to differentiate one gang from another. Many of these devices remain a secret, known only to those who 'belong'. The youths under study were not visually distinctive. Even though most gangs have adopted an American style with the latest Nikes or Reeboks, baseball caps, sweatshirts, baggy pants and leather jackets, there was no particular style or colour theme that separated one gang from another. The only overt visual signals appeared to be facial recognition, hidden tattoos on their necks and arms, or simply by the territories from which they came. Each gang had its special rules, its own salute and its own mottoes. There *were* a few visual signs and symbols which were definitive of certain gangs, but mostly the indicators were imaginary or constructed stories of belonging.

The 'Americans' were the gang which had most obviously clothed itself with various symbols, borrowing and transforming existing devices and icons. Their similated American flag, as a symbol of the American nation, defined the 'Americans' gang territory: the gang actually calls its territory 'America'. According to its members, the six white stripes of the flag are for the clean work (money) and the seven red stripes for the dirty work (blood). The thirteen stripes together stand for the thirteen presidents of the United States. The fourteen stars are the states in America, and one of the stars represents the gang. Both the flag and the Statue of Liberty are used to define a territory around which the gang can mobilise, and their territory is marked by elaborate graffiti of the statue and the American eagle. Around these symbols they have also constructed stories and mythical histories that function as a secret entrance ritual.

The gang name—the 'Americans'—stands for 'Almighty Equal Rights Is Coming And Not Standing'. Their motto is: 'In God we Trust. In money we believe'. They have an imaginary constitution, a president, a cabinet, a White House and they count their money in 'dollars'. Into the symbols of America, such as the Statue of Liberty, they construct secret myths known only to those who belong to the gang. These function as entrance rituals. Part of the litany is as follows:

> When I joined the 'Americans' I found myself in a snow white road where I walked on a thin red line. The Statue of Liberty was a lady with a seven-point crown on her head. Each point of the crown has a meaning. The first one means respect, the second discipline, the third you won't lie on your stomach when you go to prison, the fourth you won't betray your friends, the fifth you dress well day and night [he could not remember the last two]. The Statue of Liberty is a lady with a snow-white cloak, in her right hand is a torch and in her left a Bible which says *In God we Trust*. That is your passport to enter the White House. You meet with a eagle, in his claws is a dollar and on the dollar you also find *In God we Trust*. Then you kill the eagle and take the dollar and go to the White House. Two people come to ask who you are and what you want. I showed them the dollar sign and *In God we Trust* and they left me and that was my passport into the White House. I walked on the seven red-lined carpet and met another two guys and showed them my passport. Then I went in a room with a seven-point table, there were thirteen presidents sitting around the table, six were busy counting money [six white lines on the flag], and seven wiped the blood from the money [seven red lines] (Subject H).[7]

These stories add another layer to the territory over which the gang has taken possession and knowing them deepens the separation from the adult world. To quote David Cohen, 'Nothing binds a group so tightly as a closely held secret' (Cohen 1991: 173). The 'Americans' also implant various gold symbols, such as dollar signs, stars, and stripes, in their front teeth. Some members wear an excessive number of gold rings, some with precious stones, three to four on each finger, many supposedly stolen and some specially made with the stars, stripes and dollar signs.

According to the South African Police Service Gang Unit, the 'Americans' gang's use of symbols of the United States of America caused other gangs to appropriate flags of national territories. These flags have also taken on special meaning and defining myths. A member of Junky Funky Kids (JFKs) explained that his gang fell under the symbols of the U.S., except they believed they came under the eagle of America as opposed to the Statue of Liberty. Through this they believed they were different to the 'Americans' gang. JFKs could either stand for, Junky Funky Kids, Juwele Frank Crone, Join the Force of Killers, Justice, Freedom, Kindness, or John Frank Kennedy. They believed they were enemies with the 'Americans' gang because it was an American who killed John Frank Kennedy. This was given as the primary reason for their antagonism with the 'Americans'. Another opposition gang called the 'Hard Livings', live by the motto of 'rather wisdom than gold' and come under the British flag. They call themselves 'The Chosen Ones'.

Some gangs also have their own imaginary 'book of knowledge' similar to prison gangs. Knowledge of this 'book', which is a part of the gang's entrance ritual, defines the way youths are supposed to conduct their lives once a part of the gang:

> In the book of knowledge we don't run away from each other if we are in trouble, we have to stay together. We have to die together. If not others will kill you for not helping your brother. No one tells you to become an American, you do it yourself and if so you must die with them (Subject H).

The issue of respect constantly arises:

> we must respect one another—if we fight amongst ourselves what kind of impression will that give of the gang—like if I fight with another guy in the gang and members of another gang come past and say: 'Look a Dixi boy is fighting against his brother'. They will get a bad impression—tomorrow they could come and see us still fighting and they will bring guns and shoot us—then all we can say is we fought against each other but we didn't see the enemy come from behind (Subject F).

Territoriality. Acceptance of gang boundaries is central to gaining acceptance into a gang. This often necessitates gang fights to defend or appropriate territory. 'Turf' is a powerful way of bonding the group. Territories often cover no more than a hundred-metre strip of residence blocks or four to five streets. Territory defines clearly to the community who belongs to the group and who owns a particular neighbourhood or street corner. So the performance on the street corner also seems to be a performance of ownership as well as one of belonging.

Territoriality leads to certain expectations, particularly that the boys who grow up in the gang's territory will become a part of their gang. Conversely, a child living in an enemy's territory is marked out as enemy. So while one group assumes ownership over a boy, another may try to put a bullet through his head. According to one youngster, 'other gangsters who were waiting there where I live, whenever they saw me they would chase me and shoot at me' (Subject D). A similar ownership is assumed over women.

Separation, therefore, is defined by acquiring a gang disposition, gang language, posturing with other members of the gang, adopting gang beliefs and customs and mobilising around specific territory. The key motivation for the individuals seems to be 'acceptance'. This forces a young boy to go to extremes which adolescents in more 'normal' peer groups would not. Once the youth has gained acceptance he moves into a state of liminality.

Liminality

In gangs, liminality marks the beginning of 'free fall', demanding excesses which place the youth—temporarily or permanently—beyond social recall. These excesses range from full-scale gang fights and organised criminal activity to the first serious assault or kill. The youth's main concern now shifts from gaining acceptance to gaining *status* in the gang. Now freed from adult restriction, he exists in a world of betwixt and between and is required to test his young manhood and build his reputation through performances of bravery and daring.

Performance in Battle. The battlefield is a pivotal space in gang life. Battle generally happens when rivalry occurs between gangs over the issue of ownership of turf, community, women, or markets. It can range from short brief confrontations between a few members to full-scale gang wars. Personal performance is finely measured. Gang youths attempt to display both a fearless demeanour and warlike capacity, acquire visual scars of their bravery and boast of their deadly accuracy. In a sense, the battleground is an extension of the street-corner, a time and place when gang members are more conscious than ever of who is watching them:

> You build your reputation by showing people you're not afraid—like when there is a gang war and they attack me when I am standing alone with a gun, I must shoot them so that people see that I'm not afraid (Subject F).

Being seen and identified in gang fights is of particular importance in two respects: it shows warrior capacity and builds reputation, and it is important to be marked by the opposing gang as a ruthless and dangerous enemy. The aim is to be 'talked about' by their own and rival gangs, to be recognised and noticed by the community, their buddies or their enemies:

> The big gangsters stand in the front line because they are the ones that are the most hated and the most feared by the enemy—you get into the front line if you are brave and if you are scared you go to the back (Subject D).[8]

Gang youths who were interviewed relished the belief that they invoked fear in rival gangs. The more wanted and feared they were by rival gangs, the greater status they acquired in their own gang. But this had a sinister edge, subverting inhibitions against murder. According to one youth, 'I only kill my enemy, not people who want to live in peace' (Subject E).[9] Enemies 'deserve' to die. At this point, in the absence of any guidance from older members of society, what is conventionally unacceptable becomes acceptable and the thread joining them to conventional morality comes closer to breaking. Excess is praised.

Body mutilations. Another indication of liminal behaviour is body mutilation, whether it comes in the form of bullet wounds, stab wounds or teeth damage. These are a visible sign of a youth's allegiance to his new 'deviant' group and a warning to others. These scars accumulate on the young man's body, signifying his bravery and ability to perform in the face of danger. One can compare gang wounding to a traditional circumcision, or to Dinka face scarring. The purpose is the same: a 'sign of union' and a mark of manhood (van Gennep 1960: 72). An insert from our field notes is illustrative here:

> Chaka strutted in, obviously considered by the rest of the group to be quite a warrior. He was introduced as 'this one who has five bullet wounds', particular detail and attention given to the one that hit him

> between the eyes and ricocheted off his Rayban glasses. He was greatly praised by all for his warlike and fearsome spirit.[10]

These scars and markings can make individuals permanent members of a group and often plague the youths for the rest of their lives—ineradicable symbols of their membership to a deviant group. And they can serve to ensure their exclusion from the community.

First Kill. The moment that marks the youth's final and absolute break from the norms of convention is his first kill. It is a moment when a boy shows other members of his gang how deeply he is prepared to become committed to gang life; it is the single act which differentiates between those gang members on the periphery and those of the inner circle and it marks the first real test of endurance.

All the gang youths encountered were required directly or indirectly to make their first kill. Although this was not overtly defined it was an unspoken and assumed requirement. It often seemed to be undertaken casually, but it was a traumatic ordeal which came back to haunt them in their dreams. One youth, describing his first kill, recounted:

> We were sitting in a group and someone mentioned that there was a problem that needed to be sorted out, but no one tells you to go and kill someone, you must decide on your own. So I decided to take the gun because I wanted to show the other members that I can also do it ... I went to kill this 'American'. I was sitting in some other people's yard waiting for him to come home. When he came home I shot him twice in his legs but both bullets went right through his legs into a cabin and they killed someone else. The one thing is when I sleep at night this event always comes to my mind—I can't sleep at night—even when I try not to think about it, it just comes back and I feel scared (Subject A).

Killing is the moment when being labelled an enemy takes on its full and permanent form. The youth, now head-hunted by rival gangs, gets drawn into the cycle of revenge killings. 'Enemy', according to the unforgiving ethics of gang life, is a label which will follow the youths to their graves. Many gang youths who leave gangs have been found later dead in a gutter—either at the hand of their former comrades or because they have forfeited gang protection and are now fair game for other gangs. According to one youth:

> I thought about leaving the gang but then I asked myself what is the use because even if the enemies know I am not a part of this gang they will still want to kill me because I have killed their brothers (Subject A).

Confusion between reality and fantasy. In the absence of formal initiation, community support, or hope of a normal life, confusion emerges between reality and fantasy. Youths seem to get swept up in the fantasy world of dreams, movies (which they try to act out in real life) and wishful thinking:

> When we go fight with the 'Americans' I just imagine I am in a film. The last gang fight I was in, some 'Americans' came down the same road as us and we just started shooting at them. I didn't want to run away because I know on TV the main guys don't run away so I just took out my gun and shouted 'mutha fucker' and 'don't fuck with the OJs'. I started shooting at them and they ran away. I ran after them and shouted: 'Why are you running away, aren't you gangsters?' If they run they don't realise they become an easy target for us. We just shot them. If people are watching us through the windows we point the gun at them and ask them what they are looking at—that is the same as it is on the films (Subject B).

The pictures they paint of themselves are eventually what they become. The confusion and lack of clarity that defines this stage of their lives leads the young men to engage in excessive behaviour without seeming to realise it. Caught between fantasy and reality it becomes questionable where their limits lie—if they have any at all. And, paradoxically, their attempt to gain status and respect through criminal acts of violence denies what they seek: as their reputation goes up in the gang it goes down in the community. And their confusion is evident:

> There are a lot of rules that define the important things you must always remember not to do. We decided it is wrong: to rob people in our community, attacking their houses, and cars; to swear at one another; to get drunk and fight each other, you can get drunk and have a nice time but we must respect one another. You must respect the community (Subject F).

Instead of incorporation back into the community, the action of gang members leads them towards what might be termed 'eternal liminality'.

The similarities and differences between traditional rites of passage are best illustrated graphically:

Diagram 12.1: Rites of Passage Trajectories

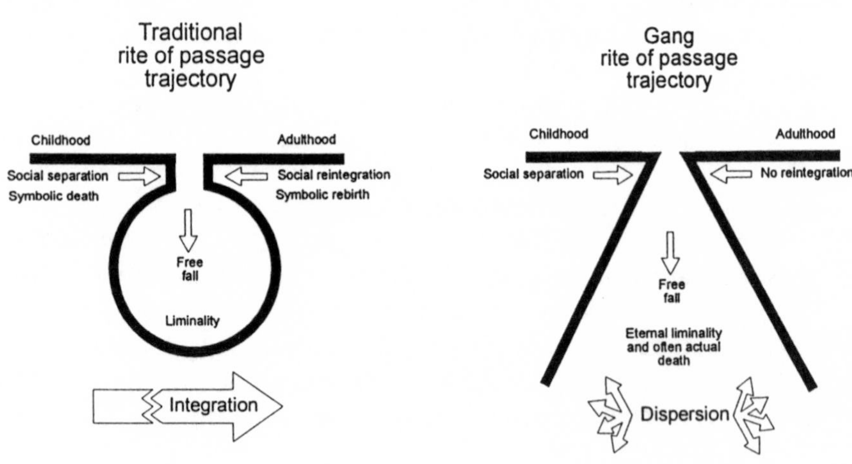

*In a **traditional rite of passage** childhood ends as the young person goes into emotional and social 'free fall'. At this point, however, social rituals and understandings take over and guide the young person through a period of liminality towards social reintegration. The process moves from symbolic death to symbolic rebirth.*

*In a **gang rite of passage** the young person invokes a break with his or her society and goes into free fall with other members of the gang. In the absence of a ritual social safety net he or she goes into 'eternal liminality', bringing about dispersion and often actual death. Reintegration into society becomes increasingly impossible.*

Eternal Liminality

By now the young man is almost inevitably destined for a permanent career of crime. What may have started as a need for ritual orientation in a period of adolescent crisis has developed into a greased pole of deviance. Life is defined by violence which knows no limits or regrets. The words of an adolescent in this deep are chilling in their callousness:

> One day quite a few of us 'Mongrels' decided to go and look for trouble in American territory. We had our weapons on us and covered ourselves in the stars and stripes flag. We covered our faces with red and white scarf's like the ones they use. We walked past the Americans' flats and shouted 'we were Americans'. This one called 'Music Maker' came out and made the American sign, greeting us with HOSH![11] That was the biggest mistake he ever made. We all went for him and he ran into the toilet in his house. Someone in the group put a shotgun in the window to shoot him but saw a pregnant lady in the toilet and said 'don't shoot!'. Instead we broke the door of the house down and the pregnant lady ran out. Everyone went in and started to stab him with the knives. Me and another 'Mongrel' friend were the last to kill him—then another guy came and finished him off with a 'pum pum' [uzi submachine-gun]. I didn't feel anything—I just forgot about it (Subject C).

Here his peers have become his father and his wise men. The prospects of ever leading a normal citizen's existence are difficult to imagine. Once the knowledge of a gang member becomes too extensive, whether it be knowledge of the dynamics of organised criminal activity or the murder of various members, they are bound to the gang by terrible necessity. According to one member:

> You can't just leave a gang because there are a lot of secrets that you share—if the police get information about a murder two or three years back the gang will think I gave the information to the police and they will come to get me (Subject A).

At this stage gang youths have either a very short life expectancy or can bank on spending much of their lives in penal institutions.

The reasons for adolescents embarking on traditional and gang rites of passage stem from similar needs and dreams. They are all young warriors. But they emerge at opposite ends of the compass and with very different life expectancies. Of these differences Robert Bly was to say: 'one man is a self-sacrificing warrior fighting for a cause beyond himself; another man is a madman soldier, raping, pillaging, killing mindlessly, dropping napalm over entire villages' (Bly 1990: 153). But both life-paths are deeply instructive in the construction of a youth justice system which works for young people and for society.

PROGRAMS AS RITUAL

The preceding discussion suggests a certain degree of prescription in designing appropriate programs for teenagers at risk. Rites of passage programs need not, of course, be a response to wrongdoing. But if they are, they should be central to initiatives to divert young people from the formal justice system. And in this context they should be restorative, inexpensive, tough, magical, emotionally powerful experiences involving meaningful rituals of transformation. They should be closely tied to the community, especially older people of influence, and they should ensure some level of commitment from the young people concerned. Importantly, they should be supported by the judiciary and all other state role-players. It is also self-evident that they should *not* be superficial, bureaucratic, punitive, expensive and seen as a soft option.

Building Young People

In their book *Reclaiming youth at risk*, Brendto et al. caution us that 'nothing we know about the human animal suggests that we have been programmed to be obedient' (Brendto et al. 1990: 24). There are better ways to change adolescent behaviour than demanding compliance and we need to move beyond labelling deviants negatively to an understanding of what it is that captures and holds adolescent attention. This understanding involves an awareness of unmet needs, discouragement, the misery of unimportance, and loss of self-esteem and self-control. But it also involves finding ways to mobilise the adventurous spirit, satisfy the deep need young people have for ritual, increase their personal social resilience, and create meaningful bonds with significant adults. We also have to realise that within the tough delinquent exterior is a need to play—with fire perhaps—but also with the world to see what it will answer.

Fostering self-esteem is critical to working with young people at risk. Its loss can begin with something as small as a sarcastic put-down from a parent, or as large as the collapse of the social support unit. In adolescence this can lead to feelings of insignificance, incompetence, powerlessness and unworthiness. (A search for the inverse of these feelings—significance, competence, power and virtue—can easily be discerned in gang behaviour). Bendtro et al., using Native American principles as a framework, suggest that any program to re-establish self esteem should involve the notions of belonging, mastery, independence and generosity (ibid: 35).

Diagram 12.2: Traditional Components of Self-esteem

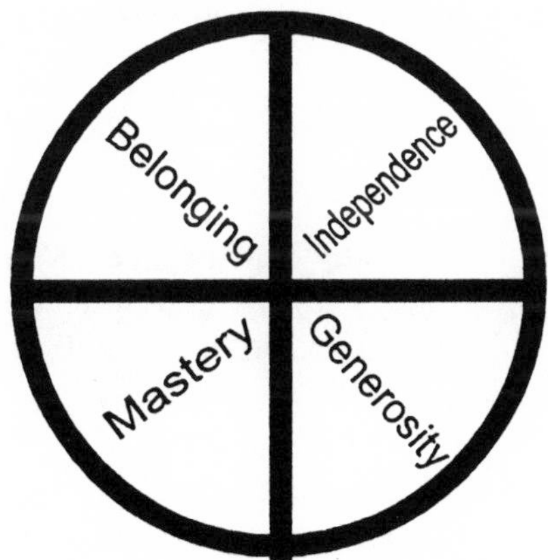

Humans are social creatures and *belonging* is the baseline from which personality develops. Two Xhosa expressions capture this. One is the notion of *ubuntu*—'a person is a person through other people', and the other is the saying 'all children are my children'. In traditional societies this sense of belonging extends beyond the human circle to animals, plants and the environment. In peasant society, maintaining balanced ecological relationships is a way of ensuring that one's own life is itself balanced. *Mastery* involves social and physical competence and opportunities for success. It is the basis of individual worth in most societies (and education systems), and if young people are deprived of the chance or ability to master their lives they retreat into helplessness and inferiority.

The spirit of *independence* is the product of both mastery and belonging, in that the purpose of any external discipline and support is to build inner discipline and social worth. Young people who lack a sense of power over their own behaviour and environment often lack motivation and seek alternative sources of power through dependence on chemicals or membership in a youth subculture (James 1976:41). Brendtro et al. suggest that self-worth is also derived from how one is viewed by others.

For this reason, being committed to the positive value of *generosity* and caring for others improves ones view of oneself through the eyes of others. Young people cannot develop a sense of responsibility unless they have been responsible *to* others. Generosity allows them to 'de-centre' and contribute to those around them in a self-affirming way (ibid: 45).

If programs for young people do not have as their goal the development of positive characteristics—unless they avoid emotional superficiality and build significance, personal power, self-esteem and self-control—they will not change the attitudes of young people and will probably fail.

Building a Support System

Rites of passage are traditionally a source of social learning and an inoculation against wrongdoing. They are conceptualised in many ways, but are generally seen as being linear and orderly. From within Western tradition, Bly finds these steps to be:

> First, bonding with the mother and separation from the mother ... Second, bonding with the father and separation from the father ... Third, the arrival of the male mother, or the mentor, who helps a man rebuild the bridge to his own ... Fourth, apprenticeship to a hurricane energy such as ... the warrior ... and fifth the marriage with the Holy Woman (Bly 1990: 182).

Within an African American tradition, Nsenga Warfield-Coppock sees these steps as being birth, puberty, marriage, eldership and death. Adolescent rituals he sees as comprising: preparation of sacred ground, separation from the mother, symbolic initiatory death, initiatory ordeals, initiatory rebirth (Warfield-Coppock and Coppock 1992: 10). Whatever form they take, these rituals involve an educational experience which takes place within family or community space and with the participation of adults known and trusted by the young people.

Many studies have shown how migration from rural areas and inner-city relocations under the *Group Areas Act* first eroded extended family—then nuclear family—networks and traditions (Pinnock 1983). Together with the industrial work-cycle these factors have placed severe strains on parents and significant elders in communities, and reduced the amount of support available for adolescents. Simultaneously, city life has increased the need young people have for support, discipline, assistance, protection, teaching and basic physical requirements as well as for experiences of trust, love, values, customs and spiritual traditions. We have seen that in the absence of this support young people create their own support structures and rituals, often with disastrous social consequences. The biggest challenge of any rites of passage program is to recreate adult and mentor support structures.

There is awesome power in relationships which work. In the development of programs for youth at risk there is a need for adults to serve in many roles, as leader, liaison, resource person, curriculum writer, teacher, facilitator, speaker, mentor, sponsor and elder. These tasks, and the need for adult training in adolescent work, point to the need for a national Mentorship Programme incorporating parents, teachers, religious leaders, community and program leaders, elders and those who have specialised skills in a range of areas such as martial arts, history, culture, sport and outdoor education.

There is a continuum of roles for mentors, from a ritual guide and teacher in a rites of passage program, through the more formal roles of probation officer, to a community buddy in a parole program. Mentors should be of good character and the same gender as the young person, often acting as a surrogate father or mother. They would have the task of transmitting something of value to the new generation, undergirding family and school support and building trust and discipline. They would have to be people known to the community and any recruiting program should include rigorous psychological and social selection filters.[12]

There is also a good argument for the formation of community Councils of Elders attached to the Mentorship Programme. These need not be 'tribal' or retrogressive groupings, and such a call for help would not only restore the self-respect of a presently marginalised sector of society but would probably provoke an enthusiastic response. All communities have within them older people whose life experiences qualify them to act as cultural, spiritual, and historical mediators and teachers. One of the greatest causes of cultural anomie among young people has not been the absence of good parenting but the absence of good grandparenting. And older people have what parents generally don't: time for youngsters. A re-valuation of old people in communities would be a powerful and progressive step towards re-balancing the lives of young people at risk.

These suggestions imply ways of dealing with adolescents in the community which are both ancient and innovative. It may be that, in the development of programs for young people at risk, to go back to tradition is the first step forward. An old African proverb says it takes a whole village to raise a child (Warfield-Coppock 1992: 152). In modern times it will take a whole community to heal one.

Building What We Do

We have established that adolescents respond powerfully to ritual and performance and abhor superficiality. Ritual or symbolic performance in a rite of passage program might better be described as *transformance*. This implies a vehicle for transformation from one status, identity or situation to another. Such a program would differ in form, depending on the young people and community involved, but our attempt here is to form a gantry of essential procedures necessary for its success. We have discussed Xhosa and gang rites of passage rituals, the latter re-creating only part of more formal ceremonies.

A comparison of this procedure for young men looks like this:

Traditional	Gang
Acknowledging ancestors/ community history	Absent
Elder permission	Absent
Induction through awe/fear	Induction through awe/fear
Sacred ground	Territory
Peer ceremonies	Peer ceremonies
Public ceremonies	Absent
Initiatory death	Dicing with death
Surviving battles with self	Surviving battles with gangs
Solo time and introspection	Discouraged
Warriorhood	Warriorhood
Scarring	Scarring
Community acceptance	Community rejection
Acceptance of older teachers	Father/adult anger
Rites or re-incorporating	Eternal liminality

Not included in these rituals are several from Native American culture which are instructive:

> *Sweat-lodge purification*—a spiritual cleansing which allows renewed closeness to the Earth.
> *Vision quest*—following the Sweat Lodge ritual a person embarks upon a journey into the wilderness, in the mountains, and sustains periods of fasting and going without water while they contemplate who they are and where they are going in life.
> *Making relatives*—a ritual for creating kinship-like bonds with friends or elders (McGaa 1990 in Warfield-Coppock 1992: 134).

Rites of passage programs are being suggested here as a diversion option for young people who have fallen foul of the law. But the rites and rituals of adolescent transformation are essential to all young people and it would be wrong to require youths to offend in order to qualify for a significant and life-affirming experience. The parameters of this paper, however, are narrowly focused on those who offend and require attention. What has been suggested in proposals for a new *Juvenile Justice Act* are family group conferences as a way of relocating youth justice issues back to communities and families (Skelton, Shapiro and Pinnock 1994). These conferences would be an important starting point in the development of a rites of passage program. Such a program would require intensive discussion at community level, but the linkages and support structures for this process are represented below.

Based on the four ritual orientations of *earth, air, fire* and *water*, processes are conceptualised under the corresponding notions of *place, learning, action* and *community*. In terms of the program, **Earth/Place** represents the sites and physical situations in which the rites of passage take place. These include the wilderness experience, the preparation of sacred ground, the vision quest experience or 'going solo', and the actual place where the young people will gather and which they will call their own. These situations connect with longer programs and more permanent places such as holding centres, shelters, a clubhouse and on-going wilderness experiences.

Air/Learning represents the rituals, rites, initiatory procedures and spiritual and temporal teaching required in a rites of passage program. These resonate with—and should link to—more aggregate programs such as parenting education, life skills training, vocational training, information centres and formal education.

Social acknowledgment and ceremonies are grouped as **Water/Community** and comprise peer, public, and kinship ceremonies as well as elder involvement and mentoring. These link with more formal programs such as victim awareness, community service work, emotional and mental support programs, foster care, counselling, mediation services, Youth Brigades (an important idea which needs urgent attention in South Africa), sex offender treatment programs, shoplifter awareness, and substance abuse treatment.

The fourth quadrant, **Fire/Action**, involves those parts of a rites of passage program where action is taken—training for a form of warriorhood (such as martial arts) and the actual induction process. Beyond the rite itself, this connects with recreational programs, gang programs, crisis intervention, behaviour management and parts of wilderness courses.

If the passing of a young person through courts to jail can be termed a Failure's Journey, what is being suggested here is the opposite: a Hero's Journey. The path of this journey could be depicted as follows.[13]

A 'youth at risk' program based on these ideas was first implemented in South Africa in late 1995 when twenty young men were nominated for a year-long pilot study. The results of this, and other similar pilot studies, can be found elsewhere, but what is important here are some of the ideas around which the program was constructed.[14] The youths were at 'at risk', some in a place of safety awaiting trial and most, probably, destined for prison. They were selected by Nicro and the Department of Welfare and discussions took place with them and their parents (where these could be found). All agreed to go on the program, called 'The Journey', which consisted of the following:

- A selection process and meeting of welcome between youths, their parents, course co-ordinators and mentors.
- A two-week wilderness experience involving strenuous physical and emotional activities.
- A community welcoming ceremony for the youths when they returned from the wilderness.
- The creation of a Club House as a base for the youths over the following year.
- Life and job skills programs run at the Club House.
- A counsellor available for mediation and support at personal and social crisis points.
- The training of the youths to mentor the next group of boys after the year's program ends.

Diagram 12.3: Rites of Passage Program Orientations

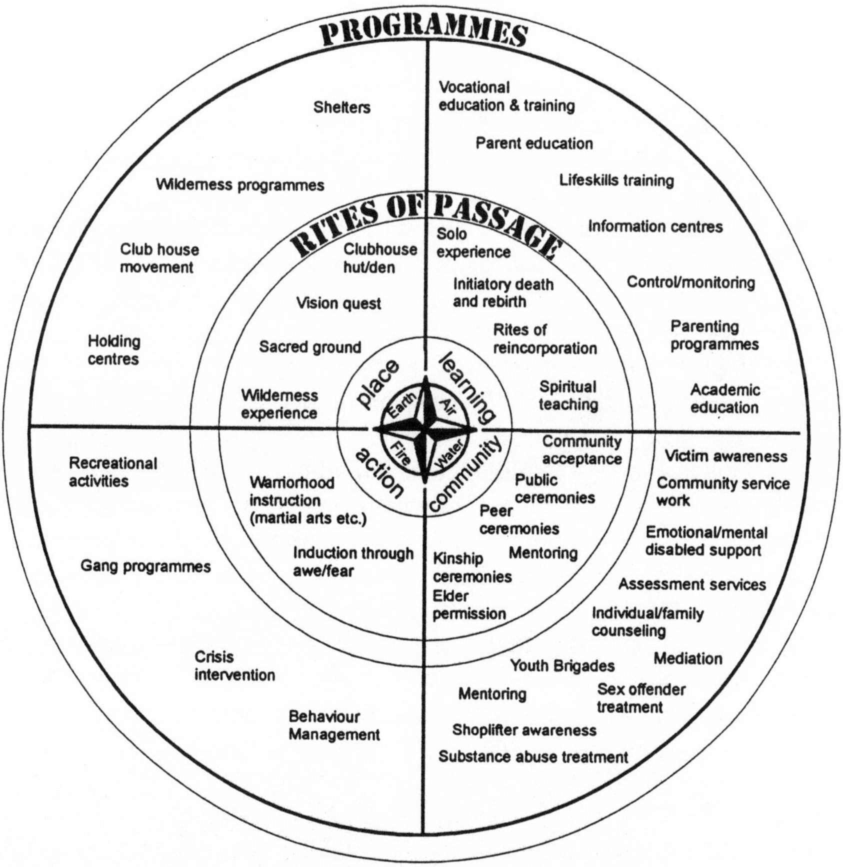

Several important guidelines emerged from discussions which established the program and from the early phases of the program itself:

Stories. When the young people joined the program, it was clear that they were very insecure in adult company. They had probably never shared their feelings and their life stories with anyone, let alone an adult. During the wilderness experience they were encouraged to share their stories—particularly at times when they were physically exhausted from their exertions and more vulnerable. These talk-sessions and their mastery of the tough environment as they climbed mountains, abseiled down cliffs and canoed down rivers, increased their self-confidence rapidly.

Physical challenge. In the wilderness the young people were physically challenged beyond all previous experience. This led to great anger and fear, but also to a sense of achievement which they had seldom, if ever, had before.

The welcoming ceremony. The young people had probably never been affirmed by adults during their time of adolescence. A welcoming ceremony was planned which attempted to draw in as many important members of the community as possible (for various reasons this was smaller than hoped). We asked: can we get the community, the parents and important *symbolic* leaders to go out of their way for these kids? And who are those symbolic leaders? The ceremony should have a particular format which should be kept secret from the youths. Most traditional rites of passage work on the basis of four orientations—say north, south, east, west—or earth, air, fire, water. But at root they celebrate death and rebirth. This last is very important and should be built into various phases throughout the year—but at the welcoming ceremony it needs to be the foremost thing. The reason is, particularly with tough youths like these, that the most damaging thing that happens to them is negative labelling (Braithwaite 1989, 1994). What we are trying to do is to allow that label, that stigma, to die and have the community indicate that they acknowledge this and grant that the young men are reborn. This is essentially a delabelling ceremony and is our best chance to end recidivism. The ceremony should avoid any superficiality and should involve the following orientations:

> *Earth*—Xhosa youths are covered in mud which is washed off during the ceremony. Older Western traditions involve burying, planting or covering with earth. Facial mud may work just as well—highly painted mud masks which are washed off during the water ceremony.
>
> *Fire*—The sense of renewal is often created by a ritual burning of the outer skin—the clothes—and the presentation of a new skin—in this case perhaps track shoes and T-shirts. Sometimes snake symbolism is used for obvious reasons. It would be ritually powerful if the young men burned their old clothes before receiving the new, or if they brought something from their past which symbolised what they wanted to leave behind and burned it.
>
> *Water*—The washing of the face masks could be part of a water

ceremony. But more powerful would be the handing round of a flagon of blessed (or in some way magically-charged) water, first to the youngsters to sip, then to the rest of the gathering.

Air—This the most difficult. Often air is symbolised by singing. But a compelling moment may be produced by one or two really big Guy Fawkes rockets, the kind which create a huge *whump* and mushroom a huge canopy of fire over the people. It's not the act, but what it symbolises, that's important.

Afterwards the young men should be encouraged to form circles and share their stories of the wilderness experience with adults and friends who are present.[15]

The *emotional* impact of ceremony is important because it resonates with deeper feelings of self-worth. Conventional punishments tend to deaden emotion in young people (other than anger) whereas a rite of passage program works with emotion as a central ingredient. This is particularly important for boys who are victims of cultural attitudes eschewing emotion. A comparison between emotional impact of imprisonment and 'The Journey' experience can be illustrated graphically:

Diagram 12.4: Journey of Adventure and Healing

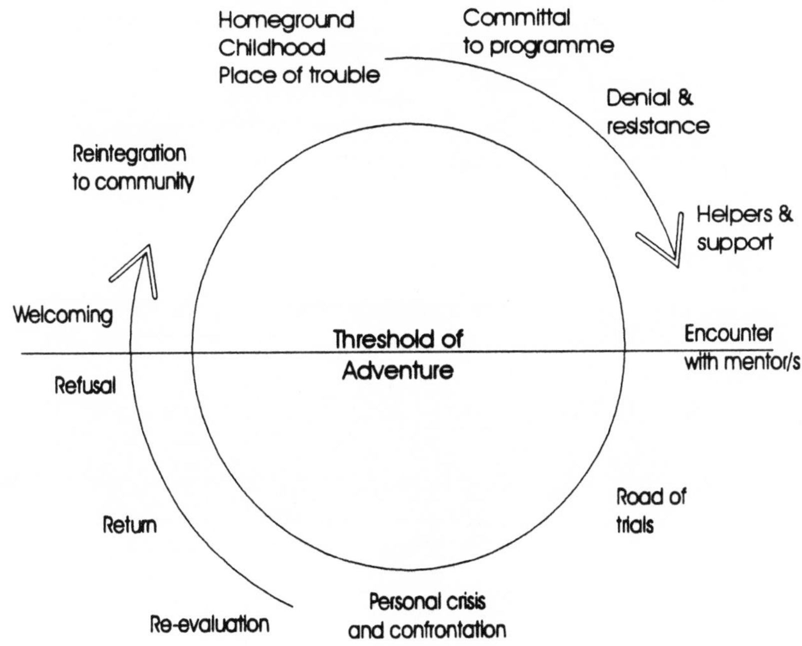

The power of names. Names in ritual space have powerful transformative qualities. The above program was named 'The Journey' and not a 'program' for this reason. The safe house was called a Club House and the young people were encouraged to find a name for it. They were asked to consider, on the basis of the wilderness experience, what new names they might like to consider for each other and what they would call their group. In African culture names are the cement of mental health and power, and their influence can be particularly seen in gang usage.

Experiential education. In both the wilderness experience and in the choice of a Club House, learning through experience was seen as essential to the program. Wild surroundings have a transformative effect on people and serve to jog young people—particularly from the city—out of their usual frame of thinking and acting. Wilderness has the added value of inducing a fear which is possible to overcome but which sharpens attention while it lasts. Kurt Hahn, the founder of Outward Bound, said of experience: 'It is a sin of the soul to force young people into opinions—indoctrination is of the devil—but it is culpable neglect not to impel young people into experiences'.[16] Central to experiential education is finding older people who have something to teach, and younger people who are appropriate role-models for youth at risk.

CONCLUSION

What has been suggested above are experiments and conceptual categories—the beginnings of a map which would require considerable discussion and planning to actualise. This map suggests a new, culturally sensitive, approach to diversion through positive experience. There is, in the end, no substitute for:

- thorough research into the rites and rituals of all cultures,
- the development of procedures based on these understandings,
- cultural sensitivity and acceptance, and
- the re-invocation of older life-experienced people who become respected by young people.

To quote Ruth Benedict: 'There has never been a time when civilisation stands more in need of individuals who are genuinely culture conscious, who can see objectively the social behaviour of other peoples without fear and recrimination' (in Cohen 1991: 56).

What is being suggested in this paper underwrites an extensive re-evaluation of what it is that our collective national cultures wish to teach our children. It is our contention that the formal education system, while essential, has become bureaucratised and is unable—indeed was never designed—to undertake the cultural transfer of life knowledges essential to the well-being of young people. And many—if not most—'modern' parents have lost the deep educational initiative without which young people lose touch with ancient inherited cultural roots and simple human wisdom. They have lost this initiative either because they do not know how to deal with their adolescent children, or because they believe school teaches these things, or—even if their children are not at school—they believe it is the school system and the state which should take responsibility to educate them. And, importantly for the many young men at risk, the notion of father as teacher is being lost. In a non-alienated culture a son does not receive a hands-on healing from a father, but a body-on healing. In more traditional societies the son's body, 'now standing next to the father, as they repair arrowheads, or repair ploughs, or wash pistons in gasoline, or care for birthing animals ... can dance to retune. Sons who have not received this retuning will have father-hunger all their lives' (Bly 1990: 94).

Of course, most urban adolescents survive in their fashion. The lucky ones have parents who act on an intuition that adolescents need both physical *and* emotional engagement. Some find mentors in their teachers or neighbours or grandparents. Others measure themselves and find adult coaching in sport or academic achievement. But many find only each other and they put together an emotional and symbolic life as best they can: music, dress, fads and fashions, drugs, romances and sexual encounters. And at the outer edge are those who do not have any support systems, who go too far, join gangs which carry them beyond the boundaries of social and legal acceptance. Some, like the eight young men who were discussed in the introduction to this paper, attack cars and people in outrageous performances. It is these we define as young people 'at risk', but any transformation of their lives requires that we look at what society provides for—and requires of—*all* adolescents. The boundary between the insiders and the outsiders is not a barrier but a continuum along which teenagers are able to move with surprising ease and speed. Unless post-apartheid South Africa reassesses its commitment to the support, education and parenting of all children—unless families, communities, and the collective wisdom of our many cultures are seen as central to this support—then *all* young people are at risk.

REFERENCES

Bly, R. (1990) *Iron John*, Dorset: Element.

Braithwaite, J. (1994) 'Resolving Crime in the Community: Restorative justice reforms in New Zealand and Australia', address to a workshop on 'Resolving Crime in the Community', Kings College, London, September.

Braithwaite, J. (1989) *Crime, Shame and Reintegration*, Sydney/Cambridge: Cambridge University Press.

Brendto, L., Brokenleg, M. and van Bockern, S. (1990) *Reclaiming Youth at Risk*, Indiana, National Education Service.

Campbell, Joseph (1968) *The Hero with a Thousand Faces*, Princeton, NJ: Princeton University Press.

Consedyne, J. (1993) *Restorative Justice: Healing the effects of crime*, Sydney: Ploughshares Publishers.

Cohen, D. (1991) *Circle of Life: Rituals from the Human Family Album*, London: Aquarian Press.

Cohen, P. (1980) 'Subcultural Conflict and Working Class Community', in *Media, Language, Culture: Working-papers in Cultural Studies*, Birmingham: Centre for Cultural and Communication Studies.

Driver, T. (1991) *The Magic of Ritual*, San Francisco: Harper.

Gluckman, M. (1962) *'Les Rites de Passage'*, in Max Gluckman (ed.), *Essays on the Rituals of Social Relations*, Manchester: Manchester University Press.

Institute of Criminology, University of Cape Town (1995) Interim Report of the Workshop on 'Confronting Crime: Innovating for Safety', Cape Town: September.

James, G. (1976) *Stolen Legacy*, San Francisco: Julian Richardson.

Kertzer, D.I. (1988) 'The Power of Rites', in D.I. Kertzer, *Ritual Politics and Power*, New Haven: Yale University Press.

Kotze, H., Mouton, J., Greyling, A., Hackmann, H., and Gouws, A. (1994) 'The Sociopolitical Beliefs and Attitudes of South African Matriculants', in L. van Zyl Slabbert, C. Malan, H. Marais, J. Olivier, R. Rioradan (eds) *Youth in the New South Africa*, Pretoria: Human Sciences Research Council.

Mahdi, L.C., Foster, S. and Little, M. (eds) (1987) *Betwixt & Between: Patterns of Masculine and Feminine Initiation*, Illinois: Open Court.

Manenberg Research Group (1988) 'Vision for the Future: Manenberg Peoples Centre', conference paper presented at Oassa conference, Durban.

Matza, D. (1964) *Delinquency and Drift*, New York: John Wiley and Sons.

McGaa, E. (1990) *Mother Earth Spirituality: Native American paths to healing ourselves and our world*, New York: Harper Collins.

Pinnock, D. (1982) *Towards an Understanding of the Structure, Function and*

Causes of Street Gangs in Cape Town, MA thesis, Cape Town: University of Cape Town.

Pinnock, D. (1983) *The Brotherhoods: Street Gangs and State Control in Cape Town*, Cape Town: David Philip.

Pinnock, D. (1995) 'Gangs, Guns and Rites of Passage: Rethinking youth programmes in South Africa', unpublished paper.

Skelton, A., Shapiro, R. and Pinnock, D. (eds) (1994) *Juvenile Justice for South Africa: Proposals for Policy and Legislative Change*, Cape Town: Youth Justice Consultancy.

Smith, K. (1988) *Street Gangs: A literature study*, unpublished B.Soc.Sc (Hons) thesis, Pretoria: Institute for Sociological and Demographic Research, Human Sciences Research Council.

Stivers, R. (1982) *Evil in Modern Myth and Ritual*, Georgia: University of Georgia Press.

Strang, Heather (1994) 'Conferencing: A new paradigm in community policing', paper presented at the Autumn conference of the Association of Police Officers, Warwick.

van Gennep, Arnold (1960) *The Rites of Passage*, London: Routledge.

Warfield-Coppock, N. (1992) 'Rites of Passage Movement: A resurgence of African-Centred Practices for Socialising African American youth', in *Journal of Negro Education*, 61(4), New York.

Warfield-Coppock, N. and Coppock, N.A. (1992) *Afrocentric theory and applications: Advances in the adolescent rites of passage, Volume 2*, Washington: Baobab.

Wieland, F. (1991) *The Journey of the Hero: Personal growth, deep ecology and the quest for the Grail*, Dorset: Prism Press.

NOTES

1. There is ample proof of this. Until lashings as a court-imposed sentence were abolished as a result of a Constitutional Court decision in 1995, between 32 000 and 36 000 young people were beaten annually through the 1990s. For the last fifteen years South Africa has consistently confined more than 100 000 people in prison and its prison rate at 333 per 100 000 of population is one of the highest in the world. The greatest number of those in prison were aged under 23. Despite these measures, a massive 91% of prison inmates reoffend within 10 years. And crime rates continue to rise. This situation is not confined to South Africa. In Britain, after nearly 1000 years of punishment-oriented retributive justice, crime is endemic. In 1982—before the time of mass unemployment—for every 1000 young people employed 56 were jailed. In 1994 only eight young people out of every 100 'went straight' upon release. For youths under 21, the reconviction rate was 71% within two years and 82% within four. In the United

States 1.5 million people are presently behind bars—0.5% of the entire population. For the last ten years the U.S. has been completing the construction of an average of one prison a week. Another 0.2% of the population—4.4 million citizens (mainly Hispanics, Afro-Americans and Native Americans)—live under correctional supervision of one form or another.

2. In the survey two in ten white youths agreed with the statement as did three in ten Indian and coloured youths.

3. In the West this head-long plunge has been taken up as bungy-jumping.

4. References to subjects A - H are from field interviews conducted by Douglas-Hamilton in 1995. For their own safety, gang informants must remain anonymous.

5. The nature of street gang ethos and language is inexorably linked to, and partly derived from, prison gangs. In South Africa there is a very close link between street gangs and prison gangs. Recently it has been alleged by the SAPS Gang Unit that many street gangs are actually run from inside prison, the bonds between prison gangs overriding those between street gangs. The rituals and structures of prison gangs seem to have filtered down to the street level and are particularly apparent in language, as well as in their signs and symbols. Even though it is unlikely that the youths, beginning their entrance into street gangs, have spent time in prison, they may pick up prison language from the older members to whom they aspire, and who are more than likely to be deeply entrenched in both street and prison gangs.

6. Douglas-Hamilton's notes 5 August 1995.

7. It seems that this imaginary entrance ritual has been influenced by certain aspects of the prison gang ritual. According to the youth in the 'Americans', when one of their members goes to prison he is only allowed to join the 26 Gang which represents the gang that seeks money. Their sign is a tattoo with dollar bills or dollar coins. This could have influenced the 'Americans' emphasis on money.

8. Most acts of bravery that attempt to prove manhood, also play a crucial role in attracting the opposite sex. According to this boy 'when you are not afraid the girls like you'.

9. Anyone who is vaguely affiliated with the gangs comes, more or less, under the category of 'deserved' and those uninvolved are 'innocent'.

10. Douglas-Hamilton's field notes 16 June 1995.

11. A greeting used by the 'Americans' to each other.

12. Charges of physical and sexual abuse would betray the trust of young people and destroy the credibility of the program.

13. A fuller treatment of the history of this concept can be found in the *Journey of the Hero: Personal growth, deep ecology and the quest for the Grail* by Friedman Wieland, 1991.

14. Nicro National, forthcoming 1996. At the time of writing these pilot projects were still in progress.

15. Foundation document for the Outeniqua rites of passage program. Don Pinnock, November 1995.

16. In: *Outward Bound-Nicro guidelines for staff and accompanying youth workers* by Lee White, November 1995: 1.

Index

Editors and Contributors

Megan Aumair completed a Master of Arts in Criminology at the University of Melbourne in August 1995. Subsequently, she has worked as a research assistant for a project sponsored by the Australian Youth Foundation documenting the impact of the criminal economy on the lives of young people living in depressed socio-economic circumstances. Her previous research has focused on the link between educational disadvantage, poverty, and crime. She is currently employed as a research officer for the Victorian Community Council Against Violence, Melbourne.

Judith Bessant (BA, Dip Ed, BEd, PhD) is a Senior Lecturer in the Department of Sociology, Social Welfare, and Administration at the Australian Catholic University in Oakleigh, Victoria. She has published in the areas of: 'youth' studies, policy studies, social anthropology, social theory and education.

Roger Burke is Lecturer in Criminal Justice Studies at the Scarman Centre for the Study of Public Order, University of Leicester, The Friars, 154 Upper New Walk, Leicester, LE1 7QA, United Kingdom. Email: rdb7@le.ac.uk. He has conducted research and published in the areas of child protection, juvenile car offending, adolescent drug misuse, crime prevention, and social and criminological theory. He is currently investigating the links between different categories of beggars and wider criminal activity in urban centres.

Sinclair Dinnen completed his doctoral thesis on Crime, Violence and State in Papua New Guinea at the Law Program, Research School of Social Sciences, Australian National University. He is currently a Post-Doctoral Fellow attached to the State, Society and Governance Project at the Research School of Pacific and Asian Studies at the same University. He has previously taught law at the University of Papua New Guinea and was Head of the Crime Studies Division of the Papua New Guinea National Research Institute between 1992 and 1994. His background is in law and criminology. Current research interests include: challenges of order in weak states, the politics of violence in post-colonial settings, development studies and comparative criminology.

Mara (Dudu) Douglas-Hamilton was born and schooled in Kenya and studied politics and criminology at the University of Cape Town in South Africa. Dudu acted as a research assistant to Dr Don Pinnock in his work on rites of passage, penetrating male youth gangs with considerable bravery and gaining their trust. She also did research into youth detention centres which acted as an important lever for legislative change on juvenile incarceration in South Africa. She is presently studying film-making in the United States.

Dr Robert M. Gordon is an Associate Professor and Associate Director of the School of Criminology at Simon Fraser University in Vancouver. He is a member of the British Columbia Interministerial Committee on Criminal Gangs and Youth Violence and was the Research Director of the Greater Vancouver Gang Project, a recently completed three year study funded by the provincial Ministry of Attorney-General and the federal Department of Justice. His recent publications in the area include, 'Street Gangs in Vancouver', in Silverman and Creechan (eds) (1995) *Canadian Delinquency*; and 'Crime, Ethnicity and Immigration' (with J. Nelson), in Silverman et al, (eds) (1996) *Crime in Canadian Society* (5th edition). Further research in the area, focusing on issues of ethnicity and immigrant status, will commence in 1997 as part of the national 'Metropolis Project', and with federal 'Centres for Excellence' funding.

Julie Hailer is a graduate student in the Administration of Justice Department at San Jose State University, San Jose, CA 95192. Email is hailerj@aol.com. She is also a full-time Public Safety Communications Supervisor for the City of Milpitas, California. The focus of her research is American Indian gangs on reservations across the United States, and the response of law enforcement agencies to these gangs.

Cameron Hazlehurst was appointed Foundation Professor and Head of the School of Humanities, Queensland University of Technology in 1992. He was previously a Senior Fellow in the Institute of Advanced Studies at the Australian National University and a research fellow at The Queen's College and Nuffield College, Oxford. He has held senior Commonwealth government appointments with the Departments of Urban and Regional Development, Communications, and Community Services and Health. He is author or editor of eight books on twentieth century British and Australian politics and history.

Kayleen M. Hazlehurst is Senior Lecturer in Cross-Cultural Studies in the School of Humanities, Queensland University of Technology. Trained in social anthropology at McGill and Toronto Universities (MA PhD), she has studied and worked with indigenous organisations and government agencies in Canada, New Zealand, and Australia. Her recent publications include *Political Expression and Ethnicity* (Praeger 1993), *A Healing Place* (CQUP 1994), and edited volumes on *Popular Justice and Community Regeneration* (Praeger 1995), *Legal Pluralism and the Colonial Legacy* (Avebury 1995), and *Perceptions of Justice* (Avebury 1995). She is the editor of *Crime and Justice: An Australian Textbook in Criminology (LBC 1996)*. With Cameron Hazlehurst she is currently undertaking a study of New Zealand gangs.

Joachim Kersten is Professor of Sociology, Hochschule für Polizei, Baden Württemberg, Germany. Email: Joachimkersten@fhpol-vs.de. He has an MA in political science (McMaster University) and a PhD in Social Science from the University of Tübingen. After research on youth at the German Youth Institute, Munich, he taught criminology at the universities of Melbourne and Munich, and European Studies at Rikkyo University, Tokyo and Limburg University, Maastricht, The Netherlands. He is the co-author of *Jugendstrafe* (1980) *Geschlossene Unterbringung* (1991, 1997), *Starke Typen* (1997) and *Gut und (Ge)schlecht* (1997). He has published in English in *International Journal of the Sociology of Law, Crime and Delinquency, International Sociology,* and *British Journal of Criminology.*

Marianne O. Nielsen is an Assistant Professor in the Department of Criminal Justice at Northern Arizona University, Flagstaff, AZ, 86011-5005, USA. Email: M.Nielsen@nau.edu. Her main research interest is Indigenous peoples and criminal justice administration. She is currently working with the Navajo Nation investigating gang activities and their prevention, and comparing Youth Justice Committees in Canada and the Navajo Peacemaker Courts. She and Robert A. Silverman have recently completed an edited book, *Native Americans, Crime and Criminal Justice* for Westview Publishing.

Don Pinnock is a specialist in juvenile justice and is one of the co-authors of the South African government's White Paper on Juvenile Justice. He also wrote the section on Victims for the White Paper on Welfare. He was consultant to a Cabinet Committee on young people in trouble with the law and was the co-convenor of an international conference on crime in South Africa. He has lectured in journalism at Rhodes University and in criminology at the University of Cape Town. He has published a number of books, including *The Brotherhoods*, a seminal work on adolescent street gangs, *Telona*, the history of a labour recruiter, *Elsies River*, a profile of a black ghetto township, and *Ruth First*, a biography of a communist journalist in South Africa. He is presently writing a book on the political and personal value of African fairy tales in times of transition. Dr Pinnock has a PhD in politics, an MA in criminology and a BA in African History. He is Senior Editor of *Getaway*, a monthly eco-travel magazine.

Paddy Rawlinson formally taught Russian and Soviet politics at Edinburgh University and is now employed at the Centre for Comparative Criminology and Criminal Justice, School of Sociology and Social Policy, University of Wales. She has also worked as a journalist in business and television (including Channel 4's *Dispatches* and ITV's *World in Action* documentary series) and has published articles in the British and Russian press. She has also acted as liaison between the St Petersburg Police in Russia and the Metropolitan Police in London.

Ros Sunley is Lecturer in Criminology and Public Order Studies at the Scarman Centre for the Study of Public Order, University of Leicester, The Friars, 154 Upper New Walk, Leicester, LE1 7QA, United Kingdom. Email: CSPO@le.ac.uk. Her background is in sociology with specific reference to young people and gender. Current research interests include: issues of power, inequality and social conflict, gendered violence, adolescence, sexualities.

James Diego Vigil is Professor of Anthropology and Associate Director of the Center for the Study of Urban Poverty at the University of California, Los Angeles. Previously, he was Director of the Center for Urban Policy and Ethnicity at the University of Southern California. In addition, he served as Chair of Chicano Studies at the University of Wisconsin at Madison. His research has focused on urban anthropology, and his publications include *Barrio Gangs* (University of Texas Press, 1988) and *From Indians to Chicanos: The Dynamics of Mexican American Culture*

(Waveland Press, 1984), as well as numerous articles in journals and edited books.

Ian Warren is a Lecturer in the School of Social Inquiry at Deakin University, Geelong. In 1995 he completed a Master of Arts in Criminology and in 1996 a Bachelor of Laws, both at the University of Melbourne. He has researched and written on youth gangs, youth culture, police culture, policing at sporting events, and ethnicity and sport. His current interests are public law theory, interdisciplinary approaches to the study of crime and law, private policing, media depictions of crime and deviance, and the implications of criminal and civil laws on the violent and racist behaviour of athletes. He is currently enrolled in a PhD in the Faculty of Law, University of New South Wales.

Rob Watts (BA Hons, DipEd, MA, PhD) teaches social theory and social policy in the Department of Social Sciences and Social Work at the Royal Melbourne Institute of Technology. He is interested in the history of social theory, comparative social policy, and the theory of ethics. Rob Watts also spent his childhood and adolescence in Footscray during the 1950s and 1960s - the place and period upon which much of his chapter is based.

Pahmi Winter lectures in the Department of Sociology and Social Anthropology, University of Waikato, Hamilton, New Zealand, in social policy, research methods, sociology of deviance, and media studies. Her doctoral research was on the introduction of a commercial ethos into news production after the public broadcaster Television New Zealand was restructured as a commercial state-owned enterprise in 1989. Her research interests include the social and institutional dynamics of penal reform and crime prevention initiatives and debates in New Zealand.

Steve C. Yun received his undergraduate degree in anthropology at the University of Wisconsin at Madison. He recently received his medical degree from the University of Southern California, but plans to continue his research with James Diego Vigil on street gangs in Southern California.

James W. Zion is the Solicitor to the Courts of the Navajo Nation, P.O. Drawer 520, Window Rock, AZ 86515, USA. Email: Jzion@aol.com. He has a law degree from the Columbus School of Law, Catholic University of America, Washington. He is an active scholar in the area of Navajo common law, Indigenous law, and Indigenous civil rights. His current research interests include Peacemaker Courts, and Navajo gang intervention. His recent publications include 'Slay the Monsters' (with R. Yazzie) in *Popular Justice and Community Regeneration*, edited by K.M. Hazlehurst, 1995; 'Hozhooji Naat'aanii: The Navajo Justice and Harmony Ceremony' (with Philmer Bluehouse) in *Mediation Quarterly*, 1993; and 'Hazho's Sokee'-Stay Nicely Together' (with Elsie B. Zion) in *Native Americans, Crime and Justice*, edited by M.O. Nielsen and R.A. Silverman.